Sustainable Development Goals Series

The **Sustainable Development Goals Series** is Springer Nature's inaugural cross-imprint book series that addresses and supports the United Nations' seventeen Sustainable Development Goals. The series fosters comprehensive research focused on these global targets and endeavours to address some of society's greatest grand challenges. The SDGs are inherently multidisciplinary, and they bring people working across different fields together and working towards a common goal. In this spirit, the Sustainable Development Goals series is the first at Springer Nature to publish books under both the Springer and Palgrave Macmillan imprints, bringing the strengths of our imprints together.

The Sustainable Development Goals Series is organized into eighteen subseries: one subseries based around each of the seventeen respective Sustainable Development Goals, and an eighteenth subseries, "Connecting the Goals", which serves as a home for volumes addressing multiple goals or studying the SDGs as a whole. Each subseries is guided by an expert Subseries Advisor with years or decades of experience studying and addressing core components of their respective Goal.

The SDG Series has a remit as broad as the SDGs themselves, and contributions are welcome from scientists, academics, policymakers, and researchers working in fields related to any of the seventeen goals. If you are interested in contributing a monograph or curated volume to the series, please contact the Publishers: Zachary Romano [Springer; zachary.romano@springer.com] and Rachael Ballard [Palgrave Macmillan; rachael.ballard@palgrave.com].

Ashish S. Galande
Elizabeth L. Rose • Sreevas Sahasranamam
Editors

Context-inspired Entrepreneurship

Cases from India

palgrave
macmillan

Editors
Ashish S. Galande
School of Business and Economics
SUNY Plattsburgh
Plattsburgh, NY, USA

Elizabeth L. Rose
ICFAI Foundation for Higher Education
Hyderabad, Telegana, India

Sreevas Sahasranamam
Adam Smith Business School
University of Glasgow
Glasgow, UK

ISSN 2523-3084 ISSN 2523-3092 (electronic)
Sustainable Development Goals Series
ISBN 978-981-95-9830-4 ISBN 978-981-95-9831-1 (eBook)
https://doi.org/10.1007/978-981-95-9831-1

This Palgrave Macmillan imprint is published by the registered company Springer Nature Singapore Pte Ltd.
The registered company address is: 152 Beach Road, #21-01/04 Gateway East, Singapore 189721, Singapore

Foreword

Amidst all the exciting opportunities presented by the rapid technological progress of the past decades, it is fortuitous that students, whether of science, engineering, humanities, or other subjects, remain deeply interested in the idea of positive societal impact. This fact is evident whether we look at the pool of applicants to or the enrollment in courses at our top universities. Consistently, over 70% undergraduate applicants to top global universities express interest in a career that leads to societal impact. Commensurately, the courses that link theory to societal impact are the most oversubscribed. Despite this demand, however, neither are our educational institutions able to prepare students adequately nor are the employment opportunities available to them allow for such careers sufficiently. How to make the youth capable of doing impactful work? Solving this puzzle is what this book is about.

Entrepreneurship has emerged as a pathway for taking ideas to impact, across all spheres like academia, for-profit, non-profit, communities, and government. Success of this pathway, however, is directly correlated with how deeply does the entrepreneur understand the context they are trying to influence. Situating an aspiring entrepreneur in the societal context, with all its complexity, is difficult for a teacher because the stories of contemporary India, where this book is situated, are not well documented. This is the missing piece of the puzzle this book enriches.

Contemporary India is shifting orbits along many dimensions. A large population is moving out of poverty. The youth is more inclined to entrepreneurship and job creation. There is a growing ecosystem to support entrepreneurial risk taking. Advancing physical and financial infrastructures are enabling market creation. The Digital Public Infrastructure (DPI) is "short circuiting" the society across many different strata. And there is the global reckoning of the opportunity India presents. Given this multi-dimensional complexity, structured story-telling—case studies—may be the only method available to us to make the lessons accessible to a wide variety of learners.

The case studies presented in this book bring out those dimensions of entrepreneurship that make it uniquely Indian. This is not to say that only those interested in India shall read this book, rather that anyone interested in bringing impact to emerging communities and nations would learn something unique from the range of cases covered here. The cases related to Rural/Social Entrepreneurship highlight how ventures are fostering economic growth in underserved communities despite societal challenges. The cases related to Digital Public Infrastructure or Technology-Enabled Inclusion illuminate their transformative power in fostering inclusion. The cases related to Cultural Entrepreneurship showcase ventures that preserve, promote, and monetize India's rich cultural heritage, indigenous knowledge, and traditional arts. The cases related to Entrepreneurship Support Organizations examine the role and impact of a diverse sample of organizations in nurturing and advancing India's vast startup ecosystem. Finally, the cases related to Making of an Entrepreneur delve into the unique journeys of individual entrepreneurs and family businesses to discuss personal challenges and dilemmas.

These case studies lower what arguably is the biggest hurdle confronting most learners of entrepreneurship for societal impact: their lack of deeply trusted relationship with the community they seek to understand. Without trust, it is impossible to gain insight about communities. While human-centered approaches to teaching and learning do use ethnography-based immersive methods to overcome the trust deficit, such immersion is not only time consuming but also resource intensive. This is a serious bottleneck! The case studies presented here overcome this bottleneck by bringing lessons through the eyes and ears of the individuals, organizations, and institutions leading each transformation.

To be clear, there is no general theory of entrepreneurship—entrepreneurship must be context-inspired. This lesson has become amply clear for me over the past few years of leading Atal Innovation Mission, the Government of India's flagship initiative for building the nation's innovation ecosystem. The yard stick we developed to assess classic business incubators, such as the Atal Incubation Centers, where the measure of success may be in number of startups supported, funding raised, patent filed, and so on, was simply not the yard stick for the community innovation centers of the small town, such as the Atal Community Innovation Centers, which are promoting innovations for, by, at, and with communities. We learned that for community innovations, context is everything.

Even so, the lessons in this book shall be useful to many other nations. In 2023, while India had the Presidency of the group of twenty nations (G20), it successfully launched the Startup20 Engagement Group, arguably the first-ever serious effort toward building a global startup ecosystem. As the nations came together and a comparative picture of the startup ecosystems of nations emerged, it was evident that what India has learned by building its startup ecosystem, making it the third largest in the world, is of value in many other contexts, not only in the so-called Global South but also in economies similar to it.

I must close this conversation by acknowledging the inflection point we stand at, where a large change is expected. The coming age of Artificial Intelligence (AI) is promising to restructure the activities and institutions that have defined the agricultural, industrial, information technology, and digital economies of the past two centuries. In the face of this "tsunami," this book rigorously documents the present context, for it to serve as the baseline against which we can measure the impact of the coming age.

Dr. Chintan Vaishnav
Former Mission Director, Atal Innovation Mission
Founding Chair, Startup20 Engagement Group, G20
Academic Director, Tata Center for Technology + Design, Massachusetts Institute of Technology
Cambridge, MA, USA

Chintan Vaishnav

Contents

Notes on Contributors

Apoorv Arora is a doctoral scholar at the Indian Institute of Management Kozhikode, working at the intersection of entrepreneurship research and practice. His doctoral research focuses on crowdfunding, alongside a strong interest in entrepreneurial mental health. He has contributed to entrepreneurship education through Zero2Entrepreneur, an international bootcamp that guides school students from opportunity identification and ideation to prototyping and startup pitching. In India, he helped execute the framework on the ground, supporting hands-on learning in innovation and venture creation. He currently works with Mind Your Business, a Durham University research-informed initiative, to develop and scale a mental health curriculum for entrepreneurs in India.

S. A. Arvind is an experienced Project Associate with a demonstrated history of working in the higher education industry. Skilled in Python, Matlab, Mechanical Product Design, C++, and SolidWorks. Strong program and project management professional with a Master of Science (MS) focused in Mechatronics, Robotics, and Automation Engineering from Indian Institute of Technology, Delhi.

Krishna Kumar Balaraman is an associate professor at IFMR GSB, Krea University, specializing in Strategy Management and Public Policy. He holds a PhD from IIT Madras in Strategic Foresight and Alliances, an MBA (PGSEM) from IIM Bangalore, a Post-Graduate Diploma in Intellectual Property Rights from NLSIU, and a BE in Computer Science from the University of Madras. With over two decades of international industry leadership experience in advanced technologies, he transitioned to research and academia more than a decade ago. His research and mentorship interests include strategic and technology foresight, entrepreneurship, institutions, AI strategies, governance, international business, and behavioural strategy with mixed method approach. He previously headed the School of Management and Entrepreneurship and the Center for Technology Foresight and Policy at IIT Jodhpur.

Sachidananda Benegal is an academic, entrepreneur, and advisor with a deep commitment to building entrepreneurial ecosystems in India. He holds a PhD and an MBA from the Indian Institute of Management Bangalore (IIMB), and a BE from NITK Surathkal. A former full-time faculty member at IIM Indore, he now teaches core and elective entrepreneurship courses at IIM Bangalore and IIM Amritsar. As Mentor-in-Residence at NS Raghavan Centre for Entrepreneurial Learning (NSRCEL), IIMB's entrepreneurship hub, he supports high-growth startups and venture-backed scaleups. He also advises emerging entrepreneurs and organizations on strategy, innovation, and scalable growth, and is a frequent speaker and trainer on entrepreneurship and innovation in India's evolving startup landscape.

Suresh Bhagavatula is Professor of Entrepreneurship at IIM Bangalore. His research explores how social networks, effectual action, and entrepreneurial scripts help understand the function of informal industries, accelerators, and technology ventures. His work has been published in academic journals, such as the *Journal of Business Venturing*, *Entrepreneurship Theory & Practice*, *Strategic Entrepreneurship Journal*, *Personnel Psychology*, and *Journal of Corporate Finance*. Further, he has trained women entrepreneurs, family businesses, and startups through various programmes at IIMB. He previously chaired the NS Raghavan Centre for Entrepreneurial Learning and co-founded Headstart Network Foundation, which has been instrumental in strengthening startup communities across many Indian cities. Currently, he is the Programme Chairperson for BBA-DBE at IIM Bangalore, the first online undergraduate programme in digital business and entrepreneurship, making management education accessible to young people across the country.

Vaibhav Bhamoriya is an agri-entrepreneurship expert and Co-PI for the Rural Agri-Business Incubator at IIM Kashipur FIED apart from mentoring and supporting over 50 startups every year. He pioneered teaching and training in agri-entrepreneurship at IIM Ahmedabad (2011–2016). He currently works at the interface of agribusiness, entrepreneurship and sustainability. He has co-authored a book *Introduction to Sustainability* and authored several cases on agri-entrepreneurship. Some of his trainees and students include the founders of Unnati Agro, Bijak, Varaha Organics, ScaNxt, Wayfield Agri etc. He is also a founder of Centre for Excellence in Agri-skills in India (CEASI) and officiates as honorary Chairperson of Pan Himalayan Grassroots Development Foundation. He is Chairperson (Economics) and Chairperson (Centre for Public Policy) at IIM Kashipur. He is a Fellow of IIM Ahmedabad and ex-faculty at IIM Indore and IIM Ahmedabad.

Tigmanshu Bhatnagar is an interdisciplinary researcher, lecturer, and innovator at the Global Disability Innovation Hub, University College London. His work pioneers inclusive, design-led solutions for disability and inclusion in disaster contexts, spanning both hardware and digital innovation. With experience across India, Europe, and the UK, Bhatnagar has developed award-winning technologies—from refreshable tactile displays for blind students and accessible mobility devices to AI-powered communication tools and inclusive fire evacuation systems—always grounded in participatory, user-centred design. He leads the Attvaran Assistive Technology Accelerator, supports global startups, and builds innovation ecosystems through strategic partnerships. His research bridges design, engineering, and social impact, delivering real-world change and shaping global standards for accessibility and inclusive innovation.

Bhaskar Bhowmick is Associate Professor and Head of the Rajendra Mishra School of Engineering Entrepreneurship at the Indian Institute of Technology Kharagpur. His research spans innovation and entrepreneurship, technology transfer, leadership, sustainability, grassroots innovation, and rural marketing, with a particular focus on technology-driven entrepreneurship in emerging economies. He has led several government-funded research and innovation initiatives and has published extensively on start-ups, innovation ecosystems, and sustainable enterprise development. As Chairman of IIT Kharagpur's Entrepreneurship Cell, he actively promotes entrepreneurial education, industry collaboration, and technology commercialization while mentoring doctoral scholars and aspiring entrepreneurs to create impactful, sustainable ventures.

Ira Chatterjee is Assistant Professor of Organization Theory at the School of Business & Economics, Vrije Universiteit Amsterdam. Her research examines entrepreneurship and the social impact of business, with a focus on how organizing enables social change, particularly in the Global South. She uses qualitative and interpretive methods to study social innovation, women's entrepreneurship, and inclusive development. Her work has been published in leading journals including *Journal of Business Venturing* and in edited volumes by major academic publishers. She holds a PhD in Entrepreneurship and Management from Hanken School of Economics.

Shantosh Cumarasurier is an innovation strategist and deep-tech advocate based in Australia. His work is focused on building inclusive innovation ecosystems, particularly within the fields of assistive technology, biomedical engineering, and venture capital.

Sujay Dixit an Instrumentation Engineer and alumnus of XLRI Jamshedpur, brings extensive experience in marketing and brand development, having worked with organizations such as Hindustan Unilever, Hindustan Coca-Cola Beverages Pvt Ltd, and Glenmark Pharmaceuticals. Currently, as CEO of TISS Incube Foundation, he leads strategic growth and ecosystem building to support social and grassroots level enterprises focused on tribal and marginalized communities. He actively mentors entrepreneurs in areas of customer discovery, business modelling, and marketing strategy and contributes to academia through teaching and advisory roles focused on marketing, entrepreneurship, and innovation.

Ebin Ephrem Elavathingal is an Industrial PhD candidate at Mälardalen University, Director at Merstra Foundation, and Coordinator for Technology and Innovation at Mälardalen Industrial Technology Center (MITC), Sweden. His work focuses on innovation ecosystems, incubation, entrepreneurship support, and industry–startup collaboration, particularly in manufacturing and technology-driven contexts. He has over 15 years of experience building and enabling entrepreneurial communities, incubators, accelerator programmes, and cross-sector innovation initiatives across India, Sweden, and broader Europe. He has also developed and led capacity-building programmes for innovation ecosystem enablers and supported startups and government stakeholders in global expansion and market access efforts for Peru, Algeria, Canada, Qatar, Belgium,

Finland, Germany, and India. He volunteers with Headstart Network Foundation, supporting grassroots entrepreneurship and ecosystem development. He contributed to building India's first SDG-focused incubator, AIC Raise. His broader interests include innovation intermediation, venture support systems, collaboration in innovation ecosystem, and the design of programmes that connect startups, institutions, and industry for inclusive and sustainable growth.

Ashish S. Galande is Assistant Professor of Marketing and Entrepreneurship at the School of Business and Economics, SUNY Plattsburgh. Previously, he served as an assistant professor at Indian Institute of Management Udaipur. His industry experience includes working as an analyst at Google (New York) and a database developer at TCS (Mumbai).

Sirish Kumar Gouda is an associate professor in the Operations Management and Decision Sciences area. He holds a doctoral degree from the Indian Institute of Management Bangalore and a bachelor's degree from NIT Warangal. He has prior work experience in the areas of supply chain consulting, EdTech, and financial inclusion.

He has several publications in leading Operations Management journals. He has trained professionals from several corporate organizations in the areas of process improvement, operational leadership, supply chain management, supply chain analytics, and sustainable operations.

Ben Hardman is Head of Innovation Ecosystems at Global Disability Innovation Hub at University College London. Ben joined GDI Hub to help translate research and emerging technology into real world impact. He is a designer and engineer with 20 years' experience of bringing innovation to market across a variety of sectors and domains such as consumer electronics, sports technology, mobility, retail, social housing, financial inclusion, and assistive technology.

Catherine Holloway is Professor of Interaction Design & Innovation at UCL and the Academic Director and co-founder of the Global Disability Innovation Hub (GDI Hub). Her work sits at the intersection of disability innovation, human–computer interaction, and global policy, with a commitment to designing technologies that expand human capability and equitable futures—particularly for communities across the Global South. Under her leadership, GDI Hub became the first WHO Collaborating Centre on Assistive Technology and has delivered a £50m+ portfolio across 41 countries, reaching more than 64 million people worldwide. Holloway has published over 190 papers and co-authored *Disability Interactions: Creating Inclusive Innovations*. She has served on the EPSRC Strategic Advisory Team for Healthcare Technologies and is Programme Committee Chair for AI and Assistive Technologies at the UNESCO Centre for Artificial Intelligence (AI). Her work continues to shape global policy, academic research, and grassroots innovation ecosystems, advancing the idea that augmentation must be designed not just for individuals, but for more just, connected, and inclusive societies.

Rakshita Honnatagi is an MRes/PhD candidate in Entrepreneurship and Innovation at Warwick Business School. Her doctoral research uses machine learning and experimental methods to study how startups signal growth and its effect on applicant attraction. She is also interested in understanding how gender bias influences startup funding outcomes. Trained as a chemical engineer, she brings quantitative and systems-oriented thinking to entrepreneurship research. Previously, she worked as a research associate at IIM Udaipur in collaboration with Deshpande Startups, where she conducted research on collective entrepreneurship, non-profit organizations, and channel strategies for micro-enterprises. She has co-authored a monograph on technology and women entrepreneurship for, SPARC, a Government of India initiative. Her research has been presented at the Academy of Management, the American Marketing Association, and the Academy of International Business.

Sumit Kumar Jaiswal is Assistant Professor of Strategy and Entrepreneurship at Ahmedabad University and holds a PhD in Strategy from IIM Ahmedabad. His research focuses on venture financing, entrepreneurial failure, and accelerator roles. He previously worked at L&T and co-founded a food venture.

Khushi Jayaprakash is an undergraduate student in Electronics and Communication Engineering at PES University, Bengaluru. Her academic interests lie at the intersection of machine learning, signal processing, and sustainable technology solutions. She has contributed to research in adversarial attack detection using deep learning models and has presented her work at international conferences. She has gained industry exposure through internships and actively engages in leadership and community initiatives, including serving as a Millennium Fellow and leading student-driven projects focused on social impact. With a strong foundation in technical problem-solving and a passion for innovation, she aims to develop scalable solutions that address real-world challenges in technology and society while continuing to advance her research in artificial intelligence and data-driven systems.

Jesudas Justin Over the last four years, Justin Jesudas has managed operations, outreach, and device commercialization at the R2D2 Center, Indian Institute of Technology Madras, focusing on assistive technology development. He was instrumental in establishing the National Center for Assistive Health Technologies (NCAHT), an experience centre dedicated to assistive technology innovation, capacity building, and user upskilling. Prior to this, he worked in research and analytics for over two decades with organizations such as UBS, RR Donnelley, and Cognizant. With 15 years of lived experience as a tetraplegic, he brings a user's perspective to his work in accessibility and assistive technology. He is also an international para-swimmer, having represented India at the World Swimming Championship and Para-Asian Games.

Srivardhini K. Jha is Professor of Entrepreneurship at the Indian Institute of Management Bangalore (IIMB). Her research and teaching interest is in Innovation and Entrepreneurship in the emerging country context. She has published extensively in top-tier international journals, written books, and authored several reports, white papers, and thought leadership articles. She has also contributed to policy formulation on innovation and entrepreneurship at both state and national levels. In recognition of her teaching excellence and her contributions to shaping India's entrepreneurial ecosystem, she was conferred the National Teachers' Award in 2025. She holds a PhD in Corporate Strategy and Policy from IIMB, an MS in Management Science and Engineering from Stanford University, and a BS is Information Science and Engineering from VTU. Prior to entering academia, she held senior managerial positions at Microsoft, Sun Microsystems, and Infosys.

Muneza Kagzi is an associate professor at T.A. Pai Management Institute (TAPMI), Manipal, India. Her expertise spans strategy, sustainability, and entrepreneurship, with a focus on innovation, digital inclusion, and corporate governance. She actively explores how emerging technologies such as artificial intelligence and blockchain influence entrepreneurial ecosystems and responsible business practices.

She teaches courses in Competitive Strategy, Sustainability, and Entrepreneurship and has designed innovative electives like Movies and Society to enhance experiential learning. She has published in reputed academic journals and is committed to fostering entrepreneurial thinking among students, equipping them to create sustainable and impactful ventures in a dynamic global environment.

Sruthi Kannan is a Senior Director of Strategy and Innovation at NatWest. Her research work with IIT Kharagpur, published papers and case studies span areas of sustainability, entrepreneurship, machine learning, and generative AI. She serves on the Board of TVS Sensing Solutions and was a member of the Executive Advisory Committee for the Startup India Seed Fund Scheme (SISFS). As the founding head of Cisco for Startups, bagging the coveted Best Startup Enabler award from the Government of India, she was recognized as one of the top 10 innovators in India and named among the top 100 women in STEM in India by the Confederation of Indian Industry.

Anupama Kondayya is Assistant Professor of Organizational Behaviour at the Indian Institute of Management Calcutta, India. Her research interests pertain to organizational and institutional change driven by concerns of diversity, inclusion, and pluralism. She also works on bringing Eastern and Indigenous perspectives to the mainstream of management. Her prior research explores phenomena such as the modernization of the Indigenous medical system of Ayurveda by entrepreneurs in India, re-examines established approaches using Eastern philosophy, and proposes frameworks to draw on and develop Indigenous concepts and perspectives for management.

Venkatesh Krishnamurthy is an entrepreneur, author, and technology professional specializing in information technology, e-commerce, and fintech. He holds a Post-Graduate Diploma from IIM Bangalore (2001), a Bachelor of Engineering in Electronics from Bangalore University (1995), and a DESU from Aix Marseille University, France (2022). He also holds a Certificate in French from Alliance Française.

A prolific author, Krishnamurthy has written several influential books, including *Information Technology Consulting and Implementation*, *A Comprehensive Guide to ECommerce*, *Create Profitable Products*, and *La Souveraineté Numérique d'une Nation* (Digital Sovereignty of a Nation—in progress), published in both English and French editions.

In June 2016, he co-founded Fee Plaza LLP, a profitable fintech startup that has successfully processed over INR 140 million in Total Payment Volume by 2023.

Kiran Kumar is a business anthropologist with a strong background in sociology and entrepreneurship. His research lies at the intersections of sociology and entrepreneurship focusing on the interplay of religion and markets in the liberalized India. He earned his PhD from IIT Madras through his study of Kashi Math and Saraswat Chamber of Commerce in the contemporary economy. Currently, he serves as an assistant professor at the Jindal Global Business School, Jindal Global University at Sonipat in Haryana.

Satyajit Majumdar has more than four decades of experience in teaching, consulting, and mentoring startups. He has been publishing research papers on social entrepreneurship, business enterprise growth strategy, and CSR. He also has award-winning case studies to his credit. He was Professor and Dean at School of Management and Labour Studies, Tata Institute of Social Sciences, Mumbai (India), and a recipient of Dr V. G. Patel Memorial Award in 2023 for outstanding work on entrepreneurship teaching, research, and mentoring. He has mentored more than 400 business and social startups and has been guiding community-based and grassroots entrepreneurs with a focus on 'technology for society'. He also participates in policy advisory roles and governing boards of organizations working on sustainability and social impact.

K. V. Mukundhan is Associate Professor of Strategy and Entrepreneurship at IIM Tiruchirappalli, teaching MBA and doctoral courses. His research examines how entrepreneurs shape institutions, how firms renew strategy amid decline, and how emerging market multinationals manage institutional complexity abroad. He has published in peer-reviewed journals and presented at major conferences (AOM, AIB, SMS). His executive education spans industries such as manufacturing, energy, and financial services, working with firms like Indian Oil, Hyundai, and L&T. Previously, he worked at Samsung R&D and Evalueserve. He also engages in inclusive development through Tamil-language training for micro-entrepreneurs and consulting on livelihood transitions, applying rigorous strategy insights across corporate and social contexts.

B. Parvathy is Assistant Professor of Marketing at the Indian Institute of Management Jammu where she teaches courses in consumer behaviour, artificial intelligence in marketing, and strategic marketing. She combines textual data from eCommerce and social media sources with lab-based experiments to understand consumer behaviour on online platforms. She applies perspectives from social psychology and consumer culture theory to understand how others' opinions on social media can shape consumer behaviour and chatter online. Before she received her PhD in Marketing from IIM Bangalore, she was a Consultant with Deloitte US. She also holds a BTech degree in Electrical and Electronics Engineering from Kerala University.

R. Pavithra is an assistant professor working in Dayananda Sagar College of Arts, Science & Commerce, Bangalore, India, with over 12 years of teaching experience. She holds a PhD from Bharathiar University and specializes in Marketing and Finance. Her research focuses on green marketing, consumer behaviour, and sustainable business practices, with publications in Scopus-indexed journals and peer-reviewed journals. She has organized national conferences and FDPs, received a grant of INR 100,000 from AICTE to conduct a six-day FDP, and worked as seminar co-director for an ICSSR-sponsored seminar. She actively contributes to academic mentoring, research development, and student guidance. She also worked for alumni initiatives, NAAC activities, and cultural programmes and guides student research projects and paper presentations.

Vedha Ponnappan is a faculty member in the Marketing area at IIM Udaipur and co-founder and co-Chair of the Centre for Healthcare, where she leads initiatives to strengthen primary healthcare through a management lens. Her research focuses on primary healthcare, health financing, nutrition, and policy analysis, with a strong emphasis on causal inference and marketing analytics.

She holds a PhD from IIM Bangalore and an MBA from NIT Tiruchirappalli and previously worked at Oracle Corporation in Bangalore as a Principal Product Manager, leading the design of enterprise-scale incentive compensation and analytics systems. At IIM Udaipur, she teaches Pricing, Marketing Research, and Causal Inference in Marketing. Her work has received over $2 million in research grants and is published in leading journals such as the *Journal of Marketing*.

Devi Premnath is an accomplished academic leader with over 21 years of experience in management education, research, and institutional collaboration. She serves as Professor and Head of Academic Collaborations at Jansons School of Business, Coimbatore. She holds a PhD in Marketing from Bharathiar University and is a university rank holder at both undergraduate and postgraduate levels. Specializing in Marketing and Systems, she has expertise in curriculum design, accreditation, international partnerships, and sustainability initiatives. She is the Coordinator of the Board of Studies, a member of the Governing Board of Jansons School of Business, and leads academic collaborations supporting research, faculty development, and student exchange programmes. A recognized speaker and researcher, her interests include marketing, artificial intelligence, and business strategy, with several publications and case studies to her credit.

Priya Tewary is an assistant professor at the Jindal Global Business School, O.P. Jindal Global University. Her research focuses on social entrepreneurship in non-Western contexts, particularly India, examining how intentions translate into behaviour and how social ventures choose and evolve their organizational forms. She is especially interested in inclusive entrepreneurship, including ventures led by persons with disabilities. She did her PhD in Strategy Area from the Indian Institute of Management Ahmedabad. Her engagement extends beyond academia through the Jagriti Yatra, where she has participated both as a yatri and as a facilitator. Her research aims to deepen contextual understanding of inclusive and impact-driven entrepreneurship.

Srividya Ramanathan is a PhD student in the Department of Health Management and Policy at the University of Iowa. Before beginning her doctoral studies, she worked as a research assistant at the Centre for Healthcare (CFH) at IIM Udaipur, where she worked on the PlusTrust case. She holds a Master's degree in Development Studies from the Indian Institute of Technology Mandi. Her research examines health systems and policy, focusing on emergency medical services (EMS), and applies quantitative, spatial, and computational methods to study access, service delivery, and policy design.

P. V. Madhusudhan Rao is a professor in the department of design, department of mechanical engineering and school of information technology at IIT Delhi. His current teaching and research interests include product design and manufacturing with a special emphasis on design of medical and assistive devices.As a coordinator of IIT Delhi Design Innovation Center (DIC), he is also responsible for initiating and driving multiple programmes in design, innovation, and entrepreneurship. He and his team's translational research efforts have led to successful products and solutions which are presently in the national and international market and have made an impact. He also serves as founder, board member, and scientific advisor of many startups and technology business incubators.

Charu Rastogi is a scholar of entrepreneurship and strategy. She holds a PhD in Entrepreneurship from the Indian Institute of Management Bangalore.Her research unpacks the mechanisms through which entrepreneurs notice and commit to particular opportunities, construct and refine those opportunities into actionable forms, and subsequently reorient them in response to shifts in the environment. Her empirical work is grounded in deep-tech and science-based ventures. In addition, she studies entrepreneurial support organizations, particularly how incubators develop the capability to support ventures, and women's entrepreneurship, with a focus entrepreneurial identity formation.Her research has received recognition in the form of Best Paper Awards at conferences and has been presented at leading academic forums such as Academy of Management (AoM) and European Group for Organizational Studies (EGOS).

Elizabeth L. Rose is Pro-Vice Chancellor and Senior Professor at ICFAI Foundation for Higher Education, Hyderabad. A Fellow of the Academy of International Business with interests in emerging-market contexts, her research addresses topics such as how small- and medium-sized enterprises internationalize and how firms compete across borders.

Oishika Roy is a graduate in Sociology and Anthropology from Ashoka University, where she also completed a PG Diploma in Advanced Studies and Research in the same disciplines. In March 2022, she joined the Centre for Healthcare at IIM Udaipur as a research assistant, where she worked on the PlusTrust case, contributing to research on healthcare systems and social impact. She currently works as an Assistant Editor at Locavore, where she engages with stories and ideas around food, culture, and communities. Roy aspires to become a food anthropologist and hopes to contribute to building food systems that are sustainable, cognizant of cultural diversity, and begets tasty food.

G. Sabarinathan is an Advisor at Foundation for Science Innovation and Development at Indian Institute of Science Bangalore. He retired from Indian Institute of Management Bangalore (IIMB) as an instructor in the finance and accounting department. He holds a BSc degree from Madras University, a Post-Graduate Diploma from IIMB, and a PhD from National Law School of India University, Bangalore. Prior to his academic career he worked in the project financing and early-stage equity funding industries in India.

Sreevas Sahasranamam is Professor of International Business and Entrepreneurship at the Adam Smith Business School, University of Glasgow. His research focuses on understanding the strategic and ecosystem enablers of entrepreneurship tackling UN Sustainable Development Goals (UN SDGs). He was recognized as a UK 40 Under 40 awardee for his contributions to entrepreneurship education, research, and policy. He serves on the World Economic Forum's Advisory Group on Social Entrepreneurship and was co-chair of the G20 Startup20 Sustainability Taskforce in 2023.

Dhruv Saidava is an educator and founder of EduNeuro, focused on advancing the critical twenty-first-century capability of learning how to learn. His work addresses a fundamental gap in education systems that prioritize rote outcomes over deep understanding and curiosity. Through EduNeuro, he designs neuroscience-informed learning frameworks that enable learners to think critically, explore independently, and apply knowledge creatively. His approach positions teaching as facilitation and learning as an active, lifelong process. Grounded in systems thinking and long-term impact, his initiatives aim to build self-directed learners equipped to navigate complexity, adapt to change, and contribute meaningfully to society.

Prakash Satyavageeswaran is Associate Professor of Marketing at IIM Udaipur, holding the Young Faculty Research Chair. With over 20 years of experience across corporates, non-profits, and academia, he specializes in healthcare, rural consumers, cross-border management, and industrial marketing. His executive education programmes are highly rated (9+), bridging academic theory with strategic industry insights.

Beyond teaching, he serves on IIMU's R&D and Executive Education committees and is a board member of IIM Udaipur's Incubation Centre board. He is also co-founder and co-chair of the Centre for Healthcare,

with over $2 million in research grants. His scholarship, published in top journals like the *Journal of Marketing*, the *Journal of International Business Studies*, and the *European Journal of Marketing*, focuses on health communication and emerging markets.

Anuradha Sharma is a PhD student in the Entrepreneurship area at IIM Bangalore. Her research focuses on entrepreneurial cognition, attention allocation, and how digitalization shapes decision-making in entrepreneurship. Her work is situated within the context of India's Digital Public Infrastructure and larger technological enablements, examining its linkages with the Indian entrepreneurial ecosystem as well as enabling cross-country comparisons. She is also a member of the Centre for Digital Public Goods at IIM Bangalore and has contributed to projects on India's digital transformation. Her research has been presented at leading academic forums, including the DRUID Academy, the India Strategy Conference, and EURAM.

Subbulakshmi Somu is an associate professor at Dayananda Sagar Institutions, Bengaluru, India. Her research focuses on human resource management, organizational behaviour, and entrepreneurship. She examines how effectuation theories can be applied to the entrepreneurial context. She completed her PhD in Human Resource Management from Annamalai University and her post-doctoral research at Putra Business School, Malaysia. Her work has been published in Scopus-indexed and ABDC-listed journals, and she has presented at leading international conferences including the Academy of Management and the British Academy of Management. Beyond research, she actively contributes to digital education as a SWAYAM MOOC instructor in HR Analytics, reaching a wide learner base across India.

Brindha Srinivasan is a doctoral graduate from the Indian Institute of Management Kozhikode, specializing in entrepreneurial well-being. Her research examines how entrepreneurs proactively craft their work and leisure to enhance well-being, enable serendipity, and improve venture performance, using a mixed-methods approach combining qualitative interviews and longitudinal data. She actively engages with both academic and entrepreneurial ecosystems. Beyond research, she is an avid reader and creative writer with a strong interest in cultural narratives. She is passionate about translating academic insights into practical impact for entrepreneurs and their ecosystems.

R. Srinivasan is Professor of Strategy and Chairperson, Centre for Digital Public Goods at the Indian Institute of Management Bangalore, India. His areas of research and teaching at the graduate and doctoral levels include platform business models, strategy processes, and digital transformation. His work at the Centre for DPG is aimed at helping India craft population-scale Digital Public Goods and Digital Public Infrastructures, as well as document its experiences for learning and replications across contexts

Mittu Tigi is an entrepreneur and startup ecosystem enabler with over a decade of experience working closely with early-stage ventures across India. He currently serves as Director at Merstra Foundation and previously led the Atal Incubation Centre at IIT Kottayam as CEO. His work focuses on advancing responsible entrepreneurship to address real-world challenges. He is also a visiting faculty member at XIME Kochi and actively contributes to initiatives such as Jagriti Yatra and Headstart Network Foundation. He is a recipient of the Global Startup Awards–Ecosystem Hero (South Asia) and has been recognized among India's 50 Most Influential Incubator Leaders. He holds an MBA from IIM Kozhikode and a BTech from MG University Kerala. He leads Kerala chapter with Headstart Network Foundation, supporting grassroots entrepreneurship and ecosystem development.

Ishan Vats is a PhD scholar in Organizational Behaviour and Human Resource Management at the Indian Institute of Management Kozhikode. He holds an MBA from Xavier Institute of Management, Bhubaneswar. Before his PhD, he worked as a Human Resource Business Partner at CARS24, handling employee experience, performance management, grievance resolution, and HR analytics, and as a research associate at Amrop India, focusing on CXO-level research. His research focuses on employment relations, employee voice, precarity, labour institutions, social entrepreneurship, and comparative systems in India, with a focus on policy and practice. He has published case studies with Ivey, The Case Centre, Springer, and Gyanodaya and presented at international conferences including the British Academy of Management, HRIC, and ILPC.

Victoria Austin is Associate Professor of Social Justice and Innovation at UCL Engineering and co-founder of the Global Disability Innovation Hub (GDI Hub), which advances disability innovation through research, teaching, and global programmes across 40+ countries, with over £120m invested. After seven years as founding CEO, she stepped down in 2024 to focus on academic work while remaining a strategic Director.

She co-directs the WHO Global Collaborating Centre on Assistive Technology at UCL and was co-PI of the £31m AT2030 programme, contributing to the first Global Report on Assistive Technology with WHO and UNICEF. Herresearch explores disability justice, technology, and urban development, grounded in participatory and practice-based approaches.

She teaches across UCL and GDI Hub programmes, supervises PhD students, and is writing a book on political engagement and technology. She also chairs the UCL East EDI Board. Previously, she spent 15 years in public service, including leading the London 2012 Paralympic Games legacy.

List of Figures

List of Tables

List of Exhibits

CHAPTER 1

Context-Inspired Entrepreneurship in India

Sreevas Sahasranamam, Ashish S. Galande, and Elizabeth L. Rose

Abstract The evolution of the Indian entrepreneurship story is deeply contextually rooted in its societal structures, colonial influence, shifting national policy regimes, and the broader global environment. Yet, much of prevailing discourse has been shaped by frameworks and case studies embedded in Western contexts, often overlooking or even undermining the distinctiveness of the Indian experience. This introductory chapter offers an overview of Indian entrepreneurship, highlighting its unique historical, temporal, institutional, spatial, and social dimensions. To ground these insights, we present a case study of the Purvanchal Entrepreneurial Ecosystem—to illustrate how regional contexts shape entrepreneurial

S. Sahasranamam (✉)
Adam Smith Business School, University of Glasgow, Glasgow, UK
e-mail: sreevas.sahasranamam@glasgow.ac.uk

A. S. Galande
School of Business and Economics, SUNY Plattsburgh, Plattsburgh, NY, USA
e-mail: agala009@plattsburgh.edu

E. L. Rose
ICFAI Foundation for Higher Education, Hyderabad, Telegana, India
e-mail: elizabeth.rose@ifheindia.org

A. S. Galande et al. (eds.), *Context-inspired Entrepreneurship*, Sustainable Development Goals Series,
https://doi.org/10.1007/978-981-95-9831-1_1

trajectories. The chapter concludes with an overview of the 25 case study chapters featured in the book, organized into five thematic sections: cultural entrepreneurship, rural and social entrepreneurship, technology-enabled inclusion, entrepreneurship support organizations, and entrepreneurial journeys.

Keywords Indian entrepreneurship • Entrepreneurial ecosystem • Rural entrepreneurship • Social entrepreneurship • Cultural entrepreneurship • Decolonization • Entrepreneurship education • Teaching cases • Contexts • Global South

SDG Links
Primary—SDG 8: Decent Work and Economic Growth
Secondary—SDG 9: Industry, Innovation, and Infrastructure, SDG 4: Quality Education

Indian entrepreneurship is deeply driven by its context, including societal structures, colonial influence, changing national policy regimes, and the larger global environment. However, for far too long, entrepreneurship education in India has been predominantly based on case studies and frameworks inspired by, or rooted in, Western contexts. While valuable, this reliance has inadvertently created a substantial gap in our understanding of how the unique contexts of India, or Bharat, inspire and foster entrepreneurship. Hence, Indian classrooms have lacked deliberations on granular insights from ventures born out of India's unique local challenges, cultural influences, and market opportunities. This book, "Context-inspired Entrepreneurship: Cases from India", is born out of this compelling need to bridge the divide. It serves as a deliberate step towards democratizing entrepreneurship education, shifting the lens to celebrate and learn from India's distinct entrepreneurial landscape.

Our core mission is to bring impactful grassroots stories to the hands of students, educators, aspiring entrepreneurs, and policymakers across the nation, particularly within its Tier 2/3/4 cities and rural towns. It is also about globalizing the lessons and practices from Indian entrepreneurship by developing a pedagogical resource that can be used in business schools around the world to understand entrepreneurship from the Global South.

The chapters are not merely stories or business narratives; rather, they chronicle context-inspired stories and compel the reader to deliberate on future courses of action by situating themself in the shoes of the protagonists of the cases. This will empower learners to grapple with the real-world, unique complexities of India, foster a deeper understanding of innovation and entrepreneurship rooted in its contexts, and thus inspire the creation of a generation of entrepreneurs who are deeply connected to their communities and envision nation-building through enterprise.

Overview of Indian Entrepreneurship

We start by looking back at a brief history of Indian entrepreneurship, to set the premise for this book. Scholarly records from the turn of the millennium, particularly from the Gupta period, highlight how entrepreneurship was influenced by social structures such as the *varna* system, an occupation-based social stratification that shaped the formation of *Srenis*, or associations of artisans or merchants (Balasubramanian, 2024; Rooney & Murthy, 2026). During this period, it was predominantly the *Vaishya* community that engaged in commercial economic activities.

Until the 1800s, the material, social, and cultural environment conducive to entrepreneurship, conceptualized in today's terminology as an entrepreneurial ecosystem, was weak in India, for multiple reasons (Tripathi, 1971). The lack of political unity, and the corresponding lack of safety for the free movement of people and goods across the country, was one key barrier. There were also customs barriers, referred to as *chowkies,* which made the cost of transporting goods expensive. Furthermore, the very act of engaging in business activities (*dhanda*) was held in relatively low esteem, with a societal distrust of those engaging in commerce.

During the British era, Agency Houses were established and served as intermediaries for promoting entrepreneurial activity (Aldous, 2023). While they were intended as mechanisms for exploiting the natural resources of India, they facilitated funding and market linkages, creating entrepreneurial ventures in indigo plantations, leather manufacturing, and coal mining. In parallel, with the increasing influence of British ideas and education, Protestant ethics began becoming infused, and thus non-mercantile classes also began viewing business and entrepreneurship more favorably (Tripathi, 1971). As Weber (2002) highlights, the evolution of modern capitalism and entrepreneurship is largely rooted in the Protestant ethic, and colonies like India became sites where its philosophy and assumptions were embedded. This shaped the creation of ventures such as the Carr Tagore Company and the shaping of cotton textile clusters in Bombay and Ahmedabad.

Fast forward to independent India while diversified business groups were an expression of larger-scale commercial activity, the government also began seeing micro-entrepreneurship as a means of addressing unemployment (Monsen et al., 2012). This saw the development of policies such as the Prime Minister's Rozgar Yojana (PMRY), the Integrated Rural Development Programme (IRDP) for self-employment generation in rural areas, and the creation of organizations like the Khadi and Village Industries Commission (KVIC) to support local craftsmen. The economic liberalization in 1991 and, with it, the establishment of foreign MNE subsidiaries in India, such as Texas Instruments in 1985, began creating the Information Technology (IT) startup ecosystem in Bangalore (Bhagavatula et al., 2019). Over time, the spillover effect of this startup activity began to manifest itself in other cities, creating entrepreneurship hotspots in Delhi, Hyderabad, Mumbai, and Chennai, among others.

During the last decade, the flagship Startup India initiative started in 2016, alongside the establishment of the Atal Innovation Mission and, through it, the creation of Atal Incubation Centres in colleges and Atal Tinkering Labs in schools; the leadership of India in creating the Startup20 initiative within the G20 in 2023; and the broader efforts towards improving the ease of doing business in India; have shaped a vibrant entrepreneurial ecosystem. Currently, India is the third-largest startup ecosystem in the world, in terms of the number of startups, and the third largest in terms of the number of unicorns (privately held ventures with a greater than US$1 billion valuation) (Sahasranamam & Kuppusamy, 2024). This buoyant entrepreneurship sentiment is echoed in statistics from multiple sources, such as the Global Entrepreneurship Monitor 2023/24 report, placing India as the second best among 49 economies on the quality of its entrepreneurial ecosystem. Furthermore, that survey highlighted a very high proportion (~80%) of responents expressing that they saw good opportunities for starting a new business in India, and an equally high proportion believed it was easy to start a business (Hill et al., 2024).

Despite this upbeat sentiment toward the intention to start a business and the perception of a conducive environment for it, a much smaller proportion were expected to act, with fear of failure being one of the key barriers (Hill et al., 2024). This highlights the need for entrepreneurship education to overcome the stigma attached to failure. Furthermore, with over 60% of the startups in five states of India (DPIIT, 2023), and more precisely in a few cities within those states, this means that entrepreneurial role modeling and support structures are largely concentrated in a few regions. For India's vision of a Viksit Bharat by 2047, entrepreneurship is a central piece, and, for that, we must democratize entrepreneurship across the country. Towards this end, as highlighted earlier, this book is an important step as a curated pedagogical resource that can be used in classrooms across the country and draws on stories from India to inspire, inform, and invoke the entrepreneurial spirit.

Context-Inspired Entrepreneurship

Context in entrepreneurship research refers to circumstances, conditions, or environments that are external to entrepreneurial phenomena but could constrain or enable them (Welter, 2011). The term 'context' comes from Latin, meaning 'weaving together' or 'to make a connection'. Context is not static; rather, it is actively created or enacted by the individual through language, cognition, and interpretations (Welter et al., 2019).

A context-inspired view of entrepreneurship helps us to comprehend it better by placing it within its specific historical, temporal, institutional, spatial, and social settings. This is important for understanding "when, how, and why entrepreneurship happens and who becomes involved" (Welter, 2011, p. 166). Broadly, to understand how context influences entrepreneurship, Welter (2011) categorizes it into 'where' and 'when' dimensions. The 'where' is about business contexts (industry, market), social contexts (family, personal networks), spatial contexts (community, village, country), and institutional contexts (formal rules such as laws and informal societal values). For instance, the institutional deficiencies in pre-liberalization India created unique entrepreneurial opportunities, including arbitrage on customs duties, seen in the role portrayed by Shahid Kapoor in the 2010 film Badmaash Company. The 'when' dimension is about the role of historical and temporal contexts in how past events and changes over time influence entrepreneurial activity. For instance, as discussed earlier, historically, in the *varna* system, the Vaishya communities, such as Marwaris and Chettiars, have predominantly engaged in entrepreneurship. To illustrate the manifestation of contextual influence on Indian entrepreneurship, we present insights from our field engagement with entrepreneurs and entrepreneurship support organizations in Purvanchal

(Eastern Uttar Pradesh), one of the least economically developed parts of India.

Brief Case Study of Purvanchal Entrepreneurial Ecosystem

We start by looking at the example of Saritha (name changed), whom we met during research related to this book, in Khanpur Masodha village. She had started a new handicrafts venture, taking up sewing and embroidery as a means to earn income for her family. If we view this just as any other entrepreneurial act, we would see it as a young woman's journey to set up a business in a low-margin, low-growth sector and attribute it to being shaped largely by the limited resources to which she had access. However, if we take the context into account, the view changes: in rural areas such as Khanpur Masodha village, women are not expected to go into business and are encouraged to stay at home. In that setting, Saritha, whom we met as part of an entrepreneurship support initiative, tells us a story of a young woman who learned a traditional craft because that was among the few vocational training opportunities that she had, and it was something that she could do from her home. This tells us how institutional and social contexts, such as the role of gender within families in this case, influence why female entrepreneurship is sometimes in low-income, low-growth industries.

Micro-entrepreneurs like Saritha also lacks the skills to deal with the complexities of tax registration and regular reporting, a reflection of the weak educational institutional context in the area. This means their ventures largely remains informal and forego digital market linkage possibilities through e-commerce platforms.

The region is also home to a newly-built temple for Lord Rama (a key character in the Indian *ithihasa* called Ramayana) in Ayodhya, which was inaugurated in early 2024. The temple construction movement had a long history of struggle and, considering its historical significance as the birthplace of Lord Rama, it attracted substantial religious tourism in 2024. Such temporal and historical contextual factors triggered the creation of entrepreneurial activity related to the temple, such as religious products, souvenirs, hospitality, and transport services for pilgrims.

In the Gorakhpur area of this region, there are communities of artisans who, for multiple generations, have been involved in terracotta handicrafts (a type of earthenware clay). This artisanal skill has seen a revival in recent years on the back of efforts by the government to market terracotta products under the One District One Product (ODOP) scheme. Entrepreneurship support organizations such as Entrepreneurship Development Institute of India (EDII) and National Bank for Agriculture and Rural Development (NABARD) have partnered to support the entrepreneurship-related skilling of these artisans and created an aggregated organization structure called Off-Farm Producer Organizations (OFPO) for marketing and selling terracotta products. This changing business and spatial context is triggering entrepreneurial activity, with the creation of new categories of terracotta products, such as terracotta jewellery.

The above case study of the Purvanchal entrepreneurial ecosystem tells us how, by considering context, it is possible to develop deeper and more nuanced insights into the phenomenon of entrepreneurship. The chapters in this book draw deeply from such business, social, spatial, institutional, historical, and temporal contexts to offer an embedded understanding of Indian entrepreneurship.

Introducing the Chapters of the Book and Their SDG Linkages

The book presents a multifaceted view of how the Indian context influences entrepreneurship. Across 25 chapters, through each of the distinct teaching case studies, we unpack critical aspects of new venture creation, growth, and impact, all with a specific focus on local contexts.

At its core, the book primarily champions SDG 8: Decent Work and Economic Growth. By inspiring and educating future entrepreneurs, it aims to contribute to job creation and inclusive economic growth. Through teaching case studies that showcase innovations in rural areas, and emerging business models, the book demonstrates how to improve productive employment (Target 8.3) and advance youth employability (Target 8.6). It documents real-world entrepreneurial journeys from smaller towns and rural regions of India to demonstrate how entrepreneurship education can directly contribute to decent work outcomes and long-term economic resilience.

Beyond the central SDG goals of the book discussed above, individual chapters have relevance to other SDGs, which we summarize below within the five thematic sections into which the book is organized.

Part I: Echoes of Heritage—Cultural Entrepreneurship

India's rich cultural heritage naturally lends itself to numerous entrepreneurship opportunities. A cultural entrepreneur is someone "who is entrepreneurial in the realization of cultural values" (Klamer, 2011, p. 141). Extant research on this theme focuses on understanding how culture-related products are created, how culture acts as a mechanism for legitimizing new ventures, and how value is created using culture as part of the meaning-making process (Gehman & Soublière, 2017). In the Indian context, research has explored the role of social capital in the craft industry (Bhagavatula et al., 2010) and circular economic practices within the indigenous Ayurveda industry (Pereira et al., 2022). More recently, technology-driven cultural ventures have emerged, leveraging AI and the Metaverse (Sahasranamam, 2024). These ventures are deeply rooted in Indian Knowledge Systems and driven by a broader trend around economic decolonization in India (Sahasranamam & Kondayya, 2026).

This section showcases ventures that are not only preserving this heritage but also reviving it by breathing a fresh lease of economic life into it. From the revival of ancient stories through gamification by **Sutradhar**, to market linkages for traditional craft forged by **Tamaala** and **Craft Mantra**, to commercializing indigenous herbal knowledge by **Bikalp Herbals**, these cases highlight how culture and heritage can be a powerful driver of entrepreneurial opportunities, while debating dilemmas around scaling and colonial mindsets.

Part II: The Grassroots Innovators—Rural and Social Entrepreneurship

This section showcases case studies of ventures that tackle India's social and environmental challenges by building sustainable models that uplift communities and steward natural resources. While social entrepreneurship focuses on realizing its social mission, rural entrepreneurship is more about leveraging place-based resources such as natural and historical assets (Korsgaard & Tanvig, 2015; Mair & Martí, 2006). Existing research on social entrepreneurship in India has explored themes such as the role of bricolage (Hota et al., 2019) and community values and tradition (Chatterjee et al., 2021), institutional contexts (Sahasranamam & Ball, 2018), and corporate involvement (Agrawal & Sahasranamam, 2016).

Similarly, studies on rural entrepreneurship have explored issues such as the well-being of rural women entrepreneurs (Chatterjee et al., 2022), customer acquisition (Chatterjee et al., 2025), and the influence of social hierarchy (Qureshi et al., 2023).

From **Bhungroo**'s ingenious solution to water scarcity and climate resilience to **Pi.kademy**'s approach to alternative education for slum children, to the **Global Himalayan Expedition** electrifying remote Himalayan villages through tourism, and **Bambrew**'s effort towards sustainable packaging, the book discusses purpose-driven ventures and debates how social, environmental, and economic objectives could be balanced. Alongside this, through case studies on **PlusTrust** creating women community health entrepreneurs, **Shivganga Samagra Gramvikas Parishad** moving from community mobilization and water conservation to entrepreneurship, and **GK Energy** bringing solar-powered agriculture, one can appreciate the dynamics and challenges of rural entrepreneurship.

Part III: The Digital Frontier—Tech-Enabled Inclusion

This section highlights case studies of ventures using technology to enable inclusion and accessibility. Considering India's distinctive socio-economic context, research on this topic has examined themes such as frugal innovation (Radjou et al., 2012), the creative adaptation of off-the shelf technologies for opportunities—often termed as "technoficing" (Qureshi et al., 2021), and the distributed co-creation of innovation ecosystems to address technological voids (Sahasranamam et al., 2024). An emerging frontier where India has assumed a pioneering role is Digital Public Infrastructure (DPI), exemplified by India Stack, which is transforming entrepreneurship by bridging identity, financial, and market voids (Sahasranamam & Prabhu, 2024).

Chapters in this section illuminate the power of digital public infrastructure (DPI), as in the case of **DIGIIT,** digitally transforming small and medium enterprises, and **Fee Plaza**, simplifying fee payments by leveraging UPI (a DPI for payments). The book also presents case studies of **5C Networks** and **Neurosynaptics**, to explore the complexities of healthcare access and technology enablement, and highlights the role of assistive technology for inclusive development through the case of **Attvaran**.

Part IV: The Architects of Growth—Entrepreneurship Support Organizations

For any startup ecosystem to thrive, it needs support organizations such as incubators and accelerators to nurture, guide, and accelerate the entrepreneurial journeys. Research on this topic has studied the role of accelerators in Bengaluru's entrepreneurial ecosystem (Goswami et al., 2018), invisible inequalities in the ecosystem (Anand et al., 2025) and characteristics of technology business incubators (Mungila Hillemane, 2020).

This section features cases of entrepreneurship support organizations in India, providing insights into the robust incubation models of **NSRCEL** at IIM Bangalore, helping to understand how the pan-India volunteer-driven startup support initiative **Headstart Network Foundation** works, and understanding the foundational grassroots ecosystem development work of the **Deshpande Foundation**. The creation of an entrepreneurship mindset and networks on the move by **Jagriti Yatra**, through an annual train journey, is another case study in this section.

Part V: Unconventional Paths—Entrepreneurial Journeys

The final section of the book engages with case studies showing individual or family business journeys that have traversed unconventional paths through entrepreneurship. From understanding the distinctive entrepreneurial ethos of a **Marwari entrepreneur**, to dilemmas of **Safai Karmacharis** (sanitation workers) undergoing an entrepreneurship training programme, to the story of a young girl pondering over what to do with her business idea after **Zero2Maker** (a pre-incubation entrepreneurship training programme), the book delves into the unique personal journeys of individuals and their choices when engaging in entrepreneurship. The case studies on the multi-generational family business of Kamaths, the **Krishna Novelty Stores**, and a **community food enterprise in Kotma** bring in the unique vantage points of how family and community, respectively, influence entrepreneurship. Overall, cases in this section bring to fore theoretical discussions around necessity entrepreneurship (Sahasranamam & Sud, 2016), entrepreneurship education pedagogies (Higgins et al., 2013), and family business characteristics (Le Breton-Miller & Miller, 2009).

In conclusion, the chapters in the book are more than just stories; they present strategic dilemmas and situations of decision-making that are designed to provoke thought, stimulate discussion, and engage the reader to appreciate the uniqueness of Indian entrepreneurship and think critically about its future trajectory.

References

Agrawal, A., & Sahasranamam, S. (2016). Corporate social entrepreneurship in India. *South Asian Journal of Global Business Research, 5*(2), 214–233.

Aldous, M. (2023). From traders to planters: The evolving role and importance of trading companies in the 19th-century Anglo-Indian Indigo trade. *Business History, 65*(5), 803–820.

Anand, P., Attri, P. S., & Sahasranamam, S. (2025). Invisible inequality in entrepreneurial ecosystems: the micro-foundations of navigating marginalization. *Business & Society*, 00076503251407016.

Balasubramanian, S. (2024). *Dharmanomics: An Indigenous and Sustainable Economic Model*. Bloomsbury India.

Bhagavatula, S., Elfring, T., van Tilburg, A., & van de Bunt, G. G. (2010). How social and human capital influence opportunity recognition and resource mobilization in India's handloom industry. *Journal of Business Venturing, 25*(3), 245–260.

Bhagavatula, S., Mudambi, R., & Murmann, J. P. (2019). Innovation and entrepreneurship in India: An overview. *Management and Organization Review, 15*(3), 467–493.

Chatterjee, A., Chauradia, A. J., & Pedada, K. (2025). Rural women microentrepreneurs, consumer acquisition, and value delivery: Evidence from a quasi-experiment in rural India. *Journal of the Academy of Marketing Science, 53*(1), 213–231.

Chatterjee, I., Cornelissen, J., & Wincent, J. (2021). Social entrepreneurship and values work: The role of practices in shaping values and negotiating change. *Journal of Business Venturing, 36*(1), 106064.

Chatterjee, I., Shepherd, D. A., & Wincent, J. (2022). Women's entrepreneurship and well-being at the base of the pyramid. *Journal of Business Venturing, 37*(4), 106222.

DPIIT. (2023). States startup ranking 2022 national report.

Gehman, J., & Soublière, J. F. (2017). Cultural entrepreneurship: From making culture to cultural making. *The Innovation, 19*(1), 61–73.

Goswami, K., Mitchell, J. R., & Bhagavatula, S. (2018). Accelerator expertise: Understanding the intermediary role of accelerators in the development of the

Bangalore entrepreneurial ecosystem. *Strategic Entrepreneurship Journal, 12*(1), 117–150.

Higgins, D., Smith, K., & Mirza, M. (2013). Entrepreneurial education: Reflexive approaches to entrepreneurial learning in practice. *Journal of Entrepreneurship, 22*(2), 135–160.

Hill, S., Ionescu-Somers, A., Coduras, A., Guerrero, M., Menipaz, E., et al. (2024). Global Entrepreneurship Monitor 2023/2024 global report: 25 years and growing.

Hota, P. K., Mitra, S., & Qureshi, I. (2019). Adopting bricolage to overcome resource constraints: The case of social enterprises in rural India. *Management and Organization Review, 15*(2), 371–402.

Klamer, A. (2011). Cultural entrepreneurship. *The Review of Austrian Economics, 24*, 141–156.

Korsgaard, S., & Tanvig, H. W. (2015). Rural entrepreneurship or entrepreneurship in the rural—Between place and space. *International Journal of Entrepreneurial Behaviour and Research, 21*(1), 5–26.

Le Breton-Miller, I., & Miller, D. (2009). Agency vs. stewardship in public family firms: A social embeddedness reconciliation. *Entrepreneurship: Theory and Practice, 33*(6), 1169–1191.

Mair, J., & Martí, I. (2006). Social entrepreneurship research: A source of explanation, prediction, and delight. *Journal of World Business, 41*(1), 36–44.

Monsen, E., Mahagaonkar, P., & Dienes, C. (2012). Entrepreneurship in India: The question of occupational transition. *Small Business Economics, 39*(2), 359–382.

Mungila Hillemane, B. S. (2020). Technology business incubators in India: What determines their R&D contributions to the national economy? *International Journal of Innovation Science, 12*(4), 385–408.

Pereira, V., Nandakumar, M. K., Sahasranamam, S., Bamel, U., Malik, A., et al. (2022). An exploratory study into emerging market SMEs' involvement in the circular economy: Evidence from India's indigenous Ayurveda industry. *Journal of Business Research, 142*, 188–199.

Qureshi, I., Bhatt, B., Sutter, C., & Shukla, D. M. (2023). Social entrepreneurship and intersectionality: Mitigating extreme exclusion. *Journal of Business Venturing, 38*(2), 106283.

Qureshi, I., Pan, S. L., & Zheng, Y. (2021). Digital social innovation: An overview and research framework. *Information Systems Journal, 31*(5), 647–671.

Radjou, N., Prabhu, J., & Ahuja, S. (2012). *Jugaad innovation: think frugal, be flexible, generate breakthrough growth.* John Wiley & Sons.

Rooney, J., & Murthy, V. (2026). Management and social order in ancient India. *Business History, 68*(3), 539–573.

Sahasranamam, S. (2024). Four ways in which history and religion are being transformed by the metaverse and AI. *The Conversation* https://theconversation.

com/four-ways-in-which-history-and-religion-are-being-transformed-by-the-metaverse-and-ai-243192

Sahasranamam, S., & Ball, C. (2018). National context matters: Influence of national business system on social enterprises in Scotland and India. In L. J. Spence, J. G. Frynas, J. N. Muthuri, & J. Navare (Eds.), *Research handbook on small business social responsibility: Global perspectives* (pp. 23–46). Edward Elgar Publishing Ltd..

Sahasranamam, S., & Kuppusamy, A. (2024). 4 emerging trends from India's booming entrepreneur ecosystem. *World Economic Forum*. https://www.weforum.org/stories/2024/12/india-startup-entrepreneur-trends/

Sahasranamam, S., & Prabhu, J. (2024). Digital public infrastructure for the developing world. *Stanford Social Innovation Review*.

Sahasranamam, S., & Kondayya, A. (2026). Understanding Hindu religious entrepreneurship: A translation perspective. *Entrepreneurship & Regional Development, 38*(5–6), 501–528.

Sahasranamam, S., Soundararajan, V., & Chatterjee, D. (2024). Co-creating innovation ecosystems in contexts of absolute uncertainty: The case of low-cost heart valves in India. *Journal of Product Innovation Management, 41*(2), 501–526.

Sahasranamam, S., & Sud, M. (2016). Opportunity and necessity entrepreneurship: A comparative study of India and China. *Academy of Entrepreneurship Journal, 22*(1), 21–40.

Tripathi, D. (1971). Indian entrepreneurship in historical perspective: A re-interpretation. *Economic and Political Weekly*, M59–M66.

Weber, M. (2002). *The Protestant ethic and the Spirit of capitalism: And other writings*. Penguin Publishing Group.

Welter, F. (2011). Contextualizing entrepreneurship—Conceptual challenges and ways forward. *Entrepreneurship Theory and Practice, 35*(1), 165–184.

Welter, F., Baker, T., & Wirsching, K. (2019). Three waves and counting: The rising tide of contextualization in entrepreneurship research. *Small Business Economics, 52*, 319–330.

CHAPTER 2

Weaving Tales from Heritage or Hanging by a Thread? The Case of Sutradhar

Anupama Kondayya and Sreevas Sahasranamam

Abstract Gaurav Tiwari founded Sutradhar (Sampatra Technologies Pvt. Ltd.) with a mission to address a perceived gap in the moral education of Indian children with content rooted in Indic heritage and made accessible through edutainment. His vision extended beyond just generating content, and embraced gamification towards the eventual development of a metaverse inspired by Indian Knowledge Systems. However, Gaurav soon realized the challenge of bootstrapping a values-driven, heritage-inspired and content-first venture in a domain dominated by high-budget productions, and of finding support for a venture promoting traditional knowledge amidst stakeholders and ecosystems influenced by modern colonial perspectives. Should he persevere, pause or pivot? This case discusses the dilemma of balancing cultural aspirations and market realities in the Indian entrepreneurship ecosystem, offering students a nuanced understanding

A. Kondayya (✉)
Indian Institute of Management Calcutta, Kolkata, India
e-mail: akondayya@iimcal.ac.in

S. Sahasranamam
Adam Smith Business School, University of Glasgow, Glasgow, UK
e-mail: sreevas.sahasranamam@glasgow.ac.uk

A. S. Galande et al. (eds.), *Context-inspired Entrepreneurship*, Sustainable Development Goals Series,
https://doi.org/10.1007/978-981-95-9831-1_2

of the challenges of building ventures in emerging categories and nascent markets such as heritage-inspired entrepreneurship. The case is particularly suited for teaching cultural entrepreneurship, heritage-inspired innovation and new category creation.

Keywords Cultural entrepreneurship • Category creation • Edutainment • Entrepreneurial ecosystems • Games • Indic Heritage • Indian Knowledge Systems • Early stage startups

SDG Links
While the central focus of this chapter is on cultural preservation, it contributes to SDG 8 by highlighting how heritage-based initiatives can create livelihood and employment opportunities around creative economy and cultural industries (SDG 8.9). The chapter also aligns with SDG 11, through its focus on safeguarding intangible cultural heritage, and SDG 4 by facilitating cultural learning.

Introduction

It was a typical morning in Gaurav Tiwari's household, with his wife and three children absorbed in the daily routine before the kids rushed to school. But he was anxious. He had a regular medical check-up scheduled later in the day and had recently been under a lot of stress about the future of his children and of his brainchild—the venture Sutradhar[1] (Sampatra Technologies Pvt. Ltd.), which aimed to address the lacuna of moral education among children in India by making Indic heritage-based content accessible through edutainment. While Gaurav had started generating and gamifying content with the ultimate vision of building a metaverse, he realized that competing with high-budget productions and maintaining his ethical goals was proving to be difficult in an endeavor primarily driven by passion and values. The result was a personal and financial toll, leading Gaurav to wonder if he should step back temporarily to prioritize family and attain financial stability before continuing to bootstrap Sutradhar. The dilemma weighed heavily on his mind that morning: should he continue or pause efforts to build Sutradhar?

[1] In Sanskrit, Sutra=thread, Dhar=holder/keeper, Sutradhar=narrator

Once Upon a Time: The Story of Sutradhar/ Sampatra Technologies Pvt. Ltd.

Once upon a time, there was a boy named Gaurav Tiwari, who grew up in a small town in India and eventually moved to larger urban centers for education and work. He studied engineering at one of India's premier educational institutes, the Indian Institute of Technology Bombay. Throughout the journey, a passion he actively nurtured was writing. Gaurav considered making a career out of it before realizing that choosing to be a professional writer in India was not pragmatic and economically rewarding. He chose financial services instead and worked for multiple leading banks in India, engaging in building products and shaping industry trends. During this time, he also dabbled in the venture capital landscape.

And then he became a parent.

As Gaurav's first child, a daughter, approached three years of age, he began to wonder what values and morals he would leave behind for her. Growing up in a joint family[2] in a small town in India, Gaurav was brought up on a staple diet of stories narrated by his grandparents. As a child, he eagerly looked forward to this daily story time, and the stories became a crucial source of values and moral education for him. Gaurav realized that his daughter, along with numerous Indian children, would not have access to this experience and moral education with the rise of the nuclear family in India. Further, while the quantity of content available to the new generation had increased dramatically through the Internet, the quality had not increased in proportion.

Gaurav wanted to change that and saw an opportunity to revive his long-held passion to bring about this change. He went back to his passion and love for writing and telling stories. Only this time, he chose stories from the treasure trove of Indic heritage—stories that he had grown up listening to and wanted the coming generations to enjoy and learn from. He chose the popular online content platform YouTube as the medium and started to create videos based on stories from the Indic heritage of India. This led to the launch of Sampatra Technologies and what Gaurav termed as the Sutradhar phase of his venture.

[2] A family structure where multiple generations and relations cohabit in the same house

Sutradhar Phase: Weaving Digital Networks with the Thread of Tradition

Gaurav's objective in the Sutradhar phase was research and feedback from and about audiences and market potential, along with the distribution of content. Thus, he focused on quantity instead of extremely high quality to gain traction on YouTube and improve chances of discovery through its algorithm. This allowed Gaurav to figure out the audience's interests and what kind of content might work going forward. Banking on an existing and popular platform such as YouTube not only created potential for reach but also kept the venture asset-light in the bootstrapped stage. But quality mattered in the online content space, especially with the rise of Over-The-Top (OTT) platforms. While Sutradhar's content had better quality than the average YouTube video, it was not enough to compete with the giants of storytelling such as Disney. Producing better content required higher investments: Gaurav was spending about INR 2000 to INR 3000 per minute of content, whereas the likes of Disney would spend a much higher multiple. Gaurav could not compete with that. This led to a need for monetization, building a competitive advantage, and finding ways to drive audiences towards Sutradhar's content, leading to the next phase. Gaurav called this the Ranbhoomi (battlefield) phase of the business.

Ranbhoomi Phase: Entering the Competitive Battle

The goal in the Ranbhoomi phase was to demonstrate that the stories could be gamified to invoke curiosity that would lead audiences towards curated and exclusive online content such as podcasts, videos, and blogs, creating a competitive advantage. Gaurav started by creating jigsaw puzzles based on stories from the Indian epic of Ramayana and the Panchatantra, eventually bundling a subscription to the Sutradhar application with the products. This would help users hear the stories related to the puzzle and move from the physical to the digital domain seamlessly. He also wanted to create online games based on the stories to fill in the lacuna of the experience of story-time for children.

Gamification, however, would require a significant investment in the range of USD 2 Mn towards production and marketing. Another challenge was the willingness to pay of the Indian consumer: people were not known to pay for casual gaming in India, and in-game advertising was the

Table 2.1 Sutradhar's products

Product	*Material/Mode*	*Price in INR (March 2025)*
Jigsaw puzzle: 2 puzzles of 35 pieces	Cardboard	399
Jigsaw puzzle: 4 puzzles of 35 pieces	Cardboard	599
Jigsaw puzzle: 4 puzzles of 35 pieces	Wooden	1099
Jigsaw puzzle: 1 puzzle of 100 pieces	Cardboard	699
Board game	Cardboard	2499
Board game	Online	Free

primary source of revenue. Real money lay in games of chance or gambling, which did not align with Gaurav's aim and moral values.

Gaurav decided to experiment anyway, start small, and test the market with a board game called Ranbhoomi Kurukshetra based on the Indian epic of Mahabharata. The game sold 1000 copies and also went on to win the DNA Paris Design Award 2025 in the graphic and communication design category, judged by a non-Indian jury and without any effort going into marketing communications, including Public Relations and Advertising. The game was also available to play online[3] in a single or 2-player format to help users experience the game and increase their willingness to pay. The game proved to be a successful low-cost experiment requiring an investment of under INR 10 Lakhs (as opposed to INR 8 or 9 crores for a digital game), having more than a 50% profit margin, and helping realize that there was a market for Sutradhar's products. This encouraged Gaurav to conceptualize Ranbhoomi Lanka (based on the Ramayana) and Ranbhoomi Mahishmati (based on the legend of Parashurama) to expand the board game offerings of Sutradhar. Table 2.1 shows Sutradhar's product offerings up to March 2025.

Plot Twist: The Changing Environment

Having tasted success with games, Gaurav started thinking about the next phase of the venture while considering the changing technological and consumer trends in parallel.

He sensed that many technological changes were impending. The preliminary version of the World Wide Web (Web 1.0) relied on Internet browsers to deliver static content, and Web 2.0, on native applications for

[3] https://ranbhoomi.mysutradhar.com/

interactive content delivery. Web 3.0 technology was still nascent, and it was difficult to predict what would emerge as its primary medium and what the nature of the content would be. What seemed clear was that Web 3.0 would be context-based instead of being keyword-based like Web 2.0, and this would have implications for content delivery. Meanwhile, 6G wireless communication technology was on the horizon, but there were no real use cases for that either.

Further, while electronic devices were moving from idiot to smart as the good old 'idiot' box was replaced with smart televisions and smartphones for content consumption, the content itself had not made that transition. There was a wave of hyper-personalization coming in, with implications even for how content was consumed and would possibly be commoditized in the following decade. The consumers themselves had changed, with low attention spans and modern-day stressors necessitating daily escapes from the grind of life (as opposed to previous generations taking vacations once every few years).

Catering to these changes would involve heavy upfront costs and foresight to predict the direction that the emerging trends would take. The entire picture would take time to emerge, but what seemed undeniable was that virtual immersive experiences were the next frontier.

Bharatverse Phase: Bridging the Past and the Future

Given the anticipated changes in the environment, Gaurav envisioned it all coming together in the next phase and endgame of his venture: a metaverse called Bharatverse, where users could interact through avatars to establish social and economic connections in a virtual simulation of ancient India. The goal was to promote knowledge about ancient India while integrating with the key activities that people engaged in online: information seeking, community building, and commerce.

As a first step, Bharatverse would enable world-building based on descriptions of ancient India provided in historical and mythological texts, powered by an AI-based engine trained using Indic texts. This would acquaint users with design concepts and ideas from ancient texts and scriptures in an immersive way. For example, a user interested in jewelry design could establish a jewelry store in Bharatverse to sell jewelry designed as per descriptions in Indic texts. This world-building would create possibilities for users to build entire cities from ancient historical and mythological descriptions, be it the city of Hastinapur from the Mahabharata or ancient centers of learning such as Varanasi and Nalanda, replete with residences, markets, gurukuls,[4] and universities.

Users would also be able to inhabit and experience these worlds and cities in their 3D avatars, engaging in both social and economic interactions. As an example, a user could rent space in Sage Dronacharya's ashram to offer courses on Vedic Mathematics that other users could enroll in and attend together using virtual reality headsets. Users would also be able to seek information and input from ancient texts and the work of specific personalities, such as Vidur or Bheeshma from the Mahabharata, through AI-based engines trained using Indic texts and avatars that could simulate their personalities. This is where the emerging technological trends and changing consumer psyches would find their culmination, with users finding their daily respite from the grind in the Bharatverse. Gaurav was excited by the possibility. But not everyone was.

The Indic-Heritage Ecosystem

Sutradhar is part of an ecosystem emerging around preserving and reviving Indian Knowledge Systems (IKS) and Indic heritage, where actors are blending traditional knowledge and perspectives with modern forms of consumption for contemporary audiences. The view of IKS in the ecosystem is that of a continuous living tradition going back more than 3000 years and continuing to hold relevant insights for modern times. The actors in the ecosystem include universities and individuals that act as subject matter experts, government departments, ideological organizations and influencers, entrepreneurs, venture capitalists, and consumers, whose interests and agendas converge and clash in this nascent ecosystem.

The ecosystem started taking shape with the distributed efforts of actors interested in exploring IKS to solve contemporary problems and reclaim Indian systems from colonial domination. In 1986, heavily influenced by the work of the Gandhian scholar Dharampal, a group of Indian scientists, professionals, scholars, historians, sociologists, philosophers, thinkers and social activists came together to form a network by the name Patriotic and People-Oriented Science & Technology (PPST) Group to explore traditions of Sciences and Technologies that existed before the

[4] An traditional educational institution where students lived in or around the teacher's house and engaged in continuous education through instruction as well as praxis

colonial domination of India.[5] One of the founding members of the group, Dr. A.V. Balasubramanian, went on to establish the Centre for Indian Knowledge Systems[6] in 1993 with Dr. K. Vijayalakshmi. Over the next two decades, the work of these and similar centers generated a critical mass of research which translated into policy support for IKS in the 2010s. In October 2020, the Government of India (GoI) established a division for IKS under its Ministry of Education (MoE), intending to preserve and promote inter–/trans-disciplinary research in IKS for societal benefit. Apart from funding the establishment of centers for IKS such as the one in the Indian Institute of Technology (IIT) Kharagpur,[7] the division facilitates internship programs for undergraduate students, and organizes faculty development programs, workshops, text mining and documentation projects, and outreach activities in partnership with other institutions.

The MoE also launched the National Education Policy (NEP) in 2020, with Indian knowledge being both its foundation and goal. The policy drew on ancient educational philosophy that held knowledge, wisdom, and truth along with the realization of one's full potential as the teleology. It also aimed to revive and extend perspectives from IKS for contemporary applications. The policy recommended integrating IKS—including tribal, indigenous, and traditional perspectives and practices—into school curricula at various levels. In particular, the policy encouraged schools to use games and videos to infuse fun into learning this knowledge. Sutradhar and Gaurav seemed poised to help realize this vision laid out in the NEP.

And they were not alone. Similar to Sutradhar and leveraging the power of storytelling and immersive engagement for children were ventures such as Vedic Pond[8] and Tiger Comics.[9] Others attempted to focus on specific texts and contemporize insights from those: Chanakya Consulting Insights[10] (Chanakya's Arthashastra), Dancing Tales (Bharata's Natyashastra) and Yogashala (Patanajali's Yogasutras). A few ventures deployed emerging technology to help realize the vision of preserving

[5] https://www.ppstindiagroup.in/ Accessed on 7th April 2025.

[6] https://ciks.org/about-us/origins/ Accessed on 7th April 2025.

[7] https://www.iitkgp.ac.in/department/KSAccessed on 7th April 2025

[8] https://thevedicpond.com/ Accessed on 8th April 2025

[9] https://tigercomics.in/ Accessed on 8th April 2025

[10] https://chanakya.one/ Accessed on 8th April 2025

IKS. These included ventures such as Brhat,[11] Mokx,[12] Who VR,[13] and Bharat Bhasha Sangathan AI.[14] Actors even launched OTT content platforms such as Prachyam[15] for streaming content based on Indic heritage. Finally, platforms such as Rediscovering Bharat helped bring various actors and perspectives together and disseminate insights.

While this emerging entrepreneurial landscape was exciting, as Gaurav began to approach and interact with Venture Capitalists (VCs) in India to share his excitement and find partners for the journey, he faced a few challenges in terms of credibility, content, and conviction. Given his prior experience with the VC world, he sensed that Indian VCs seemed to back ventures offering more assured returns compared to global counterparts. They tended to invest in sectors experiencing a rush of investment, even if it meant being another one of numerous investors rather than backing something unique. An indication of support from potential target audiences was not enough to convince investors in the ecosystem, and there was also reluctance to back something rooted in Indian culture with no comparison or past success stories available. A nascent venture like Sutradhar was being compared with giants like Disney, indicating that the investors were also in the learning phase. What also worried the VCs was the non-proprietary nature of the stories, which were available in the public domain and part of the Indian cultural fabric, being repackaged and retold by Sutradhar, thus reducing the potential for copyright and seeking higher entrepreneurial rents or profits. Gaurav also sensed an unconscious bias against Indian culture. In addition, though Gaurav did not intend it, the possible religious connotation associated with the content being marketed by Sutradhar became a point of concern, with VCs seemingly wanting to maintain neutrality. Further, the VCs were focused on getting a return on their investment within a shorter timeframe of 5–7 years, which could be inadequate for creating and demonstrating impact in cultural entrepreneurship of the kind Sutradhar and Gaurav were attempting. Pitching the envisioned journey of Sutradhar across phases and holding investors' interest and attention till the point of describing the Bharatverse phase proved to be difficult too. Gaurav wondered if there was support for

[11] https://www.brhat.in/ Accessed on 8th April 2025
[12] https://www.mokx.org/ Accessed on 8th April 2025
[13] https://www.whovr.in/ Accessed on 8th April 2025
[14] https://www.bharatbhasha.tech/ Accessed on 8th April 2025
[15] https://prachyam.com/ Accessed on 8th April 2025

passion over prototypes in the Indian VC landscape. This posed a challenge for Gaurav, who was a first-generation entrepreneur with no experience in the domain of education or cultural entrepreneurship, and for ventures such as Sutradhar that have no comparable models in the market. He needed the faith of a VC who was either working with a timeline of 10+ years to see returns or was passionate and willing to back the venture irrespective of the outcome. Thus, not only was there a lack of initial support from institutional VCs for Sutradhar but a sense of disillusionment for Gaurav that led him to avoid seeking VC funding going forward, fearing pressures and compromise on direction.

Gaurav's experience with subject matter experts was more encouraging. They continued to make efforts towards strengthening the body of work for Indic heritage and were willing to provide inputs and help. This set of actors prioritized the cause over themselves. They wrote books, created platforms to help disseminate Indic knowledge, and did not shy away from giving the stage to upcoming voices and actors in the landscape, such as Gaurav.

On the other hand, the emerging influencers seemed to operate like competitive businesses in seeking to establish themselves as unconditional advocates of the cause of reviving Indian heritage. There was a high level of gatekeeping for accessing the network. It proved to be difficult to get a response to emails or any face time with network actors, even after sending them free copies of Sutradhar's games and demonstrating vision backed by offerings. In contrast to the subject matter experts, these actors seemed to prioritize their agenda and build their personal brands using the Indic association as a vehicle. The instrumental approach to Indic heritage was also evident through a widespread Western bias among these actors. The primary driver seemed to be the opportunity that opened up in the Indic space following explicit efforts from the GoI and the MoE. The result was a fragmented, politically driven network with a high entry barrier for new actors. Gaining traction with this set of actors proved equally difficult, with many dead ends and cold leads.

In his interactions with users and customers, Gaurav discovered that customers also seemed to undervalue Indic heritage while having the willingness to pay more for Western content. He realized the key challenge in Indic heritage-based cultural entrepreneurship: while customers appreciated Sutradhar's offerings, they seemed to believe that they already knew everything there was to know about mythology since they belonged to the same culture, reducing their willingness to pay for Indic heritage-based products. Gaurav realized that the audience that would appreciate and be able to afford Sutradhar's products—the urban affluent class—were Westernized, often double-income households with little time to play games with their children, even if they bought them. Gaurav even received explicit customer feedback demonstrating unwillingness to pay INR 2000 for a game based on the Mahabharata and the perception that games based on popular Western stories and franchises such as Lord of the Rings or Harry Potter would be an easier sell.

Gaurav's initial deprioritization of sales and marketing efforts in favor of research led to challenges in building traction in this landscape. As a consequence, Sutradhar struggled to find genuine collaborators, resources, and opportunities to pursue its mission and vision.

Looking for a Happily-Ever-After

Looking back, Gaurav wondered if he should have invested in sales and marketing early on to improve his chances of VC investment later. A pitch based only on the idea of Bharat did not seem to be resonating with stakeholders and ecosystem actors. Further, VCs saw his personal journey and that of Sutradhar as baggage. Trying to enter a niche space, such as promoting Indic knowledge and perspectives in an environment dominated by Western perspectives, was proving to be a challenge. How could Gaurav understand the values and aspirations of the consumer and position his venture appropriately to speak to upstream actors, such as VCs, and downstream actors, such as consumers, while maintaining the goals and values of the venture? Gaurav wondered if he should set all his hard work with Sutradhar aside and approach the space afresh with the learnings he had gained. Or if it was only a pause and some distance he needed before continuing to build his vision for Sutradhar.

Gaurav tried to set these concerns aside as he finished breakfast and got ready to leave for the doctor's appointment. He did not want his stress levels to be flagged by the doctor. It was clear that he had some tough decisions to make.

Discussion Questions: Entrepreneurship, Ecosystems and New Category/Market Creation

1. How do childhood experiences shape a startup founder's motivations and activities?
2. What challenges did Gaurav Tiwari face while trying to start a venture in a new category, such as Indic heritage-based games?
3. Should Gaurav have prioritized quantity or quality while creating content in the Sutradhar phase? What were possible alternate approaches?
4. How does the macro environment influence the activities and direction of a new venture?
5. What is the role of different actors in a nascent entrepreneurship ecosystem around the Indian Knowledge System?
6. What is the role of personal values in entrepreneurship? How can entrepreneurs balance economic interests of a venture with values driving the venture?

Discussion Questions: Indian Knowledge Systems

1. What are the key efforts undertaken by actors and the Indian government to promote Indian Knowledge Systems and Indic heritage?
2. How is the Indic Heritage-related entrepreneurship ecosystem shaping up? What are the inherent challenges within the ecosystem?
3. How are colonial thought and Western education impacting Indian heritage-based entrepreneurship?
4. What is the role of entrepreneurs and ventures in promoting Indian Knowledge Systems?

Supplementary Reading

- Introduction to Indian Knowledge Systems—https://www.brhat.in/dhiti/indianknowledgesystems1
- McDonald, R., & Eisenhardt, K. M. (2020). The new-market conundrum. *Harvard Business Review*, 98(3), 75–83.
- Sahasranamam, S., & Kondayya, A. (2026). Understanding Hindu religious entrepreneurship: a translation perspective. *Entrepreneurship & Regional Development*, 1–28.

- How Metaverse Could Alter The Engagement With Hindu Faith—https://swarajyamag.com/culture/how-metaverse-could-alter-the-engagement-with-hindu-faith
- Four ways in which history and religion are being transformed by the metaverse and AI—https://theconversation.com/four-ways-in-which-history-and-religion-are-being-transformed-by-the-metaverse-and-ai-243192

Learning Objectives

The case helps understand the entrepreneurial journey and challenges starting with entrepreneurial motivations and identity. It also helps illustrate how entrepreneurs translate personal mission and values into a viable venture, and the dilemma of balancing economic concerns and market pressures with personal mission and values. The case brings out the choices bootstrapped entrepreneurs face due to resource constraints and high upfront costs, which potentially shape the trajectory and influence the viability of the venture. Students can evaluate the entrepreneurial choice to pause, pivot or persevere, and related implications. The case also helps see the amplified impact of the macro environment and entrepreneurial ecosystem in the early stage of a venture particularly when creating a new category.

The case is also instructive for understanding cultural entrepreneurship in the context of Indian Knowledge Systems. It helps illustrate entrepreneurial efforts to preserve traditional knowledge by employing modern technology, and the challenges therein. It helps appreciate the paradox of needing to rely on the products of modernity to further the goal of preserving Indian Knowledge Systems while encountering resistance due to colonial and modern perspectives of the consumers as well as venture capitalists. Finally, the case helps identify the myriad stakeholders and understand how political interests distributed within the ecosystem can favor or hinder cultural entrepreneurship in the Indian Knowledge Systems space (Table 2.1).

Acknowledgements The authors are grateful to Mr. Gaurav Tiwari, founder of Sutradhar, for offering generous support and inputs towards writing this case study.

Competing Interests The authors have no conflicts of interest to declare that are relevant to the content of this chapter.

CHAPTER 3

Tamaala: Preserving Heritage Through Innovation

Suresh Bhagavatula

Abstract India's traditional crafts were once an integral part of everyday life. Mass production changed that. The demand disappeared even though the artisans and their skills didn't. This case examines Tamaala, founded by Suvarna Kamakshi and Vinay Prashant, which aims to reconnect these crafts with today's buyers through hands-on workshops, thoughtful gifting options, and products co-designed with artisans. After some early success and navigating the pandemic, they're now at a crossroads: how do they grow and attract younger customers without diluting what makes the crafts special or spreading themselves too thin? Students need to find realistic ways to reach new audiences while keeping the business sustainable and ensuring that artisans actually benefit, not just get exploited in the name of growth.

Keywords Cultural entrepreneurship • Creative industries • Artisan livelihoods • Market creation • Co-creation (artisan–designer)

S. Bhagavatula (✉)
Entrepreneurship Area, IIM Bangalore, Bangalore, India
e-mail: sureshbh@iimb.ac.in

A. S. Galande et al. (eds.), *Context-inspired Entrepreneurship*, Sustainable Development Goals Series,
https://doi.org/10.1007/978-981-95-9831-1_3

SDG Link
This chapter is centrally aligned with SDG 8 by examining how an artisan-support enterprise can generate sustainable livelihoods and productive employment in rural and tribal areas. The case speaks directly to SDG 8.3 on promoting decent work through micro- and small-scale entrepreneurship, and SDG 8.9 on creating jobs that promote local culture and products. The chapter also relates to SDG 10, through its emphasis on reducing inequalities faced by rural and tribal artisans, and SDG 11, through its contribution to the preservation of cultural heritage.

Introduction

The wedding planner's eyes lit up as she watched the guests eagerly gather around the traditional games setup. It was 2024, and Suvarna Kamakshi and Vinay Prashant, co-founders of Tamaala, had just finished conducting a workshop on Indian traditional games at what they thought was a corporate event. The venue happened to be at a destination wedding location, and this chance encounter with a wedding planner would soon open an entirely new revenue stream they had never anticipated.

"We were looking for something different because we have so many expatriate weddings and NRI weddings, but those guys are tired of the same dance drama that we do," the wedding planner explained. "And they also do not have time for tourism. People from the US and Europe who come for weddings often stay for just two or three days and then return. When you recreate artisan-based traditional games, for them, some part of the tourism or cultural experience is also getting covered."

Within a month, Tamaala conducted traditional games workshops at five expatriate destination weddings, each generating workshop fees and product sales. What started as a product demonstration had evolved into a standalone revenue stream, redefining their business model.

However, this serendipitous discovery also highlighted a fundamental question that had been brewing since their founding: How could they scale their mission of supporting 10,000 artisans while preserving India's cultural heritage in an increasingly modern marketplace?

Background to the Case Organization and Founders

The Genesis of Tamaala

The name "Tamaala" emerged from deep cultural symbolism. Suvarna recalled, "Initially, the first thing we thought of when we heard 'Tamaala' was from the first stanza of Geet Govinda, which refers to the forest where Lord Krishna grew up with the Gopis and Radha. The entire symbolism was that of a shaded harbour, which enhances, encourages, and sustains any art and aesthetics."

The founders discovered that the name resonated across cultures: it was popular among Native American communities, meant "bay leaf tree" in Japanese, and held similar significance in South African traditions. This global resonance seemed prophetic for their vision of bringing Indian arts and crafts to the world while remaining firmly rooted in tradition.

"We want our traditional arts and crafts' essence not to be disturbed, but their fragrance to be shared all over," explained Suvarna. "Like the bay leaf in pulao—it spreads its fragrance around but remains intact."

Founded with the mission of cultural preservation and improving artisan livelihoods, Tamaala began as a physical retail outlet and workshop space in Bangalore. The founders, both with corporate backgrounds, had identified a gap in how traditional Indian handicrafts were being presented and marketed to contemporary audiences.

Tamaala's initial approach centered on physical workshops and retail sales. "We started doing workshops because for us, workshops meant art demonstration and learning," Vinay explained. "We realized it is easier to get people to walk into the studio when you teach some art form, because parents are always anxious that their children need to learn something new."

Bangalore proved to be fertile ground for this approach. The city's cosmopolitan population was receptive to cultural experiences, and the workshop model began to attract a steady footfall. However, the founders quickly discovered that these experiences and workshops were trapped in the traditional patterns of the Indian festival market.

"Our sales used to mirror the typical traditional market exactly," Suvarna noted. "Come Ganesh Chaturthi, our sales would increase and peak around Dussehra and Deepavali. After that, there is a total lull because the retail market goes to sleep."

This seasonality created significant challenges. While festival periods brought substantial revenue, the business struggled during the off-season. The founders were riding an emotional and financial roller coaster that many traditional craft businesses experience in a country like India.

When COVID-19 struck in 2020, Tamaala's festival-dependent model collapsed almost overnight. "When the pandemic hit, this whole thing went to zero because celebrations reduced and things were very tight for a year or a year and a half," Vinay recalled. Like many other founders across the world, they had to take a decision: "we were debating whether we should continue this or wind up and go back to corporate jobs and security."

Their e-commerce platform, while functional, had not gained sufficient traction to sustain the business. Even after being listed on Amazon Karigar, sales remained disappointing, a common experience among many handicraft businesses they were familiar with.

At this critical juncture, the founders made a strategic pivot that would fundamentally transform their business model. They began reaching out to corporate clients, recognizing an opportunity created by the work-from-home culture and the difficulties corporates were having to get the employees to return to offices. "We saw this opportunity to recreate these workshops in offices and make it easier for employees to return to work," Suvarna explained. This insight marked the beginning of their transformation from a B2C retail business to a B2B experience and gifting company.

The Corporate Discovery: From Products to Experiences

The corporate market revealed unexpected dynamics that would reshape Tamaala's entire approach. Working with companies like Sasken and Schneider Electric, they discovered that what started as workshops and employee gifting partnerships evolved into multiple touchpoints within organizations. "When we started working with Sasken, we thought we would be their employee gifting partner," Vinay explained. "Then we became the admin partner because we started doing facility management. However, we never thought that the biggest internal client would be marketing."

This evolution occurred organically through conversation and relationship-building. When a Sasken executive casually mentioned that their customer was Caterpillar, the Tamaala team proposed creating something unexpected: a handicraft representation of Caterpillar's machinery. The marketing department liked the idea and asked Tamaala to develop the product. This led to custom design work that opened entirely new revenue possibilities. The Caterpillar team was excited to see a miniature craft version of their products and wanted to know more about the crafts, which lead to an impromptu experience module. This gave them an idea to create a workshop as even local employees were excited to participate in them.

The founders soon realized that the corporate workshops served multiple purposes:

Direct Revenue:	Companies paid substantial fees for workshop experiences.
Marketing Outreach:	Workshops became paid marketing activities that educated potential customers
Product Sales:	Workshops served as retail points of sale, with participants often purchasing items
The Experience Economy:	Cultural Immersion as Business Model

The traditional games workshop became Tamaala's most popular offering. They were teaching 20–25 types of Indian traditional games. This workshop format also addressed a fundamental customer objection they had encountered: "People say, 'This is wonderful. My grandmother used to play it. It reminds me of my village days. However, I am not familiar with the rules. How will I explain to anybody else?". Eventually, the workshops solved this problem while creating significant value for multiple customer segments:

Corporate Clients:	Many of Tamaala's corporate clients had expatriate employees who visited India briefly for business. "You cannot believe that someone would travel from Europe and the US and come to Bangalore without even having a chance to visit Mysore. However, that is how it is," Suvarna observed. "If we can encapsulate a cultural experience for them in their office space, then that is extremely valuable."

Wedding Market:	The destination wedding market provided another unexpected avenue. NRI families wanted to share Indian culture with their children and relatives who had grown up abroad, but often lacked reference points beyond general statements about India's greatness.
Rural Immersion Programs:	Tamaala developed programs where corporate groups would visit artisan clusters, experience the creation process firsthand, and then place orders for gifting. This created a complete loop from cultural education to commercial transaction.

The Artisan Partnership Challenge

Central to Tamaala's mission was building sustainable partnerships with traditional artisans, which proved to be one of their most complex challenges. However, building trust required a significant investment of time. Tamaala increased trust through two different set of activities. First, they kept purchasing from the same artists. "A lot of patience and perseverance," Suvarna noted. "We kept returning to them for at least two years with each artisan. We initially kept buying their products, whatever they were making. Although years have passed and we kept returning to them, they relented and started forming the idea that these guys would not run away with our stuff."

Second and more encouraging once was that the craft industry's standard practices often kept artisans anonymous, with galleries protecting artisan identities as intellectual property. Tamaala deliberately reversed this approach. When conducting workshops, they prominently featured the names of artisans in newspaper advertisements. "We put out listings in newspapers like The Times of India, Bangalore Mirror, The Hindu and the Indian Express. All these papers carried the name of the artisans ' You are going to learn Gond painting from Rajkumar Shyam, " Vinay explained. The impact was immediate and profound. "When we sent these newspaper clippings to the artisans, they said nothing like this had happened in their lives before, not even in government exhibitions. Their names came to the fore."

Innovation Through Collaboration

Product development at Tamaala became a collaborative process with the craftsmen that respected traditional knowledge while pushing creative boundaries. The development of their terracotta mobile amplifier exemplified this approach. "There was a live workshop going on, and Suvarna sat with the potter and showed him the possibilities," Vinay recalled. "She literally did some construction with her hands and showed him that it is possible to create a mobile amplifier using clay, using the same wheel to create a conical structure sufficient to amplify sound." The creative process to develop new products required striking a balance between respect for traditional expertise and innovative thinking. "We are sharing information and respecting their skill level and knowledge," Suvarna explained. "What is possible to be fired in a kiln and what will burst at a particular temperature is something only they can tell us."

This combined approach was extended to all product development. "Design is not a one-person thing. It is never the ownership or the privilege of one single individual. It is a process that involves discussions, sitting down, and making iterations. One product may come out in a day with brilliant brainstorming, but it often takes months to be happy with what you have created."

One issue with innovations in the craft sector, if successful, many will start to imitate. It then defeats the purpose of investing time and effort to develop new products. It is not that these artifacts cannot be patented but it is not cheap nor is it quick. Also, since the collaborative innovation process raised complex intellectual property questions. How could Tamaala protect innovations while maintaining ethical partnerships with artisans?

Vinay and Suvarna decided that, after researching full patent processes that would cost ₹3.5–5 lakhs, they opted for industrial process patents at ₹5000 each, but eventually spent Rs. 20,000 due to iterations. "We get a basic level of protection, at least," Vinay explained. "It does not give you complete protection, but it is like a deterrence creator. It creates some entry barrier." Also, this level of patent is probably recoverable from a handcrafted product. The overall process involved taking photographs and documenting the design process in every step, which proved a bit of a challenge since the rural artisan was required to do some of these steps. We eventually had to go through 2 iterations, which delayed the overall process.

The Indian Handicrafts Landscape: Context and Challenges

India's handicrafts sector represents one of the world's oldest and most diverse creative economies, encompassing over 3000 distinct craft traditions practiced across the subcontinent. From the intricate Gond tribal paintings of Madhya Pradesh to the delicate pottery of Rajasthan, from Kerala's coconut shell crafts to West Bengal's terracotta work, these traditions have been passed down through generations, often within specific communities and families.

The sector employs over 7 million artisans, making it one of India's most significant sources of non-farm employment, particularly in rural areas. Unlike mechanized industries, handicrafts remain fundamentally human-centered, with each piece bearing the individual touch of its creator. This personal dimension creates the sector's greatest strength—authenticity and uniqueness—and its most significant challenge in competing with mass-produced alternatives.

India's handicrafts exports were valued at approximately $3.5 billion in 2023, representing less than 2% of global handicrafts trade despite the country's rich heritage and skilled workforce. The domestic market, although substantial, remains largely unorganized and seasonal, with demand concentrated around festivals and special occasions.

The traditional supply chain typically involves multiple intermediaries: artisans sell to local aggregators, who in turn sell to wholesalers, which supply retailers or exporters. Each layer adds markup while reducing the artisan's share of the final price. Studies indicate that artisans often receive only 10–15% of the final retail price, creating persistent poverty despite their specialized skills.

Most handicraft businesses follow predictable seasonal patterns tied to India's festival calendar. Sales peak during Ganesh Chaturthi (August–September), Dussehra (September–October), and Diwali (October–November), followed by significant lulls in activity. This seasonality creates cash flow challenges for artisans and businesses, limiting their ability to invest in innovation or market expansion.

The Artisan Community: Challenges and Aspirations

India's handicraft artisans face a complex web of challenges that extend beyond simple market access. Many belong to traditional craft communities where skills are passed down through generations rather than formally taught, resulting in deep expertise and insularity from broader market trends.

Economic Pressures
With limited access to direct markets, artisans often depend on local middlemen who provide immediate cash but at reduced prices. The lack of working capital forces many to accept whatever prices are offered, perpetuating cycles of economic dependence. Additionally, going directly to the market, while providing better returns, also carries its own levels of risk, which may be difficult for craftsmen to accept.

Generational Tensions
Younger generations increasingly question whether traditional crafts can provide viable livelihoods. Increasing access to communication and mobility through trains, roads, etc., has made access to alternative livelihoods easier. This leads to migration for factory or service sector employment in urban areas, which has depleted many craft communities and threatens the continuation of ancient traditions.

Innovation Resistance
Traditional craft communities often view design changes with skepticism, perceiving them as threats to cultural authenticity. New designs also expose them to market risks, such as whether the products will be sold. While preserving heritage, this conservatism and low risk-taking ability can limit market responsiveness and growth opportunities.

Market Knowledge Gaps
Most artisans lack an understanding of the changing urban and international market preferences. Crafts in the past have been mostly functional, but now, with many traditional ways of life changing, many of these crafts have become "showpiece" items. Therefore, craftsmen are unfamiliar with the quality standards or pricing dynamics that these new markets want. This information asymmetry disadvantages them in business relationships.

Beyond economic considerations, India's handicrafts represent valuable cultural heritage. Each craft tradition contains centuries of accumulated knowledge about materials, techniques, and aesthetic principles. The loss of a craft tradition means the disappearance of a unique cultural understanding of how these crafts were made.

UNESCO has recognized several Indian crafts as Intangible Cultural Heritage, highlighting their global significance. Some of these heritage crafts are also covered under the GI Tag, which helps identifying the place, process and people working on the art/craft form. However, this recognition alone does not ensure survival. These traditions need economic viability to continue thriving, especially since they have lost their functionality. The challenge lies in preserving authentic traditions while adapting to current market demands. Customers today seek products that fit modern lifestyles while retaining cultural authenticity. Many are likely to buy products for their aesthetic appeal without understanding the cultural history behind them.

Market Evolution and New Opportunities

The Indian handicrafts market has begun evolving in response to several trends:

Urban Consumer Awareness

The growing environmental consciousness and desire for authentic, handmade products have created new domestic market segments willing to pay premium prices for high-quality handicrafts. Many governmental agencies and organizations, such as Dastkar, organize exhibitions in metropolitan areas where craftsmen meet customers to understand which products are in demand. Outlets like DilliHaat have created awareness of products from across the country. Many government-supported craft agencies also offer discounts to make their products more affordable.

Corporate Social Responsibility

Section 135 of the Companies Act (2013) mandates that Indian corporations allocate at least 2% of their three-year average profits for CSR activities. Therefore, corporations are increasingly seeking authentic ways to demonstrate their cultural commitment and social impact, creating opportunities for partnerships with handicrafts.

Experience Economy

Consumers, particularly millennials and Gen Z, value experiences over products. This trend has created opportunities for workshops, cultural immersion programs, and experiential marketing initiatives centered on handicrafts.

Digital Platforms
E-commerce has theoretically democratized market access; however, most artisans lack the necessary digital literacy and resources to effectively leverage these platforms.

Global Interest in Authenticity: International markets are showing a growing appreciation for authentic, handmade products with compelling stories, particularly as consumers become increasingly conscious of the environmental and social costs associated with mass production.

The Innovation Imperative

For handicrafts to remain relevant, innovation becomes essential, but it must be radical in nature, meeting contemporary needs while respecting traditional knowledge. This might involve:

Product Innovation:	Adapting traditional techniques to create contemporary products (like terracotta mobile amplifiers)
Process Innovation:	Improving efficiency or quality while maintaining handmade character
Market Innovation:	Finding new customer segments or applications for traditional products
Business Model Innovation:	Creating new ways to connect artisans with markets or customers with authentic experiences. The Role of Cultural Entrepreneurs

Cultural entrepreneurs like Tamaala can serve as benevolent intermediaries operating at the intersection of heritage preservation and market innovation. However, while doing so, they are likely to face unique challenges such as:

Dual Mission Tension
Balancing commercial success with cultural preservation creates complex decision-making scenarios where profit and purpose may conflict.

Stakeholder Complexity
Managing relationships with traditional artisans, modern customers, and various intermediaries requires exceptional cultural sensitivity and business acumen.

Quality vs. Scale Tension
Growing impact often requires scaling operations, but maintaining quality and authenticity becomes more difficult with size. Market Education Burden: Cultural entrepreneurs typically must educate the market about the value of their products, a costly and time-intensive process.

This context helps explain why Tamaala's journey from traditional retail to experience-based cultural entrepreneurship represents not just a business evolution, but a potential model for addressing some of the handicrafts sector's most persistent challenges.

India's handicrafts ecosystem remains economically significant yet structurally constrained. Exports of handicrafts were valued at approximately US$3.8 billion in FY 2023–2024 (IBEF/EPCH, FY24), as reported by the Export Promotion Council for Handicrafts via IBEF, despite millions of artisans participating across thousands of traditions. Official textile data place total sectoral employment (textiles and allied crafts) in the tens of millions (Ministry of Textiles, 2024–2025), underscoring the livelihood stake. Policy frameworks and cultural institutions also matter: India's Companies Act Section 135 requires eligible firms to spend at least 2% of average net profits on CSR, creating opportunities for craft-linked partnerships (Companies Act, 2013, §135 CSR); UNESCO's Intangible Cultural Heritage lists and India's National ICH list highlight the cultural urgency of safeguarding living heritage (UNESCO ICH Lists) (Ministry of Culture, National ICH List); and the Geographical Indications (GI) registry captures dozens of craft-linked GIs, anchoring provenance and recognition for many artisan clusters (GI Registry, DPIIT).

Corporate gifting landscape in India. Estimates vary across sources, but there is consensus that corporate gifting is a significant and growing slice of India's overall gifting economy. One market study estimates the total gifting market at approximately US$75.2 billion in 2024, projected to reach around US$92.3 billion by 2030 (Research and Markets, 2024). Within this, industry sources estimate corporate gifting at roughly ₹12,000 crore in 2022, with projections of ₹18,000 crore by 2027 (Tapwell, 2025). Some reports suggest that the corporate segment could account for a mid-teens share of total gifting value by the end of the decade (Chococraft,

2025). For artisan-led brands, this channel aligns with companies' sustainability and inclusion priorities, as well as with CSR-linked engagement programs (Companies Act, 2013, §135 CSR).

Current Challenges of the Case Organization

Operational Challenges and Growth Constraints

As Tamaala's B2B business grew, they encountered new operational challenges. Payment cycles extended from immediate cash transactions to 30–75 days, creating cash flow pressures. While MSME regulations mandated 45-day payments, various administrative delays often extended the payment cycle further.

"When you are used to a cash business and become more B2B, that is one of the things that hits you, which are funding and finances," Vinay observed. Fortunately, they accessed working capital funding through nationalized banks and MSM schemes, finding the process less complicated than anticipated.

Artisan management presented ongoing challenges. "Some do not want to continue. Some are not happy doing something different from what they are used to," Suvarna explained. "Some of the younger generation do not want to continue the art form. Others enter with very radical ideas and urgency to earn the kind of money they would earn in a city doing a regular job."

These tensions required constant relationship management and education about the realities of traditional craft markets versus urban employment expectations. Market Education and Premium Positioning.

A significant challenge was educating clients about the value proposition of handmade products. Workshops served as powerful demonstration tools, showing customers exactly what went into creating handmade items.

"Suppose you were to make one bowl by yourself on a pottery wheel, it takes about 20–25 minutes for anybody to do it under guidance," Vinay explained. "That gives them an idea of what handmade means, and that is one reason we got positioned as a premium offering, especially for international clients or chief guests, because they realize there is a story behind this, an artisan's life, culture, a whole experience."

This positioning strategy proved exceptionally effective for corporate clients with international stakeholders or those seeking to showcase Indian culture authentically.

Revenue Diversification and Business Model Evolution By 2024, Tamaala had evolved into a multi-stream business model:

Corporate and Institutional Gifting
Their primary revenue source is serving companies like Sasken and Schneider Electric, among others, with customized handicraft gifts for employees and clients.

Experience Workshops
Both corporate and private workshops teaching traditional games, pottery, and other crafts, generating direct fees plus product sales. Rural Immersion Programs: Taking corporate groups to artisan clusters for authentic cultural experiences, typically resulting in large gifting orders. Wedding and Event Services: Traditional games and cultural experiences for destination weddings and special events. Retail Sales: Continuing traditional retail through their studio and online platforms, though now a smaller portion of overall revenue.

"The final outcome, which is desirable for us, is gifting, but the means to do that is also generating revenue," Vinay explained. "What we assumed to be a marketing exercise has also become a revenue stream."

The Scaling Dilemma

As 2024 progressed, Tamaala faced its biggest strategic challenge yet. Their stated goal of supporting 10,000 artisans seemed more achievable and complex than ever. Their B2B model had proven more scalable than traditional retail, but questions remained about maintaining quality, cultural authenticity, and fair partnerships at scale.

The experience economy had validated their approach as companies and individuals were willing to pay premium prices for authentic cultural experiences and products with compelling stories. However, could this model support the scale of impact they envisioned?

Several factors complicated the scaling decision:

Quality Control
How could they maintain their collaborative design process and quality standards while working with hundreds or thousands of artisans across different craft traditions?

Cultural Authenticity
Would rapid scaling dilute the cultural preservation mission that is central to their identity?

Financial Sustainability
Although the business was now profitable, supporting 10,000 artisans would require substantially more working capital, effective inventory management, and increased operational complexity.

Market Demand
Was there sufficient demand for handicrafts to support this scale, or would they need to expand internationally?

Competitive Response
As their model proved successful, how long would it take for larger players or well-funded startups to attempt to replicate their approach? Looking Forward.

As Suvarna and Vinay reflected on their journey from near-shutdown to multi-stream revenue success, they realized they stood at a critical inflection point. The wedding planner's enthusiasm had been just one of many serendipitous discoveries that shaped their path, but now they needed to make deliberate strategic choices about their future.

Their vision had remained constant: "Preservation of art and craft as cultural heritage and livelihoods was always our vision. That has not changed. It is the mechanism of revenue generation that has changed." However, the mechanisms they had discovered, such as corporate workshops, rural immersion, premium gifting, and cultural experiences, had proven far more scalable than traditional retail.

The question was whether they should focus on optimizing their current model or take the bold step toward their 10,000-artisan goal. Each path carried different risks and opportunities, and the decision would determine not just Tamaala's future but also their ultimate impact on India's cultural preservation and artisan communities.

As they prepared for their next board meeting, Suvarna and Vinay knew they needed to present a clear vision for Tamaala's next phase. The traditional games workshop taught them that sometimes the most valuable discoveries come from unexpected places, but now they must choose their path deliberately.

Discussion Questions

How should Tamaala balance tradition preservation with market-driven innovation as they scale?

What are the key risks and opportunities in pursuing the 10,000-artisan goal?

Should Tamaala focus on one primary revenue stream or maintain its diversified approach?

How can cultural entrepreneurs maintain authenticity while achieving commercial success?

What strategic partnerships or investments should Tamaala consider for its next growth phase?

Supplementary Reading

Lounsbury, M., & Glynn, M. A. (2001). Cultural entrepreneurship: Stories, legitimacy, and the acquisition of resources. Strategic Management Journal.

Rao, H., Monin, P., & Durand, R. (2003). Institutional change in Toque Ville: Nouvelle cuisine as an identity movement. American Journal of Sociology.

Kim, W. C., & Mauborgne, R. (2015). Blue Ocean Strategy (Expanded ed.). Harvard Business Review Press.

Stanford d.school. (n.d.). Design thinking resources for co-creation with artisan communities.

Dastkar & CCI (various). Reports on Indian craft clusters and artisan livelihoods.

Learning Outcomes/Objectives

- Analyze how cultural ventures balance heritage preservation with market-facing innovation and scale.
- Evaluate multi-channel growth strategies (B2B gifting, experiences, retail) for craft-based enterprises.
- Develop fair-collaboration and IP approaches that respect artisan agency while enabling product innovation.

Competing Interest The author has no conflicts of interest to declare that are relevant to the content of this chapter. Acknowledgement I thank Suvarna Kamakshi and Vinay Prashant for their openness and thoughtful reflections on the evolution of Tamaala. I am indebted to the artisans and collaborators who shared practices that animate this case. We also appreciate the encouragement from Sreevas Sahasranamam and the constructive feedback of anonymous reviewers. Any remaining shortcomings are my own.

LLM Disclosure

Parts of this chapter (language polishing and reference formatting) were assisted by ChatGPT (GPT-5 Thinking). The LLM is not an author, and no confidential or non-public data were provided.

Exhibits Relevant to *the Case*

Exhibit 3.1 Games being played at a wedding

07 Intricate work

The Shyam family from the Dindori district in Madhya Pradesh displays their centuries-old art form. Their intricate portrayal of the forest and animals reflects their animist beliefs and their oneness with nature. All members of the family have their works displayed, and interestingly, they work on each others' art works too. The next generation does justice to the illustrious and national awardwinning pedigree of the Shyam family.

WHERE: Tamaala Art Gallery, 24th Main Road, 7th phase, JP Nagar
WHEN: 11am – 8pm (closed on Tuesdays), till July 21 **CALL:** 8884816333

Exhibit 3.2 Press/ads where artisan names were foregrounded

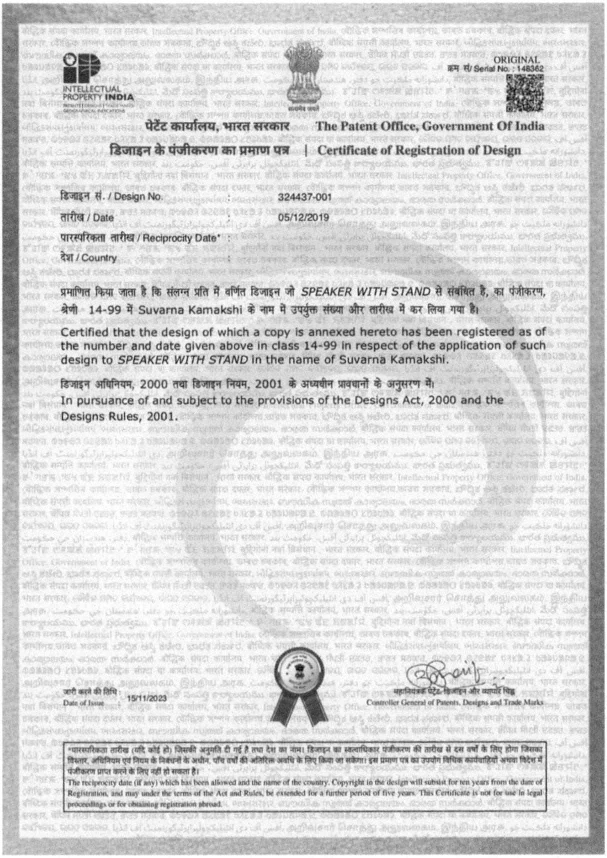

INTELLECTUAL PROPERTY INDIA

ORIGINAL

क्रम सं/ Serial No. : 148362

पेटेंट कार्यालय, भारत सरकार The Patent Office, Government Of India

डिजाइन के पंजीकरण का प्रमाण पत्र | Certificate of Registration of Design

डिजाइन सं. / Design No. : 324437-001

तारीख / Date : 05/12/2019

पारस्परिकता तारीख / Reciprocity Date* :

देश / Country :

प्रमाणित किया जाता है कि संलग्न प्रति में वर्णित डिजाइन जो *SPEAKER WITH STAND* से संबंधित है, का पंजीकरण, श्रेणी 14-99 में Suvarna Kamakshi के नाम मे उपर्युक्त संख्या और तारीख मे कर लिया गया है।

Certified that the design of which a copy is annexed hereto has been registered as of the number and date given above in class 14-99 in respect of the application of such design to *SPEAKER WITH STAND* in the name of Suvarna Kamakshi.

डिजाइन अधिनियम, 2000 तथा डिजाइन नियम, 2001 के अध्यधीन प्रावधानों के अनुसरण में।

In pursuance of and subject to the provisions of the Designs Act, 2000 and the Designs Rules, 2001.

जारी करने की तिथि / Date of Issue : 15/11/2023

महानियंत्रक पेटेंट, डिजाइन और व्यापार चिह्न

Controller General of Patents, Designs and Trade Marks

*पारस्परिकता तारीख (यदि कोई हो) जिसकी अनुमति दी गई है तथा देश का नाम। डिजाइन का स्वत्वाधिकार पंजीकरण की तारीख से दस वर्षों के लिए होगा जिसका विस्तार, अधिनियम एवं नियम के निबंधनों के अधीन, पाँच वर्षों की अतिरिक्त अवधि के लिए किया जा सकेगा। इस प्रमाण पत्र का उपयोग विधिक कार्यवाहियों अथवा विदेश में पंजीकरण प्राप्त करने के लिए नहीं हो सकता है।

The reciprocity date (if any) which has been allowed and the name of the country. Copyright in the design will subsist for ten years from the date of Registration, and may under the terms of the Act and Rules, be extended for a further period of five years. This Certificate is not for use in legal proceedings or for obtaining registration abroad.

Exhibit 3.3 Patent application journey for handmade product designs (TMAP)

Exhibit 3.4 Mobile amplifier

References

Chococraft. (2025). Corporate gifting industry in India 2025–2030: Market overview. https://www.chococraft.in/corporate-gifting-india-2025

Government of India. (2013). The Companies Act, 2013, Section 135. https://www.mca.gov.in/Ministry/pdf/CompaniesAct2013.pdf

Ministry of Textiles, Government of India. (2024). Annual report 2024–25. https://texmin.nic.in/documents/annual-report

Research and Markets. (2024). India gifting market size, competitors & forecast to 2030. https://www.researchandmarkets.com/

Tapwell. (2025). Corporate gifting statistics in India [Blog post]. https://www.tapwell.in/corporate-gifting-statistics

The Business Research Company. (2024). Corporate gifting global market report (India section). https://www.thebusinessresearchcompany.com/

CHAPTER 4

Crafting a Legacy with "Craft Mantra"

Muneza Kagzi

Abstract This case study describes the entrepreneurial journey of Ms. Renu Jayram, founder of Craft Mantra, an eco-friendly gift outlet in Udupi, Karnataka. Established in 2018, the Craft Mantra emphasizes eco-friendly practices, cultural preservation, and women's empowerment through alliance with local artisans. Leveraging her daughter Asmita's digital marketing expertise, Renu combined traditional craftsmanship with modern outreach, attracting students, travelers, and corporate clients.

As Craft Mantra evolved, Renu faced key decisions in striking the right balance between growth and her foundational principles. To extend its footprint beyond the local market, she evaluated three strategic avenues: collaborating with regional digital networks like eSamudaay, launching a dedicated e-commerce platform, or integrating with global marketplaces such as Amazon. Each route presented distinct implications in terms of autonomy, market access, financial viability, and alignment with the brand's commitment to community development.

M. Kagzi (✉)
T A Pai Management Institute, Manipal Academy of Higher Education, Manipal, India

A. S. Galande et al. (eds.), *Context-inspired Entrepreneurship*, Sustainable Development Goals Series,
https://doi.org/10.1007/978-981-95-9831-1_4

The case offers rich insights into entrepreneurial motivation, the societal impact of grassroots ventures, the role of social networks, and implementing the triple bottom-line in sustainable business practices.

Keywords Triple Bottom Line • Sustainability • Eco-friendly gifts • Women entrepreneurship • Innovation • Digital platforms

SDG Link

This chapter is aligned with SDG 8 by examining how Craft Mantra supports artisan livelihoods and employment. The case speaks directly to SDG Target 8.3, through its emphasis on micro- and small-scale entrepreneurship among artisans, and SDG Target 8.9, by promoting craft-based livelihoods that draw on local culture and heritage. The chapter also relates to SDG 5 through its role in discussion on women founder of Craft Mantra and to SDG 11 through the preservation of cultural heritage.

Introduction

On a quiet morning in March 2025, Ms. Renu Jayram, founder of the eco-friendly store Craft Mantra, sat in her quaint gift shop in Udupi, Karnataka. The coastal breeze drifted in, but her thoughts were clouded with concern. Since the store was founded in 2018, she has championed local artisans, particularly women, through sustainable, handcrafted products that reflect the region's rich cultural heritage. With the help of her daughter Asmita, a digital influencer, Renu successfully merged tradition with modern marketing to increase the visibility of her brand.

However, despite its distinctive appeal, Craft Mantra faced increasing pressure from the e-commerce giant Amazon, along with the ongoing challenge of balancing sustainability with affordability. Renu now stands at a crossroads, weighing whether to build an independent online platform, strengthen partnerships with local digital ecosystems, or collaborate with large marketplaces. Each path presented its own trade-offs between growth and preserving the brand's authentic, community-driven identity.

Visionary Start

In the coastal town of Udupi, Ms. Renu Jayram carved a niche as a visionary entrepreneur who combined tradition with innovation. In 2018, she founded Craft Mantra, a gift shop offering eco-friendly souvenirs and handcrafted products that celebrated the cultural heritage of the region. With over 20 years of business experience, Renu aimed to be a job provider, creating a platform to empower local artisans, especially women.

Inspired by the success of souvenir shops abroad and the lack of such offerings in Udupi, a town known for its temples, beaches, and academic institutions, Renu envisioned a concept store that would help preserve memories while promoting sustainability. Her visits to local exhibitions revealed how women artisans lacked consistent market access, motivating her to create a year-round platform for them through Craft Mantra.

Beyond retail, Renu was deeply involved in women's empowerment. She supported initiatives in leadership, skill building, and creativity and played a key role in launching the Platform for Women Entrepreneurs (POWER), a local NGO dedicated to promoting women-led businesses.

Platform of Women Entrepreneurs (POWER)

POWER was a registered NGO in Udupi dedicated to supporting women's entrepreneurship. It facilitated women entrepreneurs, those involved in family businesses, aspiring business owners, and local artisans, offering them a supportive network and opportunities for growth. It organized workshops, competitions, summits, and trade fairs such as *Power Parba*, providing members with valuable exposure and sales platforms. The organization also celebrated women making significant societal contributions through events such as the Empower Summit and award recognition. For more information, visit www.womenpowerudupi.org.

Renu actively associated with POWER and used it to connect with women artisans, many of whom were supported through Craft Mantra. This collaboration not only provided artisans with market access but also advanced their broader mission of empowerment, sustainability, and community welfare.

Craft Mantra: A Store That Speaks Sustainability and Soul

Walking into Craft Mantra in Udupi, Karnataka, was a very different experience. The eco-conscious store embodied upcycling and sustainability, with repurposed items such as an old autorickshaw turning sofa and a guitar-turned lamp, reflecting founder Renu Jayram's creativity and values.

The store offered more than products—it sparked reflection on conscious consumption. Its eco-friendly range included jute bags, hand-painted mugs, and framed photos of Manipal. During the COVID-19 pandemic, innovative items such as belt-attached sanitizer pouches and zippered face masks were introduced.

Renu built Craft Mantra on the ideologies of sustainability, local craftsmanship, and women's empowerment. She collaborated directly with artisans, especially women working from home, preserving traditional skills and fostering cocreation through visits and collaboration.

In addition to serving as a retail space, the gift shop served as a cultural hub and sustainability laboratory. By using natural and upcycled materials and supporting local livelihoods, Renu created a brand that honored heritage while promoting ethical consumerism and meaningful change.

The Customers of Craft Mantra

Craft Mantra began as a small venture, initially serving a limited retail customer base. Over time, strong resonance with Manipal's student community, drawn from over 30 countries through the Manipal Academy of Higher Education (MAHE), has occurred. The store's products, such as jute bags with beach scenes, coconut shell pen stands, and customized T-shirts, blend local identity with everyday utility, making them popular among students.

The brand later expanded into corporate gifting, offering personalized souvenirs that highlighted the cultural richness of Udupi and Manipal. Renu's vision was to create a space that bridged tradition and modernity, rooted in sustainability and local pride. In doing so, she built not just a store but also a vibrant movement centered on culture, craftsmanship, and conscious living.

India's handicraft and sustainable retail sector has long been a repository of cultural richness and a crucial source of income for millions of artisans, particularly women. However, despite its heritage appeal and deep-rooted authenticity, the industry continued to grapple with systemic hurdles. These included market visibility, fragmented supply networks, and mounting pressure from low-cost, mass-produced alternatives available on international e-commerce platforms such as Amazon.

A Family Affair and a Digital Touch

At the core of Craft Mantra's success was a unique blend of family collaboration and digital savvy. Renu Jayram, with her experience and passion for sustainability and local art, anchored the brand's authenticity. Her daughter Asmita, an Instagram influencer, brought a fresh, tech-savvy perspective. Together, they merged tradition with modern trends to engage diverse audiences.

Asmita transformed Craft Mantra's digital presence by sharing stories of artisans, cultural heritage, and sustainable practices through engaging in social media content. Her efforts resonated with environmentally conscious millennials and Gen Z, expanding the brand's reach across India and abroad.

Beyond marketing, Asmita digitized inventory, implemented online ordering, and helped develop an e-commerce platform. She actively engaged customers and shaped product offerings on the basis of feedback. This intergenerational partnership combined Renu's values and craftsmanship with Asmita's digital expertise, ensuring that Craft Mantra remained relevant and true to its mission.

Together, they redefined the gift shop as a platform celebrating heritage, empowering artisans, and promoting conscious living, a family-driven model of sustainable business success.

A Vision for the Future

For Renu, Craft Mantra was more than a charming gift shop—it was a legacy in the making. Her mission was to preserve Udupi's rich cultural heritage while creating sustainable livelihoods for local artisans. She envisioned the store as a symbol of community pride, blending tradition with eco-friendly innovation to inspire future entrepreneurs rooted in culture and creativity.

Craft Mantra embodied this philosophy through upcycled furniture and handmade products, each telling a story of the Udupi spirit. However, running a mission-driven business poses challenges. Renu continually sought greener practices, experimenting with biodegradable packaging and eco-friendly materials, while balancing affordability for younger, price-sensitive customers.

Craft Mantra's drive to establish a digital presence was prompted by the growing influence of e-commerce giants like Amazon. In Udupi, a promising alternative emerged in eSamudaay, a community-focused digital platform designed to strengthen regional economies (Sahasranamam, 2025). Acting as a 'business-in-a-box,' the platform enabled small entrepreneurs to set up online storefronts with integrated tools for order management, product listing, and logistics, initially serving neighborhood vendors such as pharmacies, vegetable sellers, and grocers (Sahasranamam, 2025).

The operational models of eSamudaay and Amazon differed significantly. eSamudaay emphasized local data ownership, decentralized governance, and community-driven decision-making, while Amazon relied on a centralized global system leveraging economies of scale (Sahasranamam, 2025). Amazon generated revenue through commissions and advertising, whereas eSamudaay relied on subscriptions and software leasing (Sahasranamam, 2025). In addition, eSamudaay ensured synergies between cultural events and local businesses using festivals for collaborative marketing and sales (Sahasranamam, 2025). However, its inclusive, community-centric model led to coordination challenges. Aligning diverse local actors, from entrepreneurs to community groups, required significantly more time and effort than the streamlined efficiency of centralized corporations (Sahasranamam, 2025).

Although Craft Mantra could not compete on scale, Renu remained committed to differentiating through personalized service, cultural richness, and storytelling, offering customers a genuine connection to Udupi's heritage.

Innovation was key to remaining relevant. Renu developed products such as miniature temple models and coastal-inspired jewelry that acted as cultural ambassadors, ensuring that the brand remained distinctive and emotionally resonant. Her partnership with daughter Asmita expanded her digital reach and transformed the store into a vibrant cultural experience blending tradition with technology.

Ultimately, Craft Mantra was more than commerce; it was a movement. Renu aimed to prove that purpose and profit could coexist, shaping a future where businesses honor their roots, empower artisans, and embrace sustainability. Through resilience and vision, Craft Mantra became a beacon of mindful entrepreneurship, demonstrating success without sacrificing core values.

The Dilemma

As Craft Mantra expanded, Renu faced strategic crossroads that tested the balance between growth and her core values. Scaling a handcrafted business posed operational challenges, including production limits, quality variability, and maintaining consistency, while preserving the store's mission-driven ethos.

Option 1: Launch an Independent e-Commerce Platform

By directing Instagram traffic to a proprietary website, Craft Mantra could retain full control over branding, customer engagement, and user experience, reinforcing its authenticity and eco-conscious identity. However, the financial and operational burden of building, marketing, and managing such a platform raised questions about long-term sustainability.

Option 2: Strengthen Partnerships with Community-Based Digital Ecosystems Like eSamudaay

This approach aligns with Craft Mantra's principles of local empowerment and circular economy practices, keeping economic benefits within the region. Yet, the limited geographic and market reach of such platforms could constrain the store's growth potential.

Option 3: Collaborate with Large e-Commerce Players Like Amazon

Partnering with a national platform could provide broader visibility, increased sales, and pricing competitiveness. However, it risked diluting Craft Mantra's unique identity, reducing the store to one among thousands of sellers, and potentially weakening its focus on local empowerment and sustainability.

Key Questions for Discussion:

1. How can Craft Mantra maintain its mission-driven approach while achieving profitability?
2. What role should its digital presence play in expanding the customer base?

3. How can the business scale in a highly competitive industry without compromising its authentic, eco-conscious, and community-focused ethos?

Supplementary Reading

- Casciaro, T., Gino, F., & Kouchaki, M. (2016). Managing Yourself–Learn to Love Networking. *Harvard Business Review*, *94*(5), 104–107.
- Uzzi, B., & Dunlap, S. (2005). How to build your network. *Harvard business review*, *83*(12), 53.
- Bogren, M., Von Friedrichs, Y., Rennemo, Ø., & Widding, Ø. (2013). Networking women entrepreneurs: fruitful for business growth?. *International journal of gender and entrepreneurship*, *5*(1), 60–77.
- Slaper, T. F., & Hall, T. J. (2011). The triple bottom line: What is it and how does it work. *Indiana business review*, *86*(1), 4–8.
- Sahasranamam, S. (2025, July 18). *Powering entrepreneurs in rural towns.* Financial Times. https://www.ft.com/content/be837598-ce43-4616-a12d-5fb0afa5fa14

Learning Objectives

- To understand the key drivers and motivations behind entrepreneurship.
- To explore the role of networking and social capital in entrepreneurial success.
- To understand how local communities can benefit socially and economically from grassroots entrepreneurship.
- To analyze how sustainability can be embedded into entrepreneurship to create long-term impact, with a focus on the triple bottom line approach (people, planet, and profit).

Acknowledgement The author acknowledges the use of AI-based tools for support in formatting and language refinement.

Appendix

See Figs. 4.1, 4.2, 4.3, 4.4, 4.5, 4.6, 4.7, 4.8, and 4.9.

Fig. 4.1 Craft Mantra Store from the outside. (Source: Author's photo)

Fig. 4.2 Inside look at the Craft Mantra store. (Source: Author's photo)

Fig. 4.3 Renu Jayram, Founder of Craft Mantra, showcasing her accolades. (Source: Author's photo)

craft mantra
Touching Lives while Going Green
EMPOWERing women, artisans & small businesses
Customized Eco Gifting Solutions
♠ Bags ♠ Mementos ♠ Souvenirs ♠ Decor
♠ Accessories ♠ Apparels & more

Fig. 4.4 Craft Mantra: logo and products. (Source: Provided by Renu Jayram)

Fig. 4.5 Wall paintings—a category of Craft Mantra's products. (Source: Author's photo)

Fig. 4.6 Jute bag: Corporate gifting created by Craft Mantra for a university event. (Source: Author's photo)

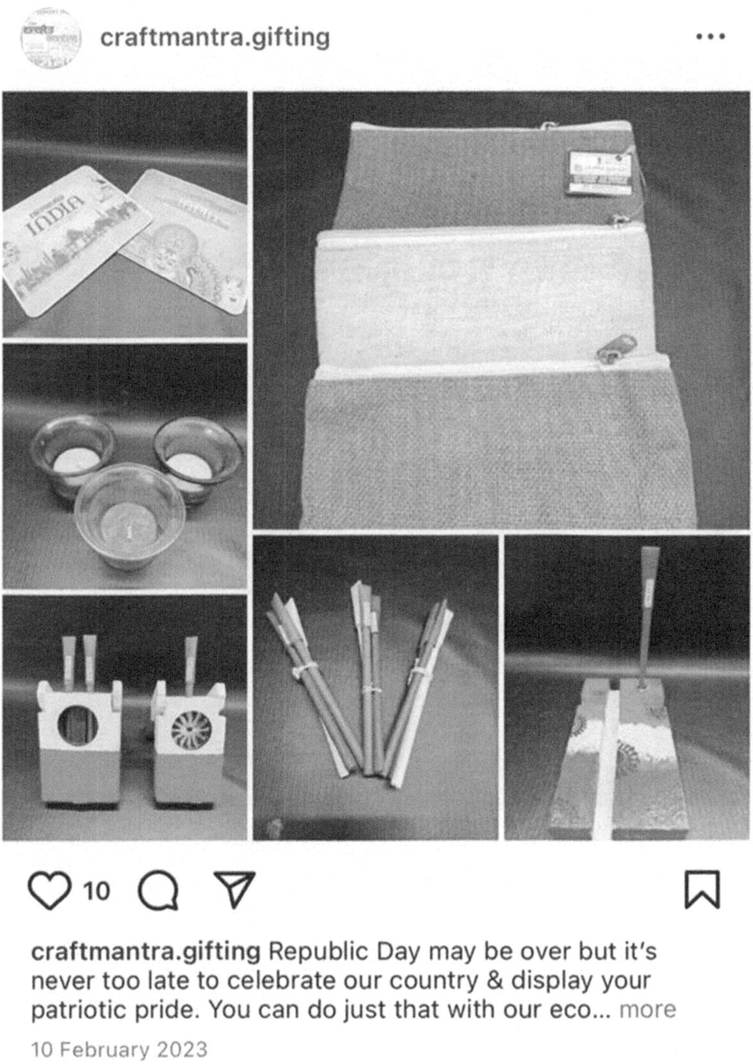

Fig. 4.7 Customized products for Independence Day. (Source: Crafts Mantra Instagram)

Fig. 4.8 Fridge magnets showing the unique tourist location in Mangalore/Udupi. (Source: Crafts Mantra Instagram)

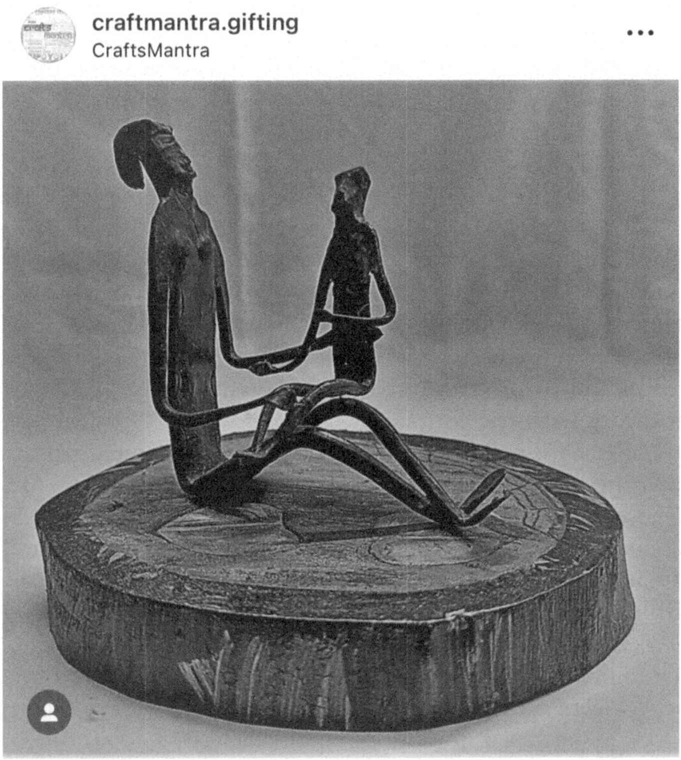

Fig. 4.9 Wooden artifacts. (Source: Crafts Mantra Instagram)

Competing Interests The author has no conflicts of interest to declare that are relevant to the content of this chapter.

Supplementary Material

Guidance for Educators on Using This Case for a 2-Hour Class Discussion

Synopsis

Craft Mantra, an eco-friendly gift shop in Udupi, Karnataka, was founded by Renu Jayram. A combination of tradition, sustainability, and creativity, the gift shop aimed to support local artisans and preserve cultural heritage through a range of handcrafted and upcycled products, including home décor and personalized gifts. The store's design, with furniture recycled from old items including autorickshaws, tires, and ladders, reflected her commitment to sustainable living.

Despite challenges from e-commerce giants, such as Amazon and Flipkart, Renu kept her offerings affordable and distinctive. Her daughter, Sneha, a popular Instagram influencer, helped extend the shop's reach by promoting it online.

Beyond retail, Craft Mantra served as a platform to empower women artisans and showcase Udupi's cultural richness. Under Renu's leadership, it demonstrated how small businesses could successfully combine sustainability, community, and tradition in a modern market.

Positioning with the course

This case study is suited for undergraduate and postgraduate students, illustrating the journey of women entrepreneurs from problem identification to successful business launch. Faculty can use it to highlight business sustainability, making it ideal for courses in entrepreneurship, strategy, and sustainability.

Possible discussion themes include the following:

- The importance of social networks: The case can be used to explore the value of social networks, in general, and women-centric networks, in particular, for entrepreneurial success.
- The utility of online social media: Discuss how social media platforms can be leveraged effectively by entrepreneurs to promote their businesses and build brand identity.
- Engaging female entrepreneurs: Examine the protagonist's motivation to involve and empower other rural women through entrepreneurship.

Relevant Readings

- Casciaro, T., Gino, F., & Kouchaki, M. (2016). Managing Yourself–Learn to Love Networking. *Harvard Business Review*, *94*(5), 104–107.
- Uzzi, B., & Dunlap, S. (2005). How to build your network. *Harvard business review*, *83*(12), 53.

- Bogren, M., Von Friedrichs, Y., Rennemo, Ø., & Widding, Ø. (2013). Networking women entrepreneurs: fruitful for business growth?. *International journal of gender and entrepreneurship*, *5*(1), 60–77.
- Slaper, T. F., & Hall, T. J. (2011). The triple bottom line: What is it and how does it work. *Indiana business review*, *86*(1), 4–8.

Assignment Questions

1. What were the key drivers of entrepreneurship for Ms. Renu Jayram?
2. How did the digital platform contribute to the growth of her business?
3. In what ways did Renu's social capital support the development of Craft Mantra?
4. Evaluate the business through the lens of sustainability via the triple bottom-line approach (People, Planet, Profit).
5. What strategies can Craft Mantra adopt to grow in a highly competitive industry?

Teaching Plan

The case can be used in the 90–100 min class. You may adjust the time depending on the audience size and level of education.

Particulars	*Details*	*Time (Minutes)*
1	Discuss what the case is about	10
2	What were the key drivers of entrepreneurship for Ms. Renu Jayram?	10
3	How did the digital platform contribute to the growth of her business?	15
4	In what ways did Renu's social capital support the development of craft mantra?	10
5	Evaluate the business through the lens of sustainability using the triple bottom-line approach (people, planet, profit).	15
6	What strategies can craft mantra adopt to grow in a highly competitive industry?	20

Analysis

Introduction

Focus the initial discussion on the case and its key aspects, while also facilitating conversations around entrepreneurship

1. What were the key drivers of entrepreneurship for Ms. Renu Jayram?

Invite students to deliberate on why entrepreneurs start a business. Most entrepreneurs begin their journey focused on profit and operating within their area of expertise. However, in this case, the motivations behind the business are notably different. Renu founded Craft Mantra not just for profit, but to:

- Empower women entrepreneurs by providing a platform to showcase and sell their art.
- Offer unique, functional souvenirs such as utility stands and fridge magnets with local cultural value.
- Promote sustainability through products made from natural and upcycled materials.
- Give it back to the community, making social impact a core part of the business mission.

2. How did the digital platform contribute to the growth of her business?

Encourage students to explore how digital platforms, particularly Instagram, played a key role in Craft Mantra's growth. Managed by Renu's daughter, Sneha, a popular influencer, the account used visually engaging posts, creative reels, storytelling, and targeted hashtags to promote the brand. By leveraging her personal brand and online network, she expanded Craft Mantra's reach to a wider, tech-savvy audience across India and beyond. This approach helped build brand awareness, customer trust, and emotional connections with those who value authentic, handcrafted, and sustainable products.

Students can reflect on how Instagram serves as a low-cost, high-impact marketing tool for entrepreneurs, supporting brand building, audience engagement, market expansion, instant feedback, and community creation.

3. In what ways did Renu's social capital support the development of Craft Mantra?

Renu's strong social networks played a key role in Craft Mantra's growth. Her ability to build relationships with individuals and organizations provided the much-needed support in overcoming challenges and expanding her business.

A major support pillar was her involvement with the Platform of Women Entrepreneurs (POWER), a local NGO in Udupi. Through POWER, she connected with fellow entrepreneurs, participated in fairs and workshops, and increased visibility for Craft Mantra. Personal relationships also contributed significantly, friends and acquaintances offered encouragement, word-of-mouth promotion, and early patronage, helping build local trust.

The store also benefited from its proximity to Manipal Academy of Higher Education. The diverse student population, including international students, formed a strong customer base and helped spread the brand's story beyond Udupi. These combined networks, community, personal, and academic, created a nurturing ecosystem for the business.

This discussion may be linked to Mark Granovetter's (1973) theory on strong and weak ties, which highlights how both close relationships (strong ties) and broader, less frequent connections (weak ties) contribute to the flow of information and opportunities across social networks.

Strong ties

- Depict close connections
- Involve frequent interaction
- Include relationships with family, friends, colleagues, and women entrepreneurs

In this case, Renu maintains strong ties with key individuals who have significantly supported her entrepreneurial journey. Her daughter, a close confidante and Instagram influencer, actively promotes Craft Mantra's products online. She also receives consistent support from family members who assist in various aspects of the business. Renu's connections with fellow women entrepreneurs provide encouragement, collaboration, and shared opportunities for growth.

Weak ties

- Involve distant connections, such as friends of friends or referrals from colleagues
- Feature less frequent interaction but can be highly valuable
- Often include acquaintances or strangers who provide new information, opportunities, or broader reach

4. Evaluate the business through the lens of sustainability via the trip bottom-line approach (People, Planet, Profit).

Invite students to reflect on Craft Mantra's journey and critically assess its sustainability using the triple bottom-line framework—*People, Planet, and Profit.*

Consider asking: Is Craft Mantra truly sustainable for the long-term? Use these questions to explore each aspect of the triple bottom-line approach.

- **People**:

How has Craft Mantra empowered local artisans and women entrepreneurs? How does its engagement with students and the community promote social inclusivity?

Craft Mantra supports local artisans, especially rural women in Udupi, by sourcing products that provide sustainable livelihoods and preserve traditional skills. Through involvement with POWER (Platform of Women Entrepreneurs), it offers a platform for women to showcase their work and strengthens community ties.

- **Planet**:

How does Craft Mantra's use of upcycling, eco-friendly materials, and local sourcing promote environmental sustainability? How can it strengthen these practices as it grows?

Environmental sustainability is central to Craft Mantra's model. Renu's creative use of upcycled materials, such as furniture from rickshaws and scrap, reduces waste and encourages reuse. The shop also offers eco-friendly products such as jute bags, coconut shell pen stands, and biodegradable packaging. By prioritizing local production, Craft Mantra minimizes its carbon footprint and supports sustainable consumption. As it grows, it can further enhance its impact by adopting more renewable materials and expanding waste reduction initiatives.

- **Profit**:

Craft Mantra has demonstrated its potential for profitability by attracting a loyal customer base and expanding into online platforms. Its unique, handcrafted offerings and focus on sustainable gifting have carved a niche market. The store's presence on social media and local digital ecosystems reflects growing brand visibility and sales. This balanced approach supports both revenue generation and mission-driven growth.

5. How has Craft Mantra balanced its mission-driven approach with profitability? What role does its digital presence play in growing its customer base?

Craft Mantra demonstrates how entrepreneurship can align sustainability with business growth by focusing on people, planet, and profit. By targeting niche markets like personalized, culturally rich corporate gifts, it differentiates itself from mass-market giants, such as Amazon and Flipkart. Listing on local digital platforms like eSamudaay and leveraging Instagram, managed by Renu's influencer daughter, has significantly expanded its reach.

Strong storytelling, authentic craftsmanship, and digital marketing have enabled Craft Mantra to maintain steady profitability while upholding sustainable practices. This case exemplifies the triple bottom-line philosophy, showing that with clear vision and community support, businesses can thrive economically while making positive social and environmental impacts.

6. What strategies can Craft Mantra adopt to grow in a highly competitive industry?

Here, the instructor can prompt discussion on strategic options for Craft Mantra's digital growth: Should it develop its own e-commerce platform, deepen partnerships with local digital ecosystems like eSamudaay, or collaborate with large platforms such as Flipkart or Amazon?

Students can weigh the pros and cons:

- Local partnerships (eSamudaay): Align with Craft Mantra's community-first ethos, support local businesses, and offer digital infrastructure with minimal cost. However, geographic reach may be limited to Udupi and nearby areas.
- Own e-commerce platform: Provides full control over brand storytelling, customer experience, and direct consumer relationships. Yet, it requires significant investment and management of logistics and fulfillment.
- Large platform (Amazon): Offer national exposure, greater sales potential, and competitive pricing. But risk diluting Craft Mantra's authentic, eco-conscious identity and may pressure pricing and craftsmanship standards.

Ultimately, Craft Mantra must balance scale with authenticity, considering its long-term vision, operational capacity, and customer expectations. This strategic choice invites students to reflect on what sustainable growth means for a purpose-driven business.

Reference

Sahasranamam, S. (2025, July 18). Powering entrepreneurs in rural towns. *Financial Times*. https://www.ft.com/content/be837598-ce43-4616-a12d-5fb0afa5fa14

CHAPTER 5

Preserving the Spirit of a Forest in a Factory: Bikalp Herbals

Vaibhav Bhamoriya

Abstract The case "Preserving the spirit of the forest in a factory: Bikalp Herbals" explores the strategic, ethical and policy dilemmas, faced by a purpose-driven wellness startup navigating the crossroads of tradition and modernity. Founded in 2021 by Stuti Lal, Bikalp Herbals (BH) sought to reimagine Ayurveda for contemporary lifestyles through its flagship product Dip-n-Sip—a biodegradable infusion that simplified ancient herbal practices for urban consumers. Rooted in cultural authenticity, environmental responsibility, and rural empowerment, BHs growth journey reveals the tension between scaling up and sustaining integrity. As BH attracted investor attention, Stuti confronted a choice between scientific validation and cultural faith, profit metrics and purpose, scalability and soul. The case situates BH within India's evolving startup ecosystem, which offers structural support but remains misaligned with tradition-based slow-growth enterprises. It further highlights policy blind spots in funding and certification frameworks for AYUSH-linked ventures. The decision moment arrives when an international investor offers significant

V. Bhamoriya (✉)
Indian Institute of Management Kashipur, Kashipur, India
e-mail: Vaibhav.bhamoriya@iimkashipur.ac.in

A. S. Galande et al. (eds.), *Context-inspired Entrepreneurship*, Sustainable Development Goals Series,
https://doi.org/10.1007/978-981-95-9831-1_5

capital—conditional on compromising raw material purity and authenticity. The case pushes students to debate how enterprises grounded in indigenous knowledge systems can pursue sustainable scaling, negotiate modern market mechanisms, and" preserve the spirit of the forest in the architecture of a factory". This case is suitable for classes on social entrepreneurship, inclusive business models and traditional-knowledge-based ventures.

Keywords Ayurveda-based startup • Sustainable wellness business • Social entrepreneurship • Traditional knowledge innovation • Startup ecosystem • Ethical business

SDG Links
This chapter is aligned with SDG 8: Decent Work and Economic Growth, by examining how Bikalp Herbals generates local employment and sustainable livelihoods through the production and marketing of natural products. The case speaks directly to SDG Target 8.3, by highlighting growth of micro-, small enterprises, and to SDG Target 8.4, through its focus on environmentally sustainable modes of production within the local economy. The chapter also relates to SDG 12, by promoting responsible consumption and production of natural products, and SDG 15, through its emphasis on the sustainable use of land-based resources.

Preserving the Spirit of a Forest in a Factory: Bikalp Herbals

On the morning of June 21, 2025—celebrated as the International Yoga Day—Stuti, founder of Bikalp Herbals, stood beside an Eco-friendly bamboo stall at a celebration venue in Lucknow. As the sun rose behind thousands gathered to perform the '*Surya Namaskara*', her team distributed about 1000 cups for free trials of Tulsi-Ginger infusion—a warming blend of immunity and clarity, served in biodegradable paper glasses printed with the message—*Svastha Jeevan, Swachh Prakriti*" (Healthy Life Clean Nature). There were many queries of "where can I buy this?" and" how did you come up with this idea?"

Stuti was then transported back to the COVID-19 pandemic days that allowed her the space and time to think over her years of curiosity, research and discovery into Ayurveda. While Ayurveda was deeply respected, she noticed it was rarely practiced, especially by the growing proportion of urban youth. Her journey has intersected with research ethics, public health policy, informal pharmaceutical sciences and traditional Ayurveda knowledge. Yet, the contradiction between its respect and its neglect remained unexplained—until she decided to act on it herself.

Thus, Bikalp Herbals (BH) was founded in 2021 and started with a limited bouquet trial experience of a prototype herbal infusion. BH was rooted in nearly a half-century of experience of her dad, Dr. V. K. Lal, and his tryst with modernizing traditions of Ayurveda. BH was formed to reimagine traditional healthcare for the modern world. Bikalp means an alternative, and BH set out to blend ancient wisdom with sustainable design and grassroots empowerment.

Stuti had recently got a seed grant proposal from an EU wellness investor and was searching for answers to strategic questions, the funding round posed: should she accept capital that drives faster scaling up but compromises cultural purity? Can the brand expand globally while remaining anchored in its social & ecological mission? She wondered if a grassroots-based ritual-driven brand could survive the competitive chaos of the wellness industry?

The Humble Beginnings

While Stuti believed in her father's faith in the traditions of Ayurveda, and it being meaningful to the current generation. But a simple solution was needed to match the needs of convenience that this current generation loved. Modern consumers, especially in Metropolitan cities, sought convenience and saw Ayurvedic formulations as hard to use, as tasting harsh, and being in outdated packaging.

At the height of the COVID-19 pandemic, Stuti saw an opportunity in the prevailing global crises. Using her father's knowledge of herbs and ayurvedic concoctions and her trust on such remedies, the duo started trials of a powdered blend for decoction or *kadha,* as known popularly, within their networks. They found that the response was immediate, but people didn't just use it; they trusted it. She was drawn back to her hypothesis that Ayurveda had trust but lacked traction. Her first product development hypothesis was to transform ancient knowledge into a form that modern users would actually adopt, without diluting its integrity.

Dip-n-Sip started to take shape based on this hypothesis. It was a biodegradable herbal infusion bag elegantly filled with curated Ayurvedic herbs, Ready to be dipped like tea—no boiling, no filtering, and no complicated rituals. It was a process innovation (as per Ayurveda) rooted in the ancient principles of Rasayana and Dosha Balance but reimagined for life on the go—Easy to carry, easy to trust and easy to sip. It appeared that the dilemma of transforming a tradition to relevance in modern living had been resolved.

Post-COVID Development and Incubation

The post-COVID scenario seemed like a fertile ground for BH through its flagship product, Dip-n-Sip. Health Consciousness seemed to be at an all-time high. Traditional medicines and remedies were in the thick of discussion for their ability to make a difference to the general wellness of modern-day humans, as well as doubts as a cure for a pandemic such as COVID. There was a mushrooming of household ventures that claimed to supply traditional or Ayurvedic remedies for various ailments, but they were most popular as immunity boosters. Even large firms such as Dabur launched several new products in the wellness market. The demand and supply were poised to come together to unleash a stage of market expansion. BH found this timing a perfect entry point to grow with the market and use quality to try and beat the market in growth.

With an idea that she believed in but faced with a challenge that her knowledge of Ayurveda was largely informal, Stuti had to develop a business model but all she knew was the positive feedback and trust of those known people who had participated in trials of Dip-n-sip. She would be a first-generation entrepreneur in a family of academicians. This led her to seek help in building a business model and she applied to The Foundation for Innovation and Entrepreneurial Development (FIED), IIM Kashipur, to be incubated under the scheme of the Ministry of Agriculture and Farmers Welfare called RKVY-RAFTAAR (Rashtriya Krishi Vikas Yojana—Remunerative Approaches for Agriculture and Allied Sector Rejuvenation). She was one of the most enthusiastic trainees in the two-month training. She was motivated by the MD of FIED when, on listening to her idea, he suggested that she approach the launch and subsequent scaling up in a more organized and planned manner. She was introduced to the real difference between a greenfield approach and a blueprint approach. While the grant itself proved to be insufficient, over the next year and a half, BH evolved into a more organized and planned business model.

The concepts given in the training were useful and because of her pre-incubation at IIM Kashipur, she sharpened the strategy and vision of BH. This helped put forth the first version of the business model in place. However, this started a see-saw game that was a business paradox for BH. The more BH moved towards a business model that would be picked up for further support and funding by the RKVY-RAFTAAR selection panel, the more it seemed certain to drift away from its mission and fitness movement as envisaged at the time of formation of BH.

While the business model took shape, it was driven by the regular concepts of growth, revenue, profits, numbers, and quantity, driven by the economics of scaling up and generating revenue from operations. However, it also pushed towards a business model that generated profit for the shareholders. This was a dilemma that was difficult back then and it remained a concern for Stuti as she attended the International Yoga Day celebrations. Stuti was not averse to scaling up. In fact, she wanted to popularize the dip-n-dip easy-to-use product suited to modern life to popularize and disrupt the wellness sector. This was the mission of BH. However, the requirement of scaling up imposed by an investor-driven business model posed other challenges as did the demands of the investors.

Investors were not ready to put money on her informal knowledge. They demanded that BH products, especially the flagship dip-n-sip, be scientifically validated. This was easy to get for a product like dip-n-sip, which was curated with the best quality raw material and the knowledge and processes overseen by a scientist, Dr. V K Lal. The efforts were directed towards this and soon BH had signed an MoU with Kumaon University, Nainital (India) and got samples tested through the Regional Food Analysis center, Lucknow. BH also received technical incubation from CSIR-IITR or the Council of Scientific and Industrial Research—Indian Institute of Toxicological Research. Validation was necessary as there was a debate about the effectiveness and purity of the formulations available, as a plethora of options, each from a small manufacturer.

Preserving the Spirit of a Forest in a Factory

The purity of the product and its raw materials and the effective processes of preparing dip-n-sip, provided an easy solution to the validation requirement, but it also pointed out that the trust of consumers was driven by this overall pursuit of excellence and zero compromise on quality. This meant that scaling up while maintaining the same purity of mission, raw materials, and products would be a challenge as operations scaled up. It would be difficult to maintain the quality of inputs or the processes, and the risk of losing the purity in favor of scale was extremely high. The need to maintain raw material integrity while scaling up was critical to the existence of BH, and this made Stuti seek help from the National Institute of Agricultural Extension Management (MANAGE), Hyderabad (India). MANAGE could prove helpful in setting up a direct farmer sourcing system at scale.

While these parts of the business model and stage of business to move ahead were coming through, the regulatory hurdles of navigating between food safety laws and AYUSH frameworks were becoming increasingly cumbersome. The government officials and concerned experts eventually supported a clear path forward, but setting up an alternative path to live was proving to be tiringly slow and difficult. BH searched widely across India and even the globe for a proper science-based AYUSH certification methodology that could trigger tests of consumer trust and feedback from them. However, this was elusive. While everyone pointed in the direction of a new institute or lab, none of them were certified for the task, and most were unwilling to carry out the validation, as they believed that the basics of Ayurveda countered science as we know it, and therefore, the best Ayurvedic products were not amenable to testing the way we were used to testing drugs and pharmaceuticals. It appeared that maintaining the spirit of the Forest and purity of Ayurveda in a growth-obsessed investor-driven startup ecosystem would be impossible.

Start-Up Ecosystem: Meaningful but Far from Perfect

It may appear that building a 'purity of culture' based business is a dream despite the presence of vibrant start-up ecosystems that provide a lot of support, both monetary and non-monetary. While many milestones of the startup journey were achieved regularly by BH, the numbers that mattered moved slowly. Both the topline and bottom line were very slow-moving. In fact, it was evident that many people would judge BH as not successful, based on the slow numbers, and even believe that BH was not profitable. BH seemed to be a business stuck in a policy vacuum where it needed a lot of support. While India had a well-defined start-up policy and supporting ecosystem for entrepreneurs and their ventures, the start-up ecosystem across the globe lacks a specialized or special policy that supports such tradition-based wellness businesses and agri-based modern products.

There is no clear policy directive on such businesses or the eligibility or requirement for such businesses that should not be evaluated on the yardsticks of only profit and scale. This was a policy blind spot, as they rarely cater to the nuances of enterprises working at the intersection of traditional medicine, rural livelihoods, and environmental stewardship. Most funding frameworks are designed for broad agri-tech or biotech interventions, which led them to sideline models like BH that blend heritage with innovation. Due to this, it was widely believed that such enterprises often remain underfunded and undervalued.

When appearing for selection for incubation and funding, BH had to deal with experts and evaluators who lacked the understanding of Ayurveda at an expert level, the economics of rural sourcing and the nuances of eco-packaging all at once, and therefore, the judgment on BH was not holistic. Stuti strongly felt that many evaluators were trying to rigidly apply the directives from the government funding agency, which was lopsided in favor of short-term and high-growth (scaling up) requirements of business. The incubators found it difficult to find enough assessors to judge the business pitches for selection.

Incubators, on the other hand, had their own anecdotes which were markedly different from those of ventures such as BH, indicating huge information asymmetry in the start-up ecosystem. The system's timeline pressure compounded the issue. Most evaluators were unable to give the requisite time to understand an innovation and its business model. Thus, the system for startup selection and inclusion is prone to both type 1 and type 2 errors. The system seemed to be misaligned as investors struggle to quantify trust, storytelling or cultural immersion—all features that help to retain the fragrance of the forest in the factory. The investor aggregation platforms have been equally disappointing. Many focus on monetizing support services—subscriptions, pitch reviews, webinars—without offering actual capital linkages. They seem to lack real understanding or interest in niche sectors like AYUSH, leading to time and resource drain for founders by participating in a lopsided selection process.

Incubation centers were seen to offer generic modules while their managers were overloaded with paperwork and often handled up to 80–100 start-ups at a time. Ventures such as BH felt that they received very little sector-specific handholding. Herbal and Ayurvedic enterprises need guidance on compliance with AYUSH norms, impact measurement and blended finance tools beyond pitch polishing and elevator speech preparation and rehearsals.

Bureaucratic processes often resulted in disbursement delays, leading to a sense of penalization amongst the better startups. BH, like many other startups, felt caught between impatient investors, ill-equipped incubators, underfunded policy windows, and evaluator fatigue. Often, many stakeholders who demanded validation and adherence to AYUSH norms were not able to help in directing the startup towards the correct information or agency to carry out these. BH was also lost in such a maze for almost a year and a half when it decided to use the fragmented services available and chart its own course. Stuti believed that the Indian startup system must evolve funding models that reward depth over hype, patience over pressure, purpose over pitch decks. Impact investing wasn't efficient, as the cost of raising funds was very high in her experience.

Lastly, she also felt that, as there were few successful ventures in the space that had scaled up, there was a dearth of domain-specific mentors as well, leaving the founder–entrepreneurs with few options of seeking advice or having a sounding board to their ideas.

Too Many Questions and Too Little Time

While there seemed to be no single body to certify ayurvedic preparations along the lines of the I.P. (Indian Pharmacopeia) system of validation of allopathic medicines, the validation of BH products was based on triangulation of multiple agencies. Table 5.1 presents its positioning in the global market.

BH was a niche player but limited by resources with identified strengths as

1. Deep cultural credibility (backed by research of the AYUSH system in India).
2. Sustainable, plastic-free packaging.
3. AYUSH-based formulations.
4. Small-batch production with a focus on quality and customization
5. Culturally grounded and AYUSH-based product innovation
6. Rural sourcing and employment.

Table 5.1 Comparative global market positioning of Bikalp herbals and selected internaltional herbal wellness brands

Brand	*Country*	*Strategy*	*Values*	*Market Position*
Pukka Herbs	UK	Ayurveda-inspired organic herbal teas	Ecological farming, FairWild certification	Sold in 40+ countries, acquired by Unilever
Neal's Yard Remedies	UK	Holistic health and beauty	Organic, ethical sourcing	Premium niche brand with a strong loyal base
Traditional Medicines	USA	Herbal medicine teas	Pharmacopoeial-grade herbs, science-backed claims	Top herbal tea brand in the U.S.
Bikalp Herbals	India	Ayurveda-based dip-n-sip infusion line	Cultural authenticity, rural empowerment	Early-stage high-integrity niche seller with export-interest

Company's Internal documents

The importance of sustainable plastic-free packaging has not been understood by most small players in the wellness sector. The prevalent packaging claimed to have an earthy feel but it also portrayed unorganized production and capabilities with little attention to detail eroding trust of probable consumers even before it had been instilled. The prevalent packaging solutions were poor in looks and functionality and contributed to market positioning as a product of poverty-ridden women full of imperfection and a scratchy attempt to be sustainable and good for the environment and society, and a unverified claim to Ayurvedic wellness. Stuti believed this was doing more harm to the sector rather than helping any brand to sell apart from charity sales to help destitute women producers without any transparency about the same. As an ambitious brand, it left BH stranded.

BH had tried to break free and break through this maze of mediocracy and downplaying, but it had limited brand recognition outside institutional and academic circles, signifying that it was yet to develop a marketing plan and sales were limited to personal and institutional networks. BH was often faced with Price-sensitive customers who preferred mass market alternatives for being cheaper rather than specific high value products.

While BH wanted to get into export, initial interactions pointed to the difficulty in communicating the benefits of AYUSH-based formulations and purity, as the international audience was unfamiliar with the tradition and had been culturally conditioned to treat anything coming from the emerging world as barbaric and uncivilized from the imperial era of subjugation of these economies and their traditions. It also meant this was a path that not many suppliers had tread with caution before BH. There were many regulatory bottlenecks for the export of dip-n-sip-like products, which were technically formulations but not medicines for curing illnesses, despite their benefits.

The export ambitions led to some business queries from various export destinations, but they brought a dilemma of their own. Stuti was soon caught between being a founder or a growth manager in a transitioning model. While export had been an ambition for growth, it posed the challenge of diluting raw material integrity and therefore the spirit of BH with which it was founded. She could either focus on maintaining purity and teaching the practices and activities to ensure there were more growers and collectors of herbs that promised the purity that dip-n-sip was based on or focus on growth by pursuing more orders and building export relationships. For BH, it was an either-or decision until there was a significant capital infusion accompanied by hiring the right talent with pure knowledge of Ayurveda or excellent skills in pursuing and building an export portfolio.

Slow but steady success started attracting larger institutional attention—invitations to international expos, policy consultations, export advisors, and many others started reaching out to BH. Each of these opportunities added to the credibility and reach of BH, yet they also demanded scalability, standardization, compliance, and formalization. Investors and international buyers sensed the subscription potential of BH and institutional partnerships as scalable assets.

This choice of preserving the ethos of BH without any dilution versus pursuing fast growth for revenue and margin improvement also imposed a choice between operating the business based on ROI metrics versus metrics of total profit. The choice is not automatic as the metrics influence the culture and ethos, and hence it could have a profound impact on the direction tread by the business. BH introduced QR-enabled storytelling to ensure that their story of purity reached customers. It, however, lacked resources to reach the customers at large. This led BH to question the path ahead—should BH strive to scale up to compete with the big players on reach and volume—or should it deepen its niche, refusing to compromise on authenticity and accepting slower growth and limited visibility?

Stuti knew that if she built too lean a structure, BH risked being seen as artisanal and unscalable; if the system built was too robust, it might lose its soul—becoming another compliant wellness brand, stripped of its cultural integrity. She kept on thinking, "How do we preserve the spirit of the forest in the architecture of a factory?

Unit Economics as the Foundation of Value Creation

The business was built on consumer readiness, efficient cost structuring and market-aligned pricing. The total initial investment on R&D, pilot testing and marketing amounted to INR 2 lakhs or INR 200,000. The pursuit for efficiency to keep the soul pure and maintain the raw material integrity meant that the cost of production of each pack stood at INR 27 which included INR 5 for labor. However, the product pack is priced at INR 110 per pack as consumer research revealed that consumers are willing to spend INR 500–1000 per month on herbal wellness solutions. This pricing looks aspirational, but it is evidence-backed, aligning the perceived value with affordability for middle-income health seekers. This would make the middle-income health seeker segment a large domestic market available for BH.

With sales expectations constrained by raw material integrity at just 5564 packets, the expected net profit stood at just INR 265,000. While this meant an ROI of 176% at the end of the year, it also meant the business did not make enough money to allow the founder a middle-income lifestyle. Growth was an imperative. 2024–25 data shows 1000+ unique buyers, 110+ repeat purchasers, and nearly 30 subscriptions. At least 10 customers have been retained from the launch of the product itself. It appears BH can transform interest into sustained value, validating its ROI based model as both culturally rooted and commercially viable, but left it looking for growth to give the founder economic viability for her skill sets and talent.

The Dilemma

It was 06:00 PM on a rainy Friday in Lucknow. Stuti Lal sat across a long wooden table at Bikalp's office, facing her team and two unexpected visitors—an EU wellness investor and a senior *vaidyacharya* (ayurvedic practitioner equivalent to a physician). The investor offered 200,000 British Pounds in seed capital—conditionally if Bikalp launched a mass-market line by Diwali (a major indina festival usually occuring around October - November based on the Lunar Calendar) using outsourced packaging and cheaper ingredients. The co-founder, Dr. V K Lal, meanwhile, warned, "this would destroy the trust in our entire community". With ten days to respond, Stuti and Bikalp Herbals must now choose, scale fast and dilute, or stay small and authentic but risk running out of money?

Discussion Questions

1. Mission vs. Market—How can purpose-driven enterprises like Bikalp Herbals balance their mission of cultural and ecological integrity with the market's demand for rapid growth and profitability?
2. Ethical Scaling—Should Stuti Lal accept the investor's offer that compromises product purity for faster scale? What ethical and strategic frameworks can guide her decision?
3. Institutional Ecosystem Fit—What does the Bikalp Herbals case reveal about gaps in India's start-up and incubation ecosystem for tradition-based AYUSH-linked ventures? How can policy better support such hybrid enterprises?
4. Innovation and Authenticity—In transforming Ayurveda into a modern, convenient product like Dip-n-Sip, how does BH balance innovation and authenticity? Where should the line be drawn between adaptation and dilution?

Supplementary Readings

V. Kasturi Rangan and Tricia Gregg, "How Social Entrepreneurs Zig-Zag their way to impact and scale? ", California Management Review vol 62(1) 53–76. 2019.

Learning Objectives of the Case

1. Understanding Strategic and Ethical Trade-offs in Mission-Driven Enterprises.
2. Explore the institutional and policy ecosystem for tradition-based startups.
3. Apply strategic management tools to Social and Cultural Contexts.

Acknowledgements The author would like to acknowledge Stuti Lal, founder of Bikalp Herbals, for offering generous support and inputs towards writing this case study.

Competing Interests The author has no conflicts of interest to declare that are relevant to the content of this chapter.

Exhibits

Exhibit 5.1 Illustrative list of plant-based beverages for healing, energy and ritual

Modern life has become very demanding, and many people are looking for alternatives to reconnect with wellness and their cultural and ecological roots. Across the globe, communities have long turned to plant-based beverages for healing, energy, and rituals. These include, but are not limited to:

1. Matcha: originated in Japan in the sixteenth century, and the green tea leaf is consumed as a whole. It is characterized by its vibrant green colour, high antioxidant content and unique flavor. Matcha, as a warm tea preparation, is consumed in the traditional tea ceremony, also known as Chanoyu. It is used by monks for mental clarity and meditation.
2. Yerba Mate: primarily consumed in central and southern regions of South America, especially Paraguay, Argentina, Uruguay, southern Brazil, Bolivia and Chile. Its use was initiated by the Guarini and Tupi tribes in Paraguay. It is known to be similar to coffee but without the jitters and is a good stimulant.
3. Rooibos tea: Has been consumed for centuries in the Cederberg region of South Africa. It is caffeine-free herbal tea with a sweet, nutty flavor, and its first written record of consumption dates back to 1772, but it has probably predated it by centuries in the tribes. It is also known for its anti-inflammatory properties. It is available in red and green versions and consumed as both fermented and non-fermented.
4. Kombucha: Probably originated in the Bohoi Sea region of China and has been used by traditional Chinese medical practitioners as a remedy for lung and stomach ailments. It's use spread from China to Russia, and from there it reached Japan and is today homebrewed almost globally. It is a fermented tea known to balance the gut and detoxify the body.
5. Zobo: Is a hibiscus tea that originated in Nigeria and Ghana and is used to cool the body and regulate blood pressure.
6. Ginger-turmeric tea in Indonesia (Jamu) is consumed daily by many for digestion and vitality benefits.
7. Chamomile and Peppermint: They are traditional sources of tonics for calming the nerves and aiding sleep.
8. Kadhas (decoction), Haldi Milk (Turmeric Latte), Thyme water and infused buttermilk have all been part of seasonable and situational health care for generations in India.

Exhibit 5.2 Cross framework strategic alignment

Framework	*Strategic level*	*Dilemma focus*	*Interlinking insight*
Porter's five forces	Industry	Competitive pressure management	External environment demands compromise between premium quality and supply chain agility
SWOT	Firm	Strategic positioning vs. scalability	Bikalp's voice-driven model competes with scale-driven players
BMC	Operational	Mission integrity vs. institutional scale	Internal systems must evolve without compromising values and cultural roots

Company's internal documents

Exhibit 5.3 Projected cash flows (2024–2025)

Particulars	*Amount (INR)*
A. Cash inflows	
Revenues from Sales (5564 units* INR110)	615,231
Total inflows (A)	615,231
B. Cash outflows	
Fixed costs	
R&D	50,000
Pilot production	100,000
Marketing	50,000
Total Fixed Costs	200,000
Variable Costs (COGS)	
Raw Materials (5564*INR12)	66,678
Packaging (5564 *INR10)	55,640
Labor (5564*INR5)	27,820
Total Variable Costs	150,228
Total Expenditure (Fixed + Variable) (B)	350,228
C. Net Cash Flow (A-B)	264,993

Company's Documents

Exhibit 5.4 Segmentation and selection

Persona	*Dip-n-Sip Bundle*	*Ideal Channel*
Urban wellness seeker	Immunity & Calm pack	Wellness stores, Amazon and Instagram.
Rural SHG consumer	Herbal Starter Box	Village Haat, SHG bazaars
Diaspora Enthusiast	Global sampler (3 flavors +QR story)	UK / US e-commerce, Indian grocery chains
Preventive Health subscriber	PCDS / Thyroid / Stress Support Pack.	Subscription model, D2C website

CHAPTER 6

Scaling Bhungroo: Naireeta Services' Expansion Strategy for Climate-Resilient Agriculture

Sreevas Sahasranamam and Ira Chatterjee

Abstract *Bhungroo* is an innovative subterranean water storage system designed to capture excess monsoon runoff and store the water underground for use during the dry summer months. Naireeta Services Private Limited (NSPL) envisioned *Bhungroo* not only as a technological intervention but also as a social innovation aimed at empowering women farmers in Gujarat, particularly within patriarchal rural settings, by giving them a much-needed voice in agricultural decision-making. This teaching case focuses on the scaling pathways available to NSPL and the strategic tradeoffs they involve. It invites students to explore the complexities of implementing technology in rural contexts, the property rights of women, and the dilemmas inherent in scaling social innovations. The case is well-suited

S. Sahasranamam (✉)
Adam Smith Business School, University of Glasgow, Glasgow, UK
e-mail: sreevas.sahasranamam@glasgow.ac.uk

I. Chatterjee
Vrije Universiteit Amsterdam, Amsterdam, Netherlands
e-mail: i.chatterjee@vu.nl

A. S. Galande et al. (eds.), *Context-inspired Entrepreneurship*, Sustainable Development Goals Series,
https://doi.org/10.1007/978-981-95-9831-1_6

for classes on social entrepreneurship, rural innovation, and climate-resilient entrepreneurship.

Keywords Social entrepreneurship • Rural entrepreneurship • Water • Agricultural innovation • Climate change • Social innovation • Scaling • India

SDG Links

This case contributes to SDG 8: Decent Work and Economic Growth by demonstrating how water access can stabilise farmer incomes and support sustainable livelihoods. By reducing crop failure and income volatility, the case highlights pathways through which agricultural technology innovation can enhance productive employment in rural economies (SDG 8.2). The case also contributes to SDG 5: Gender Equality by demonstrating how social innovation can increase women's voice, agency, and participation in agricultural decision-making within rural contexts. It also contributes to SDG 2 by highlighting sustainable agriculture and SDG 6 by discussing water management.

In the parched fields of rural Patan in Gujarat, where every year the lack of water, withered away agriculture and compelled many families to migrate to cities, the wife-husband duo of Trupti Jain and Biplab Ketan Paul envisioned a transformation. They had noticed a paradox: on the one hand, there was excess water runoff during the monsoon season, and on the other hand, there were water shortages in other seasons. With both issues hampering agriculture, they wondered if the problem of excess monsoon runoff could be transformed into a solution. Biplab, the technical lead, innovated with the local community to give birth to the idea of *Bhungroo*, a subterranean water storage system designed to hold excess monsoon water runoff underground and store it for use during the dry summer months when it could be pumped back up. Trupti soon joined him to help scale *Bhungroo's* impact, and they formally established Naireeta Services Private Limited (NSPL) to enable its wider adoption. NSPL's approach was not only about designing a technological solution for climate-resilient agriculture; rather, they envisioned a deeper social transformation aimed at empowering women farmers in traditional patriarchal communities by giving them a much-needed voice in agricultural practices. Gradually, several villages in Gujarat began to adopt the technology, and by the early 2010s, word of mouth and coverage from reputed global organizations such as the BBC helped spread *Bhungroo's* reach both in India and abroad. As demand grew, the wife-husband duo began exploring ways in which their social innovation could be adapted and scaled to address the global crisis of water scarcity, women's empowerment, and climate-resilient agriculture.

Background: The Problem and the Context

The background context that drove the wife-husband duo to act was the complex dynamics they witnessed during their field experiences and from credible reports on water scarcity, socioeconomic status, and the role of women in agriculture. For instance, in states like Gujarat and Rajasthan, annual rainfall variability had increased by 15–20% compared to the long-term average (CRIDA, 2010), leading to frequent crop failures. Groundwater resources were also under severe strain (Central Ground Water Board, 2008) due to overexploitation for irrigation and inefficient water management practices for groundwater recharge. For instance, in the Mehsana district of Gujarat, excessive use of borewells pushed the groundwater level from 200 feet to 1200 feet in just ten years (Chandra, 2016). Reports from the Planning Commission (2006) also emphasized the need for more efficient and sustainable irrigation practices to address the growing water crisis.

While water scarcity was a problem during the summer months, waterlogging and flooding were common during the rainy season. For instance, estimates in 2000 suggested that nearly 7.5% of India's arable land, mainly in Western and Northern India, was prone to waterlogging and consequently led to crop damage (UN Climate Technology Centre and Network, 2023).

Alongside the water-specific challenges, rural communities were also grappling with high levels of poverty and limited access to resources. According to the National Sample Survey Office (NSSO, 2007–2008), a significant portion of rural households relied on agriculture for their livelihoods, with many living below the poverty line. Government initiatives, while important, faced challenges in reaching remote communities and addressing the specific needs of vulnerable populations.

Another key dynamic to consider was the critical role of women in India's agricultural sector. Although constituting 73% of the rural agricultural workforce and performing nearly 70% of all agricultural activities (Agriculture Census, 2015–2016; Oxfam International, 2022), land ownership remained deeply gendered. Despite their contributions, estimates suggested only 14% of women are operational landholders and own just 11% of the total agricultural land in the country (Agriculture Census, 2015–2016; Agarwal et al., 2021). This gap severely limited women's economic empowerment and decision-making power within rural agricultural communities.

Thus, the wife-husband duo realized there was a clear and urgent need for innovative and localized solutions that could address the complex challenges of water scarcity, climate variability, gender inequality, and livelihood insecurity.

Bhungroo: Technological and Social Innovation

Bhungroo, developed by NSPL, is a unique water management system designed to capture and store excess rainwater underground (Naireeta Services, n.d.). While the company operated as a for-profit entity, its core mission remained firmly rooted in social purpose. Guided by their mission of "Antyodaya: serving the last person in the queue in the best possible way," Trupti and Biplab aimed to ensure that their innovation primarily benefited the most marginalized of farmers, especially women in vulnerable rural communities.

Bhungroo, colloquially translated as 'the big straw,' is based on the principles of aquifer storage and recovery, and vertical drainage. The technology integrates comprehensive geophysical and geological analyses with data simulation techniques "to selectively filter, inject, and store excess water" (Naireeta Services, n.d.). Occupying just one to two square meters of surface area, each *Bhungroo* unit can store between one and four million litres of water annually within its subsurface zone. On average, a *Bhungroo*, upon harvesting water for as little as 10 days a year, could support irrigation for about 7 months for 15 acres of land (Chandra, 2016). Installation of each unit takes about 3 days, and the costs of installation are estimated to break even within 3 years (Chandra, 2016). Each *Bhungroo* was expected to last for at least 25 years (Chandra, 2016).

The installation process of a *Bhungroo* involves four phases: (a) feasibility study, to evaluate the farm's location, size, and elevation; (b) geo-hydro survey, to analyse groundwater levels and subsoil structure; (c) drilling and installation; and (d) setting up a filtration chamber, to prevent larger sediments and leaves entering the *Bhungroo* from the monsoon water run-off. This simple technological innovation allowed farmers to cultivate multiple crops each year, enhancing their income and food security. In addition, *Bhungroo* also helped replenish groundwater resources and reduce soil erosion.

The initial installations of *Bhungroos* were in the Patan district of Gujarat in 2002, across 5 villages (Chandra, 2016). It was conceptualized by Biplab in the aftermath of a major earthquake in Gujarat and the water scarcity it brought with it (Christoff et al., 2018). While engaging in the relief work post-earthquake, Biplab realised how mobilizing and organizing marginalized women from villages could help facilitate high-impact social change (Christoff & Sommer, 2018). The costs of making a *Bhungroo* then were INR 7 lakhs (Chandra, 2016).

The technical innovation was complemented by close collaboration with the local communities, particularly with women's self-help groups, who played a crucial role in ensuring community ownership and participation (Naireeta Services, n.d.). Initially, Biplab, who was leading the technical development of *Bhungroo,* started testing it with male smallholder farmers. However, he soon realized that the model's emphasis on joint ownership and collective management required teamwork skills. Women in the rural communities often possessed deeper expertise in collective action compared to men, given their experiences with self-help groups (SHGs). SHGs—a transformative movement across India and other developing countries—have empowered women by fostering financial independence, social confidence, and mutual support. Recognizing these collaborative skills, Naireeta Services increasingly focused on women as key agents for implementing and disseminating the *Bhungroo* technology.

Beyond enhancing agricultural resilience, the organization saw an opportunity to improve the livelihoods, skills, and agency of poor, rural women with limited literacy. Women were trained not only to use and maintain the *Bhungroo* units but also to become trainers and leaders within their communities, further strengthening their social standing. The process of engaging women with Bhungroo included a comprehensive capacity-building programme. Training was delivered in the local language (Gujarati) using relatable terminology to explain concepts from geology, hydrology, and civil engineering. For example, as illustrated in Fig. 6.1, the placement of Bhungroo for a set of adjacent farms was

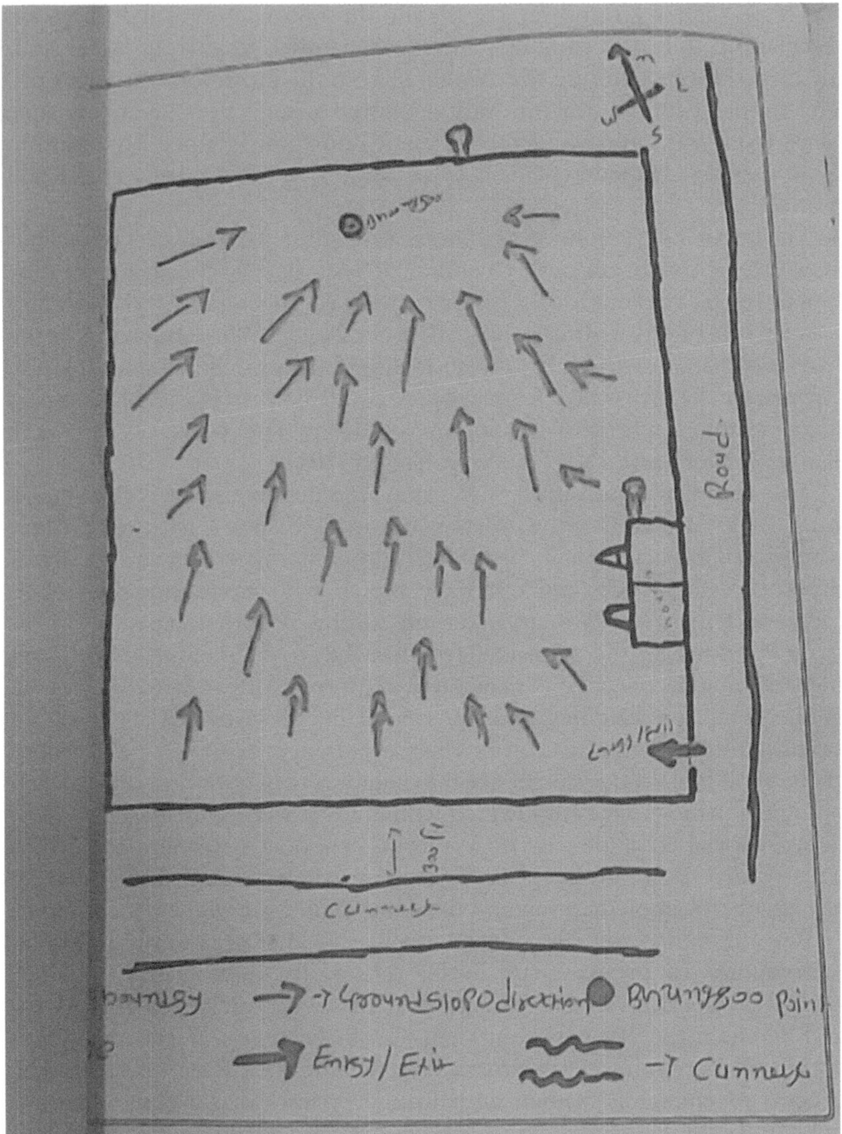

Fig. 6.1 Illustration of how the gradient of the land was visualized during a group meeting between adjacent farm owners to decide on where to set up the *Bhungroo* in accordance with the natural flow of water

determined through a participatory approach. These involved women farmers discussing areas across their farms prone to most waterlogging after rainfall, and this naturally led to conversations about the water head and natural slope of the land. This understanding enabled adjacent farm owners to arrive at a consensus on the optimal location for Bhungroo based on where the natural incline was steepest. Similarly, coloured hydrology maps were used to discuss underground water tables in a relatable and accessible way. While engaging in this process, NSPL also ensured that they gathered traditional knowledge from the community about their agricultural practices and seasonal variations, to adapt their technology effectively. This localised skill-building approach ensured the community could maintain and repair *Bhungroo* independently.

More importantly, Naireeta Services was deeply motivated by a broader social mission: to empower rural women who traditionally lacked land rights and thus, had little influence over agricultural decision-making. For instance, Trupti said,

> *I have tried, by working with NGOs, to give land rights in the name of the women, but we are not succeeding in that. Only 2% of women—those who are the single child of the family—can get that. That's the official situation.* (Christoff & Sommer, 2018, p. 3)

This fundamental barrier inspired NSPL's social innovation, wherein they granted the technology ownership rights of *Bhungroo* (and consequently water rights) to the women in the family (see Fig. 6.2). Granting women ownership rights over *Bhungroo* units—despite their lack of formal land ownership—was a transformative step. This gave the women control over a resource needed to make the land productive. This allowed them to contribute meaningfully to farming decisions and enhance their visibility and influence within patriarchal rural communities. By granting them rights to *Bhungroo* and thus indirectly to water rights (see Fig. 6.2), NSPL empowered rural women and increased their participation in decision-making processes. A core requirement of the model was that technology ownership rights be formally transferred to the women managing it, with documentation embedded in local governance structures and aligned with social norms.

Typically, a group of five women was identified from within SHGs and allotted a *Bhungroo*. Very often this would be women who owned adjacent 4–5 farm plots. These women would then agree on their roles within the

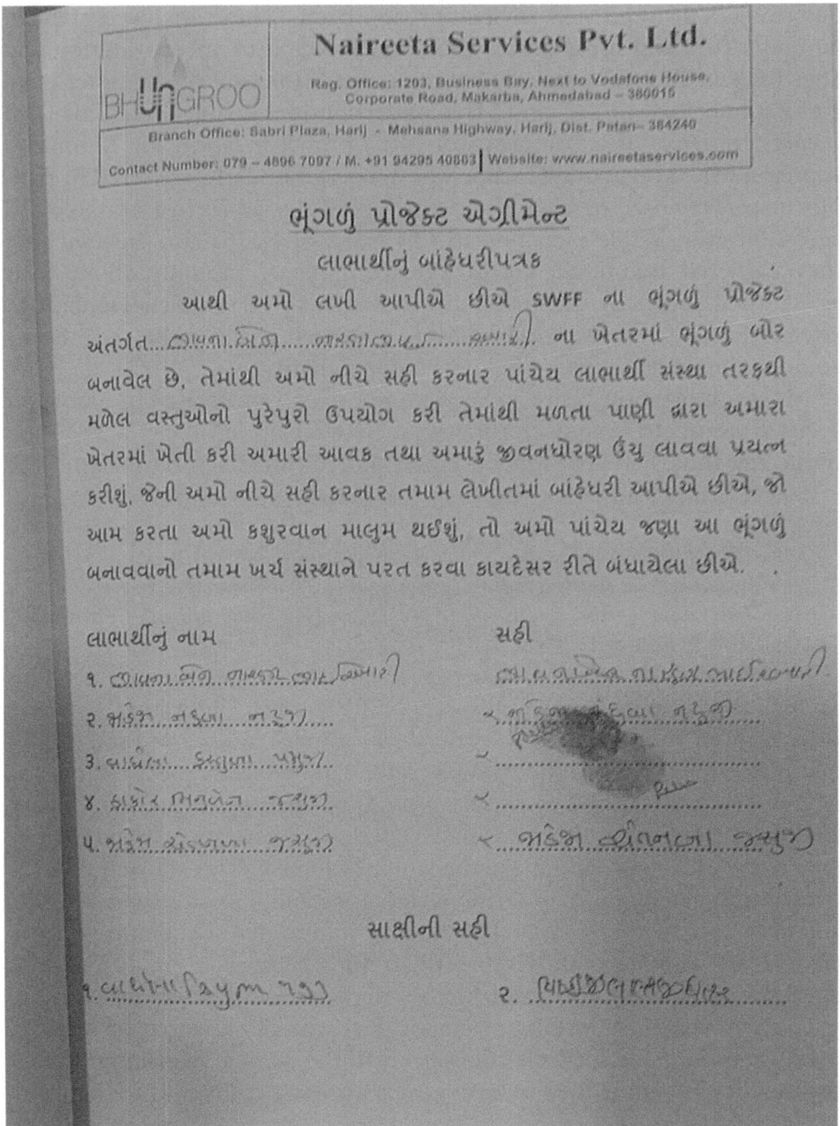

BHUNGROO

Naireeta Services Pvt. Ltd.

Reg. Office: 1203, Business Bay, Next to Vodafone House, Corporate Road, Makarba, Ahmedabad – 380015

Branch Office: Sabri Plaza, Harij - Mehsana Highway, Harij, Dist. Patan– 384240

Contact Number: 079 – 4896 7097 / M. +91 94295 40863 | Website: www.naireetaservices.com

ભૂંગળું પ્રોજેક્ટ એગ્રીમેન્ટ

લાભાર્થીનું બાંહેધરીપત્રક

આથી અમો લખી આપીએ છીએ SWFF ના ભૂંગળું પ્રોજેક્ટ અંતર્ગત [illegible] ના ખેતરમાં ભૂંગળું બોર બનાવેલ છે. તેમાંથી અમો નીચે સહી કરનાર પાંચેય લાભાર્થી સંસ્થા તરફથી મળેલ વસ્તુઓનો પુરેપુરો ઉપયોગ કરી તેમાંથી મળતા પાણી દ્વારા અમારા ખેતરમાં ખેતી કરી અમારી આવક તથા અમારૂં જીવનધોરણ ઉંચુ લાવવા પ્રયત્ન કરીશું. જેની અમો નીચે સહી કરનાર તમામ લેખીતમાં બાંહેધરી આપીએ છીએ, જો આમ કરતા અમો કશુરવાન માલુમ થઈશું, તો અમો પાંચેય જણા આ ભૂંગળું બનાવવાનો તમામ ખર્ચ સંસ્થાને પરત કરવા કાયદેસર રીતે બંધાયેલા છીએ.

લાભાર્થીનું નામ	સહી
૧. [illegible]	[illegible]
૨. [illegible]	[illegible]
૩. [illegible]	
૪. [illegible]	
૫. [illegible]	[illegible]

સાક્ષીની સહી

૧. [illegible] ૨. [illegible]

Fig. 6.2 Illustration of documentation endorsing group ownership of *Bhungroo* water rights from the local panchayat

group and commit to sharing the maintenance costs of the *Bhungroo*. One member of the group would offer a portion of their land for construction (arrived at through a mapping exercise illustrated in Fig. 6.1), while the others would contribute with labour and maintenance, creating a sense of peer support within the group (Chandra, 2016).

In essence, NSPL's model made *Bhungroo* a critical piece in advancing gender equity within rural agricultural communities. The innovation has earned several prestigious awards for its impact on women's empowerment, including the UN Global Climate Action Award, the Gender Just Climate Solutions Award, the Cartier Women's Initiative Award, and the Buckminster Fuller Challenge Grand Prize.

By the late 2000s, through multiple on-field trial-and-error experiments, Biplab, the technology lead, had developed multiple technical designs of *Bhungroo* suited for different agroclimatic conditions. These designs showed promising results across several farms in rural Gujarat, increasing farmers' incomes and empowering women. In 2011, the wife-husband duo registered Naireeta Services Private Limited (NSPL) as a for-profit social enterprise. This legal form allowed *Bhungroo* units to be sold to wealthy farmers at a profit and then use those profits to cross-subsidize and provide units at a lower price to poor farmers.

Soon after, following short documentary videos and news coverage by Indian media about the *Bhungroo* technology, they began receiving inquiries from farmers in South India interested in implementing it on their farms. Around the same time, they also began gaining global recognition, including receiving a Fulbright Fellowship and having the BBC document their story, which sparked interest in the technology from other countries in the Global South, such as Bangladesh, Ghana, and Vietnam, facing similar climate and water challenges. Thus, the family duo was now pondering how *Bhungroo* could be scaled to other regions. What should their next steps be?

Scaling Bhungroo: Options for Expansion

Option 1: Direct Replication

One option they were contemplating was whether they could replicate their model directly by setting up new operational units in different states of India and other parts of the Global South. This approach would allow control over the use of technology and ensure direct influence on the social impact mission related to women and human rights. However, this would also require hiring their own team of engineers, community mobilizers, and trainers at each new location. This option would necessitate substantial fundraising, potentially from a mix of debt, government, and grant-based financing.

Option 2: Licensing or Franchising

Another option was that NSPL could adopt a licensing or franchise model, wherein the *Bhungroo* technology is licensed to local entrepreneurs in different regions of the world for implementation in their communities. This would involve a training and onboarding programme for each potential licensee to help them understand the technology and its operational know-how. NSPL would need to develop technology documentation and standard operating procedures around its usage. The local entrepreneurs who license the technology would oversee its local implementation, staff hiring, community mobilization, and financial sustainability. In this approach, NSPL would receive a fee for any services it offered related to technology implementation or maintenance.

Option 3: Strategic Partnerships

NSPL could build strategic partnerships with established NGOs and government agencies to transfer *Bhungroo* technology. Alternatively, they could work with multinationals in the water or agriculture sectors to scale the implementation of *Bhungroo* technology to large farms. In this approach, NSPL focuses on providing technical expertise and training, while partners oversee local implementation and community engagement.

Option 4: Democratizing Bhungroo Access

Digital technologies and internet usage were on the rise across India and the Global South. Therefore, NSPL could open-source *Bhungroo* technology and develop a digital platform to disseminate knowledge, training materials, and technical specifications related to it. This would build the capacity of individuals, organizations, and communities to learn about the technology and implement it independently. The platform would include training modules, documentation, and a forum for knowledge sharing.

NSPL could then focus primarily on the training and follow-up support activities.

With several ways to scale *Bhungroo*, Trupti and Biplab needed to decide: *Which path would best help them grow their impact while staying true to their mission?*

Discussion Questions

What are the unique features and challenges of Indian agriculture? What role do women play within it?
How is *Bhungroo's* technology relevant for India's socio-economic context and its agricultural needs?
How can NSPL assess whether its social innovation is ready for scaling? What indicators can be used to evaluate scaling readiness?
What are the advantages and disadvantages of the direct replication model for scaling *Bhungroo*?
How can the organization navigate the differing regulatory and socio-cultural environments when scaling to new regions or countries?
What are the potential benefits of adopting a licensing or franchising model in terms of scalability and reach? What risks might this approach entail?
How can Naireeta Services identify and select suitable partners? What are the challenges of managing partnerships and ensuring alignment of goals?
What are the advantages of a digital platform for scaling the technology? What could be some of the disadvantages of open-source innovation?
If multiple scaling pathways are viable, how should Naireeta Services prioritize or sequence them? How can NSPL maintain its social mission of women's empowerment as it scales across different regions and organizational forms?

Supplementary Readings for Class Discussion

Dees, G., Anderson, B. B., & Wei-Skillern, J. (2004). Scaling Social Impact. *Stanford Social Innovation Review*, *1*(4), 24–32. https://doi.org/10.48558/CNNZ-7276
Steinfield, L., & Holt, D. (2019). Toward a theory on the reproduction of social innovations in subsistence marketplaces. *Journal of Product Innovation Management*, *36*(6), 764–799.

Sahasranamam, S. & Soundararajan, V. (2024) How businesses can help alleviate poverty around the world. World Economic Forum. https://www.weforum.org/stories/2024/05/5-ways-businesses-can-helpto-address-poverty/

Learning Objectives

This case is well-suited for classes on social entrepreneurship, rural entrepreneurship, agritech ventures, women's entrepreneurship, and the role of intermediaries in empowering marginalized communities. It challenges students to critically examine the dilemmas and trade-offs involved in scaling a social innovation. By engaging with this case, students will be able to:

1. Assess the readiness to scale social innovation, using appropriate indicators.
2. Compare and contrast different scaling models for social innovation (direct replication, licensing/franchising, digital platforms).
3. Examine the role of partnerships and intermediaries in scaling social impact.
4. Analyse regulatory and socio-technical challenges involved in scaling across regions.
5. Apply the conceptual learning from frameworks like Dees et al. (2004) to real-world scenarios.

Acknowledgements Authors would like to thank Trupti Jain and Biplab Ketan Paul for the time towards interviews and warm hospitality in hosting us for field visits which helped in the preparation of this case. The text is written entirely by the authors, though we had taken help of Gemini 2.5 for sourcing some of the information, which the authors engaged with deeper in the process of writing. We also took AI support from Microsoft CoPilot in improving the stylizing of the draft in certain parts.

Competing Interests The authors have no conflicts of interest to declare that are relevant to the content of this chapter.

Supplementary Material

Guidance for Educators on Using This Case for a 2-hour Class Discussion

1. Broad discussion on Indian agriculture and rural areas (5 mins)

Open the class by asking students a broad question to share their experiences or reflections on Indian agriculture or on rural areas. Based on the responses, summarise the different characteristics. One is likely to hear aspects like marginalized land holding, small farm sizes, use of technology in agriculture, agriculture mandis, Green revolution, minimum support price from the government on some agricultural produce, role of patriarchy in rural areas, farmer suicides during drought, among others.

2. Discussion on *Bhungroo*: both technical and social innovation aspects (20 mins)

Build on this discussion to get the class to think about *Bhungroo* and its role within the broader socio-economic-political context of Indian agriculture. Navigate the discussion to stress the climate-resilient nature of the technology alongside the social innovation anchored on women's empowerment in agriculture through *Bhungroo* rights.

3. Call for a snap vote using online polling or a raising of hands, asking students to put themselves in the shoes of Trupti and Biplab to choose one of the four options ahead of them. (2 mins)
4. Introduce the Dees et al. (2004) framework, and discuss it in the context of NSPL [50 minutes]

Dees et al. (2004) discussed two key aspects.

First, it discusses three different mechanisms of scaling social impact, as a continuum, namely—dissemination, affiliation, and branching. If students have not already engaged with the reading, get them to read pg. 28–29 to understand the different mechanisms of scaling social impact and ask them to summarize their understanding. Broadly, the key essence is:

- Dissemination is the simplest, least resource-intensive approach, but it offers the least control over implementation of the initiative in a new location. You may choose to discuss the example from the reading or another similar example to illustrate dissemination.
- Affiliation approach offers moderate control over implementation and comes with moderate resource commitment requirements. You may choose to discuss the example from the reading or another similar example to illustrate affiliation.
- Branching approach offers the highest level of control over implementation and requires the relatively highest level of resource commitment. You may choose to discuss the example from the reading or another similar example to illustrate dissemination.

Second, the 5Rs framework helps social entrepreneurs to find a scaling path that is most suited for them. The 5Rs are (Dees et al., p. 30)–

- "Readiness—Is the innovation ready to be spread?"
- "Receptivity—Will the innovation be well-received in target communities?"
- "Resources—What resources, financial or otherwise, are required to get the job done right?"
- "Risk—What's the chance the innovation will be implemented incorrectly, or will fail to have impact?"
- "Returns—What is the bottom line? Impact should not just be about serving more people—it should be about serving them well"

Ask students to work in groups of 3–5 to engage with pg. 30–31, to understand each of the 5Rs and get them to rate NSPL on a scale of 1 to 5 on each of them. Arrive at a consensus understanding by taking inputs from different groups.

5. Call for a snap vote again, using online polling or a raising of hands, asking students to vote again, this time, with their understanding of the 5Rs framework and the tradeoffs associated with the three approaches to scaling social impact. If there have been any changes in the voting pattern from the initial one, the educator could comment on it (3 minutes)
6. Discussion on the 4 different options ahead of NSPL (25 minutes)

Gather inputs from the 4 different camps on the voting to discuss the pros and cons, if NSPL were to choose their preferred option.

While discussing options of affiliation and branching, also bring in the discussion on the social and regulatory institutional contexts of other countries like Bangladesh, Vietnam, and Ghana. Also, discuss how the socio-economic situation within the different states of India widely differs. This could involve a discussion on state GDP and average income levels of different states.

Get the students to think about whether different options need to be considered in different contexts. Is there a case for sequencing options or considering multiple options together?

7. Debrief and summarize the learning (10 minutes)

Summarize the key learning from the class discussion—the different scaling pathways for social innovations, the 5Rs framework, and unique socio-economic contexts in Indian agriculture.

Optional—you may discuss an Epilogue of what happened by getting students to engage with the NSPL website—https://www.naireetaservices.com/.

References

Agarwal, B., Anthwal, P., & Mahesh, M. (2021). How many and which women own land in India? Inter-gender and intra-gender gaps. *The Journal of Development Studies, 57*(11), 1807–1829.

Central Ground Water Board. (2008). *Ground water resources of India*. Ministry of Water Resources.

Central Research Institute for Dryland Agriculture (CRIDA). (2010). *Annual report 2009–2010.*

Chandra, K. K. (2016, April 4). Bhungroo, a reservoir of hope for poverty alleviation, crop failure and woman empowerment in Gujarat, India. *The Weekend Leader*. https://www.theweekendleader.com/Innovation/2396/watershed-innovation.html

Christoff, P. S., & Sommer, J. M. (2018). Women's empowerment and climate change adaptation in Gujarat, India: A case-study analysis of the local impact of transnational advocacy networks. *Sustainability, 10*(6), 1920. https://doi.org/10.3390/su10061920

Christoff, P. S., Sommer, J. M., & Kaur, J. (2018). Impact report for the Bhungroo project: Highlights and lessons learned from three farming villages in Gujarat,

India. Stony Brook University. https://bpb-us-e1.wpmucdn.com/you.stonybrook.edu/dist/8/5494/files/2021/12/5IMPACT-REPORT-FOR-THE-BHUNGROO-PROJECT-final.pdf

Ministry of Agriculture and Farmers Welfare, Government of India. *Agricultural Census 2015–16: Final Report.* Source: https://agcensus.da.gov.in/document/agcen1516/ac_1516_report_final-220221.pdf

Naireeta Services Private Limited. (n.d.). About us. https://www.naireetaservices.com/about-us/

National Sample Survey Office (NSSO). (2007–2008). *Employment and unemployment situation in India.*

Oxfam International. (2022, May 25). *India: Women farmers persevere.* https://www.oxfam.org/en/india-women-farmers-persevere

Planning Commission. (2006). *Report of the working group on water resources.* Government of India.

UN Climate Technology Centre and Network. (2023). Technology and nationally determined contributions: Stimulating the uptake of technologies in support of nationally determined contribution implementation. United Nations Framework Convention on Climate Change. https://unfccc.int/ttclear/tec/techandndc.html

CHAPTER 7

PiKademy: Beyond Textbooks…Building Tomorrow's Problem Solvers

Sachidananda Benegal and Parvathy B

Abstract Uncertainties and Natural calamities are more punitive to those who are economically backward. However, the founders of PiKademy decided it was not what they wanted to see happen with kids in one of the slums of Mumbai. Beginning initially with after-school classes, they slowly built a school for the kids that was designed around project-based learning. In a short span of time, the team has not only seen enhanced learning outcomes and class attendance, but also a phenomenal increase in personal confidence of the students as problem-solvers of tomorrow. The case leaves the readers with several choices that lie in front of the founders to expand the ventures' impact—should they grow on their own? Or franchise? Coupled with the growth dilemma, the founders also need to develop a viable financial model: cross-subsidization, CSR, and alternative revenue channels were all seen as promising options.

S. Benegal (✉)
NSRCEL, Indian Institute of Management Bangalore, Bangalore, India
e-mail: sachidananda.bs14@alumni.iimb.ac.in

Parvathy B
Indian Institute of Management Jammu, Nagrota, India
e-mail: parvathy@iimj.ac.in

A. S. Galande et al. (eds.), *Context-inspired Entrepreneurship*, Sustainable Development Goals Series,
https://doi.org/10.1007/978-981-95-9831-1_7

Keywords Slum children • Scaling challenges • Education incubation • Curriculum Innovation

SDG Links
This case contributes to SDG 8: Decent Work and Economic Growth by demonstrating how equipping learners from underserved communities with relevant capabilities enables education focus enterprises to serve as pathways to productive employment and livelihood opportunities for youth, in line with SDG Target 8.6. It also highlights SDG 4 on quality education and SDG 10 on reducing inequalities.

As Humza saw students from Pi.kademy, the school he co-founded, present their ventures at *Shark-Tank Junior*,[1] in early 2025, he was pleased to see the impact the project-based curriculum at the school had created over the last two years. From struggling to get their conceptual foundation right, these students were now taking up entrepreneurial ventures with ease. Humza knew the Pi.kademy team had developed a strong model of impact delivery.

The team at Pi.kademy was not overly concerned about academic results because they were confident that their approach was providing not only conceptual understanding but also practical applications. Given this undeniable impact, Humza and Hassan, the founders of Pi.kademy, recognized that several pressing issues needed to be addressed to scale their initiative further.

Since their founding in 2022, to the present, they have relied on contributions and support from various stakeholders, including family, friends, teachers, and facility owners. However, their model thus far had been built on the goodwill or good intentions of all their stakeholders who provided resources. But on a scale, this was not something that they could assume. Developing a financial model that would ensure their initiative's stability as a priority.

One option was to charge school fees to the parents; however, this would risk a lot of the students moving back to the government schools,

[1] Sayed Mohammad Shoeb. (2025, January 29). Linkedin.com. https://www.linkedin.com/posts/sayedmohammad-shoeb_a-few-moments-from-26-jan-ugcPost-7290338541673369601-8T4u/?rcm=ACoAABrk0vgBBnwOmbWN_V3Um7lZhs-VUSEi4ys accesses on 12th May 2025.

where they would get free education. They had already tried a cross-subsidisation model, but it was not something that seemed viable currently, at least when most of the parents considered sending their children to school as a way of endowing them with a suitable network for the future. Several schools from tier 2 and tier 3 cities had reached out to them to understand the unique curriculum they had developed. However, they had not yet gotten a formal consulting assignment. Raising CSR funding was another option, however, the team had to wait a bit longer to qualify for the CSR grants from larger corporates.

Additionally, multiple methods exist to scale the initiative, each offering potential impact. Franchising was one option; another option was they develop the current school as a proof of concept and focus on pedagogical innovations, allowing their work to do the talking. If they were able to put their students across many platforms and get the attention, the story of impact could be highlighted, and more changes at an institutional level were a possibility.

However, when shaping the future, it is essential to remember the past. The team had observed that numerous social ventures had lost sight of their social mission as they expanded. The founders aimed to exercise particular caution in maintaining their focus while navigating these transitions.

Mumbai: The Socio-economic Context

Mumbai, located on the western coast of India, is India's financial and entertainment capital in addition to being the capital city of the Indian state of Maharashtra.

Historically, it was developed by the British from a small collection of islands initially dominated by the fishing community, into a major port and commercial hub. The nineteenth century had a series of firsts for Mumbai. For example: the first rail line in India operated between Mumbai (then Bombay) and Thane (about 21 km) in 1853.[2] The first cotton mill in India, Bombay Spinning and Weaving Company, was established in

[2] The Hindu: The South's first station. (2025). Archive.org. https://web.archive.org/web/20070808063353/http://www.hinduonnet.com/thehindu/mp/2003/02/26/stories/2003022600240300.htm accesses on 26th March 2025.

Mumbai in 1954.[3] The University of Bombay was one of the first modern institutes of Higher Education, established in 1857.[4]

This was followed quickly by the establishment of several banks, and a lot of commercial activities building on the cotton industry that developed there. The American Civil war in 1861 along with the opening of the Suez Canal in 1869, provided a further boost to the emerging city. The growth in commercial activity and the visionary commercial leaders led to the founding of the Bombay Stock Exchange (BSE) in 1875.[5] Today, BSE is one of the top ten stock exchanges globally by market capitalization (about $4.6 trillion with over 6000 listed companies in 2025[6]).

Despite its economic prosperity, Mumbai faces significant challenges, including overcrowding, traffic congestion, and inadequate infrastructure. A sizable portion of the economic growth of the metropolis has been fueled by the migrant labor[7] that enters the city in search of a better life but often begins living in many of the slums.[8] With a population of 21.7 million, Mumbai is the second-largest city in India in terms of population,[9] but is among the most densely populated cities globally. About 41.3% of this population lives in slums.[10] Rapid urbanization, limited affordability

[3] Hindustan Times. (2008, May 11). Web.archive.org. https://web.archive.org/web/20080511144407/http://www.hindustantimes.com/news/specials/bombay/history3.shtml accesses on 26th March 2025.

[4] (2025). Archive.org. https://web.archive.org/web/20081023203430/http://mu.ac.in/About%20University.html accesses on 26th March 2025.

[5] History and Milestones. (n.d.). Www.bseindia.com. https://www.bseindia.com/static/about/History_Milestones.html accesses on 26th March 2025.

[6] Complete History of Bombay Stock Exchange—All about BSE. (n.d.). Www.equiruswealth.com. https://www.equiruswealth.com/glossary/bombay-stock-exchange-bse accesses on 26th March 2025.

[7] Daugherty, A. (2025, February 2). What are the slum areas called in Mumbai?—Geographic FAQ Hub: Answers to Your Global Questions. Geographic FAQ Hub: Answers to Your Global Questions. https://www.ncesc.com/geographic-faq/what-are-the-slum-areas-called-in-mumbai/ accesses on 26th March 2025.

[8] "Slum" refers to densely populated informal pocket of settlements within cities that are characterized by inadequate housing and substandard living conditions.

[9] TOI Lifestyle Desk. (2024, September 30). Top 10 largest cities in India by population. The Times of India; Times Of India. https://timesofindia.indiatimes.com/etimes/trending/top-10-largest-cities-in-india-by-population/articleshow/113791114.cms accesses on 26th March 2025.

[10] Robles, B. (2025, January 30). What percentage of people live in slums in Mumbai?—Geographic FAQ Hub: Answers to Your Global Questions. Geographic FAQ Hub: Answers to Your Global Questions. https://www.ncesc.com/geographic-faq/what-percentage-of-people-live-in-slums-in-mumbai/ accesses on 26th March 2025.

housing, poverty and inadequate urban planning have been attributed to some of the factors contributing to slum formation.[11]

The life of a household in the slum is characterized by low average income levels, and working as a daily wage worker, artisan, small-scale industry worker or a service provider in the informal economy. The slum housing typically included multiple generations under one roof, with an average size of about 4 to 6 members.[12] Mumbai houses several slums that are a collection of diverse settlements. One of the more famous slums is Dharavi (which shot to fame through the Hollywood movie "Slumdog Millionaire"). Dharavi is the second largest slum in Asia (following Orangi Town in Pakistan) with a population of about one million people occupying a space that spans just 2.39 square km (535 acres, and a population density of about 2,252,164 people per square km).[13] The slum was established in 1884 during the British era and was fueled by the expulsion of factories and residents from city center and subsequently by the influx of migrant labor seeking employment. It is also renowned for its small-scale industry with about 5000 businesses and 15,000 single-room factories[14] which operated in the recycling, leather, pottery and textile[15] industries. Interestingly, the slum is the most literate slum in the country with a 68% literacy rate.[16] Other major slums in Mumbai could be found in the Mankhurd-Govandi Belt, Kurla-Ghatkopar Belt, Bhandup-Mulund

[11] Robles, B. (2025, January 30). What percentage of people live in slums in Mumbai?—Geographic FAQ Hub: Answers to Your Global Questions. Geographic FAQ Hub: Answers to Your Global Questions. https://www.ncesc.com/geographic-faq/what-percentage-of-people-live-in-slums-in-mumbai/ accesses on 26th March 2025.

[12] Slum Areas in Mumbai- A Different Side to the City of Dreams. (2022, August 24). The NoBroker Times. https://www.nobroker.in/blog/slum-areas-in-mumbai/ accesses on 26th March 2025.

[13] World Population Review. (2024). Mumbai, India Population 2024. Worldpopulationreview.com. https://worldpopulationreview.com/cities/india/mumbai accesses on 26th March 2025.

[14] World Population Review. (2024). Mumbai, India Population 2024. Worldpopulationreview.com. https://worldpopulationreview.com/cities/india/mumbai accesses on 26th March 2025.

[15] Daugherty, A. (2025, February 2). What are the slum areas called in Mumbai?—Geographic FAQ Hub: Answers to Your Global Questions. Geographic FAQ Hub: Answers to Your Global Questions. https://www.ncesc.com/geographic-faq/what-are-the-slum-areas-called-in-mumbai/ accesses on 26th March 2025.

[16] World Population Review. (2024). Mumbai, India Population 2024. Worldpopulationreview.com. https://worldpopulationreview.com/cities/india/mumbai accesses on 27th March 2025.

Slums, and Dindoshi. Several of these slums are also prone to landslides during the monsoon.

One of the smaller yet notable slums in Mumbai is the Surya Nagar Slum, which is located on a hill slope at the Lal Bhadur Shastri Marg in Vikhroli (West). Approximately 35,000 people reside in this landslide prone settlement.[17] Parksite is a smaller slum close to Surya Nagar in Vikhroli. Pi.Kademy began operations from the Parksite slum. While the exact area over which the slum extends is difficult to calculate, the population density is likely to be in the thousands.[18]

The Origins: The Tributaries

Hassan, who lives close to Parksite, had been volunteering for about 5 years (since 2016) with "Faizam Academy." He had been helping them with after-school tuition to ensure that they fared well in their academics. He had also developed a good reputation in the community. However, the COVID-19 pandemic, in 2020, put a complete break on all these activities.

The lives of several folks changed permanently, and the community here was no exception. For people surviving on daily wages, living in the slums of Mumbai, it was much worse. A family of 4 or 6 members may be living in a cramped space where they have made a shelter for themselves from the vagaries of nature while sharing the common sanitation facilities. Besides the loss of their wages, even accessing ration packets that were distributed without encountering anyone else who may be infected was next to impossible in these highly dense locations. Simply life was much worse in these slums, and education was not something that would be on people's minds during such a time.

Humza had co-founded a med-tech devices company in 2016, and was running it since his graduation in 2017. When COVID struck he felt the urge to contribute on the ground and volunteered for the health care delivery initiative. He was assisting in the process of drug delivery when he found that several intended recipients had not picked up the medication.

[17] Malik. (2021, July 20). Clearing slums along slopes in Mumbai: An uphill task. Hindustan Times. https://www.hindustantimes.com/cities/mumbai-news/clearing-slums-along-slopes-in-mumbai-an-uphill-task-101626806257279.html accesses on 27th March 2025.

[18] lewis, C. (2011, July 6). Kurla-Ghatkopar belt is king of Slumbai. The Times of India; Times Of India. https://timesofindia.indiatimes.com/city/mumbai/Kurla-Ghatkopar-belt-is-king-of-Slumbai/articleshow/9117786.cms accesses on 27th March 2025.

On further enquiry, he realized that the person would find it extremely costly to gather the medications delivered and the patient felt it would be more affordable to get admitted for treatment if health issues arose. This got him to realize how starkly the lives of people living on the margins differed from other urbanites.

The COVID lockdown also had another side effect. It had brought people closer in unexpected ways. Hassan and Humza had merely been acquaintances before COVID. The availability of time for telephonic conversations during that lockdown in 2020 proved to be very essential in the founding of Pi.kademy. The conversations with Hassan during the covid lockdowns excited Humza and Iqra, another acquaintance of the two, to commit themselves to the initiative even if Faizam Academy discontinued it after the COVID pandemic was over.

Iqra, another acquaintance who had been working on her hand-crafted gifting startup had decided to take a break and was joining the Product Design center at the Indian Institute of Technology Bombay at that time. Parkside was just a few meters away from the institute and being excited decided to be part of the initiative in any way possible.

The Confluence

As they had suspected, despite the opening of the COVID lockdowns, Faizam Academy discontinued its after-school program. This gave Humza and Iqra a reason to partner with Hassan, and all three got to work together. Their first goal was to restart the after-school program afresh and independently. In 2022, Hassan, asked his parents for a single room in their house where he could conduct the classes.

Restarting the after-school classes allowed the students who were left without an engagement during the COVID pandemic to latch on to the new initiative. Hassan and Humza had named their venture Pi.kademy. They received an overwhelming response as they reached out to the slum dwellers. Hassan's reputation played a key role. Around 150 students for the after-school program had to quickly move from one room at Hassan's home to about 3 rooms, which crammed in about 50 students in each room.

Humza, however, felt unsatisfied with the way they were engaging with the students. It did not excite their curiosity. Rote memorization dominated their intervention. Was there something that they could do? Why not try a project-based learning approach? It would help grasp concepts and apply them. The learning would be deeper and tightly tied to the application of the learning as well.

Once the founders were convinced about the shift to a project-based learning approach, it was time to get to action. They began engaging with students after school, through activities that were rolled into different themes that would form the subject of inquiry for a specific duration. However, they quickly received resistance from the parents of the students. Most of the fathers worked as drivers of autorickshaws and tempos, while the mothers would work as housekeepers at apartments and shopping complexes nearby. They complained that engaging the students in any project-based activity was unnecessary. It would be sufficient if their kids were taught the same thing as was taught in the schools during the day. Such project-based learning would not be useful if, eventually, these students had to get into the mainstream and find another job based on the academic certificates that the schooling system provided. Getting into a job through the usual schooling would allow the family to get a stable income, which was a distant dream for the family.

The potential impact of project-based learning was strongly etched in the minds of the founders, and they decided to discontinue the after-school program the next year onwards. Instead, they decided to get fully into setting up a school for the underprivileged students in the slum. It was not the most economical of decisions, but it was an impact orientation that they were for, and it would be worth taking the plunge. Their goal was to empower the future leaders with not just knowledge, but also the skills and confidence to thrive in an ever-changing world.

They got to work, beginning with trying to convince the parents to shift their wards from their existing school to the school that Pi.kademy was starting up. The founders were anticipating around 70 students in their first batch across 4th grade to 12th grade. They only managed to convince the parents of around 22 students out of the 150 and got started with their approach. They began by disposing of the furniture they had gotten for the after-school program. This generated some helpful cash to get started.

They rethought the classroom layout and removed all permanent furniture, which helped free movement that would be necessary in a project-based teaching approach. They chose the National Institute of Open

Schooling[19] (NIOS) curriculum, instead of the state or the central curriculum (ICSE/CBSE), which would allow them to adopt the project-based approach. They redesigned them and structured the classes around themes where the same theme is explored through all the subjects. For example, if water is the theme that they would engage with, they would look at the aspect of water from physics, chemistry, biology, mathematics, geography, history and even languages. Once the specific theme was explored sufficiently, they would move to the next theme and so on.

In addition to the project-based classrooms, they included weekly exposure trips, language and math labs, student-led projects and community activities, industry guides and internships. All these fueled the child's creativity and ensured that they experienced a real change in themselves and grew confident.

They also partnered with several organizations like—the American School of Bombay[20] (for the English program), the Museum of Solutions[21] (a maker space and a science lab combined), and the Indian Women Scientists Association.[22] They also formed an engagement (not directly) with the William and Mary University[23] in the US of America for their entrepreneurship program. Each partnership contributed a crucial piece of the project-based learning approach and enriched the learning experience of the students. All this involved substantial trial and error, but they had now found a model that was working well.

Once they got the usual schooling program off the ground, they realized the students were free for the rest of the day. Leaving these students free post-school meant that they would hang out with other residents of the slum and often pick up negative influences. They decided to address this issue by speaking with the parents, requesting that the students continue to stay at the school and engage in activities without any additional charges. Further, they extended the after-school program to students who were not enrolled on the full-time school itself.

[19] Home: The National Institute of Open Schooling (NIOS). (n.d.). Www.nios.ac.in. https://www.nios.ac.in/ accessed on 29th March 205.

[20] StackPath. (n.d.). Www.asbindia.org. https://www.asbindia.org/ accessed on 29th March 205.

[21] Museum of solutions. (2024). Museum of Solutions. https://www.museumofsolutions.in/ accessed on 29th March 205.

[22] Indian Women Scientists' Association. (n.d.). https://iwsa.net/ accessed on 29th March 205.

[23] William & Mary. (2019). Wm.edu. https://www.wm.edu/ accessed on 29th March 205.

To increase admissions, they had to ensure constant outreach without compromising on their mission of impactful education for the students from the slum. They had observed that the students who were part of the after-school program only (and not registered in the school program) were excited by the learning they would gain through the activities they engaged in and interactions with their peers. They knew that they had to convince the parents if they had to get their kids into the program. They began by calling the parents over to attend some of their open sessions. This itself was an arduous task, given that this meant the parents had to take time out of their breadwinning occupation and spend an entire day here. However, they knew this was necessary.

Parents in these open events were engaged in some competitive activity, example a balloon powered car race. This was followed by a reflection session where the parents were allowed to discover the joy of learning and subsequently delivered conceptual understanding. This would convince a few of the parents, and those who were yet undecided, were allowed to come back after conversations with their wards. Often, the students who attended would successfully convince their parents about the schooling.

To ensure that financial limitations do not become a deterrent to joining the program, the school fee was priced at less than 5% of the average monthly income of a single-income family within the slum. The general monthly income of a family in the locality was about INR 40,000 (approximately USD 465) if it had a double income source, and INR 20,000 (approximately USD 233) if it was a single income source. Pi.kademy charged INR 1000 (about USD 12) per student per month from its wards.

As a source of revenue to sustain its operations, the monthly fee was not going to be sufficient. On average, the initiative spent about INR 7500 (about USD 88) per month per student, and this matched with what the Mumbai municipal corporation spent on each student in the government schools. The deficit has been managed in several ways, right up to the present day. At first, the founders had put in their entire savings. Once that was exhausted, they turned to their families, who supported them. Some friends, too, pitched in, seeing the impact Pi.kademy created. They had also negotiated a lease agreement with the facilities owner, who had asked them to pay the rent once they could and not before that. Several teachers were also part timers who engaged with the initiative on a pro-bono basis. They also received a couple of grants from "The Circle"—an incubator focused on education interventions. All these have ensured that the initiative continues unabated.

But this was a crucial area that they had to find innovative ways to ensure they continue the impactful work. They had thought of a few avenues to be able to bridge this deficit. Several mentors had mentioned that the CSR mandate could help them continue with the initiative without much trouble. Applying for CSR funds required the foundation or the NGO to have completed 3 years of operations and this would need at least one more year of waiting for Pi.kademy to be apply for CSR grants.

Another option was to try to develop a monetization model to leverage some of the interests/requests from other locations asking the founders to train the teachers in their methodology. This approach would make them slightly independent of the dependence on CSR funding but was riskier in terms of the possibility of a drift in their mission.

In passing, they had also tried to adopt the approach where they could subsidize the education of the have-nots, by charging a bit extra from the haves. This attempt was met with much resistance from the parents of the haves, who were not willing to send their kids over to the school. They had thus far found only one willing parent who bought into the idea, but it looked like a dead-end otherwise.

The Scaling Dilemma

Over the past three years, there were several learnings that Hassan and Humza had gathered. They knew it would take quite some time before they would be able to get to operate at breakeven, but their resolve was strong, and they were looking out for several funding avenues to get the requisite resources. However, every idea has its own momentum, and the alternative education concept they had been championing seems to have had its own gravity. They had several options to take the venture from here, and each had its own challenges with financial resource acquisition.

Option 1: Charging School Fees

While they were charging a very nominal fee, charging a higher school fees is one potential way for this initiative to ensure its financial stability, but this included significant risks. One major concern is that parents may choose to send their children back to government schools where education is free, rather than paying the higher tier of school fees to Pikademy. This could result in a loss of students and hence revenue. Resulting in challenge for their survival itself.

In order to mitigate these risks, the initiative would need to demonstrate its value and worth to parents. This might involve showing the sustained unique benefits and outcomes that its students received, such as improved academic performance or enhanced career opportunities using their approach. The initiative might also consider offering financial aid or scholarships to families who cannot afford school fees, in order to make its services more accessible. But this would need a different funding structure.

While this model may give much better control, would this approach be most suitable for the early stages that the initiative was in?

Option 2: Cross-Subsidisation Model

The initiative has already attempted to implement a cross-subsidisation model, where students from lower-income families are subsidised by those from higher-income families. However, this approach has not been viable at present, as parents tend to prioritize sending their children to schools that will provide them with a suitable network for the future.

Cross-subsidisation can be a complex and challenging approach to implement, particularly if there is a large disparity in income between backgrounds. The approach would need a better means to access the parents who believe in the concept and the team had not yet found a means of identifying these sponsors easily.

Option 3: Developing a Proof of Concept and Then Raising CSR Funds

Developing a proof of concept is another potential option for scaling impact. By focusing on pedagogical innovations and developing a unique curriculum, the initiative can create a compelling story of impact that will resonate with stakeholders and attract support.

The team would need to highlight the initiative's impact through multiple platforms and media channels can be a powerful way to raise awareness and attract support. By telling stories of success and sharing data on outcomes, the initiative can create a compelling narrative that will resonate with stakeholders and inspire action.

Raising CSR (Corporate Social Responsibility) funding is another potential option for securing financial stability. However, this requires waiting until the initiative has met certain criteria or thresholds, such as reaching a minimum number of employees or having been in operation for certain number of years.

This approach would need the founders to leverage themselves on making their presence felt and the sponsor get their desired marketing mileage for the support.

Option 4: Training

Several schools had approached the founders to understand how they had been able to develop their approach to educating these underprivileged kids. Within the last one year about 3 schools were invited to have a look at their approach and they trained about 15 teachers in their approach.

The interest in the concept seems to be increasing, this may be one potential way to scale. Through this model, they could be an academy that would empower several teachers across different schools.

Option 5: Franchising

Franchising is a potential option for scaling the initiative's impact and reaching more students. By franchising, the initiative can replicate its model in new locations and partner with local organizations or businesses to deliver its services.

Onboarding franchise partners would not only require the team to have set up strong processes and training strength but also be able to deliver a hurdle rate of return to the franchise partners.

While the founders continued to grapple with the options for scaling and the associated resource requirements, they continued to refine the physical school that they were operating. They had decided to engage only kids from the 5th grade instead of what they started with! The 4th graders. There were several refinements that would be necessary before they scaled the school in a physical format. There were so many underprivileged students in slums in the city of Mumbai itself, and several more outside of Mumbai. It would be satisfying to create such an impact across the country and the globe!

Each approach had its own pros and cons. What would you suggest to the founders while they attempted to scale the initiative?

Discussion Questions

1. In starting up, the team seems have "made do" with the resources and relied heavily on the "good" in people to build their venture. How much of the institutional context of India affect this sort of an approach? Would it be different if one is starting up a school with a similar objective in a developed economy like the United States?
2. Do you think the founding team should consider scaling at this time? Why or why not? If they are to scale what would be the more appropriate means through which they could scale without compromising on their impact goals.
3. One important concern for Pi.kademy was securing resources. Right now, they have thought of tiered fee structures. What if Pi.kademy attempts a pay-it-forward model where graduates who go on to earn well pledge a voluntary portion to the school? Will it lead to community building and long-term sustainability? Is it enforceable purely through goodwill? How can one track and maintain alumni engagement?
4. Pi.kademy has a few more options when thinking about scaling. They might set up a franchise model- multiple branches and a standardised model. They might also expand their team by training-the-trainers. By certifying facilitators, they can take this model to other locations. Yet another option is to use technology (such as apps or online content) to take the model to other locations, while keeping the core in-person set-up lean. Which of these approaches might make sense?
5. Pi.kademy is considering partnering with NGOs. They might also think of CSR collaborations and partnerships with other private or government bodies. How much control will they retain? And what compromises would they need to make?
6. Should Pi.kademy expand to other niches? For now, they are focusing on underprivileged children. Would expanding to adult, vocational or alternative learning be a good shift? What if they were to pivot to differently-abled learners? How would Pi.kademy fund such pivots?

Supplementary Readings

The following academic articles would be helpful in developing the theoretical anchor that could be used to synthesize the case learnings.

1. Shepherd, D. A., Parida, V., & Wincent, J. (2020). The surprising duality of jugaad: Low firm growth and high inclusive growth. *Journal of Management Studies, 57*(1), 87–128.

2. Moore, M. L., Riddell, D., & Vocisano, D. (2015). Scaling Out, Scaling Up, Scaling Deep*: Strategies of Non-profits in Advancing Systemic Social Innovation. In *Large Systems Change: An Emerging Field of Transformation and Transitions* (pp. 67–84). Routledge.

Shepherd, and co-authors provide the contextual innovation aspects which helped shape the early founding of Pi.Kademy. Moore and co-authors work give a framework to explain the multiplicity of choices on the scaling front.

Learning Outcomes

Instructors could use the case:

a. To help students understand the antecedents of frugal innovation that is embedded in the contextual setting of resource constraints.
b. To highlight the role of partnerships/cocreational approaches towards generating value, and the associated role of creativity.
c. To understand the different scaling options that social ventures can pursue—based on their scaling motivation.

Acknowledgement The authors thank the reviewers for their valuable comments and suggestions, which helped strengthen the case. MS Copilot suggestions were used to improve the language. Additionally, Perplexity was used to find any academic literature that may have been relevant to the case in hand.

Competing Interests The authors have no conflicts of interest to declare that are relevant to the content of this chapter.

CHAPTER 8

Global Himalayan Expedition (GHE): At Crisis Crossroads

Sreevas Sahasranamam

Abstract Global Himalayan Expedition (GHE) pioneered a distinctive model of impact tourism in 2013, integrating adventure travel with clean energy access for remote Himalayan communities. International travelers funded the expeditions, with a proportion of the fees supporting the development of clean energy solutions such as solar microgrids or improved cookstoves. This case is set in 2020, when the COVID-19 pandemic and related travel restrictions forced Paras Loomba, GHE's founder, to reassess the venture's future and explore alternate pathways for impact and sustainability. This case will get students to think strategically about pivoting a business model in response to external shocks and evaluate emerging sustainability funding mechanisms such as carbon offsets. The case is well-suited for classes on social entrepreneurship, tourism management, rural innovation, clean energy solutions, and business model innovation.

Keywords Social entrepreneurship • Startup pivoting • Adventure Tourism • Clean Energy • Rural entrepreneurship • COVID-19 •

S. Sahasranamam (✉)
Adam Smith Business School, University of Glasgow, Glasgow, UK
e-mail: sreevas.sahasranamam@glasgow.ac.uk

A. S. Galande et al. (eds.), *Context-inspired Entrepreneurship*, Sustainable Development Goals Series,
https://doi.org/10.1007/978-981-95-9831-1_8

Climate change • Remote communities • Sustainable Development • Carbon offsets

SDG Links
This case contributes to SDG 8: Decent Work and Economic Growth by demonstrating how sustainable tourism-linked energy interventions can create local employment and livelihood opportunities (SDG 8.9). By integrating renewable energy provision with community engagement, the case also contributes to SDG 7 and SDG 11.

In early 2020, as the novel coronavirus spread across the world and lockdowns brought tourism to a standstill, for Paras Loomba, founder of Global Himalayan Expedition (also known as GHE), this unprecedented paralysis wasn't just concerning from a health perspective—it struck at the very heart of his innovative social enterprise. GHE had successfully pioneered a unique model of impact tourism in 2013 that integrated tourism expeditions with the transformative power of clean energy solutions (Sahasranamam, 2016). This model had international travelers paying for the expedition experience, with part of the fee going towards the equipment and logistics related to clean energy solutions like solar microgrids or improved cookstoves. However, suddenly, with global travel disrupted for the foreseeable future, Paras saw his carefully planned expeditions for the year vanish overnight, posing an existential question: how could GHE survive the COVID-19 disruption, more importantly, continue its mission of supporting remote Himalayan communities?

The Genesis of a Vision

The story of the Global Himalayan Expedition (GHE) began from an inspiration that Paras had on his Antarctic expedition in 2012 with Robert Swan OBE, a realization that adventure could be a catalyst for change (Economic Times, 2012). Paras Loomba, an engineer with a deep-seated desire to make a difference and a passion for sustainable development, envisioned a unique model based on it for India, combining the thrill of Himalayan expeditions with the transformative power of clean energy (Sahasranamam, 2016).

In 2013, GHE was born, with the first expedition aimed at creating an Educational Base in Ladakh powered by solar power for school children. The expedition also involved cultural and spiritual immersions, including dance and song by the local community, and visits to Hemis Monastery and Lamayuru Monastery. The adventure components of the expedition involved cycling, trekking, and rafting in the lead-up to reaching the area that was electrified. In the 2014 and 2015 expeditions, Sumda Chenmo and Shingo villages, respectively, got electrified through solar micro-grids (Sahasranamam, 2016). These efforts also had part CSR support from corporations such as General Electric (US), IEEE Smart Village, Welspun Solar, and Woodland.

Going by the testimonials of the travelers, these initial expeditions were more than just treks; they were journeys of discovery, where travelers witnessed firsthand the stark reality of energy poverty in remote Himalayan villages. These early years of GHE were about proving the concept, demonstrating that adventure tourism could be a viable vehicle for sustainable development. By 2015, GHE had established a track record of success, electrified villages, and fostered a unique cultural exchange. The challenge now was to scale this impact, to transform a promising pilot into a sustainable, scalable model.

The Ascent: Scaling Impact

By 2016, GHE had refined its micro-grid deployment strategy, implementing standardized solar installations that could be adapted to various village sizes and terrains. In 2016, 15 villages and 2 schools were electrified through solar power (GHE Impact Report, 2023). In 2017, GHE helped establish Mountain Homestays, a community tourism initiative creating homestays and tourism-related livelihood opportunities (see Fig. 8.1) in the villages it solar electrified, to act as an additional source of income for the community (Haugen, 2020).

Around the same time, GHE began exploring other sustainable livelihood opportunities such as training in pashmina weaving and facilitating market linkages for these products (GHE, 2024). Pashmina wool, renowned for its softness and warmth, is sourced from Cashmere goats, which are mountain goats native to the high-altitude regions of the Himalayas. These efforts aimed to preserve local craftsmanship and integrate cultural heritage into GHE's broader mission of community development.

Fig. 8.1 Image from an Astrostay—a GHE homestays initiative focussed on astro-tourism

In 2018, GHE formalized and expanded its homestay program, setting up 35 homestays (GHE Impact Report, 2023). GHE also began to train villagers in hospitality and tourism management, ensuring the program's long-term viability. In 2019, GHE intensified its electrification efforts, conducting expeditions that reached previously inaccessible villages in the Zanskar region. By 2020, GHE's monitoring and evaluation system showed a reduction in kerosene usage and an increase in household income among homestay participants. They also had partnerships with global organizations such as Booking.com for homestays and CSR support for providing clean energy solutions without an expedition component. GHE was getting international laurels for its unique model in remote Himalayan villages, including the UN Global Climate Action Award (see Fig. 8.2) and the World Travel & Tourism Council (WTTC) Tourism for Tomorrow Award.

Fig. 8.2 Paras addressing an audience in relation to the UNFCCC Climate Action Award

COVID-19 and the Uncharted Future

Then, the world stopped. Expeditions were canceled, and homestays were shut down. The very communities GHE had empowered were now facing dual threats—health and economic vulnerability. The pandemic's sudden onslaught left Paras facing a stark reality: One of GHE's core revenue model, built on international adventure tourism, had evaporated overnight. GHE, which was seen as a beacon of hope in the remote Himalayas, now stood at a crossroads. Paras knew that inaction was not an option. He had to chart a new course, one that would not only ensure GHE's survival but also strengthen its impact in a world that had changed. Some of the options he had ahead were:

1. **Essential Services Lifeline**

Paras considered leveraging GHE's existing solar infrastructure and deep-rooted community relationships to provide essential services. The pandemic exposed the vulnerability of remote communities, highlighting the urgent need for reliable healthcare and education. Market research suggested that the global humanitarian aid market was increasingly focused on sustainable solutions, and the GHE model had good potential there. He was also seeing a surge in telehealth and remote education during the pandemic, which was particularly suitable for the communities he was serving. He also knew GHE's strengths—expertise in solar micro-grids, its logistical capabilities in challenging terrains, and its trust with the local communities. By partnering with corporates and government agencies, GHE could transform its solar infrastructure into a network of community health centers and digital learning hubs, providing an essential services lifeline. The question remained: could GHE effectively pivot from adventure tourism to humanitarian or essential services, and could it secure the necessary funding to sustain this transition?

2. **Domestic Tourism Pivot**

As international travel ground to a halt, Paras was considering the potential of the domestic tourism market, a sector that was expected to recover much faster than global travel. Market research showed that India's growing middle class was increasingly drawn to sustainable and experiential travel. GHE could develop tailored tourism packages, showcasing the unique cultural heritage and natural beauty of the Himalayas, while ensuring that the benefits flowed directly to the local communities. This pivot, however, required a shift in GHE's marketing strategy, focusing on the domestic audience. Also, it perhaps needed rethinking of its revenue model, which was otherwise based on international travelers. It also needed to invest in skill development programs and train villagers in hospitality and tourism management. The challenge was to create authentic experiences that resonated with Indian travelers while maintaining GHE's commitment to responsible tourism. Could GHE successfully navigate this transition, and could it compete in the increasingly competitive domestic tourism market?

3. **The Digital Transformation**

The pandemic accelerated digital transformation, creating a higher potential for connectivity and remote solutions. Paras saw an opportunity to leverage technology to enhance GHE's operations and expand its reach.

For its clean energy-related efforts, GHE could implement remote monitoring systems in its installations, ensuring their reliability and efficiency. Market research showed that the digital tourism market, fuelled by virtual experiences and online content, was rapidly expanding. It could leverage that trend to create virtual tourism experiences, allowing people to explore the Himalayas from the comfort of their homes. This digital pivot, however, required significant investment in technology and digital infrastructure. GHE also needed to develop its expertise in digital content creation and online marketing. The question was, could GHE effectively build its digital skills and capitalize on the growing demand for virtual experiences?

4. **The Himalayan Resilience Fund**

Paras also considered a shorter-term option, exploring the setting up of an emergency fund, a Himalayan Resilience Fund supported by philanthropy that would provide direct financial assistance to the communities GHE served. The pandemic had exposed the fragility of these remote economies, highlighting the need for a safety net. The philanthropic sector, increasingly focused on pandemic relief and community resilience, presented a potential source of funding. GHE's strong community trust and established network of partners would be invaluable in mobilizing resources to ensure the effective distribution of pandemic relief and support. This initiative, however, required a robust fundraising strategy and a transparent system for disbursing resources and funds. Could GHE effectively raise the necessary capital and ensure that it reached those most in need?

5. **The Carbon Offset Opportunity**

Paras had recently seen a new Voluntary Carbon Markets report (Donofrio et al., 2020) that showed marked interest around corporate carbon neutral pledges (see Table 8.1). The growing global focus on climate change and carbon neutrality presented a unique opportunity for GHE, which was not dependent on tourism. The voluntary carbon market was experiencing rapid growth, driven by increasing corporate commitments to sustainability. GHE's clean cooking projects, which reduced greenhouse gas emissions, could generate valuable carbon credits (see

Table 8.1 Voluntary carbon market trends

Corporate pledges	Corporate carbon-neutral pledge had a 6x increase from 2018 to 2019
Market Value and volume	$320 million in 2019, with transaction volumes around 104 $MtCO_2e$.
Sectoral trends	Offsets associated with nature-based solutions increased 30%, while for renewable energy it decreased by 16%, but the volume for renewable energy offsets surged by 78%

Source: Donofrio et al., (2020)

Table 8.2 for a summary on carbon offset market). By partnering with carbon registries and developing a robust verification process, GHE could create a new, sustainable revenue stream. This pivot, however, required expertise in carbon accounting and certification, alongside building networks with sustainability leads of multinationals. GHE also needed to develop a compelling narrative that resonated with corporations seeking to offset their carbon footprint. The question was, could GHE effectively navigate the complexities of the carbon market and get corporations to work with them on offsetting their carbon footprint through clean energy solutions?

On a drive back home after collecting a pack of face masks and sanitizers, Paras had all these options running through his mind. Which direction should Paras take?

Discussion Questions

This case study could be used for undergraduate and postgraduate classes on social entrepreneurship, rural entrepreneurship, or entrepreneurship in emerging markets. This case study has already been tested in classroom discussions on these topics, with high engagement levels in case discussions. It could be used along with an earlier case study on the same organization—Sahasranamam, S. (2016). *Global Himalayan Expedition: Community Development Through Impact Tourism*. The Case Centre—to first discuss the scaling approaches of a nascent social enterprise set in 2015 timeline, before thinking about the COVID dilemma.

1. How could place-based dynamics be leveraged in developing social enterprise business models?
2. Put yourselves in Paras's shoes to perform a SWOT analysis for GHE around each of the scenarios outlined and create a three-year

Table 8.2 Overview of carbon markets

What are carbon offset markets?
Carbon offset markets are emerging as crucial part in the global efforts to combat climate change and transition to a net zero economy. These markets operate on the principle that individual or organization could compensate from their own carbon emissions by investing (offsetting) in other projects that reduce or remove an equivalent amount of emissions from the atmosphere. For example, this could mean investing in a afforestation programme or a clean cookstoves project.

What are the different type of carbon markets?

a. Compliance carbon markets—this is a market where entities that are required to following regulatory requirements around emissions obtain or surrender emission offsets to meet predetermined targets. This happens largely through the United National Clean Development Mechanism process, wherein saleable carbon credits are used by industrialized countries to meeting the Kyoto protocol mandated emission reduction targets.
b. Voluntary carbon markets—as the name suggests, this involves transaction of carbon offsets purchased voluntarily, without the intention to actively trade it in a regulated carbon market. Typically, corporates buy carbon offsets in this market to reduce their carbon footprint and showcase it as part of their sustainability reporting.

Who are the key actors in a carbon offset market?

a. Government and regulatory bodies: oversee the markets and establish emission reduction targets. e.g., European Union Emissions Trading System is regulated by the European Commission
b. Corporations: trying to become net zero by investing in projects that offset carbon. e.g., Microsoft investing in forestry and biomass carbon removal projects as part of their strategy to become carbon negative by 2030
c. Carbon offset project developers: create and manage projects that remove or reduce greenhouse gas emissions from the atmosphere. These could be through projects like renewable energy, reforestation or carbon capture. As part of option 5, GHE is exploring to become once such project developer through its renewable energy and clean cookstove projects.
d. Standards and Registries: offers credibility to carbon markets by ensuring that carbon offsets are measurable and verifiable. e.g., Verra (Verified Carbon Standard—VCS), American Carbon Registry

How is technology being used to monitor and track carbon offsets?

a. Satellite imaging is being used for monitoring land use and reforestation efforts
b. Sensors are deployed to monitor in real-time emissions reductions
c. Startups such as TraceX creating blockchain solutions to create traceability of carbon offset transactions to enhance transparency

Adapted from: https://tracextech.com/understanding-carbon-offset-markets/

roadmap for keeping GHE alive. Create an optimistic roadmap first, imagining that the lockdowns will be reduced by the end of 2020 itself. Second, create a pessimistic roadmap, imagining that some form of global travel restrictions is still on even in 2022. Keep in mind that you are still in 2020, and you don't know when you will have the COVID-19 vaccine or when the lockdowns will be fully lifted. You could imagine different combinations of options highlighted above, too.

3. How do carbon offsets work? What is the potential of that opportunity for GHE?
4. How could startup founders deal with sudden exogenous shocks like the pandemic?
5. If you are/were a founder yourself, share experiences from your journey through the pandemic and how you resolved the challenges it posed. If not, share the experiences of a startup friend that you know well.

Supplementary Readings

- Muñoz, P., & Kimmitt, J. (2019). Rural entrepreneurship in place: An integrated framework. *Entrepreneurship & Regional Development*, *31*(9–10), 842–873.
- Sahasranamam, S., & Soundararajan, V. (2022). Innovation ecosystems: what makes them responsive during emergencies?. *British Journal of Management*, *33*(1), 369–389.
- Browder, R. E., Seyb, S., Forgues, A., & Aldrich, H. E. (2023). Pandemic makers: How citizen groups mobilized resources to meet local needs in a global health crisis. *Entrepreneurship Theory and Practice*, *47*(3), 964–997.
- How coronavirus sparked a wave of innovation in India—https://www.weforum.org/stories/2020/05/coronavirus-covid19-innovation-technology-india/
- Stephan, U. et al. (2023). Act or wait-and-see? Adversity, agility, and entrepreneur wellbeing across countries during the COVID-19 pandemic. *Entrepreneurship Theory and Practice*, *47*(3), 682–723.
- National Geographic documentary on GHE—https://vimeo.com/403961329
- BBC short video on GHE—https://www.bbc.com/news/av/world-asia-43116948

- Understanding the carbon offsets market—https://tracextech.com/understanding-carbon-offset-markets/
- Shepherd, D. A., & Williams, T. A. (2014). Local venturing as compassion organizing in the aftermath of a natural disaster: The role of localness and community in reducing suffering. *Journal of Management Studies*, *51*(6), 952–994.

Learning Objectives
By analysing the case of GHE, students will develop their ability to:

- Critically evaluate strategic options for pivoting a business model and sustaining a startup when its core revenue stream is abruptly disrupted.
- Develop adaptive strategies to cope with external uncertainties by creating multiple scenario-based recovery and sustainability plans under varying conditions.
- Analyze and appraise the feasibility and potential of emerging mechanisms—such as carbon markets—as alternative or supplementary revenue sources for sustainability-focused ventures.

Acknowledgements The author would like to thank Paras Loomba, Jaideep Bansal, and the GHE team for their time towards interviews, supporting me in undertaking the expedition, and for sharing archival documents developed by them. Gemini 2.5 was used to improve the stylizing of the draft in multiple places.

Competing Interests This case study is based on field research that was funded by the British Academy/Leverhulme Trust Small Research Grant (SRG22\221450).

Supplementary Material—Teaching Note

Synopsis

The Global Himalayan Expedition (GHE) case examines a pioneering social enterprise that launched in 2013 with a unique impact tourism model that combined adventure travel with clean energy access for remote Himalayan communities. International travellers funded expeditions, with part of the fees supporting solar microgrids and improved cookstoves. In 2020, the COVID-19 pandemic and global travel restrictions disrupted GHE's core revenue stream, forcing founder Paras Loomba to reassess the venture's future and explore alternative pathways for impact and financial sustainability.

This case challenges students to think strategically about business model pivots under external shocks, evaluate emerging sustainability funding mechanisms such as carbon markets, and design scenario-based recovery plans for mission-driven ventures. It is ideal for courses on social entrepreneurship, tourism management, rural innovation, clean energy solutions, and business model innovation.

Guidance for Educators on Using This Case for a 90-minute Class Discussion

1. Begin with a background discussion on Global Himalayan Expedition (GHE) discussing how it was founded and its core activities. During this discussion, emphasize the critical role of place in shaping GHE's business model. (20 minutes)

- For a two-hour class: You may first introduce an earlier case study on the same organization—*Sahasranamam, S. (2016). Global Himalayan Expedition: Community Development Through Impact Tourism. The Case Centre*—to facilitate a deeper discussion on its initial phase and scaling challenges, before transitioning to the current case as a continuation.
- Use this reading to introduce the REFLECT framework of understand the role of place in rural entrepreneurship—Muñoz, P., & Kimmitt, J. (2019). Rural entrepreneurship in place: An integrated framework. *Entrepreneurship & Regional Development*, *31*(9–10), 842–873. Please refer to Table 5 of the reading.
    - The REFLECT framework consists of four key dimensions namely—Rural entrepreneurial dynamics, entrepreneurial sense of rurality, entrepreneurial rural locale and biophysical place of rural entrepreneurship.
    - Get students to map GHE against the REFLECT framework, to appreciate the role of place in GHE. This will bring out aspects such as—
        - geographical location of Himalayas forms a critical element of GHE's business model value proposition

- appreciate the constraints that remote locations pose on electrification from the main grid
- how unique place characteristics such as low light pollution enabled the development of the astro-stays idea;
- how unique local expertise around pashmina weaving and goat rearing inspired GHE's focus on handicrafts and promotion of local craftsmanship
- how local religious places (monasteries) were a key anchor in the GHE tourism experience as they were sites of cultural immersion alongside electrification efforts
- co-creating technology solutions with the local community by engaging with their social and cultural norms through on-site experiences
- experiencing energy poverty firsthand by staying in makeshift tents during village electrification project.

2. Put students into the COVID timeline. If anyone in the class had startup experience themselves or worked in a startup during COVID, ask them to share experiences from the pandemic time period and how they resolved the challenges it posed. If no one, had direct experience, ask them to share any experiences they heard from a startup friend. (5 minutes)
3. Explore how individuals and communities created ad-hoc and alternate organizing models, to create innovations and business models that met addressed the challenges posed by COVID-19. (15 minutes)

- A discussion based on the following readings could help frame this conversation:

   i. Sahasranamam, S., & Soundararajan, V. (2022). Innovation ecosystems: what makes them responsive during emergencies?. *British Journal of Management*, *33*(1), 369–389.
   ii. Browder, R. E., Seyb, S., Forgues, A., & Aldrich, H. E. (2023). Pandemic makers: How citizen groups mobilized resources to meet local needs in a global health crisis. *Entrepreneurship Theory and Practice*, *47*(3), 964–997.
   iii. Sahasranamam, S. (2020, May 11). How coronavirus sparked a wave of innovation in India. *World Economic Forum*. https://www.weforum.org/stories/2020/05/coronavirus-covid19-innovation-technology-india/

This discussion could help bring out points such as:

- Communities adopted fluid, ad-hoc, and network-based organizing models. Some of them were meant to be temporary with the intention of dissolving once formal systems gained capacity to deal handle the pandemic.
- Actors leveraged existing resources creatively by repurposing infrastructure, skills, and networks to meet urgent needs
- Temporary ecosystems were created for developing health innovations such as low-cost ventilators and telemedicine platforms
- Place-based resilience was evident with local contexts shaping the solutions
- Digital coordination, digital tools and social media became critical resources
- Close public-private partnerships helped to build and scale solutions quickly

4. Building on from those reflections, get the students to place themselves in Paras's shoes to discuss GHE's challenges during COVID as travel has come to a standstill, thus cutting off their main revenue source with no visible certainty over when it would restart. In this, focus not just on the business challenges, but also socio-economic challenges in the communities that GHE operated (5 mins)
5. Divide students into groups of 5–7 and ask them to conduct a SWOT analysis of GHE. Along with it, ask each group to develop a three-year roadmap to ensure GHE's survival. Emphasize that students must position themselves in the 2020 context, where COVID-19 uncertainties prevail with lockdowns having no clear end date, and travel resumption is unpredictable. Instruct them to consider and incorporate the five different options that Paras was mulling over while doing this. Instruct students to create two versions of the roadmap based on different COVID recovery scenarios: an optimistic quick recovery case (in 6 months) and a pessimistic case of COVID restrictions being in place till 2022. (25 minutes)

   - You could setup this activity on a Miro board, where existing templates for SWOT and roadmaps would help in creating quick visual summaries.

6. Get a couple of groups to present their roadmap plans, while other groups comment and feedback to consolidate the learning (10 minutes)
7. Summarise and debrief the discussion. In this, you could highlight the role of carbon offsets and show videos of GHE efforts from 2023 or later, alongside insights from their website. Link this to the road map discussion to highlight activities beyond impact expeditions. (10 minutes)

- GHE website—https://ghe.co.in/
- GHE YouTube Channel—https://www.youtube.com/@globalhimalayanexpedition9181/videos

References

Donofrio, S., Maguire, P., Zwick, S., & Merry, W. (2020). *State of the Voluntary Carbon Markets 2020: Voluntary Carbon and the Post-Pandemic Recovery.* Forest Trends' Ecosystem Marketplace. https://www.forest-trends.org/publications/state-of-the-voluntary-carbon-markets-2020-2/

Economic Times. (2012). International Antarctic Expedition: A night in Antarctica with Indian lanterns. Source: https://economictimes.indiatimes.com/international-antarctic-expedition-a-night-in-antarctica-with-indian-lanterns/articleshow/12974190.cms

Global Himalayan Expedition. (2023). *Impact Report 2023.*

Global Himalayan Expedition. (2024). The Pashmina Story. https://ghe.co.in/wp-content/uploads/2024/08/The-Pashmina-Story.pdf

Haugen, J. (2020). Field Report: Smart Tourism, *Stanford Social Innovation Review*. Source: https://ghe.co.in/wp-content/uploads/2024/08/Stanford-Social-Innovation-Review-GHE.pdf

Sahasranamam, S. (2016). *Global Himalayan Expedition: Community Development Through Impact Tourism.* The Case Centre. Source: https://www.thecasecentre.org/products/view?id=135543

CHAPTER 9

Bamboo to Bambrew - Brewing a Packaging Revolution

Sruthi Kannan, Khushi Jayaprakash, and Bhaskar Bhowmick

Abstract Vaibhav Anant, founder of Bambrew Technologies, transformed a moment of environmental awakening - watching a sea turtle suffer from plastic pollution - into a revolutionary sustainable packaging company. Starting in 2019 from Bangalore, Bambrew has evolved from producing bamboo straws to becoming a comprehensive sustainable packaging solutions provider, utilizing materials ranging from bamboo cellulose to agricultural waste. The case explores Vaibhav's entrepreneurial journey, including critical decisions around sourcing models, material diversification, and scaling challenges. Key dilemmas include balancing social impact with business scalability, transitioning from tribal community sourcing to structured supply chains, and expanding from a single-material focus to a

S. Kannan (✉) • B. Bhowmick
IIT Kharagpur, Kharagpur, India
e-mail: sruthi23@kgpian.iitkgp.ac.in; bhaskar@see.iitkgp.ac.in

K. Jayaprakash
PES University, Bengaluru, India
e-mail: pes1202203523@pesu.pes.edu

A. S. Galande et al. (eds.), *Context-inspired Entrepreneurship*, Sustainable Development Goals Series,
https://doi.org/10.1007/978-981-95-9831-1_9

multi-material portfolio. Through innovative manufacturing processes and their Enterprise Business Model, Bambrew achieved Rs 44.23 crore revenue by 2023 and aims for global expansion. The case illustrates how environmental consciousness can drive business innovation while highlighting the practical challenges of scaling sustainable ventures in emerging markets.

Keywords Sustainable packaging • Bamboo innovation • Biopolymer • Agricultural waste • Bioplastic • Circular economy • Environmental entrepreneurship • Plastic alternatives • Green technology • Social impact scaling

SDGs This case contributes to SDG 8: Decent Work and Economic Growth by demonstrating how eco-innovation can create productive employment and enterprise opportunities within an emerging green economy. By focusing on sustainable packaging solutions and reduction of plastic waste, the case also contributes to SDG 12: Responsible Consumption and Production and SDG 13: Climate Action. *The shocking video of a marine biologist removing a plastic straw from a sea turtle's nose was a turning point for me; I knew I had to do something impactful to address this issue.* (Krishnan, 2022)

Vaibhav Anant felt something shift inside him. The distressed marine creature's suffering wasn't just another environmental tragedy - it was a call to action that would alter the course of his life and potentially transform an industry. This pivotal moment in 2018 planted the seed for what would become Bambrew, a company at the forefront of India's sustainable packaging revolution (Bambrew, 2022).

The Genesis

Born and raised in India, Vaibhav came from humble beginnings but harbored ambitious dreams. While not initially focused on environmental causes, his education in Fashion Technology from NIFT, Bengaluru provided him with foundational knowledge about materials that would later prove invaluable (Anant, 2025). His early career in retail and manufacturing exposed him to the realities of production processes and supply chains, building expertise that would serve him well in his entrepreneurial journey.

As the shocking video of a sea turtle with a plastic straw lodged in its nostril played not just on his screen, but his mind as well, what distinguished Vaibhav from many other concerned citizens was his determination to channel his distress into action. While others might share environmental videos on social media and continue with their lives, Vaibhav saw an opportunity to create meaningful change through entrepreneurship. He envisioned a business that could deliver both commercial success and positive environmental impact.

The timing seemed perfect. In 2018, India was experiencing a growing awareness of plastic pollution. Streets in Bangalore, once known for lush greenery, were disappearing under plastic waste. Rivers that had sustained life for centuries were choking on discarded packaging. The country's vibrant markets were dulling under layers of non-biodegradable refuse. Traditional recycling efforts were proving insufficient against the mounting crisis (United Nations Environment Programme, 2021).

From Concept to Company

In 2019, armed with research, determination, and the support of a small but dedicated team, Vaibhav founded Bambrew in Bangalore's vibrant tech hub. The name itself—a blend of "bamboo" and "brewery"—reflected the company's initial focus on bamboo straws as alternatives to plastic ones (Anant, 2025).

From the outset, Vaibhav understood that sustainable solutions would succeed only if they met practical business needs. "*Our goal is to lead by example and inspire other businesses to follow suit in making environmentally responsible choices.*" With his co-founder Kunal Prasad joining the venture, Bambrew began to take shape. Despite not having formal backgrounds in sustainability or packaging, the team's professional experience and commitment to learning gave them a solid foundation. Vaibhav personally conducted extensive research and developed hands-on collaborations with manufacturers to build his expertise in sustainable materials.

Vaibhav's vision went beyond simply replacing plastic with another material. He sought to create truly innovative solutions that would revolutionize the packaging industry. The Bambrew team focused on developing sophisticated processes to transform plant fibers from bamboo and a mix of different raw materials which are all sustainable in nature into biodegradable yet robust packaging materials.

> *Our technology allows us to imbue paper with plastic-like qualities while preserving its biodegradability,* "Vaibhav explained." *This makes our packaging solutions both effective and eco-friendly.* (YourStory, 2022)

For certain applications, the company developed methods to coat bamboo papers with other sustainable materials, creating composites with enhanced properties suitable for high-strength packaging solutions (Bambrew, 2022).

Bambrew employed eco-friendly printing techniques for customization, using non-toxic, biodegradable inks and dyes to ensure the entire packaging remained environmentally friendly. Throughout production, they focused on minimizing waste; any by-products were either reused in the production cycle or processed for other uses, such as bioenergy.

The environmental imperative behind Bambrew's founding reached beyond emotional responses to hard data. Vaibhav knew plastic packaging was not just aesthetically unpleasing; it was a serious threat to human health and ecosystems. Microplastics were filtering into everyday products through their packaging, whether it was tea bags with plastic linings or frozen food containers. These minuscule plastic fragments, less than 5 millimeters across, slough off from coatings, films, and linings used in packaging (Bambrew, 2025a). Heat, friction, and storage conditions quicken their release into food, beverages, and personal care items, eventually finding their way into human bodies and ecosystems.

The science was alarming: plastic production alone produced more than 1.8 billion tonnes of carbon dioxide emissions in 2019, or roughly 3.4 percent of global greenhouse gas emissions (Bambrew, 2025a). Because the overwhelming majority of plastic packaging was never recycled, it sat in landfills for hundreds of years, gradually leaching into and contaminating natural ecosystems, eventually making their way up the food chain and creating severe hazards for wildlife and human health alike.

Yet, Vaibhav tackled sustainability with pragmatic realism rather than ideological rigidity. Early on, he realized that adopting sustainable packaging wasn't just ethical, it was smart business. Market research revealed encouraging trends. 60 percent of Indian consumers had shifted to sustainable products and were willing to pay 13 percent more for eco-friendly packaging (United Nations, 2015). Globally, 82 percent of consumers, especially Generation Z, were willing to pay a premium for products with sustainable packaging (Bambrew, 2025a). More importantly, the regulatory landscape was moving in Bambrew's direction.

In a world where Extended Producer Responsibility laws and plastic taxes were on the rise, early adoption was a hedge against future fees and penalties. Transparent sustainability initiatives foster trust, reduce buyer's remorse, and drive repeat purchases with consumers. On the business side of things, renewable, lightweight materials reduce exposure to volatile petrochemical markets and lower transport costs, strengthening supply chains in the process. Vaibhav positioned Bambrew squarely at the crossroads of environmental responsibility and business opportunity, ensuring solutions that would cater to both conscience and commerce.

Quality control became a cornerstone of Bambrew's manufacturing strategy. The company achieved remarkable metrics: a 90%+ On Time In Full (OTIF) delivery rate and a zero Parts Per Million (PPM) rejection rate—figures unheard of in the packaging sector (Anant, 2025). Their internal quality control system included multi-level checks, in-house design capabilities, and a relentless focus on functionality, structure, and aesthetics.

Why Bamboo?

Vaibhav's selection of bamboo as Bambrew's primary material along with a combination of other sustainable materials wasn't arbitrary; it was a strategic decision based on the plant's exceptional environmental credentials and versatile properties. Unlike endangered rainforest hardwood, bamboo offered a renewable and rapid-growth alternative that surpassed many traditional tree species in sustainability.

"Bamboo produces up to 35 percent more oxygen than hardwood trees," (Shop Without Plastic, 2024) Vaibhav would explain to potential investors and partners, highlighting its critical role in mitigating global climate change. This aligned perfectly with the United Nations Sustainable Development Goal 13 (United Nations, 2015) (Climate Action).

By prioritizing bamboo in combination with other sustainable materials, Vaibhav positioned Bambrew to address immediate environmental concerns while fostering a circular economy model that supported sustainable growth and resource efficiency. The company's innovative approach met market demands for eco-friendly alternatives and set a precedent for integrating sustainability into everyday business practices.

The Struggle to Scale

Early Challenges

Like any entrepreneurial journey, Vaibhav's path with Bambrew was far from smooth. In the early days, the company faced significant challenges that tested his resolve and leadership.

Developing biodegradable packaging that could compete with the durability and functionality of plastic proved complex. Vaibhav and his R&D team had to innovate and refine manufacturing processes repeatedly to create high-quality, reliable products. While certain materials offered environmental benefits, it initially posed higher costs compared to plastic, requiring creative solutions to make production cost-effective.

Perhaps the most daunting challenge was market acceptance. Convincing businesses and consumers to switch from traditional plastic packaging to biopolymer alternatives required substantial effort. Vaibhav adopted a pragmatic approach, letting the product speak for itself.

"*For customers, proof of concept and performance trump narratives*," Vaibhav observed (Anant, 2025). This insight guided Bambrew's strategy—focus on demonstrating tangible benefits rather than just telling environmental stories.

Early collaborations with environmentally conscious companies proved crucial, allowing Bambrew to test and refine their products in real-world settings. Positive feedback and successful pilot projects gradually built credibility and opened doors to larger opportunities.

The startup journey was humbling. Even years after founding Bambrew, Vaibhav maintained that the company was still in its "*zero to one*" phase—a work in progress (Anant, 2025). The road had been long, filled with experimentation, failures, and hard-won lessons. The team dedicated countless hours to developing materials that could seamlessly run on existing plastic-processing machinery, a strategic decision to address one of the major hurdles to scalability: infrastructure compatibility.

Their commitment to practical solutions led to unconventional work patterns. The team often worked during off-hours—like 3 AM slots at manufacturers' plants—to test new compounds in real-world conditions (Anant, 2025). Unlike theoretical lab experiments, Bambrew's solutions were built from day one to be commercially viable.

The Sourcing Dilemma

One of the most significant challenges Vaibhav encountered involved sourcing materials and establishing a reliable supply chain. Initially, Bambrew experimented with sourcing bamboo and handmade products directly from tribal communities (Fig. 9.1) across states like Assam, Tripura, Maharashtra, Madhya Pradesh, Kerala, and Karnataka (Krishnan, 2022; Bambrew, 2022). This approach aligned with Vaibhav's ethical values, empowering these communities with employment and economic opportunities.

However, this well-intentioned model proved unscalable in practice. Despite offering generous pay and support during festivals, Bambrew faced inconsistent workforce availability. Workers often left for months during harvesting seasons or opted out entirely due to reliance on government subsidies and traditional livelihoods.

Vaibhav faced a difficult decision: maintain the original sourcing model, which aligned perfectly with social impact goals but hindered business scalability, or pivot to a more structured approach. After careful consideration, he chose to adapt. Bambrew shifted to sourcing bamboo and other materials through more structured channels, including self-help groups (SHGs), moving away from handmade methods toward more standardized production processes. This transition, while necessary for business sustainability, weighed heavily on Vaibhav. He remained committed to

Fig. 9.1 Vaibhav with the bamboo suppliers. (Source: Bambrew website)

social impact, finding other ways to support communities while building a scalable business model.

Financial challenges also tested Bambrew's resilience. At one point, the company faced a severe cash crunch, barely managing to pay salaries. In a demonstration of personal commitment, Vaibhav took out a personal bank loan to keep the team afloat. Despite immense pressure, continued interest from major clients and the uniqueness of Bambrew's solutions helped secure investor confidence and eventual funding.

Support from early investors like Blue Ashva Capital and Supack and later by Blume Ventures, proved vital in weathering these tough times (Anant, 2025). Their belief in Bambrew's vision provided not just financial backing but also validation during the darkest periods.

Pivoting beyond Bamboo: Expanding Material Portfolio

As Bambrew evolved, Vaibhav recognized a crucial truth: while bamboo offered excellent sustainability credentials, a single-material approach would limit the company's impact and growth potential. This insight led to a strategic pivot that would define Bambrew's future trajectory.

By July 2019, just months after founding the company, Vaibhav had already begun expanding Bambrew's material scope. Though the name "Bambrew" stemmed from the initial bamboo focus, the company quickly embraced a wider range of sustainable materials (Krishnan, 2022; Bambrew, 2022; Anant, 2025).

> *Each material has unique properties and applications*, "Vaibhav explained to his team." *To truly replace plastic across different packaging needs, we need a diverse material portfolio.*

Vaibhav established four core principles to guide Bambrew's material selection: environmental impact (primarily reducing or eliminating greenhouse gas emissions), scalability (solving problems at a large industrial scale), functionality (ensuring the material performs like plastic, particularly in preserving product shelf life), and affordability (ensuring the cost doesn't deter adoption).

Bambrew's R&D team developed processes to transform agricultural waste like bioplastics derived from plant sources (Krishnan, 2022; Bambrew, 2022). Each material underwent rigorous testing to ensure it

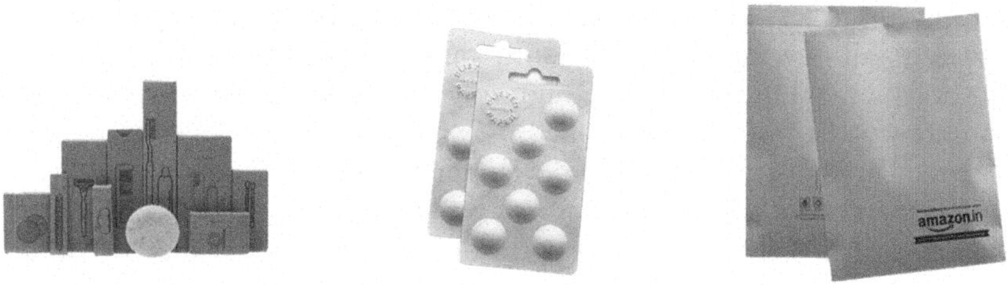

Fig. 9.2 Different products of Bambrew. (Source: Bambrew website)

met Bambrew's standards for functionality, durability, and environmental impact.

> *Sustainability at Bambrew isn't just about being eco-friendly,* "Vaibhav emphasized." *It's a comprehensive approach that considers environmental impact, scalability, functionality, and affordability.*

This multi-material strategy allowed Bambrew to target a wider range of packaging applications and customer needs. Different materials could be matched to specific use cases, optimizing performance while maintaining sustainability credentials. For food packaging requiring moisture barriers, a combination of plant derived materials might be ideal; for shipping containers needing strength, bamboo composites could be the solution (Fig. 9.2).

The pivot demonstrated Vaibhav's pragmatic approach to environmental entrepreneurship. Rather than being dogmatically committed to a single material, he focused on the broader goal: replacing plastic with sustainable alternatives across as many applications as possible. This flexibility positioned Bambrew to make a more significant environmental impact while building a more resilient business model.

Growth Strategy: From Local Startup to Global Impact

With validated products and growing market acceptance, Vaibhav turned his attention to scaling Bambrew's impact. His growth strategy intertwined innovation, sustainability, and global expansion. Vaibhav recognized that continuous innovation would be essential for Bambrew's long-term success. The company maintained substantial investments in research and development, constantly pushing boundaries in developing bio-polymer solutions. This commitment to innovation not only set Bambrew apart but also positioned it as a pioneer in the deep tech meta material (bio-plastic) sector and development of eco-friendly packaging.

"We started with 10 lakhs of business per year and now we've reached more than 40 crores," Vaibhav noted proudly in 2023 (Bambrew, 2022). *"In this financial year of 2025-2026, we're aiming for 100+ crore business".* This remarkable growth trajectory was supported by significant funding milestones. In the year 2023, Bambrew secured Rs 60 crore (approximately $7 million) in a Series A funding (Tech in Asia, 2024; Bambrew, 2025b) round led by Blume Ventures, with support from investors including Blue Ashva Capital, Mumbai Angels, Upsparks, Supack Industries, LetsVenture, and Indus Capital (Tech in Asia, 2024). This was followed by a $10 million Series B round in 2023 (YourStory, 2022; Tech in Asia, 2024).

Vaibhav strategically allocated these funds to drive growth. He established and expanded manufacturing facilities, invested in advanced machinery, and implemented rigorous quality control measures. Bambrew's market expansion efforts included extending their geographic reach, building relationships with key clients across industries, and developing robust distribution networks.

"*Each and everyone who uses packaging is our customer,*" Vaibhav declared. "*Packaging is the first and foremost thing that interacts with the customer for various brands.*" By 2024, this approach had yielded impressive results. Bambrew reported revenue of Rs 44.23 crore for Fiscal Year 2023 (The Economic Times, 2024), marking nearly a five-fold increase from previous periods. The company's valuation reached 230+ crores, positioning it as a leading player in the sustainable packaging industry (Anant, 2025).

Looking ahead, Vaibhav envisioned global expansion within 3–5 years. The short-term goals included reaching ₹100 crore in revenue, ensuring international compliance, and entering markets like the US, Middle East, and Australia (Bambrew, 2022; Anant, 2025). Significant investments were planned for product development, factory expansion, and certification standards to meet these ambitious targets.

Vaibhav's vision extended beyond business metrics. He saw Bambrew playing a crucial role in a larger environmental transformation: "*The packaging market has a tailwind, and support from Extended Producer Responsibility regulations will provide a boost for circular economy companies. I see humongous growth for this industry coming in the next few years, which will continue until 2040*" (Bambrew, 2022).

The Business Model

To execute his growth strategy effectively, Vaibhav developed an enterprise-model approach to Bambrew's business. This model targeted different market segments and needs, creating a diversified revenue stream and maximizing impact.

The Enterprise Business Model (Bambrew, 2025b) formed the foundation of Bambrew's operations. This model derived revenue from the sale of packaging products tailored for enterprise clients, ranging from high-margin items like mailer bags and carry bags (soon to be manufactured in-house) to lower-margin products like corrugated items that served as market entry points.

Vaibhav ensured operational efficiency by strategically positioning production capabilities. Since launching operations in August 2022 from their inaugural facility in Bangalore, Bambrew had positioned itself to expand manufacturing capacity (Bambrew, 2025b). The company planned to internally produce high-margin products while collaborating with outsourced vendors for supplementary offerings. This balanced approach optimized efficiency and scale while maintaining flexibility in production and cost management. To meet enterprise client demands across India, Vaibhav established a robust distribution network that integrated in-house and vendor-sourced products into nationwide delivery operations, guaranteeing Pan-India coverage.

Bambrew planned trials with an anchor customer in Q2 FY24, anticipating annual savings exceeding INR 120 crores for the client (Bambrew, 2025b). This innovation highlighted Vaibhav's ability to combine sustainability with practical business solutions, addressing both environmental and economic concerns simultaneously.

Government partnerships proved vital to Bambrew's growth. The company received lab access through India's Ashwin Bamboo Mission and the Institute of Wood Science and Technology. Vaibhav leveraged connections with government officials to access self-help groups and bamboo sourcing networks. His role as a national advisor on bamboo sector development for the Government of India positioned him to influence policy while building Bambrew's reputation.

The Road Ahead: Challenges and Opportunities

By April 2025, Vaibhav had transformed Bambrew from a small startup with a vision into a significant player in the sustainable packaging industry. The company had saved 60,000 tons of single-use plastic, 125,000 tons of CO_2, 4.30 million kWh of electricity, 115,000 barrels of oil, and over 3 million trees through its sustainable solutions (Bambrew, 2022; Anant, 2025). These impressive metrics demonstrated the tangible environmental impact of Vaibhav's original vision.

Yet, challenges remained. Despite overall positive customer reviews praising Bambrew's commitment to sustainability and innovative packaging solutions, some criticisms emerged regarding vendor relations and payment issues. Vaibhav recognized these as growth areas, emphasizing that Bambrew was "a customer-obsessed company" where improving service remained the top priority. The competitive landscape continued to evolve. While Bambrew had no direct peer in primary packaging, competition existed in secondary packaging. Vaibhav remained confident in Bambrew's position, noting the company's unmatched quality metrics and high repeat order rate of 97–98% (Anant, 2025).

Looking to the future, Vaibhav's ambitions for Bambrew extended beyond financial success. His macro vision remained unwavering: to make the world free from single-use plastics. While acknowledging plastic's usefulness in sectors where alternatives don't yet exist, he focused on responsible substitution in packaging—an area that contributed massively to global greenhouse gas emissions and microplastic pollution.

The sustainable packaging market represented a $274 billion opportunity within the $1 trillion total addressable packaging market. Vaibhav set a realistic target, aiming for Bambrew to capture 30–40% of the global sustainable packaging market (Bambrew, 2022)—a significant but achievable goal given the company's trajectory.

Beyond business metrics, Vaibhav remained deeply connected to Bambrew's environmental mission. Each avoided plastic bag, each tree saved, each ton of CO_2 prevented—these tangible impacts justified the struggles and challenges of the entrepreneurial journey. What had begun with that emotional reaction to a sea turtle's suffering had evolved into a movement capable of meaningful, measurable environmental change.

As he looked to Bambrew's future expansion into international markets, Vaibhav Anant remained grounded in his original purpose: offering practical, scalable alternatives to plastic packaging. Through innovation,

Fig. 9.3 Vaibhav at the Bambrew Headquarters at Bangalore. (Source: Author's photo)

persistence, and strategic thinking, he had built not just a successful company but a model for how business could be part of the solution to environmental challenges. The bamboo revolutionary's journey continued, with each sustainable package representing another small victory in the global fight against plastic pollution. "*We are not just a packaging company; we are a sustainability movement,*" Vaibhav quips (Fig. 9.3).

Discussion Questions

- Sourcing Strategy Dilemma: Evaluate Vaibhav's decision to shift from tribal community sourcing to structured supply chains. What were the trade-offs between social impact and business scalability?

How could Bambrew have maintained its social mission while achieving operational efficiency?

- Material Portfolio Strategy: Analyze Bambrew's evolution from a single-material focus (bamboo) to a diversified sustainable materials portfolio. What are the advantages and risks of this multi-material approach? How should the company prioritize resource allocation across different material innovations?
- Business Model Innovation: Assess the effectiveness of Bambrew's single business model (Enterprise). Does this model offer the greatest potential for scaling impact and profitability? What could be a few other models that complement this model addressing different market segments?
- Global Expansion Strategy: With plans to expand internationally within 3–5 years, what challenges might Bambrew face in different markets? How should the company adapt its products and strategies for markets like the US, Europe, and Australia while maintaining its sustainability mission?
- Competitive Positioning: As the sustainable packaging market grows rapidly, how can Bambrew maintain its competitive advantage? What should be the company's response to increasing competition from both startups and established players entering the eco-friendly packaging space?

Supplementary Reading
Academic Papers:

- Hart, S. L., & Dowell, G. (2011). Invited editorial: A natural-resource-based view of the firm: Fifteen years after. Journal of Management, 37(5), 1464–1479.
- Bocken, N. M., Short, S. W., Rana, P., & Evans, S. (2014). A literature and practice review to develop sustainable business model archetypes. Journal of Cleaner Production, 65, 42–56.

Industry Reports:

- Ellen MacArthur Foundation. (2019). Reuse: Rethinking packaging.
- McKinsey & Company. (2025). Sustainability in packaging – across the value chain, and in 2025 and beyond.

Podcasts/Videos:

- "The Circular Economy Show" - EpisodeS by Ellen MacArthur Foundation on sustainable packaging innovations
- TED Talk: "How Plastic Packaging Impacts Human Health" by Dr. Jane Muncke

Government Resources:

- India's National Bamboo Mission – https://nbm.da.gov.in
- Extended Producer Responsibility guidelines for plastic packaging – https://eprplastic.cpcb.gov.in/#/plastic/home

Learning Outcomes

Upon completion of this case study, students will be able to:

- Analyze Sustainable Business Model Innovation: Evaluate how environmental challenges can be transformed into viable business opportunities, understanding the integration of sustainability principles with commercial viability and scalability considerations.
- Assess Strategic Decision-Making in Social Enterprises: Critically examine the trade-offs between social impact and business growth, particularly in sourcing strategies, supply chain management, and stakeholder engagement in emerging market contexts.
- Evaluate Market Entry and Expansion Strategies: Understand the complexities of scaling sustainable innovations, including material diversification, customer acquisition, funding strategies, and international expansion planning in the context of environmental technology ventures.

Acknowledgments The authors gratefully acknowledge Mr. Vaibhav Anant, CEO of Bambrew Technologies, for providing valuable insights and primary data that made this case study possible.

Competing Interests The authors have no conflicts of interest to declare that are relevant to the content of this chapter. This case study was developed independently without financial support from Bambrew Technologies or any affiliated organizations.

References

Anant, V. (2025). Primary data sourced from the founder, CEO of Bambrew Technologies. LinkedIn profile: https://www.linkedin.com/in/vaibhav-anant-7474275a/

Bambrew. (2022). Bambrew sustainable packaging [Video]. YouTube. https://youtu.be/9CvMHKGofcE

Bambrew. (2025a). Blog. Retrieved from https://www.bambrew.in/blog

Bambrew. (2025b). *Pitch deck*. Unpublished internal document. Scribd. [Personal communication].

Krishnan, A. (2022). Plastic-free packaging: Bambrew Bengaluru eco-friendly startup. Retrieved from https://thebetterindia.com/285540/plastic-free-packaging-bambrew-bengaluru-eco-friendly-startup/

Shop Without Plastic. (2024). Is bamboo better than plastic?. Retrieved from https://www.shop-without-plastic.com/blogs/alternative-materials/is-bamboo-better-than-plastic

Tech in Asia. (2024). Blume Ventures leads $7.2M in Indian greentech startup Bambrew. Retrieved from https://www.techinasia.com/blume-ventures-leads-72m-indian-greentech-startup-bambrew

United Nations. (2015). *Sustainable Development Goals*. United Nations SDG Knowledge Platform. https://sdgs.un.org/goals

United Nations Environment Programme. (2021). How to reduce impacts of single-use plastic products. Retrieved from https://www.unep.org/news-and-stories/story/how-reduce-impacts-single-use-plastic-products

YourStory. (2022). Bambrew: Greentech startup making sustainable packaging for Amazon. Retrieved from https://yourstory.com/2022/07/bambrew-greentech-startup-making-sustainable-packaging-amazon

CHAPTER 10

Sustainable Impact: The PlusTrust Model and its Viability in Rural India (Part A)

Srividya Ramanathan, Oishika Roy, Prakash Satyavageeswaran, and Vedha Ponnappan

Abstract PlusTrust, a social enterprise from India, supports women from disadvantaged rural backgrounds through its microincubation program, facilitating their transition to self-sustaining entrepreneurs. Their Community Health Entrepreneurs (CHE) program, conceived after the pandemic, serves a dual purpose: training and equipping women to attain financial agency and filling gaps in healthcare access in underserved communities. Their first cohort of CHEs made significant strides, serving over 150,000 people and earning between INR 1,500 and INR 20,000 each month. However, entrenched cultural norms, familial friction over women

S. Ramanathan (✉)
University of Iowa, Iowa City, IA, USA
e-mail: srividya-ramanathan@uiowa.edu

O. Roy
The Locavore, Mumbai, India

P. Satyavageeswaran • V. Ponnappan
Indian Institute of Management Udaipur, Udaipur, India
e-mail: prakash.satyavageeswaran@iimu.ac.in; vedha.ponnappan@iimu.ac.in

A. S. Galande et al. (eds.), *Context-inspired Entrepreneurship*, Sustainable Development Goals Series,
https://doi.org/10.1007/978-981-95-9831-1_10

attaining greater agency, overlap with free government Health and Wellness Centres (HWCs), and challenges in sustaining operations after the stipend period threaten the program's long-term viability.

Part A of the case highlights the dilemmas that PlusTrust is confronted with: whether to expand to new geographies or invest more resources in existing ones, how to collaborate with government yet maintain entrepreneurial autonomy, and how to structure incentives for CHEs. While Part B of the case explores dilemmas faced by one of the CHEs: Is there merit in running her business as a health entrepreneur? Despite providing essential health services to her community, she wonders whether these offerings alone are sufficient to sustain her business and provide her with adequate profit.

Keywords Social-entrepreneurship • Women's empowerment • Sustainable livelihoods • Rural healthcare access • Health equity • Rural India • Public private partnerships

SDG Links This chapter is aligned with SDG 8: Decent Work and Economic Growth, examining how PlusTrust enables micro-entrepreneurs to build sustainable livelihoods through enterprise support. By strengthening the productive capacity of small businesses and informal entrepreneurs, the case speaks directly to SDG Target 8.3 on promoting decent work through micro- and small-scale entrepreneurship. The chapter also relates to SDG 1 through its focus on enterprise support as a pathway out of poverty, and SDG 10 through its emphasis on empowering underserved communities.

Sustainable Impact: The PlusTrust Model and its Viability in Rural India (Part A)

Introduction

It was a Wednesday morning. Simran*,[1] the Program Manager at PlusTrust, set out to Bhatoli to oversee the refresher training for the Community Health Entrepreneurs (CHEs). It was Simran's sixth year with PlusTrust, an organization with expertise in micro-incubation for

[1] Name changed to preserve confidentiality.

women changemakers from rurally disadvantaged backgrounds. An engineer by profession, Simran, stepped down from her lucrative corporate job to work in the social sector, something she always thought was her true calling. When Simran was introduced to the CHE program, she was elated by PlusTrust's collaboration with SpotSense and StepOne for enabling point-of-care diagnostics. Hailing from the peripheries of Chittorgarh, Simran has been a first-hand witness to the repercussions of health inequities. Although the CHE program was still embryonic when PlusTrust joined hands with SpotSense a little more than a year ago, Simran was confident and optimistic about the program's potential to provide quality access to healthcare and create a sustainable livelihood for the CHEs. She worked throughout the operationalization of the program. It was only in March 2022 that the first cohort of CHEs was inducted and trained, and it has already been a year, but the first year was not all roses.

The CHEs were constantly faced with issues in the community and on the personal front. Their transition from voiceless, non-earning members to respected community figures who brought in a life-changing monthly income often caused friction at home. Despite the lack of access to primary healthcare services and doctors in the vicinity, it was difficult for the CHEs to earn community trust and persuade people to pay for diagnostic services. While some CHEs had become self-sustaining in their ventures in due course, many were still struggling. Simran, however, was unrelenting and reposed faith in the CHEs and the program's potential. She was determined to position them as entrepreneurs, not just as healthcare coordinators. She brainstormed with them on how to earn from other entrepreneurial activities based on community needs. As the vehicle halted at Bhatoli and she stepped out, a question lingered in her mind: Was the current model enough to ensure long-term sustainability for these women, or did the CHE program need a deeper shift in the strategy?

PlusTrust

PlusTrust started operations in 2008 and was formally registered in 2010. The organization created opportunities in rural and remote areas for women to build a world where both genders can pursue their ambitions without bias. Particularly, PlusTrust addressed the gender gap prevalent in entrepreneurship and innovation in rural India, focusing on health and education. It offered fellowships that included monetary and mentorship support for six months and a lifelong peer network. PlusTrust also provided micro-incubation opportunities to reduce the support gap faced by for women entrepreneurs in rural, resource-poor communities. It led a peer-based support network of over 14 grassroots *changemakers* or *anchors*, each leading 5 to 10 fellows in their regions. Alumni engagement and anchor development programs helped build this network over 16 years.

Geographical Presence

PlusTrust operated in Madhya Pradesh, Rajasthan, Bihar, Uttarakhand, Uttar Pradesh, and Maharashtra (Fig. 10.1). It provided micro-incubation support through different fellowships that supported entrepreneurial mindsets in the key focus areas of health and education. The fellowship included six-month-long mentorship support from *anchors*, an opportunity to test and pilot ideas for change and training to improve technical skills, soft skills, and management skills for participating women. During the fellowship, the fellows received a minimal stipend that allowed them to provide services in their communities for free or at a nominal rate. This encouraged higher adoption that allowed the women to scale their ideas and start charging the community to become financially sustainable.

The CHE Program

The second wave of the pandemic exposed the lack of basic infrastructure and access to primary healthcare in various regions of the country, prompting the establishment of the CHE program. The CHE program was conceived to provide underserved areas with access to essential healthcare services, including diagnostic facilities and qualified medical professionals through teleconsultations. Besides, the initiative provided a unique opportunity for low-income women to embark on entrepreneurial journeys within their local communities. The program allowed them to establish their own businesses and opened doors for their social and economic empowerment.

During the program's design phase, PlusTrust realized collaboration was essential for implementing the CHE program. The problem that PlusTrust was trying to solve was complex, and it made sense to collaborate with partners who had already solved parts of the problem with a view to integrating such solutions rather than reinventing the wheel. This also meant that PlusTrust could focus on its core competencies while allowing collaborators to bring in theirs. Thus, while the primary roles of PlusTrust involved designing, managing, and executing the CHE model, they

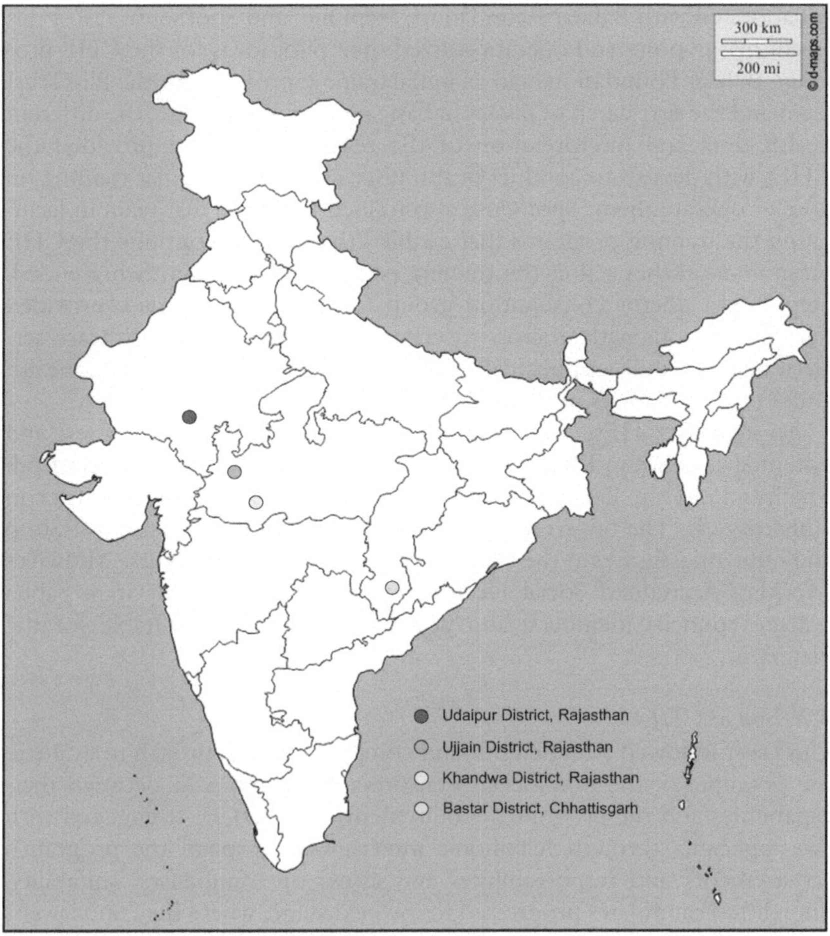

Fig. 10.1 Geographic Footprint of the CHE program. (Source—Map credit dmaps.com. PlusTrust operations layer added by case authors)

collaborated with Bahaar Foundation, StepOne, and SpotSense across different geographies and operationalized their pilot ideas for the CHE program. Bahaar Foundation held an initial training program for the PlusTrust team and the first batch of *fellows* in basic medical knowledge, the different health tests and interpretation of the results. SpotSense provided the CHEs with devices to conduct health tests, along with regular training on how to operate them. SpotSense also trained the PlusTrust team in facilitating the training programs that enabled the team to continue the CHE program workshops after the training partnership with SpotSense ended. StepOne, a doctor consultation group formed during Covid, provided teleconsultations with doctors to ensure timely access to healthcare services and last-mile connectivity for patients identified as having health issues or irregularities in the basic tests.

To identify CHEs, four locations were chosen based on interest and potential: Khalwa in Khandwa District and Nagda in Ujjain District from Madhya Pradesh, Udaipur District in Rajasthan, and Bastar District in Chhattisgarh. The on-ground partners engaged with local administration and influential figures at the village level, such as Auxiliary Nurse Midwives (ANMs), Accredited Social Health Activists (ASHAs), and Gram Sabha (village council) members, and nominated individuals suitable for the program.

Selection of CHEs

PlusTrust followed a meticulous and comprehensive approach to evaluate the potential of the nominees to ensure a harmonious fit between their capabilities and the program's requirements (Fig. 10.2). It engaged with the applicants through telephonic interviews to explain the program's requirements and responsibilities and assess the candidates' suitability. Shortlisted candidates progressed to the next stage, where they underwent comprehensive training and orientation workshops. The immersive learning experience helped PlusTrust assess the women's personal, professional, and entrepreneurial potential.

The candidates were further tasked with conducting surveys to understand healthcare challenges in their respective catchments better. These surveys covered various aspects, including healthcare challenges, travel distance to the nearest Primary Health Centre (PHC) and pharmacy, and typical health-seeking behaviors. Through the task, PlusTrust gauged the women's research abilities and the capacity to identify critical areas of intervention.

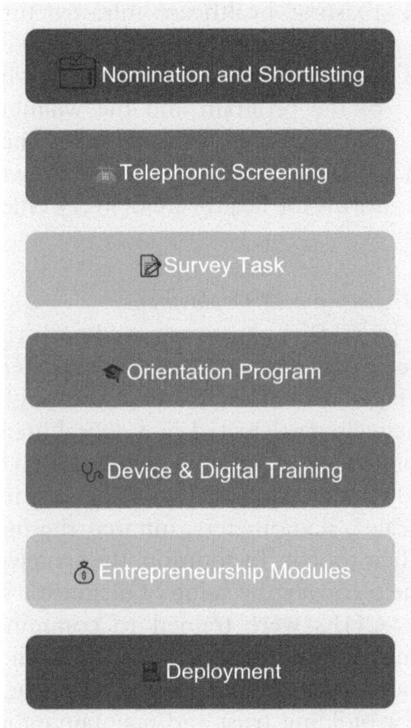

Fig. 10.2 CHE Selection and Training Process Flow. (Source—Case authors based on information provided by PlusTrust and Bahaar Foundation)

After the completion of the surveys, potential candidates were selected based on their survey findings. PlusTrust conducted further briefing sessions and provided additional insights into the program and its expectations. Notably, PlusTrust considered the candidates' family dynamics and their relationship with the community, recognizing the significance of a supportive environment in ensuring their success. PlusTrust conducted house visits to verify the information provided by the candidates and to ensure they had the necessary support system to thrive in their role as CHEs.

Throughout the selection process, PlusTrust focused on four key factors integral to the program's success.

1. Candidates' potential, encompassing their abilities, motivation, and willingness to learn.

2. Existing healthcare infrastructure, which determined the resources available for effective healthcare delivery.
3. Community's paying capacity, which would influence the sustainability of the program and the willingness of the community members to uptake the services offered by the CHEs.
4. Availability of a stable data network to leverage digital tools and platforms for healthcare delivery efficiently.

Training and Deployment

The CHEs' path was paved with rigorous training, including soft skills, technical skills, financial management, and entrepreneurial abilities (Fig. 10.2). They received thorough device training from SpotSense and actively participated in a digital literacy program. To enhance their capabilities, SpotSense equipped the CHEs with vital medical devices such as glucometers, blood pressure apparatus, hemoglobin meters, weighing scales, stadiometers, infrared thermometers, and smartphones as part of their toolkit. In addition, they received outreach and advocacy materials to help convey the value of diagnostic services to the community.

CHEs were trained to communicate their limitations clearly. They maintained a strict distinction from faith healers and untrained practitioners and refrained from prescribing or dispensing medications—essential for building trust and maintaining integrity. The training program amalgamated classroom exercises, practical immersion in the community, immersive block and village-level training, and regular virtual check-ins. Apart from the technical skills, soft skills, and physiology modules, the CHEs also delved into the world of entrepreneurial training. They became adept at goal setting and financial planning, which eventually contributed to their economic independence.

The Impact

Beginning in April 2022, 21 women started their CHE training. By September 2022, the first orientation and training were completed, and the CHEs began providing diagnostic tests in their communities by October. In Khandwa, Nagda, and Udaipur, 2291 diagnostic tests were conducted between October 2022 and March 2023 (Table 10.1).

Referred to as 'healthcare coordinators,' the CHEs assumed a vital role in enhancing health accessibility in their respective regions. In the initial

Table 10.1 CHE Program Impact Snapshot (April 2022–March 2023)

Indicator	*Highlights*
CHEs trained	21 (first cohort)
Diagnostic tests conducted	2291 (across the four locations)
Teleconsultation reach	60+ villages
Community coverage	~150,000 individuals
Monthly income range	₹1500–₹1600 (low demand) ₹6000–₹7000 (average earners) ₹20,000+ (outliers)
Additional interventions	Health camps, school screenings, *Baithaks*

Source—Case authors based on information provided by PlusTrust

phase, the first cohort received a six-month stipend, which supported their transition to self-sustaining micro-entrepreneurship. The stipend also covered essential diagnostic consumables.

PlusTrust implemented a hybrid stipend model comprising fixed and variable pay components for the second cohort to promote sustainability. Regular reviews and refresher training supported ongoing capacity building. Outreach initiatives such as health camps, school medical camps, and community *Baithaks* (community meetings) expanded the CHEs' visibility and trust.

Monthly earnings among the first cohort ranged from INR 1,500–1,600 to INR 6,000–7,000, depending on geographic and community dynamics. During the monsoon season, demand for teleconsultations surged. CHEs charged INR 50 per teleconsultation and reached over 60 villages in six months. Cumulatively, the program reached more than 150,000 individuals.

Throughout, PlusTrust ensured a high-touch implementation model with weekly data collection and on-ground support from field coordinators, enabling CHEs to resolve operational issues and maintain service quality. CHEs distinguished themselves from ASHAs and ANMs through their entrepreneurial approach, fitting into the broader health ecosystem while sustaining their service models independently.

Box 10.1 CHE-led Innovation at the Community Level
Chhaya*—Khandwa, Madhya Pradesh

Chhaya partnered with a local private doctor to set up a diagnostic point near the doctor's clinic. On Sundays, she operated near a church to serve the churchgoers. She thus earned INR 20,000 per-month from both roles, including a full-time position at a private clinic.

Sumita*—Koyal Village, Madhya Pradesh

Sumita leveraged her brother's contacts as a medical representative to help patients access necessary medicines. She conducted door-to-door diagnostic services and coordinated CHEs in the state, earning INR 12,000 from PlusTrust and an additional INR 8,000– INR10,000 from her enterprise.

Challenges

Procuring diagnostic devices and consumables after the stipend period impeded the CHEs transition to self-sustainability. The villages had unique challenges due to the social structure, harvesting season, climatic conditions, and gender-specific health issues. Additionally, the availability of free health tests in Rajasthan reduced the demand for CHE services. Earning a self-sustaining income became difficult when such unique challenges arose. However, with insights about the distinctive challenges faced by the CHEs through the Field Coordinators and Program Managers, PlusTrust enhanced the expanded the scope of work the CHEs could undertake in a given week or month.

Since the program was conceptualized as an entrepreneurial model, there was no designated number of diagnoses or hours of work the CHEs had to spend in the field in a day or a week. Inactivity or lack of proactivity also led to a drop in income. In such cases, PlusTrust had to decide whether the CHE should continue in the program.

Further, in Rajasthan, the CHE model was competing with public health centers, hospitals and ASHA workers who provided free health services, and the CHE model was unable to scale after the second batch of CHEs. Most of the CHEs from the first batch discontinued their work in health and started working in other industries to increase their income. However, some CHEs who are entrepreneurial have continued the work by providing health tests at home in villages that do not have a hospital or health center. Some CHEs also helped ASHA workers and concentrated on pregnant women, helping them monitor blood pressure, hemoglobin, and blood sugar during their pregnancy.

Family-level issues were commonplace for the CHEs as they became more vocal and brought significant income to the family. Most of the CHEs hailed from tribal or underprivileged backgrounds. Their transition during the CHE program to becoming respected and influential members of the community often did not sit well with their husbands and in-laws and caused friction in family life.

A CHE's income was directly proportional to the initiative she took. In some places, there was resistance to diagnostic services and doubts regarding the efficacy of consultations with physicians over the phone. Instead, faith healers and local practitioners were often preferred to allopathic physicians.

One of the other challenges was that villagers did not perceive the need for regular diagnostics testing. For instance, even individuals with diabetes were often reluctant to undergo monthly blood sugar testing. Once their sugar level was ascertained in a month, they would decline to spend INR 50 on another test for the next 3–4 months. This was a major roadblock on the financial viability of the model, as the entire premise of the model revolved around making regular diagnostics available to chronic patients.

Finally, the model currently took care of diagnostics and teleconsultation but did not provide for the supply of medicines to fill prescriptions. In villages where there were no pharmacies, people often preferred to go to the nearby town to get the diagnostics done, consult a doctor, and purchase medicines, instead of completing the consultations and diagnostics in the village and going to the town to fill a prescription. This led to a decrease in demand for the CHEs.

Overall, the CHEs faced complex challenges in their entrepreneurial journey, including procuring necessary equipment, navigating family dynamics, and overcoming cultural beliefs. PlusTrust's support and understanding of these challenges were crucial in ensuring the success and sustainability of the CHE program.

Road Ahead

Despite boasting an illustrious board of advisors and founders actively involved in the operations, PlusTrust's aspirations for scaling up encountered a formidable obstacle—a dearth of human resources. The lack of adequate posed a significant challenge as the organization worked to expand its presence across multiples states.

Secondly, PlusTrust had taken a geography-agnostic approach. While the approach had the potential to increase the program's reach to underserved communities, when it came to expanding its activities, it also presented several problems. Establishing and maintaining operating partners in several places, each with its unique conditions and requirements, proved to be a monumental undertaking that necessitated a significant investment of time and money.

Added to the complexity was the introduction of Health and Wellness Centres (HWCs) in the villages and hamlets that the CHEs served. These HWCs, a government program to combat Non-Communicable Diseases (NCDs), closely corresponded with PlusTrust's targeted initiatives. They provided free-of-cost diagnostic services and teleconsultations, which PlusTrust touted as a component of their unique value proposition. Although the existence of HWCs alongside CHEs provided an additional lifeline to the communities, it posed an existential challenge to expanding the CHE program. The danger of services and efforts being duplicated as the government expanded the scope of HWCs loomed large.

The future of the CHE program appeared precarious as PlusTrust was confronted with many challenges. How do they address the need for more human resources? How do they navigate the challenge posed by the HWCs' provision of free services, which directly competed with the market solution offered by the CHEs? What steps should be undertaken if certain CHEs are unable to achieve self-sufficiency over time? Finally, was the current model, without pharmacy supplies, the right one?

As PlusTrust considered the next phase of the CHE program, several strategic questions remained. While the core of the model has demonstrated promise, the organization must explore and define tangible options for adaptation and growth in a rapidly evolving rural healthcare landscape.

Should the organization deepen its focus in regions where the CHE model has flourished, or pilot new geographies with high unmet needs but without an existing HWC presence, thereby reducing direct competition?

Could CHEs supplement their diagnostic services with adjacent micro-enterprise opportunities, such as selling sanitary pads, nutrition supplements, or hygiene kits, leveraging their trusted access within households?

What partnerships, public or private, might enable scale without compromising the integrity and grassroots ownership of the CHE initiative?

Is there scope to formally integrate CHEs into existing government health initiatives (e.g., anaemia control, maternal health), while retaining their entrepreneurial independence?

Should there be differentiated models for CHE deployment based on geography, infrastructure, and local community dynamics?

How can PlusTrust design an incentive system that rewards performance but still allows CHEs to feel like independent entrepreneurs, not employees?

Supplementary Readings

- Bosco, M., Welch, M., & Prashanth, G. (2022, October 26). *Women are transforming health in rural villages in India*. Think Global Health. https://www.thinkglobalhealth.org/article/women-are-transforming-health-rural-villages-india
- Bain & Company (2020, February). *Powering the economy with her: Women entrepreneurship in India* [PDF report]. Bain & Company. https://www.bain.com/contentassets/dd3604b612d84aa48a0b120f0b589532/report_powering_the_economy_with_her_-_women_entrepreneurship_in-india.pdf
- Agrawal, A., Gandhi, P., & Khare, P. (2021). *Women empowerment through entrepreneurship: Case study of a social entrepreneurial intervention in rural India. International Journal of Organizational Analysis* 26 May 2023; 31 (4): 1122–1142. https://doi.org/10.1108/IJOA-03-2021-2659

Learning Objectives

This part of the case is suitable for discussion in entrepreneurship, social entrepreneurship, social franchising, rural marketing, or social impact courses offered at post-graduate level. It can also be used in executive education programs covering similar topics. Key learning objectives –

- The case can be used to discuss micro-entrepreneurship models in the context of social organizations working towards creating sustainable livelihoods. The case provides the opportunity to consider the pulls, pressures, competitions, and completeness of models from the protagonist's lens of PlusTrust.
- The case can also bring out competition in public welfare space, with the social impact model of PlusTrust ending up potentially competing with the government's Health and Wellness Centres. The instructor can use the opportunity to discuss what role social ventures play in these situations—supplement the government's services, act as benchmark to improve government offerings, or any other competitive response.
- Micro-entrepreneurship often is entangled in social contexts, rural institutional voids, and lack of opportunities. This case can help drive discussions around how each of these play a role in the outcome.

Sustainable Micro-Enterprise: PlusTrust's Community Health Entrepreneurs (Part B)

Abstract

24-year-old Prakriti has been working as a Community Health Entrepreneur under a program initiated by PlusTrust Foundation. The role requires her to offer and administer diagnostic tests to community members in neighboring villages for profit, while also managing input costs, sourcing of equipment, and her time. While at the start of her tenure, Prakriti saw scope for sustainable profit and growth in this work—based on initial demand for her diagnostic services—two years later, she traverses the same landscape looking for potential consumers. She finds that fewer people are expressing demand for the services she offers. Given that her costs remain unwavering, Prakriti is confronted with a fundamental question: Is there merit in running her business as a health entrepreneur? Despite providing essential health services to her community, she wonders whether these offerings alone are sufficient to sustain her business and provide her with adequate profit.

Keywords: Health entrepreneurship, Women entrepreneur, Rural micro-enterprise, Rural entrepreneurship, Community health, Primary healthcare, Diagnostic services

Introduction

On a hot and dry May afternoon, Prakriti, 22, left her home to conduct her work as a community health entrepreneur (CHE) for the day. She had spent the morning working with her mother to complete chores around the house. Now, having completed the first meal of the day at 10 am, she made her way to the neighboring village to conduct diagnostic tests.

As Prakriti walked, diagnostic kits in tow, it struck her that she would be completing 2 years as a CHE in a few days. It had been 2 years since she had been selected by PlusTrust in 2021 to be a part of the CHE program, after a couple of months of applying, studying, and surveying her village. As she walked to Ajmabad, a neighbouring village, this realization made her reflect on her time as a CHE. The last 2 years were full of varied experiences and learnings. In the first few days of becoming a CHE, Prakriti had learnt and mastered the skills of diagnostic testing of glucose levels, blood pressure, and haemoglobin count. She not only learned how to operate the devices for these tests, but also how to read the values they output, and use these values to understand key information about patients' health. She thought back to the first six months of the program, when members of PlusTrust would regularly hold financial and technical training for her and her peers, and how enriching those sessions were. In hindsight, those trainings contributed to so much of her skills today, and helped her learn how to think about her work and its problems creatively and profitably.

She felt more in control of her time and her ability to manage it, as she learned through practice what it meant for one to be self-employed. At the thought, Prakriti felt a brief surge of pride—to be able to manage housework, as well as work within the community through her CHE venture was no small task. Walking through the winding path up to her catchment area, she realized that she had begun learning how to run her own business! Through the process, she had built a sense of confidence and assurance in herself and had agency in her household as a decision-maker. It was deeply moving for her to realize that sometime in the last two years, she had begun growing into what her family had always wanted her to become.

However, in no way had these years had onlyconsisted of highs. Prakriti remembered going from house to house in her village, trying to convince household members of the importance of regular diagnostic tests. While the villagers were enthusiastic at first, they were far harder to convince when the novelty wore off.

Even today, people in the community were not willing to get tests done as regularly as they should. During certain months, it had been difficult for her to recover her travel, consumables, and time costs. She wondered, 'Is the effort worth it if I'm not able to earn properly?' Just as she reached Ajmabad, ready to interact with her peers in the community, a flurry of doubts and ideas took over her thoughts. Although she had established a business with a fair bit of credibility, could she really call this business successful? She wondered what had caused these challenges: 'Could the difficulties I'm facing be due to the business decisions I've made? What kind of a businessperson do I need to be to overcome these obstacles?' The moment of reflection turned out to be bittersweet; she was filled with a sense of concern for her venture, but she also felt excited by its potential and possibilities. As a little boy from Ajmabad eagerly called out to her, Prakriti was brought out of her reflections and into the present moment, ready to tackle her CHE responsibilities of the day.

The Community Health Entrepreneur Program of PlusTrust

The Community Health Entrepreneur program, initiated by PlusTrust, was introduced soon after the COVID-19 pandemic when the realities of poor healthcare access in rural India stood starkly revealed. The CHE program was introduced to achieve last-mile connectivity through health entrepreneurs. Along with conducting diagnostics, CHEs were to act as a channel between community members in remote locations and health professionals. With the help of telemedicine technology from partner organization StepOne, the CHEs could connect community members to doctors for higher-level care and prescriptions when required. The doctor consultations earned the CHE a minimal amount, but not enough to be considered a revenue stream.

As a key component of the program's design, the CHEs were local to the villages they serve. Recruiting and placing CHEs in such a decentralized manner ensured that the women were familiar with the region they are serving and that a pre-existing level of trust between the CHEs and customers was borne of this familiarity. However, as is true of all novel initiatives, legitimacy took time to develop; this was observed in the execution of the CHE program as well.

PlusTrust design for the program included several stages: hiring and assessment, training, and execution. To carry these stages out effectively, PlusTrust partnered with organizations that provided testing kits such as SpotSense and those that facilitated training such as Bahaar Foundation. The process, for the CHEs, involved filling out an online form that was circulated through internal community connections developed over time by field partner organizations. If a prospective CHE was selected based on their responses to this form, personnel from the field partner organization visited their families to understand whether there was sufficient support from familial networks that would permit her to do her work. Post this visit, the CHE was asked to survey her village to understand the healthcare scenario of the region, the problems plaguing the area, and the general mindset of the people.

Once hired, the CHE underwent a training process, which first involved a residential program for medical training to learn how to use diagnostic devices. After this initial training, the CHEs underwent weekly refresher sessions of these skills, and additional financial and entrepreneurial training. Some of the ideas discussed in these trainings included how CHEs could manage their finances, and any additional sources of income that the CHE could add to her basket, along with the existing diagnostic services.

These training sessions, along with day-to-day support for the CHE, were largely the responsibility of PlusTrust. For example, if diagnostic devices broke down, or diagnostic consumables were not available in neighboring towns, CHEs contacted their field partner personnel to help with such logistics concerns. However, this non-availability proved to be a persistent issue that required operational mechanisms to be put in place. PlusTrust was constructing a supply chain for diagnostic equipment as well as basic medication that the CHE could provide without prescription. Once such a supply mechanism came into place, everyday CHE work was anticipated to become much smoother.

For the first six months of the program, PlusTrust provided CHEs with INR 7000 per month to assist her in the setting-up of the venture. While the management of this money was left to the CHEs themselves, they were to ensure that they could procure the diagnostic consumables they require through this stipend. The latest phase of operation for the first batch of CHEs found that CHEs could conduct their business with a certain level of efficiency, with the most successful CHEs conducting regular haemoglobin, blood pressure, and blood glucose tests. Beginning in April 2022, 21 women started their CHE training. By September 2022, the first orientation and trainings were complete, and the CHEs started providing tests in their local communities by October 2022. In Khandwa, Nagda, and Udaipur, 2291 diagnostic tests were conducted between October 2022 and March 2023 and CHEs earned an average of INR 1200 per month. However, one must consider whether this earning, while indicative of a base level of demand and need for diagnostic tests in the catchment areas, was adequate for CHEs. This was especially important considering that the CHEs spent about INR 20 on average per day for transportation and the cost of consumables per month for the diagnostic tests averaged to INR 225. Lastly, one must reckon with the underlying fact of these numbers: while some exemplary CHEs garnered sales regularly, this was not true for all CHEs in a variety of contexts.

Headwinds

CHEs were typically young women who had completed high school or were studying further. In the latter case, they were juggling the work they are doing as a CHE along with their education.[2] CHEs had a variety of motivations to take up this role, including the desire to start their own venture, or wanting to foray into the healthcare sector, as many of them witnessed a dire absence of adequate healthcare in their towns and villages. Many younger CHEs also perceived the role to be an employment opportunity; their work as a CHE would be a possible means to earn supplemental income, along with either other sources of earning or other family members' incomes.

For most CHEs, running a business on their own was what made this role compelling. The autonomy allowed them the freedom to work based on other responsibilities, and the context they are working within. For example, in many communities, people had varied work timings, suggesting that a typical time-bound workday was not appropriate. Considering these contextual factors, CHEs were able to create a work-life scenario that suited them well. CHEs also expressed their desire to have their businesses grow through additional sources of revenue, such as training and operating as laboratory technicians, with the scope of additional blood, stool, and urine tests. Along with this, there also existed the possibility of

[2] This case was developed using primary information obtained through interviews and discussions with members of PlusTrust and Bahaar Foundation involved in the CHE program.

an interest in conducting tests for communicable diseases such as malaria, TB, dengue, etc. Together, with their supervisor organizations, CHEs were ideating on how to create additional streams of earning that would benefit them and the community both.

However, their experience also allowed them the insight that earning within these contexts was difficult, especially considering the purchasing capacity of their target group. Hence, they recognized that they could only continue to work as a CHE until it continued to be profitable. Many CHEs had come to terms with the possibility of discontinuing their CHE work if it proved to only garner consistent loss. While the financial situation of the CHE varied from person to person, for many CHEs the household was not dependent on their earnings and the money they earned was an additional income that benefited the household.

For many CHEs the average revenues were INR 2000 to INR 2500 a month. At the start of their operations, they were able to earn more and made considerable profits, given the novelty of their work. At that time, the tests CHEs conducted (glucose, haemoglobin, and blood pressure) were new to the population and they recognized the need for it. As time passed, the demand fell, and people were more reluctant to avail themselves of these services and pay for them. Over time though the services continued to be priced at INR 50 per test, and the number of people testing regularly had reduced, making it hard for the CHEs to have a constant flow of income. Further, though the CHE program had a partnership with teleconsultation group StepOne, many people in the villages did not trust online consultations. Such online consultations also could not provide the sense of comfort that people expected and often felt with in-person consultations at the local government facilities, where Patients are also able to procure the medicines. Neither the CHEs nor the online teleconsultation doctors were able to provide medicines to the patient at their home.

Adequate returns was the largest challenge for the CHE, with no provisions to provide medicines and lack of partnerships with any pharmacies being the second biggest concern. Due to the gaps in the design, many CHEs began considering this position as temporary. Many had expressed their efforts in other fields, such as education. While PlusTrust engaged in efforts to expand the CHE business beyond diagnostic services, such as eye care and dental care, and pharmacy sales, the CHE continued to be bogged down with limited income from her work.

To CHE or Not to CHE

As Prakriti wound up her work and started her journey back home, she mentally calculated her income for the day. She had earned INR 180 through four tests, after giving a discount worth INR 20 on one of them to an old woman who was only able to pay INR 30 for a blood glucose test. Prakriti estimated her consumables to have cost her INR 20 for the day. While she had walked for the onward journey in the morning, she felt too tired to carry her bag with all the diagnostic equipment and walk back after four hours of roaming in the community checking if anyone needed tests. The shared ride back home was going to cost her INR 15. She wondered if going from village to village to do these tests was really worthwhile. Should she start carrying and selling other items to supplement her income? Sanitary napkins and contraceptives seemed good choices given that she had a good rapport with the women in the villages and would be able to talk to them about and sell such products that were stigmatized in society. She could also sell over-the-counter drugs. However, she was not sure if she wanted to lug a bag made increasingly large and heavy with all of these items to the villages. Prakriti also knew that women and girls were far more enthusiastic about buying cheap jewelry and cosmetics, which she had heard from a friend who had high margins. Should she switch to selling these items door to door? But would she then lose the respect that she currently holds in these communities? Also, who would do these tests that she was currently offering?

With no clear answers in sight, Prakriti decided a meal and a nap were in order before she could marshal more energy to think this through.

Learning Outcomes

Within the case of the CHEs, there seem to be two primary challenges: their lack of legitimacy within their communities, which manifests in consumers remaining unconvinced that their services are required on a regular basis; and the lack of connectivity to a healthcare system that is deemed reliable by the consumers, and is capable of providing a complete healthcare journey, from testing, to diagnosis, to treatment. Students can be led to thinking about how to overcome these two challenges.

CHEs suffer from not being able to establish a consistent consumer base that considers their services—which largely include diagnostics for chronic illnesses such as diabetes and high blood pressure—indispensable.

Their relevance in the healthcare system is not the norm, and therefore, their services are not utilized like those of stakeholders that are considered the status quo. Students can consider what might provide CHEs this legitimacy. For example, instead of only campaigning with consumers, CHEs could be encouraged to engage with hospitals and doctors as well. Given that government-led primary and secondary healthcare providers are often overworked, CHEs might benefit from finding gaps within the existing healthcare system and attempting to fill them. If it is difficult for doctors to run diagnostics, or for a consumer to travel large distances to reach healthcare centers, doctors could recommend CHEs to patients as viable sources of diagnostic testing. Since doctors are considered legitimate sources of medical knowledge and are able to prompt patients to take medical action, they could provide legitimacy, through conversation and norm-setting, to CHEs based on their recommendation.

However, only creating narrative legitimacy by introducing CHEs within the status quo of medical providers is insufficient. CHEs would need to be able to match this with action, which would involve connecting consumers of their services with medical professionals they trust, if required. This too can be established by engaging with medical professionals within the established healthcare system, whether that involves government healthcare centers or private healthcare providers that are able to offer services at subsidized rates. Through partnerships with a few centers and organizations, CHEs would be able to connect her consumers to the next layer of care. Students can deliberate upon strategies available to a CHE to partner with a healthcare provider that her consumers may find reliable. Would it be that she would assure her partners a specific number of referrals per month, which would allow them to meet their targets as well? Thomas and Ritala (2022) would call this performative legitimacy, stemming through action.

Students, must recognize that prompting preventive health-seeking behavior, even within more affluent, urban consumer bases, is difficult. It is harder to convince consumers of health issues they may not be able to perceive. Given the presence of the former two sources of legitimacy, CHEs might benefit from conducting tests for other illnesses as well, such as dengue, cholera, jaundice, etc. To determine which tests to keep, in order to minimize costs, she might benefit from referring to her survey material on which illnesses are more common in the region she serves, allowing her to keep tests only for those illnesses, and avoid high input costs. Provided that she is able to connect patients with doctors who can complete their medical journey, her legitimacy within her community will deepen, both in terms of how she was able to action a legitimate and medically sound connection to the healthcare system, and in establishing her resourcefulness during immediate, perceptible illnesses.

How all of the above affects the CHE's sustainability as an entrepreneur is the final part of the discussion with the students. A fundamental question can be posed to students: is this even a context where entrepreneurship is possible or should this be a gap filled by the public sector without any profitability expectations? Are there ways in which the income streams for the CHE can be enhanced? Would it make sense to add a larger basket of products where there is a felt need—such as jewelry or cosmetics? Is there is a role for branding?

Competing Interests The authors have no conflicts of interest to declare that are relevant to the contents of this chapter.

Reference

Thomas, L. D., & Ritala, P. (2022). Ecosystem legitimacy emergence: A collective action view. *Journal of Management, 48*(3), 515–541.

CHAPTER 11

Building a Green Future: GK Energy's Journey in Transforming Rural Agriculture

Devi Premnath, Subbulakshmi Somu, and R. Pavithra

Abstract Gopal Kabra started GK Energy with the aspiration of using renewable energy to transform agriculture in rural India. His organization was an early developer of solar-powered irrigation pumps that allowed farmers to irrigate fields without reliance on intermittent grid electricity or expensive diesel-generated energy. Over its journey, the company grew into a mission-oriented company synonymous with sustainable rural empowerment. However, by 2025, the company found itself at a crossroads. An increase in production costs, changes to subsidy policies, technology standards, and competition in the clean energy space were jeopardizing the balance between innovation, affordability, and the social mission. As Gopal reconnected with his college friend and renewable energy expert Arvind Sharma, he faced the challenge of expanding GK

D. Premnath (✉)
Jansons School of Business, Coimbatore, India
e-mail: devipremnath@jsb.ac.in

S. Somu
St. Joseph's Institute of Management, Bengaluru, India

R. Pavithra
Dayananda Sagar College of Arts, Science and Commerce, Bangalore, India

A. S. Galande et al. (eds.), *Context-inspired Entrepreneurship*,
Sustainable Development Goals Series,
https://doi.org/10.1007/978-981-95-9831-1_11

Energy's reach without compromising the enterprise's founding mission of affordability and rural empowerment. This case explores the strategic dilemmas of scaling a social enterprise in a policy-sensitive, innovation-driven sector. It provides students with learning opportunities related to entrepreneurial leadership, policy instruments (such as PM-KUSUM), and emerging technologies in support of sustainable, inclusive business models. This case is relevant for courses in entrepreneurship, social enterprise management, and innovation in developing economies.

Keywords Solar irrigation • Sustainable agriculture • Renewable energy • Entrepreneurship • Rural empowerment • Innovation

SDG Links The case contributes to SDG 8: Decent Work and Economic Growth by demonstrating how decentralised renewable energy solutions can support rural livelihoods and enable productive economic activity. By highlighting the role of clean-energy initiatives the case also contributes to SDG 7 and SDG 13.

Introduction

At the beginning of 2025, a small town in Nanded, Maharashtra, saw an impromptu reunion. Arvind Sharma, a senior renewable energy engineer, had travelled from Coimbatore for a wedding in his native place. There he met his college buddy and classmate Gopal Kabra, founder of GK Energy, a growing business in India's renewable energy market. Though they had drifted in different career paths, Gopal's commerce degree was pursued in Pune, while Arvind's path took him to electrical and renewable energy engineering at a premier college in Coimbatore; their shared passion for green power had never waned.

Arvind had built a corporate career with multinational energy firms and worked extensively across solar and wind power projects in India and overseas over the years. At the same time, Gopal, who had always felt a pull towards entrepreneurship and was guided by his family's entrepreneurial spirit, founded GK Energy in 2008, inspired by his early interest in solar technology and a dream of revolutionising energy access across rural India.

Their reunion occurred at the solar-powered corporate office of GK Energy. As they met for tea in the warm winter sun streaming down into their rooftop garden from solar panels above, the two friends found themselves in renewed conversation, though no longer as curious students but professionals navigating a complex world of clean energy.

The mood turned from nostalgia to anxiety as they sat down in Gopal's small and efficient office. "The market is growing," Gopal said. Gopal leaned his head forward, looking proud and exasperated at the same time. "And so do the expectations. Our production costs are increasing while each new policy brings different subsidies.

We have to remain ahead in terms of innovation as well as affordability. I know we've performed well till now, but I am very concerned about how we are to scale sustainably while maintaining quality as well as the farmers' trust."

Gopal had every reason to feel anxious. A decade of consistent growth and remarkable success of thousands of solar pump installations along India's agricultural belts, among other things, had led GK Energy to a crossroads. The company had staked out a niche by solving one of the fundamental problems of Indian agriculture: unreliable electricity. There was a huge gap when it came to electrification. When urban India continued to witness higher levels of electrification, the contrast happened in the rural villages. The unpredictable power supply was the main problem. For most farmers, three-phase electricity was essential for operating electric water pumps, and this was simply not available. Moreover, the diesel pumps were very costly and polluting (Fig. 11.1).

GK Energy had answered this challenge by providing solar-powered farm pumps, allowing thousands of farmers to irrigate their fields without the grid or fossil fuels. But even as demand increased, so did complexity. Product affordability, changing technology standards, changing government subsidies, and regulatory vagueness created layers of unpredictability on top of what was already a mission-based but capital-hungry business.

Gopal presented three crucial questions that would frame GK Energy's future:

- How can GK Energy stay competitive in a rapidly changing clean energy world dominated by innovation and scale? What is the ideal balance between cost-effective technology and affordability for rural farmers? Would the increasing pressures of scale, policy change, and cost dynamics decelerate its progress?
- For Aravind Sharma, it was no longer a casual reunion. It was an invitation. His engineering skills, business acumen, and analytical

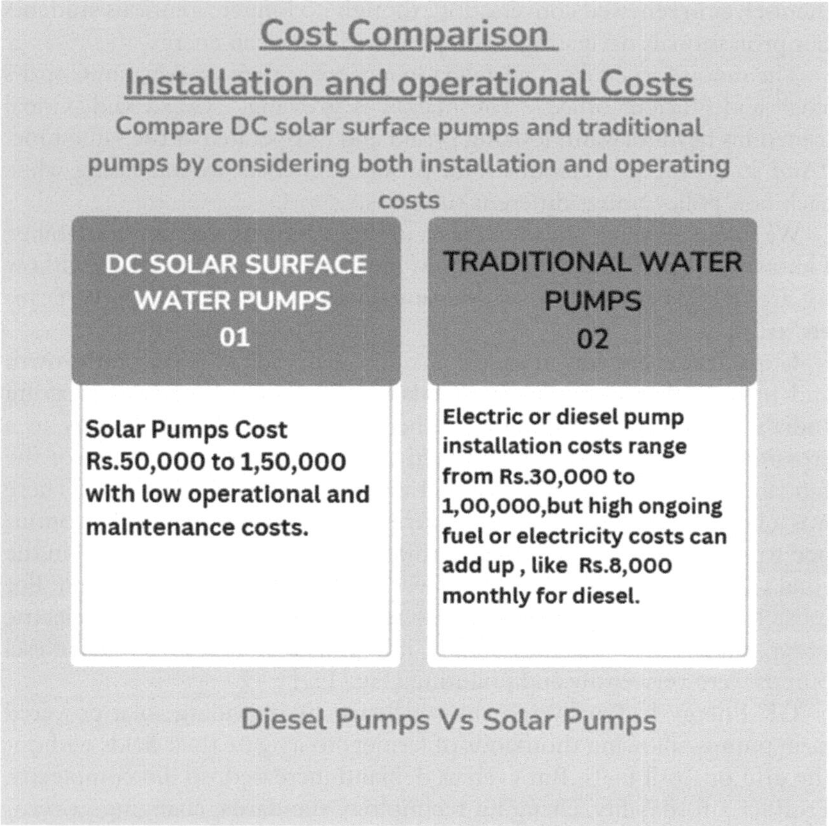

Fig. 11.1 Cost Comparison: Diesel Pumps vs. Solar Pumps

thinking were now being required to assist GK Energy through its most unprecedented chapter in history. When the sun had set below the horizon and the solar street lights outside GK Energy's office automatically lit up, a greater question hung in the air: How could this mission-based social enterprise scale up without compromising its mission? Would GK Energy keep illuminating rural India, literally and metaphorically?

Background to GK Energy

GK Energy is an India-based pioneering renewable energy company, dedicated to providing decentralized, sustainable power solutions for rural and agricultural communities, in general. Founded in 2008, the company's inception was in making solar water heaters and has since become a leading player in the clean energy sector, contributing enormously towards solar-powered irrigation and rural electrification in multiple Indian states. While promoting solar pump technology is core to GK Energy's raison d'être, the company finds itself at a key inflexion point: It has successfully installed tens of thousands of solar pumps and systems under prominent government programs such as Atal Saur Krushi Pump Yojana and PM KUSUM, but now needs to maintain these installations that it feels are moving towards financial sustainability (Table 11.1).

However, the renewables sector is becoming increasingly competitive, and GK Energy has critical challenges to overcome in cementing its position. The firm has to be careful about over-reliance on government schemes, while pushing innovation, if it is to stand up against incumbent energy majors and scrappy start-ups simultaneously in next-gen technologies such as solar storage or smart grids. These are strategic challenges facing GK Energy at a pivotal point in its market maturation, where its innovation capability will determine whether it remains competitive or still lags behind.

The venture is poised at a fork in the road, between its formidable heritage and the imperative of revolutionary change in India's fast-changing renewable energy environment. With an IPO in the offing, GK Energy is faced with the dilemma of achieving its social goal of offering cheap, clean energy to Indian farmers while keeping its finances in check.

Table 11.1 GK Energy's Solar Pump Installations (2022–2024)

Scheme	*Year 2022*	*Year 2023*	*Year 2024*	*Total installations*
PM KUSUM	6975	10,392	22,860	**40,277**
Mukhyamantri Saur Krushi pump Yojana	245	103	1043	**1391**
Magel Tyala Saur Krushi pump Yojana	413	105	642	**1160**
Total	**7633**	**10,600**	**24,545**	**42,828**

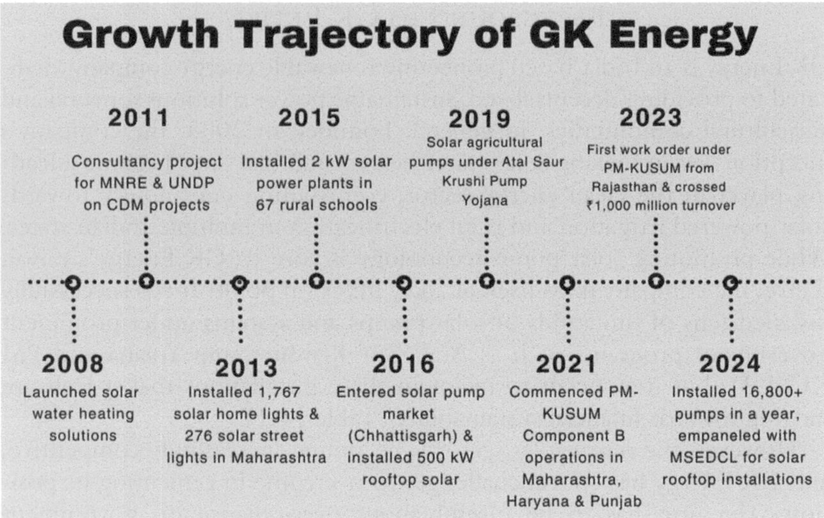

Fig. 11.2 GK Energy's Growth Trajectory

"I belong to a business family, and I did my commerce in the college stream. Right from school days, there used to be a great craze to study science, and I also received awards for a solar project. Also, in business studies, my first project report was on solar energy," Kabra added. "The Sun was always at the back of my mind, but I've learnt that communication and energy are two essential apps for the basic needs of human life."

This individual's enthusiasm was the building block for GK Energy's corporate odyssey. Its foray into solar water heaters in 2008 was the harbinger of a grander enterprise to transform India's energy landscape, a quest as pertinent as ever in the company's present strategic and financial juncture (Fig. 11.2).

Industry and Ecosystem Landscape

The Backbone of Indian Agriculture: A Sector at the Crossroads

In India, farming is not a livelihood; it's a way of life that pulses through the country's religious, economic and cultural spirit. In gold wheat fields in Punjab and rice paddy terraces in Kerala, farming is what fills not just the stomach of Indians, but identity and tradition too. Even today, this sector contributes approximately 18–20% of Gross Domestic Product (GDP) and provides the livelihood to over 50% of the Indian population. But beyond this charming landscape, a vulnerable and precarious reality lies in store. Indian agriculture is still highly susceptible to the whims and fancies of monsoons, as they remain the lines that connect millions of small and marginal farmers in India with the intensifying forces of climate change.

Farming is not for the faint-hearted in a country where a failed monsoon can mean not just missed harvests, but missed meals. Intermittent rains, longer dry periods than ever and sudden floods are now more frequent, leading to greater volatility in both crop yields and farmer incomes. These climate hazards are compounded by the small uptake of risk management tools such as crop insurance or adaptive farming technologies.

Its agriculture, even if it is one of the world's leading suppliers of commodities and exports a lot of cotton, rice and seafood, suffers from deep structural problems. Only 48% of the country's arable land is under irrigation, and only 63% of this irrigation is tube well and canal irrigation (Ministry of Statistics and Programme Implementation (MoSPI), n.d.). This form of irrigation is widespread, but quite wasteful and leads to over-extraction of groundwater.

The balance land is purely rain-fed and falls either in drought-prone or flood-affected areas. It is further strangled by fragmented land holdings, outdated farming methods and lack of access to marketing networks and storage. This has led to a fragile, inflexible infrastructure that is preventing the sustainable, climate-resilient agriculture necessary for the vast majority of rural people who are chronically insecure.

Energising Fields: The Reality

In the last decade or so, India has done reasonably well in providing electricity to rural areas. In 2014, the average was just 12.5 hours of electricity a day across the country's villages; by 2023, it had risen to almost 22.5 hours/day (Shri Manohar Lal, n.d.). This increase in coverage is due to the combined efforts of the central and state governments under initiatives like Deendayal Upadhyaya Gram Jyoti Yojana and Saubhagya.

While the extra availability is, on paper at least, an improvement, it has not resulted in a consistently better rural service for consumers. Satisfaction with the quality of power provided by state-owned utilities remains unsatisfactory, as not even 40% of rural consumers were satisfied with the quality of electricity in a 2019 report on electricity access released by Smart Power India and Initiative for Sustainable Energy Policy. So it's not just the volume of supply; it's the quality and reliability of supply.

This disparity has a massive impact on the productivity of the farming community, as power for irrigation pumps, cold storage, and crop processing is essential for the agricultural sector. The diesel-based alternatives, on the other hand, although they are widespread, are expensive and polluting. This also adds up as a handicap for the smallholder farmer.

The bottom-line issues of this reality check are those of an unreliable service, frequent outages and fluctuating voltage, the result of what amounts to a more fundamental problem: the infrastructural shortfall between electrification and usable power, which is particularly unsatisfactory at present for energy-demanding agriculture.

A Sector-Wide Crisis: Disappearing Water, Diminishing Hope

India's agricultural sector is undergoing what many analysts are calling a profound structural crisis. Agricultural growth is low, farmer incomes are not rising, and agrarian distress has become a recurring topic of policy dialogue today. The industry, which was once the epitome of India's self-reliance and food security, is now grappling with growing problems that threaten to set back decades of progress. Their concerns extend beyond the economy. There is a tremendous fear that the country will soon move from an exporter of food to a net importer of food, with unsettling implications for its stability and nutrition.

Several factors are colliding to propel this crisis:

- Growing exposure to climate change and unpredictable rains
- Liberalized import policies are compromising domestic producers
- Retraction or diminution of farm subsidies
- Widespread farm indebtedness and access to formal credit are limited
- Deterioration in public investment in rural infrastructure
- Rapid land conversion of good agricultural land for industrial and real estate purposes

The crisis is exacerbated by water shortage. India is not a water-rich country, and its agriculture has been out of sync with its hydrological realities for a long time. Groundwater over-extraction, particularly in states such as Punjab, Haryana, and Maharashtra, has assumed dangerous levels. Mismanagement of water resources, ineffective flood irrigation, and low investment in micro irrigation technologies are further compounding the problem.

Additionally, excessive focus on water-guzzling crops such as rice, wheat, and sugarcane, which account for more than 90% of crop output, has contributed to unsustainable groundwater extraction (Estimating the Productivity of India's Agricultural Waters Towards Water and Nutritional Security Through Crop Choices, n.d.). This unsustainable trend requires immediate action in water governance, diversification of crops, and investment in climate-resilient, water-efficient agricultural technologies to safeguard the future of Indian agriculture.

The Market for Solar Irrigation

The market for solar irrigation has grown significantly, and several competitors have emerged:

1. Oorja Development Solutions: Founded in 2016, this company offers "irrigation-as-a-service," in which farmers pay for each use rather than up front. More than 1000 smallholder farmers in various Indian states have been impacted by their strategy.
2. Sun Culture (since 2018): Has drawn more than $35 million in venture capital and primarily operates in Kenya and East Africa. Their RainMaker2 solar pump with Climate Smart Battery combines scheduled irrigation automation with weather insights.
3. Claro Energy (India): Developed a mobile solar pump trolley that can be moved between water sources and installed over 10,000 solar pumping systems.
4. Future Pump: This project encourages independent smallholder farmers to use portable small solar pumps and is backed by social impact investors, including the Acumen Fund. They demonstrate a 30% cost reduction using their tiny SF2 model; they have rolled out this model in 15 African countries to date, and it is significantly lower than competitive solar pumps in the sub-1 HP category (Futurepump SF2 Product, n.d.).

These innovative ventures address critical challenges faced by small farmers across the globe by offering a wide range of solutions from

Pay-per-use service to ultra-affordable solar models. The transformative potential of the solar-powered irrigation that is helping in building a resilient and climate-smart farming community is underscored by these enterprising players like Oorja, Sun Culture, Claro Energy, Future Pumps, and GK Energy.

Current Challenges and Strategic Dilemmas

The Risk of Obsolescence of Technology

An even faster rate of improvement in solar irrigation technology may put in place an obsolesce risk. Since 2020, the rate of improvement of solar PV modules' efficiency has accelerated (1.2% per annum, as opposed to only 0.6% per annum in the previous decade (Zhang et al., 2023). The rapid evolution is reshaping and redefining the solar equipment market and thereby puts a lot of pressure on the manufacturers and service providers like GK Energy to stay ahead. For small and marginal farmers, this also opens a new set of problems and paradoxes. These solar phenomena bring a bag of paradoxes, and although there are short-term prospects with an early adoption, the threat of long-term obsolescence is still real.

With the permanent solar input variance nature of pumping systems, helical rotor pumps provide 40% more water per day than conventional centrifugal pumps under similar operational circumstances. Explanation of pump science is always improving. Smart irrigation controllers and the Internet of Things are another growing trend. Mohammed et al. (2023) found that AI-optimization of irrigation schedules can save 30–45% of water while increasing or maintaining yield, depending on whether one has an AI-based or timer-based irrigation system. While the technological horizons keep growing, it remains a test for companies like GK Energy.

As evolutionary and revolutionary technology frontiers unfold from time to time, it is a challenging task for companies like GK Energy. These firms are compelled to supply technologically sound services; yet they also need to make the supply accessible to small farmers. Heavy & everlasting R&D infrastructure has become an exacting necessity because of the competitiveness that has thrived in this space.

Moreover, a lack of standardisation and interoperability issues further complicate the deployments in these rural areas.

Policy and Subsidy Volatility

Solar irrigation is an area of renewable energy that is highly conditioned by government policies and subsidies. According to the 2023 report by the Global Subsidies Initiative of the International Institute for Sustainable Development, schemes for renewables subsidies in developing countries have an "average lifetime of 4.3 years before they undergo radical revision."

Aklin and Urpelainen (2022), in a Nature Energy publication, say that election timing and political instability heavily impact renewable energy support policies, with this political risk mostly afflicting developing markets where GK Energy operates.

In March 2019, the PM-KUSUM scheme was launched with ₹344 billion by the central government, and this was a major reason that paved the way for the growth of GK Energy. The scheme has 10 GW of solar capacity installation under its four components, including 1.4 million standalone solar pump systems (Ministry of New and Renewable Energy, n.d.).

Further, there is a gap in the implementation of some central schemes by the State Electricity Boards due to the regional political dynamics. These often lead to bottlenecks and discrepancies in subsidy approvals and infrastructure readiness. Additionally, the evolving compliance norms, such as technical specifications and vendor eligibility, require constant adaptation and monitoring from the companies, leading to increased administrative costs. For GK Energy, for long-term success, it becomes imperative to build a resilient model that will help in striking a balance between agility and operational stability.

Economic Downside Risks

The solar pumping market, as a subset of the agricultural economy, is especially exposed to macroeconomic shocks and fiscal uncertainty. History demonstrates that in periods of economic decline, investments in agricultural technologies decline more than overall GDP. As de Janvry and Sadoulet (2022) note, agri-tech investment decreases by a factor of 2.3 for each one percent decline in GDP, a troubling multiplier for outfits GK Energy in Tanzania. On top of that, the currency exchange rate is a serious financial threat. Ibrahim and Odusanya (2021) note that currency exchange rate (FX) uncertainty has led to an overcost for solar projects in African markets between 18 and 27%, where the majority of the components that make up the system are imported.

In addition to these economic factors, the uncertainties generated by climate further compound the issue. Burke and Emerick (2016) show that the adoption of new capital-intensive agricultural technology is delayed by as much as 2.3 years by droughts or floods, even after taking account of publicly or privately provided subsidies. It is this clash between climate and capital constraints that hinders long-term growth and resilience in the off-grid sector. It not only brings about a delay in the critical transition to clean energy in agriculture, but it also affects the vulnerable stakeholders, the small farmers. As a result, there is an urgent need for innovative financing models, localised manufacturing, and climate-resilient planning to derisk the solar irrigation investment in these potential but risky markets.

Strategic Scaling and Growth Dilemma

Finally, GK Energy needs to consider the transformation of its business model from "Selling solar irrigation systems" to "Irrigation as a service" model, where farmers prefer to rent and use it rather than purchasing it. This would provide regular income to the company and minimize the effect on market maturity. GK Energy is assuming market saturation and projecting revenue to increase at a 50% rate in FY26, then drop that growth down to 30% in FY27 before reaching 20% in FY28. This has Arvind thinking about the various growth strategies and the trade-offs associated with them. One of the key issues GK Energy needs to weigh up is the innovation-cost trade-off. Due to the rapid maturing of AI-based smart irrigation and IoT-connected pump controllers, it stands at a crossroads: whether to heavily invest in such new technologies or continue developing its more affordable solar pump solutions? (Table 11.2).

A further major strategic issue is the expansion geographically. Having built its forte in some areas of India, GK Energy needs to consider whether it should focus more efforts in those areas or expand into other Indian states and possibly look at opportunities abroad in other developing nations.

New markets have a higher logistical, regulatory, and operational complexity, but they may also present good growth opportunities and reduce reliance on a small number of areas. On the other hand, expanding into more established markets may result in better distribution channels and increased brand affinity, but it may also restrict overall growth potential.

The third major concern is product diversification. Its business focus has mostly been on solar-powered irrigation pumps, but there is an

Table 11.2 GK Energy's Financial Parameters and Financial Projections

GK Energy Financial Parameters						*Financial Projections*		
Financial Parameter	*Units*	*FY22*	*FY23*	*FY24*	*6MFY25*	*FY 26*	*FY 27*	*FY 28*
Revenue from operations	₹ billion	0.7	2.85	4.11	4.22	6.33	8.23	9.88
Revenue from operations growth	%	NA	304.63	44.23	139.76	50%	30%	20%
Operating EBITDA	₹ billion	0.05	0.17	0.54	0.78			
Operating EBITDA margin	%	7.12	6.03	13.09	18.56			
Profit after tax (PAT)	₹ billion	0.02	0.1	0.36	0.51	0.89	1.15	1.38
Profit after tax (PAT) margin	%	2.2	3.53	8.75	12.06	14%	14%	14%
Return on equity (ROE)	%	17.08	50.73	64.49	47.72			
Return on capital employed (ROCE)	%	15.73	29.36	50.1	29.67			
Net debt to equity ratio	Times	2.3	1.93	0.94	1.5			
Total borrowings	₹ billion	0.24	0.43	0.62	2.03			
Net debt to operating EBITDA	Times	4.18	2.24	0.98	2.05			
Net working capital days	Days	113	51	80	118			
Receivable days	Days	224	144	135	135			

increasing need to consider diversifying into other rural-specific renewable energy options, such as solar lighting systems, decentralized microgrids, and solar cold storage devices. Such wider services would increase rural productivity and strengthen the financial sustainability of farmers while decreasing the company's exposure to irrigation-specific risks.

However, diversification requires huge investment in research, market training, and distribution channels, where there are concerns about resource allocation and implementation.

Strategic Options Ahead: Classroom Debate Prompts

GK Energy is at a crossroads. Which way should it go?

- Leap of Innovation or Incremental Innovation

Should GK Energy go all the way with AI-IoT-powered systems, even if it finds itself struggling with increased costs? Or would it be better to invest in improving the current technologies so that it can maintain its low prices?

- Policy Dependency or Market Autonomy

Should the company just bet all on winning more subsidies and government programs? Or should it start exploring partnerships, micro-finance models, or lease-based offerings to have a market-independent model?

- Product Focus vs. Portfolio Diversification

Should GK Energy continue as a niche solar pump leader, or should it provide rural renewable complementary solutions?

- Traditional Sales vs. Service-Oriented Model

Will a shift to "irrigation-as-a-service" help build customer loyalty and recurring revenue? Or will it strain the company's capital?

Discussion Questions

1. To maintain its position in the expanding solar irrigation market, what steps should GK Energy implement to separate itself from its market rivals?
2. Should GK Energy dedicate resources toward AI and IoT technologies for irrigation systems, or should they concentrate on lowering costs to serve more small-scale farmers instead?
3. How can GK Energy increase its agricultural energy solutions in rural areas by extending its work beyond irrigation systems?

4. What should the social enterprises learn from GK Energy's path to maintain their financial health while delivering positive social results?

Supplementary Reading

1. GK Energy Limited. (n.d.). *Official website*. https://gkenergy.in/
2. Tata Power Solar. (n.d.). *Solar water pumps*. https://www.tatapower-solar.com/solar-water-pumps/
3. GK Energy Limited. (2024, December). *Industry research report on solar equipment and renewable energy* [CRISIL Report]. https://gkenergy.in/wp-content/uploads/2024/12/CRISIL-Research_Industry-report.pdf
4. Ministry of New and Renewable Energy. (n.d.). *National portal for PM-KUSUM*. https://pmkusum.mnre.gov.in/landing.html [pmkusum.mnre.gov.in]
5. Uttar Pradesh New and Renewable Energy Development Agency. (n.d.). *PM-KUSUM C-1 Scheme portal*. https://pmkusum.up.gov.in/
6. Punjab Energy Development Agency. (n.d.). *Benefits of solar pump for farmers*. https://www.peda.gov.in/benefits-of-solar-pump-for-farmers
7. Verma, S., and Shah, T. (2022). "India's Energy-Groundwater Nexus and Solar Irrigation Pumps," Environmental Research Letters
8. Chandel, R., Naik, M. N., and Chandel, S. S. (2023). "Evaluation of solar photovoltaic water pumping system technology for community drinking water supplies and irrigation," Reviews of Sustainable and Renewable Energy.

Learning Objectives

- Understanding the Role of Renewable Energy in Agriculture—Explore the critical challenges in irrigation and rural development that can be addressed through solar energy.
- Analysing Entrepreneurial Leadership—Examine how GK Energy has developed the strategies to capitalize as a market leader in solar energy.
- Evaluating the Impact of Government Policies on Entrepreneurship: Analyse how policies like PM-KUSUM have promoted sustainable agriculture solutions.
- Exploring Innovation and Technology in Business Growth—Investigate how AI and IoT integration can enhance the efficiency and effectiveness of renewable energy solutions in agriculture.

Competing Interests The authors have no conflicts of interest to declare that are relevant to the content of this chapter.

References

Aklin, M., & Urpelainen, J. (2022). Political instability and effectiveness of renewable energy policies in developing countries. *Nature Energy, 7*(5), 409–417. https://doi.org/10.1038/s41560-022-00991-7

Burke, M., & Emerick, K. (2016). Adaptation to climate change: Evidence from US agriculture. *American Economic Journal: Economic Policy, 8*(3), 106–140. https://doi.org/10.1257/pol.20130025

de Janvry, A., & Sadoulet, E. (2022). The puzzle of lagging sub-Saharan Africa agriculture: Toward a theory of connectedness. In H. de Gorter, J. McCluskey, J. Swinnen, & D. Zilberman (Eds.), *Modern agricultural and resource economics and policy* (Vol. 55). Springer.

Estimating the Productivity of India's Agricultural Waters Towards Water and Nutritional Security Through Crop Choices. (n.d.). https://www.orfonline.org/research/estimating-the-productivity-of-india-s-agricultural-waters-towards-water-and-nutritional-security-through-crop-choices

Futurepump SF2 Product. (n.d.). Engineering for Change. https://www.engineeringforchange.org/solutions/product/futurepump-sf2

GK Energy Limited. (n.d.). Initial Public Offering. Securities and Exchange Board of India. https://www.sebi.gov.in/filings/public-issues/dec-2024/gk-energy-limited.

Ibrahim, A. A., & Odusanya, I. A. (2021). Financial Integration and Growth Outcomes in Africa: Experience of the Trade Blocs. African Governance and Development Institute Working Paper Series, WP/21/052. Online: https://ideas.repec.org/p/agd/wpaper/21-052.html

Ministry of New and Renewable Energy. (n.d.). Pradhan Mantri KisanUrja Suraksha evamUtthanMahabhiyan (PM-KUSUM). https://mnre.gov.in/en/pradhan-mantri-kisan-urja-suraksha-evam-utthaan-mahabhiyan-pm-kusum/

Ministry of Statistics and Programme Implementation (MoSPI). (n.d.). Chapter 12: Irrigation. Source: https://www.mospi.gov.in/sites/default/files/Statistical_year_book_india_chapters/Irrigation.pdf

Mohammed, M., Hamdoun, H., & Sagheer, A. (2023). Implementing artificial intelligence to predict optimum water and energy requirements for sensor-based micro irrigation systems powered by solar PV. *Agronomy, 13*(4), 1081. https://doi.org/10.3390/agronomy1304108

Shri Manohar Lal. (n.d.). Average Electricity Supply in Rural Areas Has Increased from 12.5 Hours in 2014 to 22.6 Hours in 2025 and in Urban Areas to 23.4 Hours in 2025. https://www.eqmagpro.com/average-electricity-supply-in-rural-areas-has-increased-from-12-5-hours-in-2014-to-22-6-hours-in-2025-and-in-urban-areas-to-23-4-hours-in-2025-shri-manohar-lal-eq

Zhang, Y., Kumar, P., Rao, N. D., & Singh, R. (2023). Technological Progress in solar PV modules: Trends and implications for energy access. *Renewable and Sustainable Energy Reviews, 169*, 113072. https://doi.org/10.1016/j.rser.2022.113072

CHAPTER 12

Shivganga Samagra Gramvikas Parishad: Bridging Indigenous Community Mobilization and Entrepreneurship

Sujay Dixit, Satyajit Majumdar, and Sreevas Sahasranamam

Abstract Shivganga Samagra Gramvikas Parishad was founded by Padmashree Mahesh Sharma Ji and Harsh Chauhan Ji as a grassroots community mobilization initiative that aimed at restoring the self-confidence of indigenous (tribal) communities in Jhabua, Madhya Pradesh. While initially focused on collective action around local problems like water scarcity and forest conservation, the founders recognized that long-term transformation required more than mobilization—it demanded economic independence. To break the cycle of seasonal migration to cities in search of manual labour, they envisioned fostering local entrepreneurship that is

S. Dixit (✉) • S. Majumdar
TISS Incube Foundation, Mumbai, India
e-mail: sujay@tissincubefoundation.com; satyajit@tissincubefoundation.com

S. Sahasranamam
Adam Smith Business School, University of Glasgow, Glasgow, UK
e-mail: sreevas.sahasranamam@glasgow.ac.uk

A. S. Galande et al. (eds.), *Context-inspired Entrepreneurship*, Sustainable Development Goals Series,
https://doi.org/10.1007/978-981-95-9831-1_12

rooted in indigenous knowledge and community needs. However, the pathway to enabling such bottom-up livelihood creation was unclear, presenting the strategic dilemma for discussion in this case. This case is well-suited for classroom discussions on community-led venturing, social entrepreneurship, and indigenous knowledge-inspired business models.

Keywords Community-based enterprise • Social entrepreneurship • Indigenous communities • Tribal India

SDG Links The case contributes to SDG 8: Decent Work and Economic Growth by demonstrating how rural entrepreneurship rooted in indigenous knowledge can support rural livelihoods and productive economic activity. By highlighting sustainable natural resource management and water conservation, the case also contributes to SDG 6 and SDG 15.

Introduction

On a quiet morning in early 2017, outside Rishi Bhavan in the heart of Jhabua, Mahesh Sharma ji—widely regarded as the Gandhi of Jhabua and a recipient of the Padma Shri, India's fourth highest civilian honour—sat sipping his customary cup of tea. Across from him sat Harsh Chauhan ji, co-founder of Shivganga Samagra Gramvikas Parishad, a non-profit social enterprise working for the development of indigenous communities in Jhabua. The two men had worked side by side for over a decade.

The familiar Jhabua air around them still reverberated with chants and sounds of an awakened indigenous community from a Halma, a community gathering that Shivganga had organized a couple of weeks back. The Halma involved a massive voluntary community mobilization for water conservation. Voluntary labour for common good had become a source of pride rather than compulsion. Rituals and cultural values that once appeared destined for extinction were now celebrated as foundations of resilience. It was perhaps one of the rare examples in India where cultural revival had preceded economic development—and not the other way around. Quite clearly, the movement they spearheaded was demonstrably empowering the local tribal community, building social capital and confidence among them.

They had mastered the art of mobilizing the community for collective action around local problems like water scarcity and forest conservation. However, they knew that mobilization alone wouldn't secure the community's future. The community needed to achieve economic independence to move away from the cycle of migration to cities every year during the lean agricultural season in search of manual work (*'maz-doori ki majboori'*). Mahesh Sharma ji and Harsh Chauhan ji were acutely aware of the fundamental paradox: Mobilization had restored confidence, solidarity and environmental stewardship; however, confidence without income could not secure dignity—at least not in the long run.

They had an idea in mind—If Shivganga's philosophy was truly grounded in swabhiman (self-esteem) and swavalamban (self-reliance), then livelihoods and entrepreneurship had to become a central pillar of the movement. Yet, they were unsure of the path to doing it. This was not about social engineering anymore, but rather about business skills, financial management, and market links—a fundamentally different domain for the community. As they sipped their tea, they were discussing this strategic dilemma in preparation for an upcoming community gathering of tribal youth:

> *How could Shivganga, an organization built on indigenous community mobilization, effectively*
> *uplift the people of Jhabua, while maintaining its core collectivization principles?*

This tension between cultural integrity and economic aspiration, between voluntarism and entrepreneurship, lies at the heart of the Shivganga case. To appreciate the strategic dilemma fully, it is essential to understand how Shivganga emerged, how its philosophy evolved, and how it is situated in the contemporary landscape of tribal development and tribal entrepreneurship in India.

The Genesis and Evolution of Shivganga

The Founder's Journey: Mahesh Sharma Ji's Early Years and Philosophical Formation

The story of Shivganga cannot be separated from the personal journey of its founder. Mahesh Sharma Ji was born in Ghughsi village, Datia district, in a household of six brothers. Right from his formative years in Gwalior he was actively involved in social service through participation in student councils. His early association with Rashtriya Swayamsevak Sangh (RSS) got him deeply engaged in grassroots mobilization, community welfare and the foundational notion that social transformation must rise from within rather than arrive from outside.

These ideological foundations - self-reliance, collective duty, and the centrality of indigenous knowledge—would later become core to Shivganga's approach. What distinguished Mahesh ji's philosophy from mainstream development discourse was his conviction that communities possessed not only problems to be solved, but also assets to be unlocked. This insight would profoundly shape his work in tribal India.

Immersion in Bhil Heartland (1998–2003): Founder's Transition from an Observer to Leader

In 1998, Mahesh ji moved to Jhabua, one of India's most socio-economically challenged tribal districts (a map of the Jhabua region is provided in Fig. 12.1). Jhabua is home predominantly to the Bhil community—proud, culturally rich and historically self-sufficient, yet battered by decades of ecological deterioration, shrinking livelihoods and structural neglect. As General Secretary of the Forest Residents Welfare Council, Mahesh ji spent five crucial years living in villages, walking long distances through forested pathways, staying with tribal families and observing the rhythms of life from close quarters.

During this immersion period, he began understanding their challenges firsthand. He identified pressing issues such as water scarcity, deforestation, seasonal migration, and socio-economic struggles. During this time, he also built strong relationships with tribal families and gained their trust.

In this process, he observed untapped potential. He encountered deep ecological knowledge passed down through generations, strong kinship bonds that organized reciprocal labour, fierce community loyalty, and an ingrained ethic of sharing and mutual responsibility. What was missing was not talent or motivation, but social capital and confidence. This insight challenged the dominant development narrative of the time, which often blamed tribal communities for their own poverty. Instead, Mahesh ji understood that structural neglect, historical exploitation, and repeated failed interventions had eroded the community's belief in its own capacity for change. Through continuous engagement, he began empowering the villagers to acknowledge their strengths and explore solutions rooted in their own traditions.

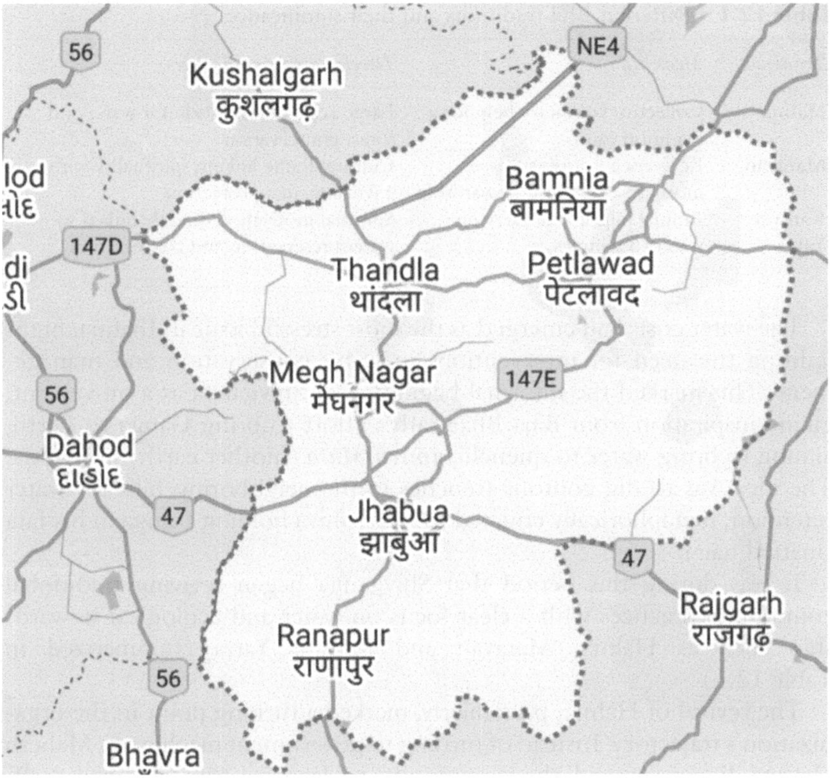

Fig. 12.1 Map of Jhabua district

A Turning Point: Revival of Community Traditions (2005)

By 2005, Mahesh Sharma Ji, along with Shri Harsh Chouhan Ji, a tribal himself, and other tribal social leaders, began organizing training camps for youths in Jhabua. These gatherings were not skill-workshops in the conventional professional sense; they were platforms for collective reflection and shared visioning. They gave young people a space to articulate the pain points of their communities—water scarcity, disappearances of forests, loss of cultural memory, family fragmentation due to migration, alcoholism and dependency on external patronage.

Table 12.1 Different Bhil traditions and their significance

Tradition	*Meaning*	*Development significance*
Halma	Collective voluntary help for a common cause	Large-scale mobilization for water and forest conservation
Matavan	Reverence for forests as mother - ecological stewardship	Cultural frame linking spirituality with environmental protection
Kanwar Yatra	Annual pilgrimage carrying water to temples	Spiritual motivation directly linked to water preservation and conservation

The water crisis had emerged as the most stressful issue in Jhabua, highlighting the need for interventions in water conservation and management. This marked the informal beginning of Shivganga as a movement, taking inspiration from Raja Bhagirath's effort to bring Ganga to Earth, aiming to bring water to quench *Jameen Mata* (mother earth) of Jhabua. The idea was to dig contour trenches in the neighboring hills for water retention, metaphorically equated to Lord Shiva holding Ganga in his Jata (matted hair).

It was during this period that Shivganga began reviving traditional community practices with a clear focus on water and ecological stewardship such as Halma, Matavan and Kanwar Yatra (summarized in Table 12.1).

The revival of Halma, particularly, marked a turning point in the organization's trajectory. Instead of turning to government machinery, Mahesh Sharma Ji encouraged the community to lean on Swavalamban (self-reliance) and revive the tradition of Halma, where community members unconditionally helped one another in large collective tasks.

When an annual Halma call was made for large-scale community projects like water or forest conservation, thousands of community members came together, providing for their own travel and contributing a small fee towards managing the event, indicating their commitment to the cause. The collective voluntary help began to attract very large scale participation that surprised even Mahesh ji and Harsh ji.

This meant entire hillsides were covered with contour trenches in a single day, storing water and regenerating landscapes that had been degraded by decades of neglect. See photos from different Halma efforts in Figs. 12.2, 12.3, 12.4, and 12.5. It was one of the rare instances where development happened without funding—powered only by belief, pride and collective purpose.

Fig. 12.2 Photograph of a Halma gathering digging contour trenches

The Halma movement restored three critical psychological and social foundations: pride (in tribal identity and community capability), ownership (over community resources and decisions), and confidence (that collective action could produce tangible results). These three elements became the psychological bedrock upon which Shivganga's later interventions would rest.

Formal Establishment of Shivganga Samagra Gramvikas Parishad (2007)

By 2007, the scale and momentum of the of grassroots work demanded more structure and legal organizing, leading to the formal registration of Shivganga Samagra Gramvikas Parishad under the Madhya Pradesh Society Registration Act. Importantly, the new organization did not drift toward a conventional NGO model focused on service delivery. Instead, formal

Fig. 12.3 Photograph of a mountain after contour trenching

Fig. 12.4 Photograph of Halma gatherings where trees are replanted

Fig. 12.5 Photograph of a mass gathering in preparation for a Halma

structures were created to protect and amplify the grassroots philosophy rather than replace it.

Shivganga expanded gradually into five mutually reinforcing domains, each designed not merely to deliver services but to increase the community's self-confidence and self-reliance:

1. Water Conservation: Large scale contour trenching, watershed management projects and earthen dams
2. Community Leadership Training: Training for tribal youth to become social leaders to carry forward development initiatives
3. Healthcare Initiatives: The Arogya Rath (Mobile Medical Unit) providing healthcare access to people across villages
4. Cultural Exchange Programmes: Bridging gaps between tribal and urban communities through initiatives such as *Image vs Reality*, where students from IITs, IIMs, and TISS interact with tribal communities
5. Environmental regeneration: Reviving community forests and village ecological stewardship

A timeline of key activities is provided in Fig. 12.6.

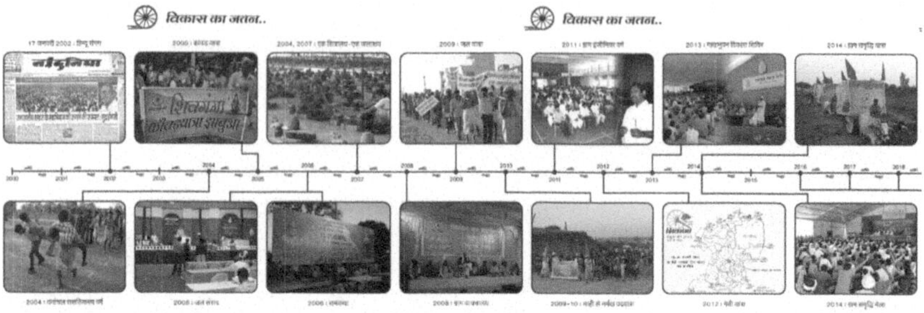

Fig. 12.6 Timeline of key activities in Shivganga's journey (Original image shared by the organization was adapted for purposes of this case study)

The Philosophical Foundation of Shivganga—Four-Stage Development Model

Shivganga's work is anchored in a distinctive four-stage progression model that clarifies how individual and community transformation must unfold, as summarized in Table 12.2.

This framework clarifies something that development researchers often miss: economic outcomes are not the starting point of transformation—they are the culmination. Conventional development practice often reverses this sequence, introducing livelihood programmes or microfinance without first addressing convergence of psychological readiness, social cohesion, and cultural foundations.

The implications are profound: Livelihood programmes fail if they are not layered upon restored self-belief and community cohesion. A person without confidence will not take entrepreneurial risks. A fractured community cannot sustain collective enterprises. A community that has lost faith in its own potential will not invest effort in uncertain ventures. Shivganga's four-stage model turns this logic on its head: create the psychological and social foundation first, then livelihood programmes become catalysts rather than impositions.

This philosophy shaped Shivganga's slow, organic, culturally anchored expansion over the years. However, it also created an inevitable next step. If the movement was to honor its own internal logic, Swavalamban (self-reliance) had to eventually take economic form. The question was never whether entrepreneurship should happen, but when and how.

Table 12.2 Four stage development model of Shivganga

Stage	*Hindi/Sanskrit Term*	*Meaning*	*Outcome*
Stage 1	Parmarth	Serving others without expectation of personal reward	Creation of a spirit of contribution and collective purpose
Stage 2	Swabhiman	Pride, self-esteem and recognition of one's own worth and dignity	Development of inner confidence and belief in one's capacity
Stage 3	Swavalamban	Self-reliance and the ability to sustain oneself and one's community economically	Capacity for economic independence and sustainable livelihoods
Stage 4	Sustainable development	Holistic progress encompassing economic, social, environmental and cultural dimensions	Long-term prosperity that honors both material and non-material needs

To understand the next phase of Shivganga's journey, it is necessary to situate the organization within the socio-economic landscape of tribal communities in India.

The Context of Tribal India and Tribal Entrepreneurship

More than 8.6% of India's population belongs to Scheduled Tribes, yet tribal regions consistently rank among the lowest in income (average income 30–50% below national average), literacy, and health indicators (Kijima, 2006; Kumar et al., 2020). The paradox is striking: regions rich in natural resources and indigenous knowledge remain economically marginalized.

Key structural constraints affecting tribal entrepreneurship include:

- Geographic Remoteness: Limited infrastructure, poor road connectivity, restricted market access
- Financial Exclusion: Low access to capital, weak relationships with formal banking institutions, high collateral requirements
- Informational Gaps: Limited exposure to external networks, markets, and technology
- Institutional Disruption: Historical erosion of community governance systems and collective decision-making structures

- Skill Mismatches: Education systems that devalue indigenous knowledge and prepare youth for external labour markets rather than local enterprise

However, the tribal economy also contains powerful, underutilized advantages that represent the foundation for alternative development pathways:

- Strong Reciprocity Networks: Deep trust relationships and informal credit systems rooted in kinship
- Ecological Knowledge: Intimate understanding of local ecosystems, climate patterns, soil conditions, and sustainable resource management
- Artisanal Traditions: Rich heritage of craft and natural material processing (textiles, bamboo, lac, pottery)
- Collective Identity: Strong sense of group cohesion and willingness to work for community benefit
- Demographic Dividend: Large youth population with energy, education, and desire for better futures

By early 2010s, a shift had begun across policy, NGO, and academic discourse: from viewing tribal communities as beneficiaries of development to viewing them as stakeholders in value creation (mostly through entrepreneurial route). This shift began to recognize tribal capabilities and acknowledged the limitations of top-down development models. This began to shape support structures for developing tribal entrepreneurship such as:

- Farming: Cooperative farming models such as Farmer Producer Organizations began getting supported by National Bank for Agriculture and Rural Development in 2011. This supported models such as Sahyadri Farms in Nashik, which began gaining traction.
- Artisans: Companies like FabIndia began creating community-owned companies by 2007, the first one being Rangasutra. This made artisans and tribal communities shareholders, and making them active participants in the development process.
- Retails outlets: Through initiatives like Tribes India retail outlets for tribal crafts getting popular in cities, giving tribal craftsmen market linkages.

- Tribal tourism: Eco-tourism began getting promoted by state governments in tribal regions such as Araku Valley and Madumalai, creating opportunities for tourism linked tribal entrepreneurship.

Such efforts began to directly influence Shivganga's thinking and strategic choices.

Shivganga at a Strategic Inflection Point

Unlike many other tribal entrepreneurship efforts in India, where entrepreneurship and market logic get imposed before building the psychological and social foundations necessary for it, by 2017, Shivganga had deliberate foundation-building within the community. This involved:

- Voluntary Collective Action: Communities have demonstrated capacity for mobilising thousands without financial incentives through Halma
- Village-Level Governance Structures: Halma committees and youth leadership groups provided organizational infrastructure
- Youth Motivation and Engagement: Young people are actively participating and seeking economic opportunity
- Reclaimed Cultural Identity: Tribal culture was celebrated rather than hidden through Kanwar Yatra and other festivals. Their traditions were consciously revived
- High Social Capital and Trust: Networks of reciprocity and mutual obligation remained strong

However, the transition into entrepreneurship came with multiple potentially destabilizing risks that could undermine what has been carefully built, as summarized in Table 12.3.

Thinking of these risks from an prospective young tribal entrepreneurs' perspective, Mahesh ji and Harsh ji, saw several dynamics that could come into play:

- Profit Distribution: Economic returns may be reinvested in the business or for private use, how would community be factored in it?
- Cultural authenticity: Markets often demand standardization and branding that may feel inauthentic to community members or distort the cultural meaning of products

Table 12.3 Risks associated with transition to entrepreneurship

Existing strength of Shivganga	*Potential risk during livelihood transition*
Collectivism and shared decision-making	Entrepreneurship may encourage individualism and competition; profit motives may erode collective spirit
Voluntary participation and intrinsic motivation	Market incentives may change motivations; participation may become transactional rather than relational
Cultural pride and identity	Commercial pressure to "modernize" and adopt non-tribal branding may dilute authenticity
Community-controlled decision-making	Dependence on external experts (bankers, consultants, markets) may shift power away from communities
Slow, organic, locally-driven growth	Markets demand speed, consistency, standardization; local rhythms may be incompatible with commercial timelines
Emphasis on relationships and solidarity	Formalization of contracts and market relationships may replace mutual, relational trust

- Competitive Dynamics: If multiple entrepreneurs from the community are interested in the same sector and similar opportunity, competition may emerge. How will this fit with collectivisation principles of Halma?
- Time Allocation: Entrepreneurs will need to invest personal time and effort into the venture and this could reduce availability for community activities like Halma gatherings or youth training
- Power dynamics: Successful entrepreneurs would gain resources and influence. But will it be accessible to all and benefits existing networks and relationships or will it create new forms of inequality within the community as was the case with land previously? Also, some of these resources needed would external (e.g., banks, traders) and will it shift agency and power away from community to external actors.

In essence, these were not peripheral concerns and could strike at the heart of whether Shivganga can maintain its philosophical coherence while embracing entrepreneurship.

The Strategic Options before Shivganga

As Mahesh Sharma ji and Harsh Chauhan ji contemplated the future, they recognized three fundamentally different pathways forward, each with distinct benefits and risks:

Option 1: Expert Partnership Model—Engaging with External Institutions (E.G., TISS)

A compelling option was to forge a partnership with a reputed academic institution like TISS, which was already offering a social entrepreneurship training programme. Shivganga could leverage TISS's expertise in curriculum design, training, and business skills.

Prospective Benefits:

- Access to proven curriculum and training methodologies developed in academic settings
- Academic institute like TISS comes with a background of developing social sector changemakers over a number of years, a powerful alumni network
- Institutional legitimacy that could attract external funding and donor support
- Professional business training in financial management, marketing, and operations
- Potential for rigorous documentation and research that could scale the model
- Reduced internal capacity-building burden on Shivganga staff

Key Risks:

- Dependency on external partners and Shivganga's autonomy may be compromised
- Community may perceive training as "top-down" despite Shivganga involvement, reducing ownership
- External curricula may not be culturally adapted and could risk of imposing urban business logic onto tribal contexts eroding their core values
- Uncertainty over the duration for which the support will be needed: Will partnership be temporary or permanent? When does dependency end?
- Power dynamics: Will community members become subjects of academic study rather than partners in design?
- Uncertainty about whether internal organizational capacities for entrepreneurship support will be built over time

Critical Question: How can external expertise be leveraged without recreating the "expert-knows-best" development paradigm that Shivganga was originally created to overcome?

Option 2: Organic Growth Model—Community-Led Enterprise Development

This approach involved building entrepreneurship support, leveraging existing Shivganga networks—engaging self-help groups and creating micro-clusters for agri-based or handicraft products. This will support entrepreneurs to emerge organically from within the community.

Prospective Benefits:

- Maximum community ownership with no dependency on external partners
- Entrepreneurship support aligned perfectly with Shivganga's grassroots philosophy
- Business models grounded in indigenous knowledge, local resources, and community needs
- Risk of cultural dilution minimized as the enterprises will be designed by and for the community
- Builds internal institutional capacity helping Shivganga become a hub of entrepreneurial knowledge

Key Risks:

- Slow progress: organic growth may be too gradual to meet community economic needs urgently
- Weak market linkages: Entrepreneurs may produce excellent products but lack channels to reach buyers
- Limited business expertise within the community could risk wasted resources and failure of enterprises
- Risk of repeated failure eroding community confidence and willingness to try new ventures

Critical Question: Can community members develop sufficient business acumen quickly enough to create viable enterprises, or will multiple failures discourage further entrepreneurial attempts?

Option 3: Focussed Sectoral Development

This involved identifying sectors of entrepreneurial potential within Jhabua (e.g., organic agriculture or traditional crafts) and channeling training of the youth (Paramarthis) into these sectors. Further, complement the specialized training with market linkages, and financial support concentrated on a few high-potential areas, and draw on external networks where needed in those specific areas.

Prospective Benefits:

- Focusing the resources on to a few high-potential activities creates efficiency
- Specialization allows for deeper expertise development and professional support
- Higher probability of quick wins—focus on creating a couple of community-led ventures to serve as role models in chosen sectors to create visible momentum and confidence
- Draw on sectoral external experience and financial support (e.g., government schemes, donor funding, market partnerships)
- Sectoral networks (e.g., organic farmers association, handicraft clusters) can create peer learning possibilities

Key Risks:

- Risk of ignoring diverse interests in the community, as sectoral choices may not match individual aspirations
- Dependence on a one or two sectors creates economic vulnerability. If the sector fails or is too seasonal (e.g., tourism) livelihoods could collapse
- Wasted effort and resources if sectoral choice proves commercially unviable
- Loss of collective ethos - sectoral specialization may fragment community unity in silos
- Risk of creating beneficiary dependency on specific external schemes or programmes

Critical Question: How can sectoral focus be pursued without narrowing opportunities and creating new forms of economic vulnerability?

Discussion Questions

1. How could social or community venturing emanate from social movements?
2. How does the shift to venturing conflict with original values? Can economic aspirations and indigenity genuinely co-exist? Or is some dilution of Shivganga's original values an inevitable cost of economic development?
3. Can entrepreneurship strengthen rather than weaken the value of Parmarth (service and collective good)? Or does the introduction of markets fundamentally change the spirit of participation?
4. How should Shivganga evaluate trade-offs among the three strategic options to sustain long-term impact?
5. If they work with external partners, how can such relationships be structured to ensure equitable power dynamics and cultural sensitivity?
6. What metrics should Shivganga use to evaluate success? Traditional business metrics (profit, growth, market share) or alternative metrics (community satisfaction, cultural vitality, social cohesion)?

Supplementary Reading

- Korsgaard, S., Müller, S., & Tanvig, H. W. (2015). *Rural entrepreneurship or entrepreneurship in the rural–between place and space. International Journal of Entrepreneurial Behavior & Research, 21(1)*, 5–26.
- Peredo, A. M., & Chrisman, J. J. (2006). *Toward a theory of community-based enterprise. Academy of Management Review, 31(2)*, 309–328.

Learning Outcomes/Objectives

By engaging with this case, students will be able to:

1. Understand how community-based enterprises can emerge from grassroots social movements
2. Analyze strategic decision-making in hybrid social organizations balancing collectivist values and entrepreneurship
3. Evaluate partnership models and stakeholder engagement strategies in culturally rooted contexts
4. Critique conventional development approaches and articulate alternative paradigms centered on cultural integrity and community agency

Acknowledgements The authors would like to thank Mahesh Sharma ji, Harsh Chauhan ji, Nitin Dhakad ji, Rajendra Dindod ji, and Shivganga Samagra Gramvikas Parishad team for their time towards interviews and warm hospitality in hosting us for field visits, which helped in the preparation of this case. The text is written entirely by the authors, though we had taken help from Gemini 2.5 and Microsoft Co-pilot in improving the styling of the draft in certain parts.

Competing Interests The authors have no conflicts of interest to declare that are relevant to the content of this chapter.

References

Kijima, Y. (2006). Caste and tribe inequality: Evidence from India, 1983–1999. *Economic Development and Cultural Change, 54*(2), 369–404.

Kumar, M. M., Pathak, V. K., & Ruikar, M. (2020). Tribal population in India: A public health challenge and road to future. *Journal of Family Medicine and Primary Care, 9*(2), 508–512.

CHAPTER 13

Empowering Small and Medium Enterprises Through Digital Enablement: The Case of DIGIIT

Anuradha Sharma and R. Srinivasan

Abstract India's digital ecosystem is rapidly advancing and pushing growth in the regional, agricultural and Small and Medium Enterprise (SME) sector. A large part of it is being driven by India's Digital Public Infrastructure (DPI) movement. This case study examines DIGIIT, which began its digital operations as a SaaS provider and later leveraged DPI to customise solutions for sector-specific challenges. This study observes DIGIIT's journey and the impact of environmental factors like the COVID pandemic and India's digital transformation on its evolution. It studies how DIGIIT leveraged the changes to create solutions for the obstacles hampering its growth and expansion. The journey also describes how pivoting helped enhance its business proposition and aided in refining its business model for fulfilling its larger mission and vision. DIGIIT's story helps explore and understand concepts like first-mover advantage and network effects as applicable to India's current digital economy, while

A. Sharma (✉) • R. Srinivasan
IIM Bangalore, Bengaluru, India
e-mail: anuradha.sharma22@iimb.ac.in; srini@iimb.ac.in

A. S. Galande et al. (eds.), *Context-inspired Entrepreneurship*, Sustainable Development Goals Series,
https://doi.org/10.1007/978-981-95-9831-1_13

showcasing how business ventures can leverage proprietary business tools in combination with public resources like the DPI to obtain both commercial gains and societal outcomes.

Keywords Digital enablement • Digitalisation • Digital public infrastructure (DPI) • Networks • Social outcomes • Platforms • COVID-19

SDG Links This chapter is aligned with SDG 8: Decent Work and Economic Growth, examining how DIGIIT leverages digital public infrastructure to enable the digital transformation of small and medium enterprises. The chapter is also aligned with SDG 9, through its focus on industry, innovation, and digital infrastructure, and relates to SDG 10 by promoting digital inclusion for underserved businesses.

Karthikeyan Arumugam (Karthik) founded DIGIIT (http://digiit.ai) in his hometown, Trichy, in the state of Tamil Nadu, close to a decade ago (in 2015). Though it had a different purpose and scope, the enterprise and the founders had pivoted enough to reach where they were in early 2025. Karthik had been selected for incubation in the Velocity programme at the NSRCEL[1] Indian Institute of Management, Bangalore's (IIMB) entrepreneurship centre & incubator. As part of the programme, NSRCEL had organised a demo day (a match-making fair between investors and enterprises/founders), and Karthik was flying into Bangalore to attend the same. He knew that he would meet potential investors who would be interested in what he was doing. Along with the value that he was adding/capturing, many of them would also be interested in the past (evolution of the enterprise) and the future (sustainability of the enterprise). He needed to have his strategy, business plans, and impact metrics ready.

On the long drive from the airport to NSRCEL (IIMB), Karthik was reminiscing about his entrepreneurial journey—from being a consultant to DIGIIT's co-founder, and the journey of DIGIIT, which was nowhere near predictably linear. What started as a training centre to improve youth employability went on to create a large-scale industrial impact while promoting digital enablement in India's Small and Medium Enterprises through India's digital public infrastructures (DPIs). DIGIIT had achieved multiple milestones in a few years and made its name in both public and

[1] Velocity - Kotak BizLabs: Incubation Program for Revenue Stage Startups | NSRCEL

private sector initiatives. It had also transformed and expanded into new sectors and geographies, enabling multiple business segments which needed new digital capabilities. The impact that DIGIIT had created by helping small businesses use digital platforms was both social and commercial, and aligned very well with DIGIIT's vision and mission.

Seeding of the Idea

When the COVID-19 pandemic struck in 2020, Karthikeyan Arumugham (Karthik) already had a well-established Learning Centre at the Indian city of Trichy with more than 15,000 students enrolled for learning multiple skills through SMACT (Social, Mobile, Analytics, Cloud, and Internet of Things). He and his well-trained and knowledgeable team were in contact with colleges, which provided them a large student base from Trichy and neighbouring districts of Perambalur, Ariyalur, and Thanjavur in the Indian state of Tamil Nadu. They conducted workshops and presentations in colleges where graduates from all disciplines used to attend. Their mentorship and learning programmes (started in 2015 as a means of Karthik's giving back to his home district) helped the students apply theoretical knowledge to practical, real-world scenarios. Identifying the gap between classroom teaching and practical learning, Karthik and his team aimed to make these students employable through their hands-on learning programme. Karthik was joined by Sivakumar Thiyagarrajan (Siva), an old acquaintance, who led the business on the ground in India, while Karthik provided contributions from Singapore, where he also continued as a full-time consultant. The classes were conducted in-person, either at the Trichy learning centre or at different college campuses. Karthik and Siva developed the curriculum and teaching programmes for colleges and also created the latest tech-based products and prototypes with the students for college presentations.

The programme gradually got converted into a hybrid business model in 2017, where the founders used their technological expertise from their consulting and product development backgrounds. They envisioned the Learning Centre as a digital platform that connected employers, institutions, and students. The learning programmes developed into mini businesses by letting the students apply their knowledge in the market and become job-ready. They also started supplying these resources to both local businesses and MNCs for a fee, which generated revenue for the centre. These revenue streams, though not steady and sustainable in the long term, were still instrumental in scaling up their learning programmes and providing some subsidies/compensation to the learners. The next obvious step was to scale the business and enter into new geographies.

COVID-19 struck India in early 2020, and the entire learning and skilling industry came to a standstill. The Indian government declared a lockdown,[2] which resulted in a large number of students shifting back to their native places, which led to a drop in attendance at the Learning Centre. The education system of the country frantically went online, and so did Karthik's learning programmes. They finished the programmes that were mid-way, but realised that continuing the classes online did not seem viable. Many of the students, especially those from rural areas, lacked devices like smartphones and stable internet connections. Difficulties in reaching out to students, persistent connectivity issues, and problems in sharing study materials online did not work out for the centre.

On the other hand, the COVID-19 pandemic was proving to be a catalyst in the adoption and implementation of new innovative technologies in industries, especially in a country like India.[3] As businesses went either online or hybrid, online sales in India saw a huge boost across multiple sectors.[4] This, coupled with several government initiatives since 2016[5] had nudged India towards a technologically robust and innovative path. The entire scenario forced Karthik and others to think about pivoting. But pivoting required new ideas, a new set of resources, a new stream of capital inflow, and an overhaul of their entire entrepreneurial strategy. Given that the entire world had migrated to online solutions, Karthik and Siva decided to do the same.

Founding of the Enterprise: LDT Programme - Networking, Mentoring, and New Business Ideas

Karthik and Siva had known each other since 2005, when they were colleagues at Credit Suisse Bank in Singapore. Karthik moved out of the bank in 2008 and focused on consulting roles where he developed niche expertise in Business Application Technology Consulting and Professional

[2] Press Release: Press Information Bureau

[3] How COVID-19 Has Accelerated The Digital Transformation Of Industries | nasscom | The Official Community of Indian IT Industry

[4] India: COVID-19 impact on e-commerce sector by categories | Statista

[5] Digital India: Driving The New Wave Of Entrepreneurship Across The Nation

Services. Though Siva moved back to India in 2011, both kept on working in the consulting services area and were joined by a common friend in the founding of the Learning Centre. At this stage, their consulting and professional services were on a contract basis with U.K. and U.S.-based clients, and they were able to generate revenue of US$600,000 between 2011 and 2015. They had decided to start a product company in 2014 and invested heavily in infrastructure, skills, and resource development. They set up base in Karthik's hometown, Trichy, where they constructed an office spanning 10,000 sq. ft. and invested around US$750,000. They simultaneously used it for the Learning Centre (Fig. 13.1). In 2017, while Siva took care of the Learning Centre at Trichy, Karthik had joined Accenture (Singapore), where he led digital transformation for government and government agencies in the Asia-Pacific (APAC) region. Post that, he joined a cloud security platform startup in San Francisco and led their APAC business stream. The company got acquired by a big MNC for 400 M USD, and Karthik also received payment in the form of shares due to his role in initial team building.

Keeping the Learning Centre as a common objective, both Siva and Karthik took parallel journeys. Encouraged by his experience and driven by his passion, Karthik kept searching for avenues to enhance his skills in the domain of digital platforms. He was admitted to the Indian Institute of Management, Bangalore for the programme called "Leading Digital Transformation (LDT)", which focused on honing digitalisation skills for managers and provided mentorship and insights on platform businesses. In the LDT programme, he met Kiran VP (Kiran), who was leading digital transformation for Sapient, India, and Regims Mohammed (Regims), who was the Digital Transformation lead for Qatar Airlines. They encouraged his interest in building a product company for the platform business and also gave valuable mentorship, guidance, support, and assistance.

As a part of the programme's deliverables, they were required to develop a new business idea in the context of digitalisation and platforms. The three of them came up with the idea of creating a digital platform that would provide digitalisation capabilities and transform businesses. They initially named it HIGGS since they conceptualised it as an 'invisible, hardly-there field which provides capabilities to others while working in the backdrop'. This idea was awarded the title of the 'Best project for Unified Business Management Platform- Retail Domain' in the LDT programme for the year 2019. The idea won so much appeal that it succeeded against great minds and leaders from across India, Singapore, Dubai, Qatar, Kuwait, Oman, UAE, Germany, and Australia. Unlike many executive education programme projects, this idea did not die down once all the fanfare ended. The idea of HIGGS did not evaporate with the end of the course, and Karthik decided to do something about it.

Kiran fondly recalled:

> Karthik had a lot of passion in this field, and he decided to take this passion forward. The idea was still at the development stage at that time, but after initial discussions about the technical aspects, architecture, marketing, and business model, we decided to invest time, energy and money in it and took it forward.

Thus, the business idea underwent iterations and improvements and got renamed as DIGIIT.

Evolution of DIGIIT (Phase I): Platform as a Service

By 2019, Karthik had enough knowledge about digital platforms as a transformative force. He and Siva were trying to fix bits and pieces of what their Learning Centre as a platform might look like, and were also developing platform-based solutions to be used by businesses at scale.

Regims recalled the decision as one of the early innovative pivots in their business model, which led to the strengthening of what was to come in the future.

> Karthik already had a background in digital transformation and had a team that was already working on similar things at the Learning Centre. We thought that maybe we could take that as the backbone of our business and develop something on top. This was basically an architectural innovation. They already had the technology and the team. All we had to do was to apply a new business model and look for probable markets.

The period 2019–2021 was an important time for them. It was during this time that they identified a significant gap in the Indian Micro, Small and Medium Enterprise (MSME) sector.[6] During and even before COVID-19, bigger firms were gradually shifting towards technological upgrades and usage of platforms.[7] The market saw the growth of technological giants, digital marketplaces, online teaching platforms, and similar initiatives. Some businesses wanted to own (internalize) capabilities for developing digital platforms and scale online. But for the Indian medium and small-scale business sector, the shift was hardly visible.

Karthik mentioned the gap and how it inspired his team to build something.

> There were bigger players in the market that were leveraging their online platforms to transform their businesses. On the other hand, some MSMEs needed to digitally transform their businesses by leveraging a platform to survive in the digital economy. But they were left out.

COVID-19 gave a push to this movement. But this mission was fraught with challenges. First and foremost, how do they develop sustainable and affordable solutions at scale? DIGIIT's founders did not want their solutions to be restricted to certain segments of the economy. They wanted to go extensive and cover all segments of businesses while providing support in the space of agricultural and women entrepreneurs as well. Secondly, how do they establish a big enough network that helps entrepreneurs leverage the platform advantage? So far, they had operated in Trichy and neighbouring districts. Their network was spread as far as their own connections went. But to be successful, they needed to build solutions deployable at a population scale. And thirdly, how to build a low-cost model to generate enough revenue for it to sustain itself? Until that time, they were not focused on key elements like cost and revenue, as the entire origins of the enterprise were rooted in their Learning Centre's mission of improving employability.

[6] MSME: Fail to scale: India's manufacturing aspiration confronts the 'missing middle' - The Economic Times

[7] India: COVID-19 impact on start up funding 2020 | Statista

DBaaS (Digital Business as a Service) (Phase II): Development and Networking

From 2018 to 2020, the Learning Centre witnessed a slowdown and an eventual halt due to COVID-19. The year 2020 saw them investing INR 20 million from their sources to start DIGIIT's product development journey. "Digital enablement" and "operationalisation" were the two key words for DIGIIT when it started offering Digital Business as a Service. A village-based rural entrepreneur, a city-based *Kirana* shop[8] owner, and even a multi-store showroom owner, DBaaS could provide digitisation tools to every businessperson. DBaaS as a tool offered every user a custom solution, while being deployable on a large scale across geographies. Simultaneously, it was low-cost and efficient for the business users. Karthik already had his existing team and an established Learning Centre spanning 10,000 square feet in Trichy, which now also served as an office for his new business. Moreover, Karthik had the support and partnership with experts like Siva, Regims, and Kiran.

Using their resources and investments, they created four products in 2020. (1) UNITY—for manufacturers and brands; (2) OMNI—for retail operators; (3) Infinity—for aggregators focusing on Dairy and Agri Industries; and (4) ZEAL—for social ventures with environmental, social, and governance (ESG) use cases. These were given as a subscription-based service, which started generating a revenue stream. Since the products/services were cloud-based and easy to implement, the uninformed (businesses) 'novices' could use both the cloud-based solutions for a subscription fee and mentorship by the DIGIIT team, to enjoy the benefits by turning into digital 'native' enterprises. Thus, "Digital Native Enterprises" both defined DIGIIT's objectives and represented the level of digital literacy they aimed to build among businesses across different strata of society. The first 50–60 subscriptions were provided free of cost to encourage adoption and increase awareness about the solution. DIGIIT started strong in the fast-moving consumer goods (FMCG) segment, but even at this stage, DIGIIT's business was not scaling at the speed at which Karthik and his team wanted. The market witnesses the growth of many other platform-based models and marketplaces, and DIGIIT's vision of

[8] Small, local or neighborhood grocery stores that sell everyday essentials like groceries, household items, and sometimes personal care products.

digitalising the MSME, rural, Agricultural, and Women entrepreneur segment seemed like a daunting task. They were making all efforts by meeting multiple entrepreneurs and providing mentorship classes for their solutions, but the speed and scope were not what they had expected to achieve by 2021. DBaaS was a uniquely placed solution with a good subscription-based earning potential, but would prove to be a suboptimal product if DIGIIT could not reach out to a wider customer base and spread its network.

Platform as a Service (Phase III): New Projects, New Breakthroughs[9]

Throughout this period, Karthik and the co-founders sustained their focus on building a platform, as they believed that a multi-sided platform model had the potential to attract and retain users with very little capital investment and technical expertise. The founders had continued their engagement with the faculty at IIM Bangalore, and Prof. R Srinivasan (Srinivasan), one of the LDT programme directors, joined the firm as an advisor. Srinivasan had been steadfast in advising Karthik and DIGIIT to stay focused on building a platform. He remarked:

> One of the key design elements of the DIGIIT business model had been the seamless transition from digital business as a service to platform as a service. By leveraging its existing human and technological resources, DIGIIT was uniquely positioned to empower small and medium businesses,..., and push for the transformation of 'digital novices' to 'digital native enterprises'. While a lot had been said about digital transformation at large enterprises, DIGIIT's mission was to take all the benefits of digital transformation to the smallest of (even unorganised) businesses through leveraging open networks.

The purpose of DIGIIT is outlined in its mission as follows.

> *To empower businesses by providing affordable, easy-to-use, Artificial Intelligence (AI)-powered digital platforms and business networks that enhance efficiency, scalability, and innovation, enabling them to thrive in the digital economy.*

[9] (Refer to Fig. 13.2 for milestones and journey).

The tide turned in their favour post 2020 when DIGIIT got selected as one of the promising "Innovative Digital Platforms" at an event organised by the Indian High Commission and the Government of Singapore, and they got a chance to show the product demo to important government and business delegates across the globe. DIGIIT's work and recognition led to NITI Aayog[10] and other organisations inviting them for a demo, which facilitated the onboarding of select entrepreneurs onto the DIGIIT platform. This further strengthened DIGIIT's image as the digital enabler of Small and Medium Enterprises (SME). And soon enough, it was granted the award of the best Digital MSME by the Tamil Nadu (an Indian state) government.

DIGIIT, since the days of the initial Learning Centre, has always had a prosocial objective behind its operation. And this was reflected in the programmes it ran for women and agricultural entrepreneurs. DIGIIT got its first big prosocial breakthrough in 2021 in the form of 'GENIE CSOs for climate change'[11] to promote women entrepreneurs at the grassroots level. This was a TREC-STEP[12] initiative promoted and funded by the European Union as a part of a larger global drive touching base in about 15 countries. This programme aimed to productively engage women entrepreneurs in the promotion of social enterprises for climate change. This was done through specifically designed capacity development actions, incubation support, technological tools, and other essential methods. The programme was operationalised through 430-odd Climate Social Organisations (CSOs), and each CSO was connected to approximately 1000 women entrepreneurs at the grassroots level. DIGIIT was approached through Karthik's network in Trichy, and they leveraged their DBaaS-based product 'Zeal' to develop the platform support, capability building, and value-added service integration. Thousands of women entrepreneurs thus commercialised their businesses through digital branding, marketing, and

[10] The NITI Aayog is a policy think tank of the Government of India, established with the aim to achieve sustainable development goals with cooperative federalism by fostering the involvement of State Governments of India in the economic policy-making process using a bottom-up approach. Objectives and Features | NITI Aayog

[11] GENIE: GeoEngineering and NegatIve Emissions pathways in Europe | GENIE | Project | Fact sheet | H2020 | CORDIS | European Commission

[12] TREC STEP (in the state of Tamil Nadu) is an organisation promoted by the Government of India in 1986, for spearheading the promotion of science, technology, and Innovation.

sales. And this was achieved by DIGIIT's team in 6 months, which was a feat in itself. The programme helped DIGIIT establish new networks in 7 more Indian states and other countries, which took guidance from DIGIIT's approach for this project. Post this breakthrough, they sold Unity to a few manufacturing companies, OMNI to some Retail outlets, and Infinity to aggregation businesses.

The next breakthrough (in 2021) came in the form of an INR 1 million seed fund from the government of Tamil Nadu, which had recognised DIGIIT's efforts in transforming MSMEs through Digital Platforms. This created wide visibility for DIGIIT across industries, MSMEs, government and government agencies, entrepreneurs and others. At this stage, DIGIIT's initial challenges regarding networking, speed and scope seemed to have largely been overcome.

Piggybacking on DPI Wave (Phase IV): Leveraging Multiple DPIs

It could be said that DIGIIT founders were present at the right time and the right moment to leverage the environmental changes. The third and biggest breakthrough for DIGIIT came in 2021–2022 when India started the Digital Public Infrastructure (DPI)[13] revolution. DIGIIT got selected as one of the first five startups to drive a pilot launch of the Open Network for Digital Commerce (ONDC)[14] in the cities of Bangalore, Bhopal, Delhi, Shillong and Coimbatore. This was promoted by the Department of Commerce, Government of India. In the course of the process, the DIGIIT team got to work with the ONDC leadership team and prominent people from the ministry (Department of Commerce). DIGIIT both contributed to the open-source network development and also adopted the network at a population scale.

Prospects continued to grow for DIGIIT when it leveraged other DPIs in the year 2022–2023. It was chosen as one of the first nine startups to develop the minimum viable product (MVP) for the Unified Logistic Platform (ULIP).[15] The proposed prototype was selected as the best one

[13] Decoding India's Digital Public Infrastructure - Protean
[14] ONDC | Open Network for Digital Commerce
[15] Ulip Portal

from among over 600 candidates. This helped DIGIIT obtain access to 27 systems across 6 ministries and a chance to develop the prototype as a use case. Thus, the integrations to both ONDC and ULIP gave DIGIIT an opportunity to promote its mission and vision of providing digital enablement services to a large share of India's MSME network in both digital commerce and supply chain.

The year 2022 saw them working actively in the ONDC network. This led them to participate and lead the nationwide adoption drive of ONDC across India, and even run an ONDC pilot in Bangalore, Karnataka, while onboarding over 30 sellers and integrating with leading logistics players. DIGIIT participated in workshops conducted by state-level governments and also became part of their digital transformation and MSME initiatives. DIGIIT worked closely with government agencies, open network stakeholders and top-level decision makers. DIGIIT, represented by Karthik, also got a special invitation to the launch of the National Logistics Policy (NLP)[16] by the Prime Minister of India at New Delhi.

DIGIIT's ONDC impact got wide coverage in media and news articles (Fig. 13.3). Apart from commerce and logistics, DIGIIT also became an early mover and integrated with other DPIs like Open Network for Employment, Skilling and Transformation (or ONEST)[17] for skilling and education, the Open Credit Enablement Network (or OCEN)[18] for credit, Transport4All[19] and Agri Digital Mission.[20] By connecting to several DPI initiatives, DIGIIT was able to level the playing field for both small and big businesses in the context of digitalisation, and received special recognition from the Ministry of Commerce. Thus, over these years, DIGIIT witnessed a surge of opportunities which pushed them to create the required capabilities.

[16] Press Release: Press Information Bureau

[17] Inside ONEST, a decentralised network that hopes to shake up the education sector | YourStory

[18] OCEN - Open Credit Enablement Network | OCEN

[19] Transport4All Challenge

[20] Press Release: Press Information Bureau

Leveraging Open Networks

By 2023, DIGIIT had made its presence felt in multiple areas and was one of the pioneers in the wave of digital public infrastructure-based actors. It provided Karthik and his team with all that was lacking before 2022 in terms of network and visibility. For each of these multiple DPIs, he had different subscriptions. Ulogistics (logistics integration), eBiz (mobility integration), Hgateway (payment solution integration), Imobility (first mile logistics), skill and education, and ePay (UPI integration). They built everything by connecting it to a DPI. There was a platform at the core level, and the digital native enterprises plugged into the platform to carry out multiple services through the use of the open network integration (every DPI as a service). Karthik describes the network's growth in four phases.

> The first set of connections was in the way of some like-minded entrepreneurs coming together in Trichy and starting the Learning Centre. The second set of connections got formed through the centre's businesses when we got in touch with local resources, colleges, students, and even the district administration. The third set for me was when I joined the LDT programme at IIM Bangalore. It was an eye-opener in terms of both knowledge and networking. And finally, the biggest network required for DIGIIT's growth came in the form of leveraging the DPIs, which gave it the network, connections with policy makers and tech giants, and all that was required.

Thus, DIGIIT became the master of leveraging the newfound network effects and solved the earlier challenges of integration. It became one of the only ventures that got integrated into six DPIs for its work. Karthik wondered:

> Would an offline venture have been able to garner the same kind of advantage from the phenomenon? It's hard to say.

Furthering their Prosocial Mission: Projects and Funding

DIGIIT was involved in the development of women-led businesses through their women entrepreneurship development programme, even before they engaged with DPIs. They got in touch with the Department of Industries and Commerce (Government of Kerala) and engaged with many women entrepreneurs to spread awareness about how to build sustainable and scalable platform businesses through ONDC and other DPIs. They met multiple district-level functionaries to develop solutions for the same. Karthik got in touch with technological leaders from various sectors: industrialists, bureaucrats, diplomats from different countries, and potential investors to scale DIGIIT's operations within Tamil Nadu. Since the city of Coimbatore in Tamil Nadu was a part of the ONDC pilot, DIGIIT was able to onboard big clients and sustain coverage and growth.

Transze, one such client, needed logistics support as they had a fleet of 20 vehicles providing logistics services to MSMEs. Through ONDC, they were able to leverage the channel to receive more orders and connect with businesses that required logistical support. DIGIIT was also able to support the onboarding of hyperlocal delivery services from the city of Trichy by providing them with 'platform enablement'. The subscription products of DIGIIT, built on ONDC, helped connect logistics service providers to carry out deliveries at a large scale. Iway was one such player that conducted same-day deliveries through both its own platform and ONDC, all supported by DIGIIT. Similarly, ShipXGuru was also a specialised logistics platform built on ONDC and provided logistics services in the southern part of the state of Tamil Nadu. This opened up possibilities to onboard 10,000+ pan-India logistics players across India within a year, and DIGIIT was able to generate over INR 5 million in revenue.

The year 2023 saw DIGIIT enter into collaborations with the National Digital Agri Mission and the Tamil Nadu Digital Mission. These two collaborations provided DIGIIT with inroads into the agricultural and rural sectors, which were also a part of DIGIIT's original vision and mission. Participation in the MANAGE programme of the Ministry of Agriculture and Farmers Welfare of India allowed DIGIIT to develop digital platforms (integrated with ONDC) for agri value producers and women entrepreneurs across India. DIGIIT also partnered with the Tamil Nadu

Agricultural University incubation centre to empower Agri value producers with digital platforms. DIGIIT got selected for the Startup Tamil Nadu (StartupTN) Mission to develop DPI-enabled platforms for the startup ecosystem of the state of Tamil Nadu. These initiatives helped DIGIIT receive seed funding worth INR 2.5 million for platform development under the welfare programmes for farmers (Rashtriya Krishi Vikas Yojana). They further received INR 15 million funding from one of the world's biggest software corporations, which helped in the acquisition and onboarding of over 100 clients across 7 states in India, and a revenue generation of over INR 10 million.

The impact of these initiatives was multi-fold. Not only was DIGIIT now a pan India name, but it also made progress in its social mission of (a) empowering women Agricultural entrepreneurs (see Fig. 13.4), contributing to gender equality and improving socio-economic status in rural areas; (b) community development by creating local employment opportunities and supporting local producers while fostering enhanced living standards and social cohesion (see Fig. 13.5); and (c) sustainability by promoting sustainable agricultural practices benefiting the environment and ensuring long-term viability of agricultural lands. DIGIIT had become a commercially viable business model with a strong prosocial mission of digitally enabling underserved segments of India.

Challenges and the Way Forward

The DBaaS solutions were adapted to make DPI integrations easy. India's DPI approach followed the principles of inclusivity, interoperability, modularity, and scalability. After integrating with DPI-based networks, DBaaS was being used at a population scale through a 'plug and play' approach. DIGIIT created a blended solution that operated both as a standalone business unit and via DPI integrations. They provided solutions to MSMEs by bundling the existing business into platform solutions within 3 months of onboarding a customer. Digital enablement and networking helped them respond to such requests in a fast and efficient manner. This increased their legitimacy and trust in the market. These success stories also helped them gain more customers. In the financial year 2024–2025, DIGIIT started focusing on top-line use cases with 7 ready-to-launch DBaaS subscriptions, including Digital Women Entrepreneurship, Agri Digital

Mission, Digital Supply Chain, and MSME Digital Transformation. They increased their base to 258 clients across 11 states and created new avenues for revenue. The DBaaS subscription model created success stories, creating revenue of over INR 10 million in 2024–2025.

Karthik participated in more than 100 outreach (see Fig. 13.6) programmes and gained more insight and knowledge from the grassroots level. It helped in curating the solutions to meet market requirements (Fig. 13.7).

Their revenue streams included consulting, where they gave advisory services; subscription services for their products and platforms; and implementation services, which were customised to every client. They diversified into commerce, logistics, fintech and mobility, and provided subscriptions based on the merchant's product lines.

Their team in 2025 consisted of 25 full-time employees, 7 consultants, and 10 interns who provided professional, advisory, and customer engagement services. 75% of their workforce were women from Tier II and Tier III cities, who managed pan-India domains. And not surprisingly, most of the full-time employees were students of the original Learning Centre. They also had a dedicated sales team that managed on-the-ground issues. Thus, what began as a SaaS or PaaS solution before 2022 had evolved into a multifunctional solution, integrating multiple customers.

DIGIIT's team was operating from 4 locations by 2025: Trichy, Coimbatore, Chennai, and IIMB's NSRCEL, and was serving multiple states like Tamil Nadu, Kerala, Karnataka, Punjab, Odisha, Maharashtra, J&K, Gujarat, and Pondicherry. They spent about 30% of their revenues on cost of goods sold, and their operational expenses stood at 15% of their revenue, which was expected to reduce as they scaled further. The 2025–2026 projections for revenues were strong at INR 30–50 million. With an expected future funding of INR 100 million from a Bangalore-based incubator, they hope to actually grow 10x of their projections!

As he landed in the Bangalore International Airport and took a taxi to NSRCEL (Indian Institute of Management, Bangalore), Karthik began reviewing his presentation deck for participation in the demo-day (where his Velocity cohorts will meet with potential investors), and had three specific questions in mind. First on his mind was the immediate business growth trajectory—should they focus on deepening their presence in their existing markets, or should they focus on widespread growth? Secondly, he was cognizant of the fact that resolving the dilemma between penetration and geographical expansion had significant ramifications for its resources, especially for the local feet-on-street employees/associates. He was fairly confident that his DPI-based products were packageable in a box, and therefore, rapid deployment would not be a problem. The major challenge was likely to be local adaptations of the services, including pre-sales, on-site implementation support, and after-sales support. He was reminded of what his mentor, Prof. Srinivasan, would ask him, “Do you want to become world-famous in Trichy before you step out?” Third on his mind was the question of profitability. Should he expand/diversify now, or focus on improving DIGIIT’s profitability— through increasing the wallet-share of their customers or up-selling/cross-selling more products and services— before even thinking of expansion and diversification?

He looked out of the window and saw that his taxi had covered only 8 km of the 42 km-long journey. The traffic was piling up, and he realised he had a long way to go. He needed answers, but had time to make up his mind.

Discussion Questions

1. What are the next steps for scaling and the future evolution of DIGIIT? Is it market penetration or geographical expansion? Should DIGIIT focus on leveraging existing entrepreneurial networks and DPIs within their current geographical markets, or should they expand to other geographies?
2. How can DIGIIT expand geographically and even become international in future while sustaining profitability? Does it have the resources to serve these markets? Given that DPI-driven products and services are packageable (as in a box), what are the challenges/opportunities in growing through a franchisee-led model?
3. At a more fundamental level, should DIGIIT expand at all? Or should they focus on profitability in their current markets (increase their share of digital spends of their customers and/or upsell/cross-sell more products/services to their existing customers)?

Supplementary Reading Material

- Airan, A., Hodigere, S., Sridharan, S., & Natarajan, S. (2024, June 15). The governance of digital public infrastructure: India paper. *Aapti Institute*. https://aapti.in/blog/the-governance-of-digital-public-infrastructure-india-paper/
- ANI. (2024, November 9). Public digital infrastructure helped micro-level players grow in India: FM Sitharaman. *ET Retail*.

https://retail.economictimes.indiatimes.com/news/e-commerce/e-tailing/public-digital-infrastructure-helped-micro-level-players-grow-in-india-fm-sitharaman/115111606

- Baker, T., & Nelson, R. E. (2005). Creating something from nothing: Resource construction through entrepreneurial bricolage. *Administrative science quarterly*, *50*(3), 329–366.
- Cardon, M.S., Wincent, J., Singh, J. and Drnovsek, M., 2009. The nature and experience of entrepreneurial passion. *Academy of Management Review*, 34(3), pp. 511–532.
- Collis, D. (2016). Lean strategy. *Harvard Business Review*, *94*(3), 62–68.
- Fréry, F., Lecocq, X., & Warnier, V. (2015). Competing with ordinary resources. *MIT Sloan Management Review, 56*(3), 69–76.
- Iyer, B., & Davenport, T. H. (2016). A new way for entrepreneurs to think about IT. *Harvard Business Review.*
- Kirtley, J., & O'Mahony, S. (2023). What is a pivot? Explaining when and how entrepreneurial firms decide to make strategic change and pivot. *Strategic management journal*, *44*(1), 197–230.
- McDonald, Rory, and Cheng Gao. "Entrepreneurship: Every Pivot Needs a Story." *Harvard Business Review* 95, no. 4 (July–August 2017): 24.
- Parekh, K. (2022). *The core of being an entrepreneur: Finding passion in what you do.* Forbes.
- Sahasranamam, S., & Prabhu, J. (2024). Digital Public Infrastructure for the Developing World. *Stanford Social Innovation Review.* https://doi.org/10.48558/XDTX-PW77
- Video: "How ONDC can create a $100B E-commerce Revolution in India | Bigger Than Nykaa & Zomato?" https://youtu.be/OU2UFyo30bc?feature=shared
- Video: "The Power of Platforms" https://youtu.be/4foEZgAOzJY?feature=shared
- Video: "Will Flipkart become PhonePe before PhonePe becomes Flipkart? | Two by Two | The Ken" https://youtu.be/EiL9s8VjZ4I?feature=shared
- Video: "What is Digital Public Infrastructure" https://youtu.be/8CACZ4tCJWg?feature=shared

Learning Outcomes
This case is best suited for an MBA class, providing the following insights-

1. Introduction to the concept of Digital Public Infrastructure as foundational, interoperable and inclusive digital systems which are deployable at a population scale.
2. How can entrepreneurs use the DPI and multiple DPI-driven initiatives to create, sustain and capture value? This can be in terms of expansion and market reach, low cost, high speed, and bundling of new offerings.
3. To highlight how digital entrepreneurs in emerging markets like India can enable digital have-nots and bridge the digital divide.
4. To highlight how the DPI embeds 'public purpose' in its foundational rails upon which the entrepreneurs can create initiatives which are both commercially viable and pro-social.

Competing Interests Srinivasan, R is on the advisory board and is a nominal shareholder in the firm, DIGIIT.

Annexures

Fig. 13.1 The Learning Centre. (Source: DIGIIT Website)

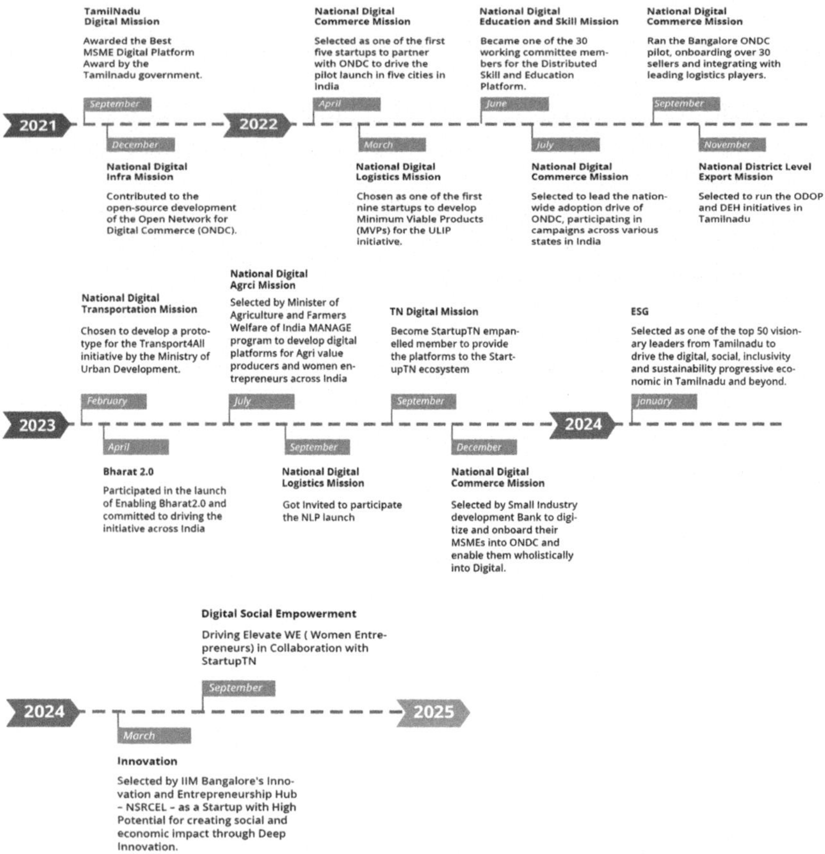

Fig. 13.2 Milestones and Trajectory. (Source: Company documents)

Fig. 13.3 DIGIIT coverage in popular media. (Source: Company documents)

Fig. 13.4 Women Entrepreneurs enabled by DIGIIT; Beta launch of their business platform. (Source: Author's Pictures - March 2025)

Fig. 13.5 A small-scale Kirana Store operating on DIGIIT's platform. (Source: Author's Pictures - March 2025)

Fig. 13.6 Outreach programme with Startup TN representative for one of the Women Entrepreneurship initiatives named- 'Tholozhli'. (Source: Author's Pictures - March 2025)

Fig. 13.7 Outreach Programme at Chamber of Commerce in Coimbatore. (Source: DIGIIT website)

CHAPTER 14

5C Network - Revolutionizing Radiological Workflows in India with AI

Sachidananda Benegal and Parvathy B

Abstract What started of a personal experience with delayed Radiology reporting, triggered Kalyan, the founder of 5C Network, to pay attention to the dearth of radiologists to cater to the increasing demand for diagnostics in a growing health care market like India. Coupled with this insight the case highlights the development of a suitable workflow for radiology diagnostics in India and the resource acquisition journey of the venture. The case sheds light on the challenges of deep-tech venture building in emerging markets like India where the ecosystem itself is nascent. The case leaves the readers to help Kalyan, find his way to continue the phenomenal growth rate demonstrated thus far, while tackling the ever-changing environmental landscape. What should Kalyan do?

S. Benegal (✉)
NSRCEL, Indian Institute of Management Bangalore, Bangalore, India
e-mail: sachidananda.bs14@alumni.iimb.ac.in

Parvathy B
Indian Institute of Management Jammu, Nagrota, India
e-mail: parvathy@iimj.ac.in

A. S. Galande et al. (eds.), *Context-inspired Entrepreneurship*, Sustainable Development Goals Series,
https://doi.org/10.1007/978-981-95-9831-1_14

Keywords Radiology diagnostics • AI • PACS • Regulatory clearance • Contextual data

SDG Links While the primary focus of this case is on improving access to healthcare through digital health infrastructure, it contributes to SDG 8: Decent Work and Economic Growth by demonstrating how expanded healthcare access can strengthen workforce health, productivity, and economic participation. By leveraging digital platforms to bridge healthcare gaps between urban and rural areas, it also contributes to SDG 3 and SDG 10.

Introduction

Kalyan had returned from the European Congress of Radiology (ECR) 2025[1] to his Bengaluru office. ECR was a week of intense discussions with several peers in the field of Radiology, and he had learnt a lot. In the last 8 years of running 5C Network, the connections from the ECR conferences have infused him with a lot of new threads to think about.

This time, however, he was looking forward to reading about the IndiaAI Mission 2024[2] which had been recently approved by the Indian Parliament. The media had spoken a lot about it, with much speculation and anticipation. Understanding the implications of the Mission would be useful to consider, as it could change the ecosystem for the AI companies in India.

He had started 5C Network in 2017, and he had seen a lot of changes in the ecosystem since. There weren't a lot of AI companies based out of India in the healthcare industry itself, and regulation was nonexistent. The world, however, was taken by an AI storm since 2022 when people began using AI tools like ChatGPT, and a large number of individuals were playing around with the several options that had become publicly available. Several larger organizations had begun investing in developing an AI

[1] sima. (2024, August 27). ECR 2025: Registration and Abstract Submission are open - ESR | European Society of Radiology. ESR | European Society of Radiology. https://www.myesr.org/ecr-2025-registration-and-abstract-submission-are-open/ accessed on 10th April 2025.

[2] *India's AI Revolution*. (2025). Pib.gov.in. https://pib.gov.in/PressReleasePage.aspx?PRID=2108810 accessed on 10th April 2025.

strategy. Suddenly, even the governments across the world had woken up to the power of AI and begun doing their bit in regulating AI.

All these posed several new considerations that kept Kalyan occupied. In India, the digital public infrastructure has gained increased attention after the success of the Unified Payment Interface and the associated adoption. The Indian government was taking proactive steps to embrace AI, and the AI mission was one of those initiatives. It is quite possible that the government could encourage the adoption of AI in healthcare with zest. If this were the case, it could render some of the advantages 5C had built and acquired over the decade a challenge. Finding new resources that would provide a competitive advantage was going to be crucial.

If 5C were to expand globally, there would be similar challenges as well. Privacy had emerged as a major concern with the growing adoption of AI, and in healthcare this would have to be incorporated more foundationally. European countries had begun a proactive approach to developing an AI policy and wanted all companies operating in the European Union to adhere to it. This would be an important consideration if 5C were to extend globally.

Back to the present, as he read the announcements in the Mission closely, he had to also consider several aspects of the industry and 5C's capabilities to think of the next steps.

The Radiology Diagnostics Industry in India

Healthcare diagnostics plays a vital role in modern-day medical care, offering an avenue for monitoring, diagnosis, and well-being tests. The Indian diagnostics market is valued at around 13 billion USD in 2023.[3] The rising number of chronic diseases, the growing ageing population and the increased adoption of government-backed insurance programs are some of the drivers of this growth.

80–85% of the market is unorganized, and the remaining is split between a few large, organized players, and many smaller regional players. The major notable national players include Dr. Lal Pathlabs, Metropolis Healthcare and Thyrocare Technologies. The COVID outbreak in 2020

[3] Topic: Diagnostics market in India. (2024). Statista; Statista. https://www.statista.com/topics/12366/diagnostics-market-in-india/#topicOverview accessed on 30th March 2025.

increased the demand for testing services across the country and consequently increased the volumes and realization of diagnostic companies.[4]

Broadly, the healthcare diagnostics space can be segmented into two—pathology and radiology.[5] Pathology relates to testing of all major illnesses and accounts for nearly 58% of the revenues in the industry. Radiology relates to imaging diagnostics and accounts for about 42% of the industry revenue.[6] The radiology segment (which is currently estimated to be Rs 425 billion in FY 23) is likely to have higher growth in the coming years.[7]

India has approximately 8876 medical diagnostic imaging centers, as of January 2025, out of which nearly 80% are single-owner, operated, standalone centers. The remaining 20% are part of larger brands. Maharashtra (1114 centers), Uttar Pradesh (1077 centers) and West Bengal (770) are the top three states by the number of diagnostic imaging centers.

Radiology and Imaging diagnostic centers offer a wide range of tests that help visualize internal structures and diagnose various conditions. Some of the primary tests offered by such a center are:

1. X-Ray: A common imaging technique used to detect fractures, infections, and abnormalities in bones and organs.
2. MRI (Magnetic Resonance Imaging): Provides detailed images of soft tissues, including the brain, muscles, and internal organs.
3. CT scan (Computed Tomography): Combines X-rays to create cross-sectional images for detecting tumors, injuries, and other conditions.
4. Ultrasound: Non-invasive imaging used for monitoring soft tissues, organs, and pregnancies.
5. Mammography: Specialized imaging for breast health and early detection of breast cancer.
6. PET Scan (Positron Emission Tomography): Used for detecting cancer, heart problems, and brain disorders.

[4] India, in. (2022). *Overview of diagnostics Industry in India*. Groww. https://groww.in/blog/overview-of-indian-diagnostic-industry accessed on 30th March 2025.

[5] Topic: Diagnostics market in India. (2024). Statista; Statista. https://www.statista.com/topics/12366/diagnostics-market-in-india/#topicOverview accessed on 30th March 2025.

[6] India, in. (2022). *Overview of diagnostics Industry in India*. Groww. https://groww.in/blog/overview-of-indian-diagnostic-industry accessed on 30th March 2025.

[7] India, in. (2022). *Overview of diagnostics Industry in India*. Groww. https://groww.in/blog/overview-of-indian-diagnostic-industry accessed on 30th March 2025.

7. Bone Density Test (DEXA Scan): Measures bone strength and helps diagnose osteoporosis.
8. Fluoroscopy: Provides real-time moving images of internal organs, often used in gastrointestinal studies.
9. Echocardiogram (ECHO): Uses ultrasound to assess heart function and structure.
10. Color Doppler: Evaluates blood flow in vessels and organs.
11. Interventional Radiology: Minimally invasive procedures guided by imaging, such as biopsies or stent placements.

In simple terms, radiology allows doctors to "see inside" the human body. Diagnostics using radiology typically involves the use of waves, like X-rays, sound waves or magnetic waves, from a source, which the target receives. A picture of what is inside the body is created based on the waves that are received by the target. Each type of test uses dissimilar sources and varies in the end image construction approach.

For example, in ultrasound scans, the ultrasound machine uses sound waves of much higher frequency to understand the body's internal structure. The waves bounce off tissues and organs, and the machine turns these echoes into pictures. In contrast, in an MRI scan, the MRI machines use magnets and radio waves to make hydrogen atoms in your body "dance." The machine listens to the signals these atoms send back and creates detailed images of soft tissues.

Given the diagnostic importance of these tests, turnaround time following the radiological test is an important parameter. The average turnaround time for a radiology test would be about 120 minutes for an X-ray and about 240 minutes for a more complex test like CT scans and MRI in 2015.[8] Subsequently, technological advancements and digitization have helped reduce the turnaround time of these reports. Most centers now have integrated into a Picture Archiving and Communication System (PACS) and have begun relying on Artificial Intelligence (AI) to enhance diagnostic accuracy and efficiency.

[8] Ahamed, A. (2019). Radiology EVALUATION OF TURNAROUND TIME (TAT) AND WAITING TIME (WT) FOR GENERAL RADIOLOGICAL INVESTIGATIONS IN OUR HOSPITAL. Academia.edu. https://www.academia.edu/88947964/Radiology_EVALUATION_OF_TURNAROUND_TIME_TAT_AND_WAITING_TIME_WT_FOR_GENERAL_RADIOLOGICAL_INVESTIGATIONS_IN_OUR_HOSPITAL accessed on 30th March 2025.

The turnaround time, more recently, for an X-ray is about 30–60 minutes, while for the more complex tests, it is about 90–120 minutes.[9] Turnaround times are, however, a function of the availability of the skilled workforce who operate the diagnostic labs. Operating a radiology diagnostic center requires at least a team of two—a radiologist and a radiation technician.[10] Radiologists are physicians who specialize in the field of radiology; while radiation technicians assist the radiologist and manage the instruments used to produce images.

As of January 2025, India had about 2687 radiologists[11] (which was about a 5.63% increase from 2023 numbers). Among the top three states with the most radiologists in India were Maharashtra (584) and Gujarat (270), followed by Uttar Pradesh (245). Despite the growth in demand and the number of medical diagnostic centers, there is a huge shortage of trained workforce to manage the load on radiology-led diagnostics.

The Genesis

Kalyan had taken an uncommon path after his graduation from a prestigious NIT off the west coast of India in 2015. Instead of taking up a job, he decided to work with the health department of the Government of Karnataka, as a consultant in developing the Healthizen app. Through Healthizen, any citizen could point out a potential health hazard and the health department would work with the administrative bodies concerned to resolve the identified issue.

In 2015, Kalyan's future co-founder was involved in an accident and subsequently admitted to a reputable hospital in Bengaluru. He was mandated an MRI scan, but the report would take two days to be processed and shared. It was when Kalyan was awaiting the MRI report that the idea of 5C Network first emerged. Kalyan wondered—if this were the case in Bengaluru, a city with so many medical enterprises and facilities, how

[9] UFO Themes. (2018, October 14). *Report Turn-Around Time*. Radiology Key. https://radiologykey.com/report-turn-around-time-2/ accessed on 30th March 2025.

[10] Baysson, H., Etard, C., Brisse, H. J., & Bernier, M.-O. (2012). Expositions radiologiques à visée diagnostique pendant l'enfance et risque de cancer: bilan des connaissances et perspectives. *Archives de Pédiatrie*, *19*(1), 64–73. https://doi.org/10.1016/j.arcped.2011.10.023 accessed on 30th March 2025.

[11] Smartscraper | Rentech Digital. (2025). *Radiologists in India - 2687 Available (Free Sample)*. SmartScraper. https://rentechdigital.com/smartscraper/business-report-details/list-of-radiologists-in-india accessed on 30th March 2025.

much worse would the situation be in many other cities and towns? Kalyan decided to explore how big the opportunity was, and his confidence only increased as he compared the growth rates of scanning machines and the radiologists who were required to operate them.

Having decided to start Kalyan began using these connections in the health care segment, through his work with the government, to make inroads into the early set of medical centers who would help him detail out the problem better. These discussions helped the founders to better understand the issues surrounding the radiology services in hospitals, and an acceptable positioning of the solution that they intended to develop.

The next phase involved a lot of hustling to begin getting the first set of centers to partner with. Hustle is a favorite for entrepreneurs during their ventures' early days, and Kalyan was no exception. Once, when attending a friend's wedding in Jaipur, while most of the friends were having fun in the prewedding activities and sightseeing, Kalyan went missing for about an hour. When he returned to join them, his friends were surprised to know that he had gone to a radiology center nearby to have a discussion and try to get them interested in the solution they were developing.

The conversations confirmed that patients struggled with the issue of the timely report generation, delaying the treatment by a few hours, if not days, in some cases. Turn-around time had to be reduced, but there were not many radiologists who could perform the analysis. Technology was an answer in this case, especially when he had seen that the output radiology solution was in a digital format to begin with. That is, a CT scan output would first be synthesized in a computer and later reproduced into a physical color printout. This output thus rendered itself for a direct analysis if one could ensure that the data was collected from these centers systematically with high fidelity, which could then be analyzed with the help of AI.

In fact, this approach could grant them a strategic advantage overall, too. Most of the current AI algorithms used in analyzing radiological scans were not trained on data that was specific to India. The algorithms often extended what was built on publicly available data or built using the data that is available from developed countries like the United States of America, or even those in the East, like Japan and South Korea. If 5C solved the issue of gathering the local data, it would help them get a first mover advantage, even if a follower organization enters.

This was the first task 5C got to work on, developing a reliable data gathering solution which could then be used for the AI analysis. Following the aspiration of vertical integration, 5C got to developing a cohesive data system- increasing efficiency and control further enhancing 5C's value creation.

The three layers of 5C's data strategy include data collection, data curation, and data augmentation. Data collection gathers raw data from across sources, recording the full spectrum of user and system behavior. Data curation organizes, cleans and labels to ensure it is accurate and reliable. Data collected across sources and systems "talk" to each other, maintaining connections between these previously siloed pipelines. The data augmentation layer brings in additional insights such as attributes or context. Tightly integrating these three layers together ensures that the data is clean, connected, and context aware, making sure your systems are ready for AI-based decision making.

While initially they began developing AI algorithms for the analysis of the data they had collected, a growth in their partnerships allowed them to increase the efficiency of the AI models. These AI models also needed to pass through the regulatory clearances by the Central Drug Standard Control Organisation (CDSCO) to be effectively deployed at scale. These clearances would take time, but their approach to data collection was proof enough to begin working towards raising investments that would be necessary as they progress.

Over time, the focus on data integration and the development of AI algorithms was packaged into a solution with several subcomponents. They developed their VORTEX platform which would enable the partner organization (a hospital or diagnostic center) to push their high-fidelity image and other relevant patient details to 5C's system. It then pushes the anonymized Digital Imaging and Communications in Medicine (DICOM) images into 5C's PACS. These images are then analyzed by the AI algorithms that 5C develops. These AI algorithms are stored and retrieved based on the nature of the case from 5C's Bionic Inference Engine. The AI algorithms then generate the required radiology report. The radiology report is then checked by their internal team of radiologists for quality issues and only then made available on the 5C platform. The hospital radiology team could then access the radiology reports from 5C on this platform within a couple of hours in most cases (and within an hour in urgent or emergency cases). Figure 14.1 captures 5C's workflow with the hospitals.

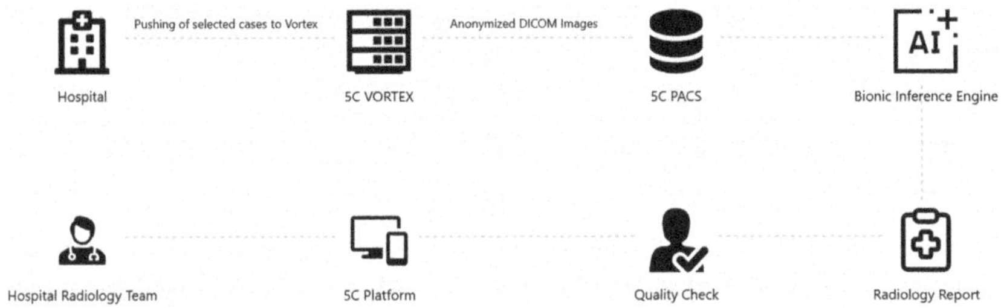

Fig. 14.1 5C's workflow (*5C - Network*. (2025). 5cnetwork.com. https://www.5cnetwork.com/explore-5C/ accessed on 12th April 2025.) for radiology reporting with hospitals

Organizational Culture and Team

5C prides itself in being a market leader in AI-driven radiological reporting. However, there seem to be several offbeat aspects that the founders seem to have used in building their team and culture. As startup founders, the speed to market is extremely crucial, and many times it challenges the conventional approaches of mature organizations. Here are two instances that highlight such choices in 5C's story.

The tech talent 5C was able to attract formed the backbone of the solution that they developed. Surprisingly, however, the product development team does not have any radiologists in it (who are the domain experts). This approach was risky, but they seem to have managed to find their path since the technology talent they hire is encouraged to question every assumption and think fundamentally. A sizable number of radiologists are part of the quality check team for radiology reports that the product generates, but the product development is entirely a technology team.

Classical models which have studied effective delegation suggest the development of a strong middle management that ensures that tasks are completed in time and effectively. 5C, however, has ensured that the management does not become an exclusive function. Every individual who leads a team must not only manage the team but also bear individual contributor responsibility. Even Kalyan must deliver in an individual capacity on the sales front in addition to handling the management of a few teams and performing the role of chief executive.

Despite the uncertainty that surrounds a startup, it may be such idiosyncratic choices of founders that cumulatively evolve into a part-dependent advantage for the firm if it survives to become a larger organization.

Leveraging Investors as a Risk Mitigation Approach

As a first-time founder in a rapidly shifting landscape that is powered by AI, it is important to get all the support you can. Investors form a vital cog in the strategic decision-making of startups. 5C boasts an illustrious set of investors. The cap table features Tata 1 mg, Vikram Vuppala (Nephroplus), Om Manchanda (Lal Pathlabs), Viren Prasad Shetty (Narayana Health), and others.[12]

The following table details the different investment rounds and the amount raised.[13]

Date	*Funding round*	*Amount raised*	*Investors*	*Valuation*
April 2017	Seed round	$842,400	Axilor ventures, Angel Investors	Not disclosed
October 2017	Seed round	$767,260	Axilor ventures, Angel Investors	Not disclosed
January 2019	Seed round	$564,000	Capria ventures, Axilor ventures	Not disclosed
November 2020	Seed round	$1.22 million	Capria ventures, Axilor ventures	Not disclosed
January 2022	Series A	$1.01 million	Tata 1 mg, Vikram Vuppala	$20.2 million
September 2022	Series A	$4.6 million	Celesta Capital, Capria ventures	$20.2 million
April 2024	Series A	$3.06 million	Not disclosed	Not disclosed

A look at the table indicates that 5C has a variety of investors. While some are pure-play financial investors, some others, like Tata 1 mg, have a more strategic alignment with what 5C does. In fact, 5C powers all the

[12] Kaur, J. (2023, February 23). *Tata 1 mg-Backed 5C Network Acquires Healthtech Startup Krayen*. Inc42 Media. https://inc42.com/buzz/tata-1mg-backed-5c-network-acquires-healthtech-startup-krayen/ accessed on 30th March 2025.

[13] Tracxn. (2021, August 17). *5C Network*. Tracxn.com; Tracxn. https://tracxn.com/d/companies/5c-network/__urUNKy836saXV4z0roBJobP9GclO5Qip-C6OwFFvRGo accessed on 30th March 2025.

radiology diagnostics on Tata 1 mg medical application. Yet others are domain experts and seem to have made investments, having understood the domain 5C operates in. In tandem, these investors ensure that they can guide and support the capable team that 5C has been able to assemble in navigating the uncertain territory.

Developing Capabilities through Acquisition

In February 2023, 5C Network completed the acquisition of "Krayen", an artificial intelligence health tech startup based in Los Altos, United States. The purpose of this acquisition is to enhance 5C Network's digital scanning services, with an ambitious target of achieving one billion scans annually by 2025.[14]

Established in 2021 by Bargava Subramanian and Kirthiraj Yuvaraj, Krayen leverages computer vision and natural language processing (NLP) to assist hospitals and healthcare providers in delivering personalized treatment plans. The platform analyzes patient data, including medical history, genetic information, and lifestyle factors, to recommend customized treatment plans accordingly.[15]

Krayen, much like 5C, primarily serves hospitals, diagnostic centers, and healthcare providers. Their solutions are designed to seamlessly integrate into existing medical workflows, thereby enhancing efficiency and accuracy. This allowed 5C to extend Krayen's offerings to its customers.

Following the acquisition, Bargava took over as the Chief AI Officer, and Kirthiraj became the CTO of 5C Network, reinforcing the leadership team.[16] Additionally, they set up their Coimbatore office, named NeoCortex, in December 2023.[17] Highlighting his vision for NeoCortex,

[14] ETtech. (2023, February 23). *Tata 1MG-backed 5C Network acquires AI healthtech startup Krayen*. The Economic Times; Economic Times. https://economictimes.indiatimes.com/tech/startups/tata-1mg-backed-5c-network-acquires-ai-healthtech-startup-krayen/articleshow/98187918.cms accessed on 30th March 2025.

[15] Kaur, J. (2023, February 23). *Tata 1 mg-Backed 5C Network Acquires Healthtech Startup Krayen*. Inc42 Media. https://inc42.com/buzz/tata-1mg-backed-5c-network-acquires-healthtech-startup-krayen/ accessed on 30th March 2025.

[16] *5C - Network*. (2025). 5cnetwork.com. https://www.5cnetwork.com/company/about-us/ accessed on 30th March 2025.

[17] Hariharan, S. (2023, December 12). *5C Network launches AI R&D centre in Coimbatore*. The Times of India; Times Of India. https://timesofindia.indiatimes.com/city/chennai/5c-network-launches-ai-rd-centre-in-coimbatore/articleshow/105917488.cms accessed on 30th March 2025.

which is the AI R&D center for 5C, Kalyan said: "Neocortex will serve as a hub for our AI-powered solutions, enabling us to enhance our efficiency, contributing to our mission of making healthcare more accessible and efficient across the region."

5C chose Coimbatore as the base for Neocortex for a couple of reasons. Firstly, though Tamil Nadu (the state in which Coimbatore was located) was not among the top three states in terms of number of medical imaging centers, it did have the highest number of CT and MRI scan machines. Secondly, Coimbatore offered additional advantages when it comes to recruiting and competing for talent. Basing themselves out of Coimbatore allowed them to be among the top two favored recruits[18] at several of the engineering colleges around the city. In a city like Bengaluru, competition for talent was high, and Coimbatore provided them with a strong hold in terms of having better negotiating power and access to the talent they sought for R&D work.

Looking Ahead

5C has had a remarkable journey over the last 8 years. It has connected itself with 2300 hospitals, and diagnostic centers to power its radiology services. They had generated reports for more than 98.6 lakh (9.86 million) cases and onboarded over five hundred radiologists as partners.[19] About 1 in 5 CT and MRI scans, as well as about 5 in 100 X-ray scans are analyzed by 5C's algorithms. Their platform today has about seven hundred radiologists onboarded and analyzes anywhere between 5000 to 6000 scans daily.[20]

In the journey, the approach of internalizing the data layer and analysis, instead of working on a publicly available data set had set them apart. At 250 LLMs, all trained on Indian data - they have the largest number of regulator (CDSCO[21]) approved AI models in India. The combination of data and AI does lend AI startups an advantage. However, the constantly evolving landscape of AI with new models requires one to be at the

[18] The other one being Zoho Inc.

[19] *5C - Network*. (2025). 5cnetwork.com. https://www.5cnetwork.com/ accessed on 12th April 2025.

[20] Informed during the interview with the founder - Kalyan.

[21] CDSCO—Central Drug Standard Control Organization.

forefront, especially when AI forms a core ingredient of your value creation process.

Beyond the organization's product strategy and competitive landscape, there are several challenges that plague AI-based startups in general. These include the dearth of readily available trained talent in areas like data science, machine learning and domain knowledge of health care. This often leads to prohibitive cost of human resources where lots of aspiring AI firms chase a few people. In addition to the human resources challenge, regulations, and the amendments therein influence several aspects of healthcare startups.

An example in context here is the IndiaAI Mission 2024.[22] This policy was passed with the intention of making computing power (GPUs) and research opportunities more accessible at an affordable cost. Under the scheme, as on 6th March 2025, about 10,000 GPUs were made available, and were focused on the creation of indigenous AI solutions tailored to Indian languages and contexts. Currently, the government estimates the provisioning of compute at the rate of ₹100 (about $1.2 USD) per hour to users. In addition, several focus areas and initiatives have been kick-started.

Awareness of AI in general is on the rise. The Medical space is no exception, and with the entry of competition it promises to be an interesting time ahead. Kalyan had many things to tackle in the times ahead. What do you think he has to do if he has to continue the present rate of growth or accelerate from here?

Discussion Questions

1. How has Kalyan evolved with the venture since its founding? How much of his thinking dominated by technology and how much of it with business? What are the implications of these changes for the organization?
2. How has the product evolved since its early founding? Why did it take a long time for the team to build a first deployable version of the product? How has the product development kept pace with the evolution of the ecosystem for companies like 5C Network?
3. If analyzed using a classical strategy framework like the Porters' 5 forces, where do you see the threats emerge for a company like 5C?

[22] *India's AI Revolution*. (2025). Pib.gov.in. https://pib.gov.in/PressReleasePage.aspx?PRID=2108810 accessed on 12th April 2025.

What resources would be crucial in the changing landscape to gain a competitive advantage?
4. What could be the potential growth avenues for 5C now that they seem to have acquired a significant market share in India?

Supplementary Readings
The following academic articles would be helpful in developing the theoretical anchor that could be used to synthesize the case learnings.

1. Kulkov, I. (2023). Next-generation business models for artificial intelligence start-ups in the healthcare industry. International Journal of Entrepreneurial Behavior & Research, 29(4), 860–885.
2. Mariani, M. M., Machado, I., & Nambisan, S. (2023). Types of innovation and artificial intelligence: A systematic quantitative literature review and research agenda. Journal of Business Research, 155, 113364.
3. Ibeh, A. I., Oso, O. B., Alli, O. I., & Babarinde, A. O. (2025). Scaling healthcare startups in emerging markets: A platform strategy for growth and impact'. International Journal of Advanced Multidisciplinary Research and Studies, 5(1), 838–854.

Learning Outcomes
Instructors could use the case:

(a) To understand the evolution of deep-tech products in an ecosystem that is still nascent and evolving.
(b) To understand the challenges of innovation and scaling for venture in the deep-tech space.

Acknowledgement The authors thank the reviewers for their valuable comments and suggestions, which helped strengthen the case. MS Copilot suggestions were used to improve the language. Additionally, Perplexity was used to find any academic literature that may have been relevant to the case in hand.

Competing Interests The authors have no conflicts of interest to declare that are relevant to the content of this chapter.

CHAPTER 15

Attvaran: Accelerating Assistive Technology Start-Ups in India

Tigmanshu Bhatnagar, Arvind S. A., Shantosh Cumarasurier, Justin Jesudas, Ben Hardman, Victoria Austin, P. V. Madhusudhan Rao, and Catherine Holloway

Abstract This case study examines Attvaran, an assistive technology (AT) startup accelerator launched in mid-2024 through collaboration between University College London's Global Disability Innovation Hub, IIT Delhi, and IIT Madras. Addressing the needs of over 26.8 million people with disabilities in India's growing AT market (projected to reach $2.76 billion by 2030), Attvaran functioned as both an accelerator program and

T. Bhatnagar (✉) • J. Jesudas • V. Austin • P. V. M. Rao • C. Holloway
University College London, London, UK
e-mail: t.bhatnagar@ucl.ac.uk; j.jesudas@ucl.ac.uk; victoria.austin@ucl.ac.uk; pvmrao@design.iitd.ac.in; c.holloway@ucl.ac.uk

Arvind S. A.
Indian Institute of Technology Delhi, New Delhi, India

S. Cumarasurier • B. Hardman
Global Disability Innovation Hub, London, UK
e-mail: s.cumarasurier@ucl.ac.uk; ben.hardman@ucl.ac.uk

A. S. Galande et al. (eds.), *Context-inspired Entrepreneurship*, Sustainable Development Goals Series,
https://doi.org/10.1007/978-981-95-9831-1_15

an action research initiative. Attvaran supported 20 startups while studying systemic barriers to AT innovation in India. The program revealed three critical dilemmas: tensions between social impact and commercial viability in AT ventures; complexities of effective mentorship for founders lacking traditional business backgrounds; and mismatches between short-term accelerator models and long-term ecosystem building requirements for AT innovation success. Through qualitative analysis of program design and participant experiences, this case demonstrates that supporting AT ventures requires moving beyond traditional startup acceleration toward sustained ecosystem building that bridges research, user communities, policy frameworks, and investment mechanisms. The case provides valuable insights for practitioners working at the intersection of disability innovation, social entrepreneurship, and inclusive technology development in emerging markets.

Keywords Assistive technology • Startup accelerator • Disability innovation • Social entrepreneurship • Ecosystem building

SDG Links This case contributes to SDG 8: Decent Work and Economic Growth by demonstrating how innovation in assistive technology can support enterprise creation, startup development, and job generation within an emerging health-tech ecosystem. With a focus on improving health and inclusion through assistive technologies, the case also contributes to SDG 3 and SDG 10.

Introduction

In mid-2024, a group of academics and innovators came together to launch a bold experiment: Attvaran, an accelerator program designed exclusively to support assistive technology (AT) start-ups in India. The name, a fusion of AT and *tvaran*, the Sanskrit word for acceleration reflected both its thematic focus and its ambition: to test whether a startup accelerator could catalyse sustainable, scalable innovation in one of the most overlooked and underdeveloped sectors of Indian entrepreneurship.

But Attvaran was never just an accelerator. From its inception, it was conceived as a form of action research: a live experiment in building, running, and studying an intervention to learn what it truly takes to nurture inclusive innovation in a fragmented, resource-constrained context. Developed by the Global Disability Innovation Hub[1] (GDI Hub) at University College London (UCL) together with Indian Institute of Technology Delhi[2] (IITD) and Indian Institute of Technology Madras[3] (IITM), Attvaran[4] responded to a growing recognition that while assistive technology is an essential enabler of rights, livelihoods, and inclusion for disabled people, the ecosystem that supports its development and adoption remains deeply underdeveloped.

India is home to an estimated 26.8 million people with disabilities, though the true number is likely far higher due to systemic underreporting (Saikia et al., 2016). Despite policy reforms like the 2016 Rights of Persons with Disabilities Act and campaigns such as Accessible India, access to affordable, high-quality AT remains limited (Acts, Rules & Regulations, 2016). Even as the Indian AT market is projected to grow to $2.76 billion by 2030 (India Disabled and Elderly Assistive Device Market Analysis, n.d.), the pipeline of ventures bringing AT products to market remains fragile, with many startups unable to secure sustained funding, reach diverse user communities, or navigate complex regulatory and procurement pathways.

By contrast, India's pharmaceuticals and vaccines sectors have achieved global dominance through well-oiled hospital, physician, and pharmacy channels, while AT operates in a different reality, the end-users often cannot pay, insurance rarely reimburses, and there is no nationwide clinician-led distribution network. Essential devices from powered wheelchairs to digital hearing aids are thus absent from hospital formularies and roadside pharmacies alike. The result is a need-demand gap where the people most in need generate the weakest market signals.

For many founders, particularly those working outside elite metropolitan bubbles, mainstream startup support mechanisms are a poor fit. Generalist accelerators lack expertise in disability innovation. Investors are often sceptical of the market's viability, citing high R&D costs, long sales cycles, and unclear exit pathways. The needs of users, many of whom are low-income, rural, or multiply marginalised are rarely well-understood in

[1] www.disabilityinnovation.com

[2] https://www.ncaht.in/

[3] https://r2d2.iitm.ac.in/resources/ncaht

[4] https://at2030.org/attvaran-india-launch/

product development processes. And few support structures exist to help AT startups manage the dual burden of social impact and commercial sustainability.

Attvaran set out to explore whether a contextually grounded, sector-specific accelerator could address some of these issues by engaging deeply with startups, mentors, funders, and user communities over a six-month journey. What emerged was not just a program, but a platform for learning about the systemic frictions that shape disability innovation in India: where it succeeds, where it stalls, and what kinds of scaffolding are needed to enable lasting progress.

This case traces that journey of discovery, missteps, pivots, and provocations offering students and practitioners alike a unique window into the real-world dilemmas of disability innovation. At its heart lies a simple question with far-reaching implications: what does it take to accelerate not just assistive technology startups, but the very systems that allow them to grow?

Background: Founding Attvaran

The idea of Attvaran emerged from a shared frustration about how hard it was for disability-led or disability-focused technology ventures to gain traction in India. While many of these innovations had promise ranging from frugally engineered mobility aids to AI-powered vision tools, most struggled to move beyond pilot stages, often falling into the chasm between proof-of-concept and market readiness. It wasn't just about lack of capital or weak business models; it was about the absence of an ecosystem designed to support assistive technology ventures on their own terms.

This frustration resonated deeply with researchers and practitioners across three institutions: the GDI Hub, IIT Delhi and IIT Madras. Each brought a unique institutional logic and body of experience to the table. At UCL, the GDI Hub had been leading the AT2030 programme[5] - a £50 million UK Government-funded initiative testing "what works" to improve access to life-changing AT globally. Operating in over 60 countries, GDI Hub's work bridged research, innovation, and systems change. It supported the development of open-source AT products, worked with governments to reform policy, and incubated early-stage ventures. But India posed a particular puzzle: despite a booming startup culture and

[5] https://at2030.org/

growing attention to inclusion, few AT ventures were breaking through. Meanwhile, IIT Delhi and IIT Madras had spent over a decade at the coalface of AT innovation.

At IIT Delhi, the Assistech Lab had built landmark devices like the SmartCane, which is an affordable electronic mobility aid for people with visual impairments and a refreshable Braille display designed for digital inclusion. These projects weren't just engineering marvels; they were also case studies in co-design, policy engagement, and public-private collaboration.

At IIT Madras, the R2D2 Lab (Rehabilitation Research and Device Development) had taken a similarly holistic approach. It developed the Arise Standing Wheelchair, the NeoFly (a custom-fit wheelchair), and the NeoBolt (a wheelchair-motorbike hybrid add-on), all now commercialised via the startup NeoMotion. These innovations reflected a strong emphasis on frugal design, user input, and scalable manufacturing blending academic rigor with entrepreneurial ambition.

Conversations between these institutions intensified during late 2023. GDI Hub had been exploring contexts for deeper engagement in South Asia and identified India as a high-priority country. IITD and IITM were independently grappling with a common challenge: while they had incubated impressive products and occasionally helped spin off startups, they lacked a sustained structure to support scale, market entry, and systemic impact. Incubators existed, but none were fully tuned to the specific needs of AT ventures. Most general accelerators struggled to support disability-focused products that required regulatory approvals, embedded user feedback, or low-margin business models.

The missing piece was orchestration: a mechanism to bring together mentors, investors, user communities, corporates, policymakers, and research expertise into a single, purpose-driven platform. As discussions continued, the idea of Attvaran crystallised, not as a conventional accelerator but as an ecosystem experiment. The program would be temporary yet ambitious, rooted in India but connected to global learnings, and focused as much on learning what doesn't work as on celebrating success. Early conversations also surfaced a stubborn pattern that no single start-up team could cover all five lenses—medical, technical, social, business, inclusive-design—that successful AT development demands. In India's entrepreneurial culture, founders are quick to add co-founders but slower to engage users, mentors or institutional collaborators. Attvaran therefore positioned itself as a talent broker, filling the gaps with expert mentors, user test beds, and stakeholder workshops.

Crucially, the program was born not only from strategic alignment but also from human alignment. Relationships among key individuals across GDI Hub, IITD, and IITM many of whom had collaborated on research, prototyping, or policy projects previously helped build trust and momentum. The timing was also fortuitous. Funding from AT2030 was available. Institutional interest was high. And India's AT landscape was showing signs of ferment (An overview of Assistive Tech startups in India—Tracxn, 2025): grassroots inventors, newly formed startups, and a few catalytic funders were beginning to shift the discourse around disability and design.

By early 2024, Attvaran had moved from concept to commitment. Its foundational question—what kind of accelerator does AT need? remained open. But its mode of inquiry was clear: learn by building, support by doing, and interrogate every assumption.

Background: India's AT Ecosystem

AT is often referred to as the "infrastructure of inclusion." From screen readers and mobility aids to prosthetics, communication devices, and accessible software, AT enables millions of people with disabilities to participate more fully in society. Yet globally, access to these technologies remains shockingly low. The World Health Organization estimates that over one billion people currently need AT, and this number will rise substantially as populations age and chronic conditions increase (Disability, 2023). Despite this demand, the sector is often overlooked - underfunded, poorly regulated, and fragmented across geographies and market segments (Albala et al., 2021; Holloway et al., 2021).

India is no exception. Although officially home to 26.8 million people with disabilities according to the 2011 Census, actual figures are likely much higher. National policy has gradually shifted toward a rights-based approach - most notably with the Rights of Persons with Disabilities (RPwD) Act of 2016 (Narayan & John, 2017), which expanded recognised disability categories and mandated accessibility across education, infrastructure, and employment. Government schemes such as ADIP (Assistance to Disabled Persons for Purchase/Fitting of Aids and Appliances) (ADIP | Department of Empowerment of Persons with Disabilities (DEPwD) | India, n.d.) and campaigns like Accessible India have attempted to improve access to devices, particularly through subsidised distribution models (Accessible India Campaign | Department of Empowerment of Persons with Disabilities (DEPwD) | India, n.d.).

Yet despite these efforts, the market for assistive technologies remains immature. A 2023 study estimated that more than half of Indians with severe disabilities lack access to even basic AT (Senjam et al., 2023). Key barriers include high device costs (often due to import dependence), lack of awareness among users and service providers, weak distribution infrastructure - especially in rural areas - and limited public or private financing to support innovation (Senjam et al., 2019, 2021). Moreover, regulatory processes for assistive devices are poorly defined, especially for products that are on the line between medical devices, consumer goods, and accessibility solutions.

Ironically, the demand signals are strong. India's AT market was valued at $716.2 million in 2023 and is projected to grow at a CAGR of 20%, reaching $2.76 billion by 2030 (India Disabled and Elderly Assistive Device Market Analysis, n.d.). This growth is fuelled by multiple demographic and social trends: an ageing population, increased diagnosis of learning disabilities and neurodivergence, greater expectations of inclusive workplaces and schools, and rising digital penetration. These trends suggest that AT is not only a moral imperative but also a strategic economic opportunity - a chance to build a high-impact sector serving both domestic and global markets.

Despite this, investor engagement remains lukewarm. Many mainstream venture capitalists see AT ventures as high-risk and low return, especially those developing hardware or devices for low-income users (How Sovereign Funds Could Empower the Future of Assistive Technology and Disability AI, 2023). Concerns include small addressable markets, low purchasing power among target users, long development cycles, and limited exit pathways. These perceptions, while not always accurate (The Case for Investing in Assistive Technology, n.d.), have real consequences: AT startups often struggle to raise capital, relying instead on grants, Corporate Social Responsibility CSR funding, and philanthropic capital. Meanwhile, even impact investors, who might be better aligned in values, frequently lack the domain knowledge to evaluate AT ventures effectively.

In this vacuum, a patchwork support ecosystem has emerged (India Is Prime Ground for Impact Investments. Here's Why, 2023). Organisations like Villgro, Social Alpha, and the Assistech Foundation (ATF) have run programs targeting disability tech or health innovation. Academic incubators - such as NSRCEL at IIM Bangalore, CIIE at IIM Ahmedabad, and BIRAC-supported bioincubators—have occasionally supported AT ventures, especially those that intersect with health or edtech. These initiatives have helped seed early-stage ideas and build proof-of-concept prototypes. However, they often fall short in providing sustained, sector-specific support particularly in areas like clinical validation, accessibility testing, regulatory navigation, and distribution partnerships.

Crucially, many of these incubators operate on short-term cycles and are unable to commit to the kind of user, ecosystem-level engagement required to move AT ventures from prototype to scale. Moreover, few explicitly focus on connecting startups to real users, especially those outside urban centres meaning that product-market fit is often assumed rather than earned.

At the same time, funding mechanisms are shifting. India's mandatory CSR law, which requires companies to spend 2% of profits on social development, has emerged as a potential funding avenue for AT ventures. Some companies have begun moving from direct donations of devices toward more strategic engagement with AT start-ups - co-developing pilots, funding user research, or integrating solutions into workplace inclusion strategies. This trend, while still nascent, signals a broader shift in how disability innovation is understood: not just as charity or compliance, but as a strategic lever for social and business value.

It is into this complex, fragmented, and shifting ecosystem that Attvaran was launched. Unlike prior efforts, Attvaran aimed to build a dedicated AT accelerator, shaped by sector-specific knowledge and embedded in long-standing academic networks. It sought not only to support startups, but to test new ways of building markets, aligning stakeholders, and transforming innovation pathways. Positioned at the intersection of academia, practice, and systems change, it offered a rare opportunity to examine the limits of conventional acceleration - and what might lie beyond.

Current Challenges and Dilemmas

While Attvaran began with a clear mandate - to support AT startups in India - the experience of running the program quickly revealed a series of structural tensions that were far more complex than anticipated. These tensions were not simply operational hurdles; they reflected foundational questions about how to support innovation in a sector shaped by market failures, policy gaps, and profound social inequality. Below, we outline three core dilemmas that emerged during the program. These are not unique to Attvaran but echo across global disability innovation ecosystems, but the program's experience brings them into perspective.

Dilemma 1: Impact Vs. Profitability—What Kind of Growth Should be Accelerated?

A recurring challenge for Attvaran was how to support ventures whose value lies in social inclusion, not just commercial return. Many startups in the cohort were founded by individuals with lived experience—disabled entrepreneurs, caregivers, therapists who identified deep user needs but operated in markets with limited paying capacity. Their innovations were often impactful but not immediately attractive to traditional investors, particularly those seeking fast returns or large addressable markets. For example, a startup creating low-cost educational devices for disabled children had clear social value but no obvious path to monetisation. Another team building a motorised wheelchair add-on faced manufacturing costs that far exceeded what most users could afford without subsidies or institutional buyers.

Attvaran faced a difficult choice: Should it steer these startups toward profit-first models, helping them reshape their offerings to appeal to mainstream capital? Or should it help them lean into impact-first strategies, including CSR partnerships, grant funding, and NGO collaborations—even if that meant slower or less scalable growth?

The program tried to do both. Providing sessions on revenue models and pricing strategy while also facilitating access to grant-makers and CSR funders. But this balancing act surfaced a deeper strategic question: What does success look like for an AT accelerator? Is it a high-growth company with investor backing, or a small, mission-driven venture that improves lives but never becomes "VC-ready"? And can a single accelerator design truly serve both?

> *We've been trying to reach out to investors who would be interested in funding ... but a VC is going to look at a business which is gonna grow 20 to 50X in the next four to five years... Having that kind of a growth in assistive technology or in rehab is actually a bit... not seen. – Participating Startup Founder*

Dilemma 2: Mentorship as Support Vs. Mentorship as Dependency

Mentorship was widely praised by Attvaran participants. Many startups credited their mentors with opening doors to pilot sites, refining product designs, or navigating tricky questions around pricing and procurement. However, mentorship also surfaced hidden asymmetries of power and expectation.

In a sector where many founders come from technical or clinical backgrounds rather than business schools or startup hubs, the mentor often became the most experienced person in the room, and their guidance held significant weight. While some mentors were highly engaged in testing products, visiting teams, making warm introductions, others were less responsive or constrained by time, creating gaps in continuity. In some cases, mismatched expectations or inconsistent engagement led to confusion, demotivation, or over-reliance.

Attvaran had to ask: What kind of mentorship architecture is appropriate for this context? Should mentors be rotated or assigned in panels to avoid dependency? Should there be structured mentoring curricula rather than ad hoc check-ins? And how should the program support startups when mentorship becomes inconsistent or counterproductive?

The challenge was not just logistical but relational. Mentors had the power to shape narratives, steer strategy, and legitimise ideas. This created value, but also vulnerability.

> *Our mentor was one of the first to test our product - before we'd even finished internal testing. That kind of feedback was invaluable. But for some other teams, mentor contact started too late… it's a missed opportunity when time is limited. – Participating Startup Founder*

Dilemma 3: One-Time Boost Vs. Long-Term Support, When Does Acceleration End?

Most accelerators operate on a short-cycle model: a fixed duration of intensive support, culminating in a demo day or pitch event. Attvaran followed this format but quickly realised its limitations. AT startups rarely follow the trajectories of SaaS or fintech ventures. They require longer product development timelines, complex regulatory clearances, and more time to build trust with users - especially when working with marginalised or medically vulnerable populations.

By the end of the formal program, many startups were only just beginning to enter procurement conversations, refine pricing models, or navigate early pilots. Some had secured grants or user feedback, but few were investor ready. The program team was faced with a difficult truth: short-term interventions, no matter how well-executed, were insufficient to bridge the valley of death between pilot and scale.

Should Attvaran have extended support beyond its original scope? Introduced a lightweight alumni program? Created sector-wide platforms for follow-on investment or product validation? These questions remain open, but they expose the underlying tension between programmatic design and sectoral need. For AT ventures to succeed, support needs to extend beyond acceleration and into sustained ecosystem building.

> *You can't do this in three months and move on. AT is not like SaaS or consumer apps. If we're serious about this sector, we need long-term scaffolding. – Participating Startup Founder*

Together, these dilemmas point to a deeper question that Attvaran had to confront: Was it building startups, or was it building a sector? The answer, increasingly, was both. But each direction came with its own set of trade-offs—between scale and depth, speed and trust, capital and care. For accelerators working in mission-driven spaces like disability innovation, these tensions are not peripheral. They are central design questions that must be wrestled with openly, iteratively, and with humility.

Discussion Questions

How should accelerators operating in impact-driven sectors like assistive technology define success?

Should success be measured by startup scalability, funding raised, or social outcomes delivered? What tensions arise when these metrics conflict, and how can accelerator programs navigate them?

In contexts where user needs are high but purchasing power is low, how can AT ventures develop viable business models?

Should accelerators push startups toward commercialisation, or help them build non-profit or hybrid pathways? What trade-offs are involved in each approach?

What risks emerge when mentorship becomes a central component of an accelerator program, particularly in sectors where founders have limited business experience?

How might accelerators balance the value of personalised mentorship with the risk of over-dependence or inconsistent support?

Given the long development cycles and regulatory complexity of AT ventures, is the typical short-term accelerator model fit for purpose?

What alternative program structures (e.g. tiered support, alumni networks, embedded partners) could better serve startups in slow-moving but high-impact sectors?

Attvaran aimed to build both startups and a broader ecosystem. Is this dual ambition realistic or overstretched?

What are the risks and opportunities of combining venture acceleration with market shaping, policy engagement, and ecosystem building within a single program?

Supplementary Reading

These readings offer a combination of academic theory, policy analysis, and sector-specific insights that support deeper classroom engagement with Attvaran's dilemmas. They help frame the challenges of assistive technology innovation in India and beyond and ground the case in current thinking on inclusive entrepreneurship and market shaping.

Assistive Technology Ecosystem and Innovation Strategy

- Albala, S., Holloway, C., Austin, V., & Kattel, R. (2021). *New economics of assistive technology: A call for a missions approach* [Working paper]. Institute for Innovation and Public Purpose. https://apo.org.au/node/311062
- Holloway, C., Morgado Ramirez, D. Z., Bhatnagar, T., Oldfrey, B., Morjaria, P., Moulic, S. G., Ebuenyi, I. D., Barbareschi, G., Meeks, F., Massie, J., Ramos-Barajas, F., McVeigh, J., Keane, K., Torrens, G., Rao, P. V. M., MacLachlan, M., Austin, V., Kattel, R., Metcalf, C. D., & Sujatha, S. (2021). A review of innovation strategies and processes to improve access to AT: Looking ahead to open innovation ecosystems. *Assistive Technology*, *33*(sup1), 68–86. https://doi.org/10.1080/10400435.2021.1970653
- Mazzucato, M. (2016). From market fixing to market-creating: A new framework for innovation policy. *Industry and Innovation*, *23*(2), 140–156. https://doi.org/10.1080/13662716.2016.1146124

Market Growth and Policy Landscape in India

- *An overview of Assistive Tech startups in India—Tracxn.* (2025, March 19). https://tracxn.com/d/explore/assistive-tech-startups-in-india/__zD_H3GnXQKkNKjgUy9Bfv_0lhxVbnbp_V9Iyl4QD5VU
- *India is prime ground for impact investments. Here's why.* (2023, March 15). World Economic Forum. https://www.weforum.org/stories/2023/03/impact-investors-india-new-research/
- Saikia, N., Bora, J. K., Jasilionis, D., & Shkolnikov, V. M. (2016). Disability Divides in India: Evidence from the 2011 Census. *PLoS ONE, 11*(8), e0159809. https://doi.org/10.1371/journal.pone.0159809

Accelerators, Mentorship, and Learning

- Sarasvathy, S. D. (2001). Causation and Effectuation: Toward a Theoretical Shift from Economic Inevitability to Entrepreneurial Contingency. *The Academy of Management Review, 26*(2), 243–263. https://doi.org/10.2307/259121

Investment and System Transformation

- Lave, J., & Wenger, E. (1991, September 27). *Situated Learning: Legitimate Peripheral Participation.* Higher Education from Cambridge University Press; Cambridge University Press. https://doi.org/10.1017/CBO9780511815355
- Diamond, D. W. (1984). Financial Intermediation and Delegated Monitoring. *The Review of Economic Studies, 51*(3), 393–414. https://doi.org/10.2307/2297430

Learning Outcomes and Objectives
By engaging with this case, students and practitioners will:

1. Understand the distinctive challenges of disability-inclusive innovation and assistive technology entrepreneurship in emerging markets.
    (a) Grasp the structural barriers AT startups face—such as fragmented markets, affordability constraints, complex regulatory requirements, and low investor familiarity.

   (b) Reflect on how disability innovation differs from conventional tech or health innovation and why sector-specific accelerators may be necessary.

2. Critically evaluate the design, purpose, and limitations of accelerator programs in complex, low-infrastructure environments.
   (a) Analyse the mismatch between short-term acceleration cycles and the long-term support needs of ventures working on inclusive, hardware-intensive, or socially impactful solutions.
   (b) Debate whether accelerators should focus narrowly on startups or adopt broader ecosystem-shaping roles (e.g., market creation, investor education, CSR engagement).

3. Explore strategic trade-offs in building social ventures: impact vs. profitability, mentorship vs. dependency, and short-term support vs. long-term accompaniment.
   (a) Examine how accelerators like Attvaran balance diverse models of value creation—commercial, social, and systemic—and how they adapt to different types of ventures and founders.
   (b) Identify how support programs can be intentionally designed to mitigate over-dependence and promote founder resilience, particularly for underrepresented or non-traditional entrepreneurs.

This case is ideal for graduate-level courses in Social Entrepreneurship, Inclusive Innovation, Startup Ecosystem Design, Disability and Technology and Global Health Innovation. It supports both business and public policy teaching tracks and can be used in sessions exploring frugal innovation, mission-oriented acceleration, or inclusion-centred product development (Table 15.1).

Table 15.1 List of Attvaran Start-ups

Category	*Start-ups*	*Brief description*
Spark: Five young startups that are early stage but brimming with promise.	Euphelity Private Limited	Euphelity focuses on creating educational solutions for specially abled students, like those with Cerebral Palsy, Dyslexia, blindness, deafness, voicelessness, etc. students, for their education till class 5th. Founder: Anant Vaish
	Exobot Dynamics	Exobot Dynamics offers "Exobot Hand," an advanced bionic prosthetic for upper limb amputees. This lightweight and durable bionic hand mimics natural hand movements using myoelectric sensors, providing intuitive and precise control. It features an adaptive grip, high load capacity, and long-lasting battery life, making it a practical and empowering solution for users. Founder: Munish Kumar
	Panoculon Labs	Panoculon Labs creates AI-powered smart glasses and navigation for better environmental perception without GPS. Founders: Sreeraj R and Rishabh Sharma
	Wheel Ease Solutions	Wheel Ease Solutions provides "Clip Ease," an innovative electric clip-on kit that transforms manual wheelchairs into electric-powered ones. This solution aims to enhance mobility and independence for wheelchair users by offering features such as a lightweight construction, 25 km range per charge, quick charging capability, and a 25 km/h top speed. Founders: Maqool Saifi, Taha Nafees & Ayan Baig
	uDot Braille Tech Pvt Ltd	uDot is making education equitable for the visually impaired by developing a dynamic tactile interface. Founders: Kaviraj Prithvi and Lalika

(*continued*)

Table 15.1 (continued)

Category	*Start-ups*	*Brief description*
Start: These startups were originally selected for acceleration because of their ideal timing and promising innovations, which are beginning to disrupt their respective fields.	Nirvesh Enterprises Private Limited	Enhancing stroke survivor care with Synapsil, a multimodal wearable system for comprehensive physiological assessments. Founder: Dr Anvesh Jallapally
	Sahayatha HealthCare	Innovating wheelchairs with integrated cleansing systems and recline capabilities for enhanced hygiene and comfort. Founder: Sruthi Babu
	Next Skills 360	Bridging educational gaps by teaching twenty-first - century skills to underserved students, including accessible coding tools for the visually impaired. Founder: Suraj Meiyur
	PhonoLogix	Addressing communication disorders with the Speech Ally app and platform, offering early intervention through gamified activities and teletherapy. Founders: Elizabeth Jean Thomas and Jijo John
	Grailmaker Innovations	Helping the visually impaired navigate spaces with the Spacefelt app, offering personalized navigation through QR labels. Founders: Vivian Manohar, Prathyusha Potharaju
	IWAYPLUS	Providing geocoded indoor maps and positioning solutions for seamless navigation in large indoor spaces like hospitals and airports. Founders: Vikas Upadhyay and Pulkit Sapra
	Thryv Mobility	Specialising in accessible and sustainable transportation solutions for people with disabilities. Founders: Justin Jesudas and Sujatha Srinivasan
	Insighte	Offering personalised therapy for children with autism and ADHD through a platform that supports home, school, and online services. Founder: Midhun Noble
	Enable Me Access Association	Advocating for accessibility and inclusion by providing training, assessments, and solutions for various needs. Founders: Anubha Singhal and Peter Gibson

(*continued*)

Table 15.1 (continued)

Category	*Start-ups*	*Brief description*
Scale: These startups are on a trajectory for growth and are have provide a purposeful, well-built, and robust solutions.	BeAble Health	BeAble Health addresses the challenge of monotonous and time-consuming rehabilitation for upper limb motor deficits caused by strokes or spinal cord injuries. Their solution, ArmAble, combines hardware and software to create interactive therapeutic games that engage patients in high-repetition exercises essential for neuroplasticity. Founders: Habib Ali and Sreehari K.G
	TRUE Assistive Technology	TrueAT focuses on innovative solutions for vehicles and spaces, like its patented TurnPlus swivel seat mechanism for cars. This award-winning product has improved mobility and independence for over 500 users in India, including employees at Microsoft and Titan. Founder: Naina Padaki
	Sunbots Innovations	Sunbots addresses the educational and employment gap for 9.5 million blind and visually impaired children, of whom less than 1% achieve braille literacy and formal education. Their solution, SMARTON, is a mobile application and camera-enabled device that connects to any glasses. It uses camera vision and generative AI to make physical and digital content accessible. Founders: Suket Amin and Deep Parmar
	SignAble Communications	SignAble addresses the challenge faced by 63 million deaf or hard-of-hearing individuals in India who struggle to access essential services due to a lack of sign language interpreters. Their app offers an on-demand Indian Sign Language interpretation service using Video Remote Interpretation and Video Relay Service. For businesses, SignAble provides a web-based application that allows employees to access ISL interpretation via laptops or desktops without needing mobile devices. Founders: Tarun Sarwal and Rupmani Chhetri
	SaralX	SaralX addresses the issue of digital inaccessibility, which prevents brands from reaching the $13 trillion market potential of people with disabilities, who make up 15% of the global population. SaralX provides technology and expert feedback to ensure digital assets are accessible and compliant. Founder: Akashdeep Bansal
	lifeandlimb.ai	LifeandLimb.ai leverages AI and machine learning to develop functional and customisable prosthetic limbs, making advanced prosthetics affordable and accessible for people with limb differences. Founder: Nishant Agarwal

Acknowledgements The authors acknowledge the use of Claude 4 Thinking to assist with drafting the abstract and structuring content analysis. All AI-generated content was reviewed, edited, and approved by the human authors, who take full responsibility for the accuracy and integrity of the final manuscript.

Competing Interests This project was part of AT2030 and was funded with UK International Development from the UK government. The authors have no conflicts of interest to declare that are relevant to the content of this chapter.

References

Accessible India Campaign | Department of Empowerment of Persons with Disabilities (DEPwD) | India. (n.d.). Retrieved January 19, 2025, from https://depwd.gov.in/accessible-india-campaign/

Acts, Rules & Regulations. (2016). https://depwd.gov.in/acts/

ADIP | Department of Empowerment of Persons with Disabilities (DEPwD) | India. (n.d.). Retrieved January 19, 2025, from https://depwd.gov.in/adip/

Albala, S., Holloway, C., Austin, V., & Kattel, R. (2021). New economics of assistive technology: A call for a missions approach [Working paper]. Institute for Innovation and Public Purpose. https://apo.org.au/node/311062

An overview of Assistive Tech startups in India—Tracxn. (2025, March 19). https://tracxn.com/d/explore/assistive-tech-startups-in-india/__zD_H3GnXQKkNKjgUy9Bfv_0lhxVbnbp_V9Iyl4QD5VU

Disability. (2023). World Health Organization. https://www.who.int/newsroom/fact-sheets/detail/disability-and-health

Holloway, C., Morgado Ramirez, D. Z., Bhatnagar, T., Oldfrey, B., Morjaria, P., Moulic, S. G., Ebuenyi, I. D., Barbareschi, G., Meeks, F., Massie, J., Ramos-Barajas, F., McVeigh, J., Keane, K., Torrens, G., Rao, P. V. M., MacLachlan, M., Austin, V., Kattel, R., Metcalf, C. D., & Sujatha, S. (2021). A review of innovation strategies and processes to improve access to AT: Looking ahead to open innovation ecosystems. *Assistive Technology, 33*(sup1), 68–86. https://doi.org/10.1080/10400435.2021.1970653

How sovereign funds could empower the future of assistive technology and disability AI. (2023, August 15). World Economic Forum. https://www.weforum.org/stories/2023/08/sovereign-funds-future-assistive-technology-disability-ai/

India Disabled and Elderly Assistive Device Market Analysis. (n.d.). Retrieved April 5, 2025, from https://www.nextmsc.com/report/india-disabled-and-elderly-assistive-device-market

India is prime ground for impact investments. Here's why. (2023, March 15). World Economic Forum. https://www.weforum.org/stories/2023/03/impact-investors-india-new-research/

Narayan, C. L., & John, T. (2017). The rights of persons with disabilities act, 2016: Does it address the needs of the persons with mental illness and their families. *Indian Journal of Psychiatry, 59*(1), 17–20. https://doi.org/10.4103/psychiatry.IndianJPsychiatry_75_17

Saikia, N., Bora, J. K., Jasilionis, D., & Shkolnikov, V. M. (2016). Disability divides in India: Evidence from the 2011 census. *PLoS One, 11*(8), e0159809. https://doi.org/10.1371/journal.pone.0159809

Senjam, S. S., Foster, A., & Bascaran, C. (2021). Barriers to using assistive technology among students with visual disability in schools for the blind in Delhi, India. *Disability and Rehabilitation: Assistive Technology, 16*(7), 802–806. https://doi.org/10.1080/17483107.2020.1738566

Senjam, S. S., Foster, A., Bascaran, C., & Vashist, P. (2019). Awareness, utilization and barriers in accessing assistive technology among young patients attending a low vision rehabilitation clinic of a tertiary eye care Centre in Delhi. *Indian Journal of Ophthalmology, 67*(10), 1548–1554. https://doi.org/10.4103/ijo.IJO_197_19

Senjam, S. S., Manna, S., Kishore, J., Kumar, A., Kumar, R., Vashist, P., Titiyal, J. S., Jena, P. K., Christian, D. S., Singh, U. S., & Kamath, R. (2023). Assistive technology usage, unmet needs and barriers to access: A sub-population-based study in India. *The Lancet Regional Health - Southeast Asia, 15*, 100213. https://doi.org/10.1016/j.lansea.2023.100213

The Case for Investing in Assistive Technology. (n.d.). ATscale. Retrieved April 5, 2025, from https://atscalepartnership.org/investment-case

CHAPTER 16

Neurosynaptic: Creating Affordable, Accessible Healthcare Delivery Via Digital Innovation

Sachidananda Benegal and G. Sabarinathan

Abstract Healthcare delivery to the remotest of villages in a vast country like India has been a grappling problem for decades. Over two decades the founders of Neurosynaptics have faced numerous challenges, made strategic pivots, grappled with funding challenges, and developed a platform that today promises to be a model that can be taken global. The case highlights the challenges of the health care delivery system and how passionate technology entrepreneurship could solve grass-root challenges, leveraging existing players and focusing on quality. It leaves the reader to help the founders manage their possibility of mission drift while tackling multiple stakeholders on-boarded during the ventures' growth phase. Additionally, it asks what

S. Benegal (✉)
NSRCEL, Indian Institute of Management Bangalore, Bangalore, India
e-mail: sachidananda.bs14@alumni.iimb.ac.in

G. Sabarinathan
Institute of Management Bangalore, Bangalore, India
e-mail: sabari@iimb.ac.in

A. S. Galande et al. (eds.), *Context-inspired Entrepreneurship*, Sustainable Development Goals Series,
https://doi.org/10.1007/978-981-95-9831-1_16

changes would be necessary in the business model going ahead, given the observed environmental munificence over the years.

Keywords Implementation partners • Grass-root delivery • Technology platform • Grant funding • Investor expectations

SDG Links While the case is on improving health outcomes through remote diagnostics, it contributes to SDG 8: Decent Work and Economic Growth by demonstrating how health technologies can enhance healthcare in rural areas and in turn improve economic productivity (SDG 8.2). With a focus on healthcare innovation, the case also aligns well with SDG 3 and SDG 9.

Introduction

It was June 2021, right in between the COVID-19 lockdown, when the phone rang. Rajeev had just finished his afternoon lunch and was planning to watch the news. It was Sameer, his partner who wanted him to get on a conference call with one of their investors.

There was a sudden spur of medical practitioners offering telemedical consulting using existing mobile applications. The COVID-19 anxiety had gotten a lot of people paying for the teleconsultation clarifying their doubts with the doctor. It was an opportunity that could help generate revenue, especially when their well-oiled ReMeDi (Remote Medical Diagnostics) solution was not currently being used in the rural markets, due to the lockdown restrictions.

The ReMeDi solution was their most recent version of the product, which was developed over several years working towards a low-cost high fidelity diagnostic accessories kit, which enhanced telemedical consultation effectiveness. Their diagnostic kits transmitted accurate health parameters to the expert doctors in urban hospitals, even when operated on by a low-skilled volunteer who may be from the village. With COVID-19 disrupting the usual operations of Neurosynaptics in rural areas, the spurt in telemedical consultations by doctors and the large pool of urban families who could afford a stepped-down version of ReMeDi kit[1] along with the mobile application for their family, the situation seemed well suited for a pivot.

The two founders however, had committed to Neurosynaptics for a much more personal cause. They had spent the last decade and half

[1] The kit is to be thought of as a platform (not just a set of devices and the software)—which can enable a lot of possibilities in the health care at the bottom of the pyramid.

developing the reliable and robust kit that was a solution which would work within the context of the available health care ecosystem in rural India. They recently began servicing other developing countries with similar infrastructure challenges in healthcare delivery. Their growth had convinced them that they were delivering impactful results where health care access was a challenge.

The COVID 19 opportunity looked like something that if chosen would give their investors a very lucrative return. Given that they already had their production facility, it would not be very challenging to cater to the increased demand (even though its deliveries could be slightly delayed, getting official permission to operate the facility would not be challenging as they were already in the healthcare segment). However, on a personal front, pursuing the opportunity meant they would need to budge them from their mission of improving the reducing the infrastructural constraints in rural healthcare delivery.

Some of their investors were first time social impact investors who would carry a return expectation that operated for the commercial sector. They had been very patient with the team since they saw the impact created on the ground and the headway the team had been making. Sameer and Rajeev had to decide how long they could continue creating an impact through their social venture without having a clear exit for these investors.

As they finished the call with the investor and borrowed time to think about the opportunity and get back, they continue to reflect on their journey and make the appropriate choices for the future.

The Health Care System in India—A Brief

Government has been the primary provider of health care in India, since Independence, spending about 1.9% of the GDP on health care in FY24.[2] The task of providing a strong delivery of health care for the large population of the country, through government infrastructure has, however, always been a challenge.[3] Health care is part of the concurrent list, where both the central and the state governments play an active role. However, implementation is the responsibility of the state government in almost all cases.

[2] IBEF. (2023). Healthcare Industry in India, Indian Healthcare Sector, Services. Www.ibef.org. https://www.ibef.org/industry/healthcare-india accessed on 30th March 2025.

[3] Bureau, E. N. (2019, April 1). *Evolution of Indian healthcare in last 70 years.* Express Healthcare. https://www.expresshealthcare.in/blogs/guest-blogs-healthcare/evolution-of-indian-healthcare-in-last-70-years/410530/ accessed on 30th March 2025.

Today, the public health infrastructure is composed of five levels[4]:

1. **Village Health guides and ASHA**: Accredited Social Health Activists (ASHAs) are the first point of contact in rural areas, who work at the grass root level—offering basic health education, promoting hygiene, and providing initial medical advice.
2. **Sub-centers**: Each sub-center carters to a population of about 5000 people. It serves as the first point of contact between the Primary Health Center (PHC) and community. The sub-center is the most peripheral unit of this system and has an Auxiliary Nurse Midwife (ANM) and one male Multi-purpose Worker [MPW (M)]. A lady health worker is in charge of six sub-centers. These sub-centers are expected to provide services in relation to maternal and child health, family welfare, nutrition, immunization, diarrhea control, and control of communicable diseases.
3. **Primary Health centers (PHC)**: Each PHC serves a population of 30,000 in plains and 20,000 in hilly, tribal, and difficult areas. They provide integrated curative and preventive health, with emphasis on preventive and promotive aspects. State Governments establish and maintain these PHCs under various programs. They are the first point of contact between village communities and a medical officer. A medical officer is in charge of the PHC and is supported by fourteen paramedical and other staff. It also acts as a referral unit for six sub-centers and often has four to six beds for in-patients.
4. **Community Health centers (CHC)**: They serve a population of about 120,000. Four medical specialists including Surgeon, Physician, Gynecologist, and Pediatrician are supported by twenty-one paramedical and other staff at each CHC. There are around thirty indoor beds with OT, X-ray, labor room and laboratory facilities. A CHC is a referral center for four PHCs within its jurisdiction, providing facilities for obstetric care and specialist expertise.
5. **District Hospitals**: They are the tertiary level of health care and provide comprehensive secondary health care facilities.

[4] *Health Care Delivery System in India: Structure and Function • BNS Institute*. (2024, March 22). BNS (B.Sc in Nursing) Institute. https://bns.institute/community-health-nursing/health-care-delivery-system-india/ accessed on 30th March 2025.

The idea of a ASHA worker had been introduced only as recently as 2005 under the National Rural Health Mission (NRHM),[5] and they have since been a formidable force to recon in ensuring rural health delivery. Most of these sub-centers, PHCs and CHCs are in government buildings, and a small portion are located either in rented buildings or rent-free Panchayat/Voluntary Society buildings.

In addition to the above infrastructure, India's rich heritage of traditional and indigenous health care systems also provides an alternative for of the rural population. Collectively called AYUSH (Ayurveda, Yoga & Naturopathy, Unani, Siddha, and Homoeopathy) these form an integral part of the country's health care delivery.

The government has introduced several national health programs over the last 75 years. Some notable ones are:

(a) **National Health Mission (NHM)**—an umbrella program that encompasses the NRHM and National Urban Health mission; that works to improve access, equity, and quality of health care services.
(b) **Ayushman Bharath**—aimed at providing health insurance coverage for the economically vulnerable families, enduring free access to secondary and tertiary health care services.
(c) **Reproductive, Maternal, Newborn, Child, and Adolescent Health (RMNCH+A)**—a strategy to focus on reducing child and maternal mortality, as well as improving health outcomes across the life stages.
(d) **National Vector Borne Disease Control Program (NVBDCP)**—aimed at the control of vector borne diseases like malaria, dengue, and chikungunya.
(e) **Revised National Tuberculosis Control Program (RNTCP)**—aimed at reducing the tuberculosis cases and deaths rapidly through comprehensive care and prevention strategies.

Despite these efforts by the government (both the central and state) a substantial portion of the rural population finds it extremely difficult to have access to quality health care through the public system.

The private health players include large corporate hospitals, as well as small private-owned clinics and nursing homes. They are also often more

[5] *About Accredited Social Health Activist (ASHA): National Health Mission.* (n.d.). Nhm.gov.in. https://nhm.gov.in/index1.php?lang=1&level=1&sublinkid=150&lid=226 accessed on 30th March 2025.

expensive and may be more specialized. Located mostly in metros, tier 1 and tier 2 cities, these often cater to those who can afford out-of-pocket expenses or have health insurance coverage.

To provide comprehensive coverage for such a large population, the government has had to strengthen its health care delivery. In the rural areas where it is a predominant health care provider, several challenges continue to haunt the delivery like—accessibility, affordability, quality of care, human resource shortage and infrastructure. Any private players developing solutions for the rural areas need to grapple with these challenges and have been a strong deterrent to their efforts in this direction. Further, Government has a mandate to provide free health care at the primary level, which the private providers would find challenging (to develop a sustainable model).

The Genesis

When Sameer and Rajeev met for the first time during their post-graduation at the Indian Institute of Science (IISc), Bangalore in 1993, little did they know they were to embark on an entrepreneurial journey together almost a decade later, that too in a domain they were completely unfamiliar with! In 2002 after nearly a decade of technological experience they started Neurosynaptics.

Their initial idea was to interface the human nervous system with electronics in applications like prosthetic limbs, artificial retina, etc. However, this transformed in unanticipated way as they met Prof Ashok Jhunjhunwala who was heading the Telecommunications and Computer Networks (TeNeT) group at the Indian Institute of Technology Chennai at his lecture in IISc. TeNeT group was set up with a vision to develop low-cost technologies to enable telecom growth in India.

The lecture by Prof Jhunjhunwala was pivotal in the journey of these two nascent entrepreneurs who had their roots in villages that were distant from the major cities. They connected immediately to the nature of the problem TeNeT initiative could empower! The solutions that TeNeTs' group developed could be fundamental technology layer which could be the building blocks for other entrepreneurs to build specific solutions that were needed in the rural areas like health care, education, utilities and many more.

The founders decided, to quote—"At that point of time we thought and realized that it was much more impactful to do something for the masses rather than to do something niche though it has its own advantages." They took up the challenge of getting health care in rural areas of the country in an affordable and accessible manner with quality. This has since remained a Neurosynaptics mission, allowing them to overcome several technical and institutional barriers as they encountered them.

Product and Delivery Models Evolution

Given their academic and professional background, technology was going to be a prominent driver of their product innovation. While technology was a strong point for the team, and any technology automatically enables a level of scale, it was unclear what was likely to be the manner in which technology itself would evolve over time. This meant the team had to be flexible and open to adopting challenges to emerging technologies.

The TeNet initiative in pursuit of developing a low-cost affordable solution that would operate in a rural setting, decided to install a few kiosks that would be powered by Wireless in Local Loop technology (WiLL) instead of telephone lines, which required huge upfront investments to serve rural areas. It took Neurosynaptics nearly two years to develop a technology solution which could be deployed on the kiosk that had developed and installed as part of the TeNeT initiative. They launched this first peer-to-peer teleconsulting solution in 2005 though the WiLL powered kiosk.

Building on TeNeTs' infrastructure; WiLL kiosks formed their first value delivery channel. There was a lot of positive media coverage of the enormous value delivery possibility that telemedicine promised in a vast country like India. Many hospitals, who were crucial to deliver end-value, were willing to be part of this transformation.

After their first installation at the WiLL kiosk failed to sustain the initial euphoric reception. There were several other complementary capabilities that needed to be integrated. The team realized that (a) integrated pharmacy service, (b) a well-trained and dedicated kiosk operator and (c) incorporation of numerous social concerns—were essential to ensure their telemedicine solution would deliver value. Such customization and specialization in delivery would eventually rule out multi-service kiosks as a viable and long-term delivery channel.

The founders decided to focus on technology and products, while they were willing to improve the delivery by partnering with various implementation agencies—whom they called implementation partners (IPs). Understanding the ground realities was extremely important to solve for the colossal set of challenges that are involved in ensuring teleconsulting-based healthcare delivery. The team found a few partners - IL&FS, Piramal, Janani and Drishti; they could work with in delivering the promised value and decided to experiment with some of their own centers as the last mile delivery in rural health care. With their initial experiments, and the success of some of their partners better than their own attempts at health delivery, they realized that they could rely on implementation partner who were more evolved at ground level delivery of health care.

When Neurosynaptics approached Janani as a partner, Janani was engaged in putting up a large-scale health care network across Bihar. In these attempts while on the one hand the founder encountered some imposters who claimed to be doctors, there were also other individuals who were well versed with what it takes to scale an initiative on the ground. This gave Neurosynaptics their first scalable project in 2008.

World Health Partners (WHP), another IP, was an offshoot of Janani. WHP raised grants from different funding agencies, the donors, and set up telemedicine centers as a focal point in the project delivery area to attract people to come to the center for general health issues. It organized health care programs according to verticals - for example family planning, tuberculosis, pneumonia or diarrhea etc., and set up telemedicine centers which became the focal point for attracting patients to the center.

The funding for these initiatives by IPs came from multiple sources - in addition to donors, WHP also tapped into government funds for various schemes. For example, for family planning there is an incentive given to people who are going through the sterilization procedure. For Tuberculosis there existed an incentive for the health worker to deliver the drugs. Programs like RNTCP (the Rajeev Gandhi National Tuberculosis Control Program) and DOTS (Direct Observational Treatment System) incentivized health workers to make sure that the patient would take the medicine and complete the course of antibiotics. In addition to the donor and government funding, WHP also generated its own revenue from telemedicine centers through consultation fees, sale of medicines, diagnostics etc.

Neurosynaptics also helped other Non-Governmental Organizations (NGO)s set up their telemedicine centers to develop health care in the project area across various parts of the country. It also had centers in other states like Tamil Nadu, Andhra Pradesh, Maharashtra etc. Beyond the connectivity necessary for teleconsultation, the team worked to increase the variety of medical scopes that would help the consultant specialist to get more real-time and accurate measurements. These different scopes formed the diagnostic kit that could be used by a minimally trained worker at the telemedicine center.

The partnership model became a learnt yet strategic decision they built their business on. The more deliberate choices were on the product front where they worked to improve their service quality. Initially, Neurosynaptics included essential fail-safe mechanism and graceful degradation to address the variations in the telecommunication infrastructure (network coverage and its strength) in a vast country like India. To ensure this, the team had move away from a peer-to-peer network and developed client server architecture and dedicated servers which powered the services of their IP.

On boarding partners also imposed constraints on Neurosynaptics' technology. In one such instance WHP decided to go ahead with using satellite connectivity to provide telemedicine for primary care, despite Neurosynaptics suggestion of a terrestrial connectivity. However, the exorbitant upfront capital expenditure and limited communication capabilities eventually convinced WHP to adopt terrestrial connectivity.

The journey with WHP allowed Neurosynaptics to scale up rapidly. WHP developed around 1100 telemedicine centers all over the country and Neurosynaptics was able to sell around 1600 units to these telemedicine centers. At its peak Neurosynaptics was installing around 20 units, and training 40 operators per month as part of this partnership.

Around early 2012, the team decided to embrace cloud technology over web server-based operations. As the adoption of cloud became a common place, Neurosynaptics was early to make the transition. Through, effective leverage of cloud technology has enabled Neurosynaptics not just drive down the costs of ownership but also allow a dynamic configuration model which gives extreme control to the implementation partners.

A few years later, another major trend that took front stage was the penetration of the internet via smartphones. People in rural areas had adopted smartphones quickly and this proved to be extremely useful for the venture. The capabilities of mobile phone had increased sufficiently to perform a larger quantum of computation on the Smartphone itself.

Having adopted mobile as an essential part of their value delivery, they have developed a mobile kit which helps the on-field health care assistants to diagnose in remote locations than possible earlier. This was done with support from a Department of Biotechnology grant.

Riding on the learning from early IPs, Neurosynaptics continued to partner with numerous hospitals and NGOs to ensure effective rural healthcare delivery. Constantly updating the technology ensured the product suit was ready it to move beyond the national boundaries and deliver health care benefits to international locations who had similar challenges like India. For example, in countries like—Ghana, Senegal, Kenya, Philippines, Myanmar, Bangladesh, and Nepal. The list of IPs showing interest in partnering was only growing.

IPs contributed to the health care delivery beyond the last mile delivery. These partners take care of the health-related operator trainings, local regulatory clearances, and additionally ensured a minimum patient pool size which the Neurosynaptics catered to and made the business viable in the region. In some cases, the IPs treated telemedicine delivery as a not-for-profit initiative, while in other cases the IPs benefited by creating a pool of referred patients for their main hospitals.

The following table summarizes Neurosynaptics' product evolution.

Year	*Product variant*	*Channel*
2005	P2P communication	WiLL based kiosk in rural areas
2006	1st version of the complete product using P2P	WiLL based kiosk in rural areas
2007	1st client-server version + fail safe mechanism of communication	Janani, Drishti and other similar partners
2008–2009	Graceful degradation under varying conditions of bandwidth	World health partners (WHP), an implementation partner
2009–2014	Developed a host of diagnostics kits to be deployed in the telemedicine centres	
2015	Web-version of the platform	WHP
2018	Cloud-version of the server	Various implementation partners
2015	First version of integration of undated USB and bluetooth tech to the cloud-based solution	Various implementation partners
2019	ReMeDi bluetooth version of the kit	Various implementation partners

The initial market discovery, product development, research and growth have all imposed different financial pressures on Neurosynaptics.

Financing the Venture

The first round of funding from Venture East TeNeT fund, in 2003 helped the founder focus exclusively on product development without distractions. Following the initial experimentation with the WiLL Kiosk, and their subsequent decision to go ahead to build a parallel delivery system equipped for health care delivery –they needed additional funding.

The team raised another round of funding from APIDC Venture Fund in 2006 and got a soft loan from Technology Development Board (TDB). The second round helped them develop a scalable solution that worked with IPs like WHP. They also reached an operationally self-sufficient stage. However, to improve the quality of service, they needed to improve their diagnostic tools, and this meant they had to develop an additional product suite, which further translated to a new funding round!

In 2013, the team was on the verge of getting a soft loan from the Department of Biotechnology (DBT) worth 4 Crores, on condition of a matching investment. Around the same time, situations so emerged that they had to provide exit to one of their investors. These sudden change in the situations derailed the fundraising efforts.

With no immediate alternative available, the founders approached a Pune based company e-Zest headed by Devendra who was Sameers' friend. With e-Zests' timely help, the founders bought over the shares of their initial investor. This helped them give their investor the exit that was required but put them behind in their journey. In Sameers' own words, "this set us back by around 3 years." The setback meant their growth aspirations would have to be postponed, and the focus would be on building a cash flow which would help them maintain the technological innovations that are essential to continue the value that their business model delivered thus far.

At the time, the founders also decided to invest in R&D only through grants and not through investment funds. They began actively looking for grants to fund the R&D, which would ensure that their solution would maintain its edge in the market. The team went head got a small grant from the Canada Grand challenge in 2014; they also applied for grant through the DBT—'Sparsh' scheme. The team also received the Millennium Alliance award for innovative technology development. In all over the course of the next two and half years they raised a total of INR 1.8 Crores (around USD 0.225 Mill) through these grants to sustain their R&D, which their usual operation would not have supported.

The turbulent times ended in 2016, when they found a reliable investor in Naga Prakasam of the Indian Angel Network. Naga was impressed by the field visit he made to see the ReMeDi solution in action - Neurosynaptics was enabling its implementation partner, the Meenakshi Mission Hospital and Research Center of Madurai, deliver rural health care services to the remote villages. Impressed by the quality of service on the ground, and the team Naga decided to lead an investment round through the Indian Angel Networks. The ask from Neurosynaptics was for INR 6 Crores (around USD 7.25 mill). Three investors, IAN (3Cr), HealthQuad (3Cr) and Accelor (1Cr) coinvested to provide an investment of 7 Crore in the round.

This gave the team a much-needed breather but meant that there was a ticking clock on the exit. Around 2025, the usual venture financing cycles would come to mature, and it was imperative that they need to think of providing their investors with an exit (at least some if not all of them!).

Organizational Needs and Challenges

Functional for over two decades, Neurosynaptics had only 20 odd employees. While a part of this was due to the need to remain lean to sustain primarily on operational revenue, a larger part of it is also due to their geographical scaling approach. Neurosynaptics had leveraged their IPs on the ground level to deliver the benefits of telemedicine.

IPs like WHP helped them get a national scale and the documentaries which covered the impact had given Neurosynaptics with a good list of partners. The lean operational team had found it difficult to live up to the increasing number of implementation partners to be able to work together and ensure delivery. The focus thus far had been on improving the quality of technology at the end user points and introduction of a number of new diagnostic probes in their ReMeDi suite.

Their experience had gotten them to realize the complementary capability that an implementation partner would get to the table. A typical implementation partner could be a hospital or an NGO or even a doctor who intends to cater to a set of 20–30 locations. The implementation partner help with setting up the ground level operations and in many cases sponsors the upfront investment. However, with the cloud-based solution and Bluetooth enabled kit, the customizability quotient of the product offering is almost a hundred percent. The initial capital expense is entirely subsumed in the operational expense making the product more attractive to the new implementation partners.

While Neurosynaptics had been extremely successful in creating and delivering such technologically enabled components, the conversion of the pipeline was still a major concern. They had faltered several times in hiring their Business Development head who could move the needle for them. Sameer has had to fill in the role even after two decades! It is a challenge the team had not overcome yet.

Revenue Model Changes over the Years

In addition to the growth over the last two decades, the founders had also played with the revenue model several times.

In the early days when the health care delivery was through the N-log kiosks, it was a pilot phase where TeNeTs' existing business model would compensate Neurosynaptics for the services that were consumed. When Neurosynaptics made the decision to take the solution to the end market through implementation partners, the implementation partners became the primary revenue source, however technology continued to dominate how they could be charging their implementation partner.

The server versions of the ReMeDi platform required the IP to make an upfront payment for the server installation at IPs' premises to Neurosynaptics and additionally pay an annual maintenance fee to ensure that the server was running without glitches. This also meant that IPs would need to be of a significant size to afford the payment of upfront server costs. Any major server failure meant the service would be down for a few days when the Neurosynaptics team would have to visit the location and fix the issue.

As Neurosynaptics developed a web-based platform, the upfront server requirement was reduced, when all the disaggregated server locations could not use the power of shared servers to ensure Neurosynaptics more actively monitored cases of failure and increase responsiveness. While the upfront investment decreased, the annual maintenance became the significant stream of revenue. A greater number of medium sized IPs could now benefit from the platform Neurosynaptics had developed.

As Neurosynaptics embraced cloud computing and mobile technologies to deliver health care benefits, it enabled Neurosynaptics transfer the cost savings and customization benefits derived to even a medical doctor (thus a small sized IP!). This didn't just ensure that they could onboard more IPs but along with them came the benefits of increased reach. Neurosynaptics, through its ReMeDi portfolio could not only charge the IP for individual consultation, but also for specific tests that were conducted on each patient!

With almost two decades of work with several implementation partners, the team had realized several aspects they could do better by implementing the last mile themselves. This also meant an improved quality of health delivery. The ReMeDi solution had become more powerful and robust. This, however, meant they had to work with the sponsors more closely and develop new organizational capabilities. Following this thought, they had considered hiving off the R&D part and the manufacturing of the ReMeDi kits into a separate foundation called the ReMiDi foundation. This foundation could seek CSR funding and then Neurosynaptics would execute the project on the ground. The pros and cons were still to be weighed before making a final decision.

Options Available

Several unanswered questions continued to haunt the founders as they look to chart their future course of action.

Balancing Social Impact with Investor Expectations

A major challenge the founders faced was regarding their social venture's impact and the return expectations of their investors. As first-time social impact investors, these stakeholders have been patient with the team, allowing them to create an impact on the ground. However, the founders must decide how long they can continue creating impact without having a clear exit for these investors.

Pivoting the Business Model

The COVID-19 pandemic has created opportunities for them to pivot their business model and expand into new areas, such as teleconsultation services through an app and the ReMeDi kit. While this could be a lucrative opportunity, it would require deviating from their core mission of making an impactful solution that leaves no rural area devoid of necessary medical attention at an affordable price. Would the founders be willing to compromise their social mission?

Scaling the Business

As they grow and look to expand into new markets, they face challenges in scaling their business while maintaining quality. They need to find reliable implementation partners (IPs) who share their mission and can handle the increased demand. However, sourcing high-quality IPs at a rate that their system can handle may be difficult.

If they are considering taking on the last mile delivery themselves to ensure quality standards are met, it would provide them with more control over the delivery process, but it comes with significant implementation costs. Are they ready to internalize this cost and activities?

Foundation Status and CSR Funding

To access CSR funds on a larger scale in India, they would need to become a foundation that can raise finances only after completion of three years. While this would provide access to significant funding resources, it would require the company to wait longer and adapt to new regulations and requirements. It is a trade-off between short-term financial needs and long-term strategic goals, that the founders needed to resolve.

Additionally, two other operational challenges may emerge to keep the founders on their toes such as - emergency of stronger competition as the ecosystem becomes more favorable, increasing complexity of navigating regulatory requirement as they scale into new geographies.

However, one thing they knew for sure - the journey had just started. There was still a lot that needed to be done in the health care delivery if they had to make a difference in the ecosystem.

Discussion Questions

1. What excited the founder duo to jump into tackling the massive challenge of health care? Have the held themselves true to the core mission they focused on during the journey? What has allowed them to manage with all the distractions and opportunities that they encountered during the journey?
2. When the founding team started their venture the ecosystem lacked severely in its ability to support any innovation. During their journey

the team has managed to deal with these drawbacks in the ecosystem and growth in strength over the years. Are there some repeated patterns you see here? How have they managed to continue their growth story?

3. In the light of the various financial challenges the founding team faced, they have been innovative with tackling their resources requirements. How have they dealt with the financing challenges while they continued to grow?
4. The team has been able to grow well using the implementation partners, and have also been able to reach to several developing countries across the globe that face health care challenges like that in India. Yet, they seem to think of letting go of partners and forming a CSR funding-based approach to take serve the masses. Do we see elements of mission drift here? What would they need to keep in mind as they make this transition?

Supplementary Readings

The following academic articles and books would be helpful in developing the theoretical anchor that could be used to synthesize the case learnings.

1. Shepherd, D. A., Parida, V., & Wincent, J. (2020). The surprising duality of jugaad: Low firm growth and high inclusive growth. Journal of Management Studies, 57(1), 87–128.
2. Cornforth, C. (2014). Understanding and combating mission drift in social enterprises. Social enterprise journal, 10(1), 3–20.
3. Krishnan, R. T. (2010). From jugaad to systematic innovation: The challenge for India. Rishikesha T Krishnan.

Learning Objectives

Instructors could use the case:

(a) To help students understand the antecedents of frugal innovation that move beyond Jugaad that is embedded in the contextual setting of resource constraints.
(b) To highlight the role of partnerships/cocreational approaches towards generating and capturing value.
(c) To understand the challenges of being true to the social orientation and the entrepreneurs mindset in dealing with the mission drift issues.

Acknowledgement The authors thank the reviewers for their valuable comments and suggestions, which helped strengthen the case. MS Copilot suggestions were used to improve the language. Additionally, Perplexity was used to find any academic literature that may have been relevant to the case in hand.

Competing Interests The authors have no conflicts of interest to declare that are relevant to the content of this chapter.

CHAPTER 17

Fee Plaza LLP - Part A: A Ready to Use Fintech Platform

Venkatesh Krishnamurthy and Krishna Kumar Balaraman

Abstract The case Fee Plaza LLP (Part A and Part B) discusses the origin, operations, strengths and growth challenges of Fee Plaza LLP, a FinTech start-up based in Bangalore, India. Fee Plaza is bootstrapped (self-funded by the founders) and this case discusses the dilemma faced by the founder of Fee Plaza in scaling up the business, and the choices and consequences based on his orientation as an entrepreneur in an emerging economy—India. The latter part of the Fee Plaza case is about the growth options, dilemmas and efforts of Fee Plaza LLP. It explains the platform extensions, alliances and further challenges that the founder and collaborator faced in structuring technology alliances and being equitable in doing so.

V. Krishnamurthy (✉)
Aix Marseille University Graduate School of Business - IAE, Aix en Provence, France
e-mail: venkatesh.krishnamurthy@iae-aix.com

K. K. Balaraman
IFMR GSB, Krea University, Sri City, India
e-mail: krishnakumar.balaraman@krea.edu.in

A. S. Galande et al. (eds.), *Context-inspired Entrepreneurship*, Sustainable Development Goals Series,
https://doi.org/10.1007/978-981-95-9831-1_17

The case highlights challenges in internationalizing the platform for launching in the USA with a subscription model.

Keywords Entrepreneurship • FinTech • Technology platform • Alliance • International business • Emerging economy • Digital payments

SDG Links This chapter is aligned with SDG 8: Decent Work and Economic Growth by examining how financial technology innovation can enhance productivity and support sustainable economic growth (SDG 8.2). The chapter also aligns with SDG 9 through its focus on digital payment infrastructure and innovation in financial services, and relates to SDG 17 by enabling partnerships that support other enterprises.

Fee Plaza LLP - Part A: A Ready to Use Fintech Platform

Introduction

Venkatesh, the founder of Fee Plaza LLP, was a lifelong Bangalorean, the Silicon Valley of India. Sitting in his home office, he was occupied with thoughts on the travails of bootstrapped ventures such as where to spend limited money—in building the platform or on marketing—and the regulatory hazards in Fintech startups. At the same time, he was wondering how much resource to reallocate, to increase the total addressable market. He also contemplated how to restructure the business model of Fee Plaza to unlock its potential and appropriate the value. It was also necessary for Fee Plaza to become more attractive to merchants to adopt. Considering that Fee Plaza was a white-labelled product platform, the end customer seldom realized the core value provided by Fee Plaza. The merchants intentionally tend to downplay the value of a platform of Fee Plaza and try to drive down the system usage charges payable to Fee Plaza, even if it is borne by the payer. He was wondering how he could increase the value proposition for the payer to increase the usage of Fee Plaza as a preferred payment platform. What will it take to increase Fee Plaza's value? Will Fee Plaza's value increase by converting it into a multi-sided platform?

Beginnings

Fee Plaza was co-founded in June 2016 by Venkatesh and his father Krishnamurthy. Venkatesh was an electronics engineering graduate and a post graduate in software enterprise management, He had worked in many functions in the Information Technology (IT) industry, such as sales, software development, software design, technical support, technical marketing, product engineering and program management. In his employment career, He had worked almost entirely on Internet related technologies and businesses - networking, Internet software development, sales of Internet infrastructure software & hardware, Internet security, Internet banking and Internet gaming. He enabled the launching of several products in as many as 17 languages. He also taught technology courses in many business schools from 2003, and authored a book on marketing of IT. Venkatesh's father Krishnamurthy, after his retirement from government service, co-founded Collaborative Infotech Systems Private Limited, a company that offered software product engineering services in mobile and web technologies, in 2008. Venkatesh always had an entrepreneurial approach to work even when he was employed in the industry. His entrepreneurial orientation along with his educational experience and professional background nudged him join Collaborative in 2012. Over time, his product experience encouraged him to think of launching a Software as a Service (SaaS). This thought was the genesis of Fee Plaza in 2016.

His idea for Fee Plaza emanated from the challenges he observed while paying the school fees for his daughter. In a city like Bangalore that was considered the technology capital of India, he still had difficulty paying the fees online. "It is really tiring to go to school, wait in the queue, pay with a cheque and get the receipt, four to five times a year. The school does not even allow ECS. Why cannot the school just let us pay online?" Venkatesh expressed his displeasure to his wife. He was genuinely tired of paying the fees at the counter, for many years. His wife, as he had expected, responded with a challenge "Instead of complaining, why don't you do something about it?". Though this challenge was a trigger for the Fee Plaza idea, the solution potentially was to address a much larger scope. He noticed that the organizations such as schools that collect fees and subscription payments needed an entire range of integrated solutions from payment portal to backend transaction history generation and traceability.

Venkatesh had thought many times that the younger generation, especially in Indian cities, aspired to get their children to better schools, upgrade to bigger apartments, cars, and were willing to pay for their convenience, with their disposable incomes. He had seen many of his colleagues and friends standing in queues to get application forms for school admissions. He had also found out that a few of his colleagues and senior executives of various companies were misusing resources - like asking their team members to stand for them in those queues! He was wondering if he could create a "portal" where parents could pay and fill the application forms for their schools of choice.

He discussed this with his uncle, Nagaraja Murthy, a retired Karnataka Administrative Services officer and a career education administrator. His uncle indicated that there was a law in the state (Karnataka) that prevented schools from charging fees for application forms. Apparently, this law was enacted to stop private schools from charging exorbitant amounts towards applications, a free non-refundable income to schools even if they rejected applications in ratios such as a few hundreds to one! So that admissions applications portal seemed an infeasible idea. Hence, he dropped the applications-fee-only portal idea. He repurposed the portal idea for schools to collect tuition and other fees, after a student was offered admission.

While teaching about market segmentation at various business schools and other institutes of higher learning, Venkatesh had elaborated on the merits and demerits of market segmentation. "Market segmentation, by definition, is limiting, but should be made only when absolutely necessary", he had thought and taught. His wife's challenge made him think "When collecting money online, why restrict it only to application payments? Why not facilitate all types of payments that schools collect under multiple heads? After all, every business will be happy to collect payments and I can facilitate that online. Moderate success should not be difficult". He discussed this idea with family and the uncle. The family, satisfied with Collaborative Infotech Systems' moderate success, left it to him to decide whether to start a company and how much to invest. Checking with the domain registrars, he found that the domain name feeplaza.com was available and booked it. Thus, Fee Plaza began taking shape. He told his close friends that he was on to his next venture but didn't disclose much. Without his asking, two of his friends blindly offered to invest INR 2 Million each. He refused squarely, because he did not like to bet his friends' hard-earned money on an idea that may not succeed. He convinced his father to co-found Fee Plaza and incorporated with limited liability in June 2016, thus giving Venkatesh the autonomy for independent action in pursuit of his vision. Soon, he designed the platform and wanted to build in stealth mode. So, Venkatesh drafted an NDA and contracted an engineer to build the platform. Fee Plaza enterprise followed a minimalist model by clear ownership of roles and responsibilities. Venkatesh managed product roadmap, merchant on-boarding and marketing, while the other co-founder (his father) managed the administrative and banking matters. Venkatesh shared the software engineering work with contractors. This saved Fee Plaza the expense of fixed salaries, thus contributing to the shortened payback period.

Challenges in Online Payment Collection

Merchants face multiple challenges and barriers to collect payments online. These challenges have multiple consequences such as challenge to growth (owing to the merchant's lack of online payment collection), financial exclusion and loss of taxes to the government. There were a few more limitations associated with the services provided by the existing Payment Service Providers (PSPs).

- IT investment: The payment gateways tend to be minimalistic systems put in by the PSP. The merchants have to build their IT infrastructure to connect their systems to the payment gateway and to maintain the systems. This presents serious barriers to enterprises that do not have their own IT and often are excluded from the benefits of online payment collection. Another challenge is fixed cost the merchant incurs irrespective of the Total Payment Value (TPV) or frequency of transactions. This cost includes cost of IT maintenance, charges payable to the PSPs and many others.
- Lack of non-financial data: To further complicate the situation, the PSPs only give limited data pertaining to the transactions such as the unique transaction ID, amount, timestamp of the transaction, success/failure of the transaction, but nothing beyond. This means that the merchant has to build the IT to collect the non-financial data pertaining to the payments, such as, the name of the payer, e-mail address, phone number, address, age, purpose of the payment, specific remarks and any other data as required for the merchant to sell the product/deliver the service, as the case may be. The cost of associating payments to payers and of reconciling the non-financial data pertaining to payments is significant and cumbersome.

- Lack of merchant branding: Merchants that use PSPs, even with those that allow the collection of limited non-financial data from the payers, offer such services at higher price than the plain PSPs, are often inflexible in the type of data collection and operate with their brands. This deprives the merchants the opportunity to extend branding experience in the payment screens shown online.

The Fee Plaza Platform

Fee Plaza went live with customer transactions in October 2016 for collecting structured and collection of unstructured payments (invoice billing) was launched a few months subsequently. It was quite a significant accomplishment for Fee Plaza to go live with a real customer transaction on its fintech platform within 90 days of incorporation. This quick time-to-market was possible primarily for three reasons: very clear definition of product specifications, customer relevant innovation, and active pre-launch marketing.

Fee Plaza's plug-and-play service, with zero cost of adoption to merchants, facilitated structured payments such as school fees, library membership fees, where non-financial data needs to be collected from the payer along with the payment. Fee Plaza launched a few technology-enabled business innovations, such as zero investment, zero cost of reconciliation, white-labelled payment services. The structured payment service of Fee Plaza enabled payments collection from existing and new customers, along with the necessary non-financial data, with zero cost of data reconciliation. Unstructured payment is one where a merchant can demand payment from a known party, like in sending an invoice online with a demand for a specific amount. Fee Plaza's services are white-labelled, which means the merchants can reinforce their brand identities, during the online payment process, which is not available with many PSPs. All the merchants need to collect structured payments is to share the payment link provided by Fee Plaza. To receive payments against proforma invoices (for advance payments), invoices and to offer payer-specific discounts (for groups, bargain hunters, etc.), the merchant simply has to login to its Dashboard on Fee Plaza system and upload the demand.

Merchants, such as enterprises and other entities in fintech terms, use payment gateways from banks and third-party PSPs to collect online payments. PSPs charge merchants fees like setup costs, annual maintenance, and a transaction fee—usually a percentage of each transaction—known as the Merchant Discount Rate (MDR) or Transaction Discount Rate (TDR). Some banks may waive setup and maintenance fees based on a merchant's TPV, or even the MDR/TDR for very high transaction volumes, like tens of millions INR weekly. PSPs may also profit from the PSP's float—the time gap between a transaction and when the merchant receives the funds.

International and Future-Ready Platform

From the very beginning, Venkatesh was actively thinking of how to scale up Fee Plaza globally. Accordingly, his objective was to make this a truly international product that can function in several countries. This proactive approach would also help Fee Plaza look at different business models that catered to different jurisdictions and financial institutions. An important objective was to make Fee Plaza a truly international product that could accommodate several languages, currencies, financial regulations and financial supply chains in as many countries as possible.

Internationalization and Localization: Internationalization pertains to engineering the product or platform to support the requirements of various countries/regions, such as languages, currencies, business rule and storage formats. Localization pertains to delivering content such as user interfaces, manuals and instruction video of the product or platform in local languages.

Venkatesh had worked on internationalization and localization of products during his employment at Aventail and Adobe. He had always thought of building a company that operated globally. With his experience, he had decided to make the Fee Plaza an internationalized platform and ready for localization. Fee Plaza was internationalized to support multiple currencies and languages from the first line of code, except for right-to-left text (RTL) formatting necessary to accommodate languages like Arabic, Hebrew, Kurdish, Persian, Urdu, Sindhi and a few African languages. This limitation is due to the limited budget of Fee Plaza and higher priorities of other features such as delegated fee administration, and revenue analytics for merchants. The price listings are not published in local languages as there was no perceived requirement for it.

Data storage: Venkatesh had studied finance subjects in his postgraduate course. Therefore, he knew that the finance sector is often highly regulated by every country with its own laws, both in conjunction and diversion from international regulations. He thought that sooner than later, it was likely that the Government of India (GoI) would demand that the data pertaining to its users be stored in India. So, though during initial development Fee Plaza subscribed to Amazon Web Services (AWS) hosting in the US, he ensured that all the hosting was moved to AWS Mumbai in India as early as within a few weeks of incorporation of Fee Plaza, but before the commercial launch of the service. After the launch of Unified Payment Interface (UPI) in India, in April 2018,[1] the GoI set a deadline for all e-commerce companies and related businesses, to store the user data within the Indian territory.

Experience-Centric Innovation
Fee Plaza has been mindful of the needs of its merchants. This led to many innovations, driven both by itself, its merchants and its users. Fee Plaza continued to innovate and a few of its innovations are listed below.

Visualizing the design of Platform for low cost of ownership: To avoid complying with PCI DSS[2] requirements, Venkatesh designed the Fee Plaza platform with neither visibility nor storage of payers' debit card and credit card data in Fee Plaza's systems. If Fee Plaza's system were either to view or to store the payers' card details, then it should have implemented periodic information security audits as required by the Reserve Bank of India (RBI) and PCI DSS. This would have cost a significant additional investment in platform engineering as well as in the recurring cost for PCI DSS audit (upwards of INR 2 million per quarter). As CCAvenue is PCI DSS complaint, the Fee Plaza platform was designed to hand off the payer to CCAvenue's payment screen seamlessly, where the payer enters her/his card data. This is done by loading CCAvenue's payment page as an iFrame in a Fee Plaza page or by redirecting to CCAvenue's payment page. By avoiding PCI DSS requirements compliance, Fee Plaza could achieve operating profit in the third full year of operations, i.e., in 2019.

Merchant-driven innovation: Rotary Club of Bangalore Charitable Trust (RCBCT) was the first merchant to sign up to use Fee Plaza in 2016. RCBCT had the need to collect participation fees from golfers for their charity golf tournament and this was accommodated easily in the system. However, RCBCT requested Fee Plaza to collect additional data from golfers such as handicap number, T-shirt size, T-shirt type preference (male, with collar/female with round neck), along with the payments. As

[1] https://www.medianama.com/2021/02/223-data-localisation-compliance-delay-whatsapp-pay-npci-3/

[2] Payment Card Industry Data Security Standards - https://www.pcisecuritystandards.org

RCBCT was the first merchant and a charity organization, Fee Plaza decided to enhance the system to facilitate this requirement, free of cost. Upon completion, the team decided to formalize this as a feature in the Fee Plaza system. With this feature, Fee Plaza has a facility to insert custom pages in the payment workflow, to collect any non-financial data from the payers. This feature enabled Fee Plaza to charge the merchants for custom non-financial data collection. Fee Plaza enabled the merchant to demand and collect non-financial data such as e-mail address (by default), phone number, address, school related parameters (stream, grade, section) along with the name of the payment collected (membership fee, quarterly fee, etc.).

One of the early merchants of Fee Plaza, Suchitra Film Society, Bangalore (SFS), signed up to collect membership fees and season tickets for its film festivals, on Fee Plaza. However, SFS was issuing photo identity cards to its members upon the payment of membership fee. Collection of payments offered only part service and thereby part benefit to SFS. Fee Plaza then decided to allow payers to upload their photographs, if the merchants demanded, by including the photos on the payment receipts, thereby eliminating the need for issuance of photo identity cards. Photo became a part of the readily configurable non-financial data that Fee Plaza offers to its merchants, for a premium convenience fee.

The Fee Plaza Advantage

Zero investment and zero cost of ownership: Fee Plaza offers plug 'n' play payment collection facility to merchants - this means zero investment, zero cost of IT maintenance and zero exit cost. The merchants had to provide the price list to Fee Plaza in the specified format and Fee Plaza updated and maintained the price list online, resulting in zero cost of operations for the merchants. Fee Plaza charged only for successful transactions. Fee Plaza charged convenience fee only on transactions, so that the merchants do not incur any fixed cost. Fee Plaza gave the merchant the choice to absorb, add or pass on the convenience fee to the payer. Availing Fee Plaza service was totally free, if the merchant decides to add the convenience fee to the basic price or pass on the convenience fee to the payer. To top it all, Fee Plaza published merchant-branded payment collection apps free on Google Play Store. Later, Fee Plaza introduced a nominal sign-up fee of INR 5000/– to new merchants and intended to charge for publishing the merchant-branded app on Google Playstore.

Pre-reconciled non-financial data: Fee Plaza enabled merchants to acquire non-financial data pertaining to the payment, with its vast readily available array of data types. In addition, Fee Plaza had the ability (priced extra) to collect additional non-financial data on-demand from the merchant. The non-financial data reported by Fee Plaza is pre-structured and associated with the payments, which resulted in zero cost of data reconciliation for the merchant.

Seamless branding of merchant franchises and chains: The payment collection pages provided by Fee Plaza and the app were all branded with a merchant logo. This gave a sense of trust to the payer and significantly expanded the brand reach of the merchant. In addition, as the payment link will remain the same for all the products/services listed by the merchant, the merchant could simply put this link on their website and direct all the users to their website in their marketing campaigns. This greatly improved the online branding and page rank of the merchant website. Fee Plaza enabled merchant franchises and chains to collect payment under common branding, independent of whether the payments were remitted to franchisor, franchisee, or a specific outlet of the chain.

Founder's Anticipation of Future Trends

By 2017, almost every bank and PSP in India launched a wallet. Wallets, classified by the Reserve Bank of India (RBI), came under fewer regulations and scrutiny. RBI had made user approval via authentication (either with password in net banking or with an One Time Password - OTP sent by the bank/card issuer to the payer's registered mobile phone number) a compulsory requirement for completing a payment transaction, to fraudulent payments online. Many e-commerce companies found this restrictive. For example, taxi aggregators could not auto-charge their riders upon completion of rides. Wallets, initially, didn't have the requirement of authentication and could be auto debited. The tie-up of a few wallet providers with taxi aggregators gave a major fillip to the rise of wallets as payment instruments. A few wallet service providers went overboard, started collecting cash at payers' doorsteps, to load their wallets. Merchants and customers of Fee Plaza began demanding the facility to use wallets, as wallets were giving a "cash back" to the payers to grow their wallets' share of the market. Facilitating wallet payments on Fee Plaza was going to require additional funds. Fee Plaza used the payment gateway CCAvenue for acquiring payments, but CCAvenue gave transaction rates that were not competitive in the market. Also, the launch of Unified Payment Interface (UPI) was on the horizon and the impact (which proved to be tectonic later) of UPI was not known. Venkatesh proactively weighed in on all these factors. He correctly analysed that people would sense that keeping money in wallets was depriving them of interest and they would dump wallet use. He decided to put the demand of wallet payments on hold.

GoI and the RBI subsequently realized that wallets could and were being used to launder money and collection of bribe & extortion amounts. This led RBI to take many measures such as to:

- limit the amount of money a person could load into a wallet per month and per year
- disallowing of loading the wallet with cash
- verifying the identity of every wallet holder with Know Your Customer (KYC) process.

With the above restrictions, all wallet providers, including those mainstay business was money laundering for a wallet transaction fee, were dealt with a severe blow. By the April of 2018, the wallet business had diminished except purpose-specific wallets such as *Fastag*®. It was only upon the launch of UPI, the wallet providers made their wallets compatible with UPI and eventually wallets entered the formal economy. Then, Fee Plaza received favourable rates from CCAvenue for UPI transactions. Fee Plaza began allowing UPI transactions and therefore practically all wallets (compatible with UPI). This in hindsight proved to be among the best innovation priority decisions made by Venkatesh.

Fee Plaza innovated and enhanced its services during its existence, with multiple benefits like:

1. Equated Monthly Instalments (EMIs) for payments higher than INR3,500/–. Fee Plaza only facilitated this for the payers through 10 credit card issuing banks. The banks assessed the creditworthiness online and offered or declined EMIs to the payers. The merchants received complete payment at once after the payment while the payer pays the card issuer in EMIs. Neither Fee Plaza nor the merchant assumed the credit risk, which was borne solely by the card issuing bank.
2. Showing discount coupons for payers on the payment success page, which also opened up a referral marketing revenue stream to Fee Plaza.

Challenges of Fee Plaza

As one can expect with all business, Fee Plaza too faced a few challenges. A few of these challenges were unique to the industry and a few others were unique to India.

Domestic Challenges

Reaching the market: The decision to collect payments online is a policy decision for enterprises (merchants). The decision is often made by the management. As money is a sensitive matter, managements prefer to speak with the top person at Fee Plaza and not a young sales professional, at least till Fee Plaza became well known in the market. For this reason, many fellow entrepreneurs that did policy sales, similar to that of Fee Plaza, advised the co-founders to not hire junior sales professionals.

In addition, the managements have many queries, and their accounts staff too pose many more. Fee Plaza found that the marketing cycle was typically 1 month per merchant and any longer duration often meant that the merchant was not interested in signing up. The nature of business, the limited staff and the time available with the co-founders limited the number of merchants that could be met and marketed to.

The problem of parallel economy: This was one of the biggest challenges for Fee Plaza. A business like Fee Plaza had to depend on the volume and TPV for growth. With much persuasive skills Fee Plaza signed up with many merchants. However, after signing up, the merchants simply did not use Fee Plaza. Many merchants still preferred cash to collecting payments online, to evade taxes.

Cyclical nature of payments: A few of the merchants collect payments seasonally, like the beginning of the year, quarter, month, etc. This means that the revenues tapered down in a cycle before ramping up. There were related challenges such as merchants not updating their price lists upon expiry of their old price lists, despite multiple reminders. This was due to lack of interest on the part of the merchant, staff change and other reasons.

Growth Challenges

Fee Plaza's growth is shown in (Table 17.1). The growth seemed astronomical, owing to the low base of the founding year, as with every start-up. The revenue was sufficient for Fee Plaza to operate, but the low absolute revenue was limiting the growth prospects.

Table 17.1 Fee Plaza's growth trajectory

Base year June 2016 to March 17 (part)	*April 2017 to March 2018, over the previous year*	*April 2018 to March 19 (first half), over the previous year*
# of merchants	1.8x	1.3x
TPV	10x	3.2x
Revenue	10.42x	10.62x
Net profit (from operations)	Negative	Positive

Fee Plaza Future Prospects

The co-founders were considering potential business models for the future of Fee Plaza. A few of options included seeking funds, launching abroad, and getting acquired.

Launch Fee Plaza Abroad

Fee Plaza offered its services in India and supported English, with INR payments. Fee Plaza was ready to be localized. This meant that with very little investment (about US$20,000/–) in incremental IT, Fee Plaza would be enabled to add a payment gateway - currency - language set.

Set-up Fee Plaza subsidiary in the US/another country: Fee Plaza could establish a subsidiary abroad and launch its services, with the US as a prime choice due to no language changes and widespread online transactions. After checking with US contacts, Fee Plaza expected reasonable success there.

Challenges in establishing US operations of Fee Plaza: the co-founders were not US citizens or permanent residents, startup and compliance costs were estimated to be at least $40,000, and annual operations would require $100,000 minimum. This could strain Fee Plaza, especially if growth slows and payback delays. This was an ideal option that will help Fee Plaza retain its independence. This could give Fee Plaza the much-required international footprint and market and the possibilities will be almost limitless.

License Fee Plaza to any other entity that can launch Fee Plaza in another country: With this option, a licensee could use Fee Plaza to launch online payment services. The $20,000 localization cost could be paid by the licensee or shared with Fee Plaza. This would shift Fee Plaza from just FinTech to a FinTech + SaaS model. Licensees might request non-citation rights — replacing Fee Plaza's branding with their own—for a higher fee, which Fee Plaza could agree to. The fee could scale with the licensee's transaction volume, infrastructure use, or other metrics. Fee Plaza began talks with a few potential licensees for the US and EU regions. This option seemed suitable as Fee Plaza could retain its independence and the cost of customizing for another country was not upfront. This could give Fee Plaza a steady stream of licensing revenue that was much needed for innovation and growth.

Seek Funding

Fee Plaza could seek external investment to boost growth, but advice varies. Some recommend avoiding venture funding, while others suggest trading equity for it. One of his advisors, Krishna Kumar, kept suggesting to Venkatesh that the latter should go in for professional funding. Venkatesh was unsure. He thought no VC would be interested because the revenue was small to attract any VC. At Series A, VCs might invest but typically bar co-founders from drawing salaries or cashing out equity, offering only a notional valuation increase for less control and possible investor meddling—unappealing to the founders. South East Asian VCs interested in Fee Plaza demand a legal base in Singapore or Malaysia, but Fee Plaza saw no clear potential there and was prioritizing other regions. This option does come with the advantages that generally do with venture funding, such as capital required.

Get Acquired

Fee Plaza was a super-white-labelled system (for example, a bank could brand itself on it and offer white-labelled payment apps and web pages to its merchants) and offers the non-financial data associated with the payments, all plug'n'play, without needing a penny investment from the merchants. Most payment gateways are plain vanilla and do not offer any of these advantages to the merchants. Fee Plaza made online payment collection a breeze! Not just that, if a bank could buy Fee Plaza, it gets two additional streams of income - transaction fees on the payments and also gets a float on the money transacted through it. Fee Plaza similarly could be a great addition to the third-party payment service providers like the wallet providers. However, Fee Plaza was not approached any such potential match. The advantage of this option was that the co-founders could exit with a profit for all they achieved with Fee Plaza. The disadvantage was that the co-founders could not completely implement what they envisioned for Fee Plaza. The acquirer's priorities would decide the future course of Fee Plaza.

Quo Va Dis?

It was extremely difficult for any analysis to have shown the true behaviour of small business owners in money matters. The urge to collect cash so as to not account was deep among the small business that Fee Plaza was had not expected at all. Therefore, Venkatesh's premise that "all business will be happy to collect payments online" was to prove largely incorrect. So, he wondered what Fee Plaza's additional value proposition to its merchants could be.

The digital payment usage was increasing in India. He began thinking about what can be done - changing the business model, shifting the headquarters to a different country, widen the portfolio of services within the payments space? This could become the proverbial trillion-dollar question or worth nothing at all.

Abstract

Fee Plaza Part B case is about the growth options, dilemmas and efforts of Fee Plaza LLP. It explains the platform extensions, alliances and further challenges that the founder and collaborator faced in structuring technology alliances and being equitable in doing so. The case highlights challenges in internationalizing the platform for launching in the USA with a subscription model.

Keywords: Entrepreneurship, FinTech, Technology platform, Alliance, International business, Emerging economy, Digital payments

Fee Plaza LLP - Part B: The Challenge of Scaling up and Expanding Abroad

Fee Plaza Growth Phase

In 2019, Venkatesh struggled to scale Fee Plaza despite signing up many merchants with his sales skills, as revenue growth lagged. He consulted a serial entrepreneur, noting only 10% of merchants actively used Fee Plaza, while most had not in years, and asked for advice. The entrepreneur replied, "You're lucky—typically only 2–3% of signed-up merchants use platforms in India. Fee Plaza's doing great!" Unconvinced and uncomforted, Venkatesh found some relief in an industry report showing payment processing margins averaged below 2%, while Fee Plaza consistently hit 2.36% or more, sometimes much higher, with some transactions yielding thousands in profit. He mused, "A business that earns while I sleep—build it, launch it, forget it—is ideal. Fee Plaza could be that, but only if it scales."

Fee Plaza in the US

In early 2019, Venkatesh shared Fee Plaza's growth plans with Raghavendra Rao, a trusted friend of 20 years and a former colleague. Known as Raghu, he had exceptional traits: integrity, diligence, business savvy, and a strong work ethic. After weeks of thought, Raghu proposed launching Fee Plaza in the USA, citing its favorable market characteristics — a strong formal small and medium business (SMB) economy, valuing the convenience, and demand for structured non-financial data.

The Structure of Entities

After weeks of talks, Raghu and Venkatesh agreed to proceed. The co-founders had put in Fee Plaza a paid up capital that was the minimum amount required by law. Venkatesh had invested all amount beyond this as debt to Fee Plaza. Venkatesh, reluctant to invest more due bootstrapping and the repayment due from Fee Plaza, also found setting up a US subsidiary for Fee Plaza LLP (India) costly—especially as a non-US resident/citizen. Dual audits in India and the US would spike compliance costs. So, they opted to create a separate entity in USA. Raghu, who ran his own US software consulting firm, chose not to use it for Fee Plaza, to keep finances distinct and allow the new US entity—created to market Fee Plaza's services — free to be sold independently. Thus, Raghu would establish a new US entity Fee Plaza Inc.

Who Will Market and Sell?

Raghu, like Venkatesh, was a solopreneur with no professional investors. While managing his US software consulting firm, Raghu had limited time. Venkatesh, with US contacts, proposed Raghu recruit contacts to market and sell Fee Plaza's services for a commission. Since commissions were small, Venkatesh suggested recurring commissions tied to merchants' ongoing use of the US entity's services, which Raghu accepted. This commission structure avoided fixed salary costs, would keep sales reps motivated to onboard merchants, and leveraged recurring commissions for retaining customers.

What about the Investment?
Neither Raghu nor Venkatesh had struck it rich from their employers' IPO during their careers, both hailing from modest means with only personal savings as a safety net. Venkatesh insisted their agreement be fair, especially in sharing costs. He suggested Fee Plaza LLP license its brand, software, and IP to the US entity. Customizing the platform for the US would entail costs, which Raghu's new entity would incur in the beginning. This cost would be recouped, without interest, by offsetting royalties owed to Fee Plaza LLP, while all the IP remained with the Indian entity.

Fee Plaza Inc., USA
With the agreement on licensing, royalty and numbers in place, Raghu registered Fee Plaza Inc. in the US in Jan 2020. Fee Plaza Inc. and Raghu licensed Fee Plaza's name, logo and software for offering services in the US. The agreement also accommodated for the launch of additional services that the Indian entity would develop in future. Such additional services would be guided by the corresponding addenda, with the first agreement overriding any potential conflicts.

Change in the Business Model

In India, customer payments went to Fee Plaza LLP's escrow account at IDFC FIRST Bank, set up with a hefty one-time fee. Fee Plaza LLP deducted its charges and passed the rest to merchants, offering services to Indian clients without sign-up or subscription costs.

Raghu found out that in the USA, the cost of maintenance, audit and compliance of such an escrow account (called Money Services Business—MSB account) would be USD75,000 per year to begin with and expected to increase in subsequent years. This expense was neither bearable by Fee Plaza Inc., nor was desirable. So, Raghu and Venkatesh discussed how to avoid this expense. They both decided to change the business model. In India, Fee Plaza LLP was a Fintech. In the US Fee Plaza Inc. would be a Software-as-a-Service (SaaS) provider. This meant that the money paid by customers would be paid by the payment gateway in the US directly to the merchants. Fee Plaza Inc. cannot take any cut in transaction amounts as the payments were direct. So, Fee Plaza Inc. would offer the payment collection service as a subscription to the USA merchants. As the amounts were paid from consumer directly to the merchants, Fee Plaza Inc. need not maintain the MSB account and therefore not incur corresponding expenses. To meet the new requirement of direct settlement of amounts to the merchants, Fee Plaza Inc. had to create additional software to integrate the USA merchants to the payment gateway(s) directly. This was an additional item in the customisation list of Fee Plaza LLP's software for Fee Plaza Inc.

Due to shift in the business model, Fee Plaza LLP's merchant settlement module became unnecessary in the US, cutting customization efforts for the software platform by about 25%. Raghu registered Fee Plaza Inc. with a US bank, and a payment gateway, to collect subscription fees from US merchants.

Venkatesh introduced Raghu to two persons: SR and CB. CB, a web marketing expert and altruistic entrepreneur, reviewed Fee Plaza Inc.'s website, made valuable changes, and suggested a U.S. marketing roadmap. She declined to be a reseller, citing time constraints. SR, who was also an entrepreneur for some time, showed a lot of enthusiasm. She listed Fee Plaza Inc. on various USA commerce portals. She brought in two prospects. Venkatesh and Raghu demonstrated the Fee Plaza Inc. platform to both these prospects prior to official launch. However, before the prospects responded, SR gave a shock; she said that she wanted equity in the USA entity, without her investing any amount! This unsettled both Raghu and Venkatesh. While they were struggling, they were equitable in sharing the revenues with their associates. Asking for equity, without a proven contribution, seemed a little unreasonable. So, Raghu and Venkatesh thought that associating with SR could become untenable. Raghu then dissociated with SR. Venkatesh had already committed to marketing support in the background, willing to demonstrate Fee Plaza platform to prospects in the US daytime from India. There is something about entrepreneurs. Call it hope, aspiration, unreasonable optimism, competitive aggressiveness, sense of unreal adventure or whatever, they cling on to their ventures as long as possible. Without salespersons, Raghu decided to go on, trying his luck with his contacts.

The Modification of Software for Fee Plaza Inc. USA

Venkatesh asked Fee Plaza LLP's contract engineers to work on Fee Plaza Inc. software requirements. He set up the engineering infrastructure, issue trackers (on Trello and Asana). He and Raghu held regular status checks, and progress was swift at first. Then, during India's Covid-19 lockdowns, the lead engineer got stuck in his hometown without his computer, delaying the planned Dec 2020 US launch. When the lead engineer returned to Bangalore, he ran into an unexpected technical roadblock on Amazon cloud, due to the change in business model (merchant subscription in the USA). He could remove the roadblock only by May 2021. Of the Fee Plaza LLP's two services viz., structured payments (like in school fees) and invoice billing (for merchants), the structured fees module was ready for launch by Nov 2021. The invoice billing module was ready for launch two months later. Raghu paid for all the customisation work, at actuals.

When Venkatesh and Raghu demonstrated the structured fees service to the prospects that SR introduced, both the prospects said that they wanted to configure the structured fees, instead of requesting Fee Plaza Inc. every time they needed a new structured fee (like the fee for a school event). This feature, called "Delegated Administration" was in the pipeline. The lead engineer enabled took another two months to enable the view of structured fee listings but did not complete the "add new fee" feature for merchants.

Venkatesh suggested Raghu to launch the services as they were (i.e., without the Delegated Administration feature). Raghu said that he would like to launch only after both the services viz., structured payments and invoice billing, were complete. He reasoned that selling Fee Plaza's services, without the Delegated Administration feature, would be difficult, as experienced with the initial prospects. Venkatesh thought Raghu's decision was reasonable, as Raghu did not have a team to market Fee Plaza Inc.'s services in the US.

Future Dilemma

While the customization of Fee Plaza LLP's software for Fee Plaza Inc. was progressing slowly, Venkatesh thought of taking more control of engineering before things worsened. He discussed this with Raghu, who concurred. Venkatesh then began working on a few other ideas in the payment space.

The New Product Lines

Venkatesh, skilled at building platforms solo, collaborated with Raghu to create three new ones without relying on Fee Plaza LLP's engineers. First, a classifieds site—later tied to payments—gained traction with Indian

SMEs. Second, a platform for independent garages. He also made US versions of both. Raghu advised waiting for the Delegated Administration feature to launch all four platforms in the US together. By then, Raghu had spent heavily from his personal funds on Fee Plaza Inc.'s software customization, auditing, compliance, and other costs.

The GoI Factor

While Venkatesh planned Fee Plaza LLP and Fee Plaza Inc.'s future and built new platforms, India's market shifted. The Government of India (GoI) launched a mandatory invoice billing system for firms with INR 500 Crore (INR 5 Billion) turnover, rivalling Fee Plaza's service. Venkatesh foresaw the threat, as GoI aimed to monitor payments for better indirect tax enforcement. He predicted, correctly so, that GoI would lower the threshold once stable, which it did, dropping it to INR 50 Crore (INR 0.5 Billion) about 2 years later. GoI enhanced it by linking it to the GST network and E-way Bill logistics platform, offering a superior, free alternative. Further investment in Fee Plaza's invoice billing service became impractical.

With all this going on, Venkatesh was wondering when Fee Plaza Inc. would formally launch any of its services in the USA. While Fee Plaza won awards from Acquisition International magazine UK for three years in a row (two in the first year), engineers hired to work on a few product lines and to complete the remaining work did not show commitment and quit. Fee Plaza LLP's revenues stagnated as many of its merchants shut down during Covid-19 and its aftermath and never recovered. Venkatesh had to decide on the future steps for Fee Plaza.

Discussion Questions

1. What are the challenges faced by an entrepreneur in bootstrapped ventures?
2. How does the entrepreneurial orientation of an individual help visualize startups?
3. What were some the actions taken by the founders that helped be cash flow positive?
4. What were the things that in retrospect, founders could have done differently?
5. How can you build a team when revenue is low and valuation is non-existent?
6. Should the entrepreneurs have sought funding and if so, at which stages?

7. Was the structuring of India—US entities most appropriate? Why?
8. Where should the founders spend limited money—platform or marketing?
9. What are the regulatory hazards in fintech startups?
10. What are the challenges in scaling a fintech venture?
11. Options considered by Indian founders before extending to the US
12. Should Indian entity set up a US subsidiary?
13. Should Indian entity license the brand, technology?

Supplementary Reading

- Lumpkin, G. T., & Dess, G. G. (1996). Clarifying the entrepreneurial orientation construct and linking it to performance. *Academy of management Review*, *21*(1), 135–172.
- Clark, D. R., Pidduck, R. J., Lumpkin, G. T., & Covin, J. G. (2024). Is it okay to study entrepreneurial orientation (EO) at the individual level? Yes!. *Entrepreneurship Theory and Practice*, *48*(1), 349–391.
- Sarasvathy, S. D. (2001). Causation and effectuation: Toward a theoretical shift from economic inevitability to entrepreneurial contingency. *Academy of management Review*, *26*(2), 243–263.

Learning Objectives

This case can be used to discuss the challenges and choices faced by an entrepreneur in the fintech space in an emerging economy. It can be used to discuss entrepreneurial orientation, internationalization choices, digital business models, start-up challenges, trust among partners and entrepreneurial effectuation processes.

Competing Interests The authors have no conflicts of interest to declare that are relevant to the content of this chapter.

Supplementary Material

Epilogue

Part A

Fee Plaza LLP in India continued to earn revenues to sustain itself and to repay some of the debt to its co-founder Venkatesh. Fee Plaza LLP had recently been granted a significant free usage credit from Amazon Web Services which brought the cloud hosting cost to zero. Other expenses included paying the software engineering contractors, auditors, and compliance charges to the government. At this rate of repayment, the recovery of Venkatesh's remaining debt from Fee Plaza LLP would require about 6 years, excluding interest amount.

Entrepreneurs should neither underestimate their potential, services, ability to command a price however new the firm is, not give away free for goodwill, as not generating revenue, that too from multiple streams will reduce the life of the venture.

Part B

- Fee Plaza Inc. has not formally launched any of its services in the USA.
- Fee Plaza continued to win awards, such as from Acquisition International magazine
- Other engineers hired to work on a few product lines and to complete the remaining work did not show commitment and quit.
- Fee Plaza LLP's revenues stagnated as many of its merchants shut down during Covid-19 and its aftermath and never recovered.
- This was not a recoverable situation and Fee Plaza closed operations in 2024

Teaching note to guide some of the discussion questions

1. What were some the actions taken by the founders that helped keep cash flow positive?

- No cash incentives to customers, merchants
- Each unit transaction was profitable
- No requirement of expensive PCI-DSS by design, huge savings of PCI-DSS audit money (about INR 4 M per year as in the founding year)

- Equitable sharing of risks among Venkatesh and Raghu
- Hired contractors to avoid salary commitment

2. What were the things that in retrospect, founders could have done differently?

- Made merchant registration free; should have been priced, even if nominally
- Made the merchant-branded apps free, should have been priced, even if nominally
- Did not charge both the merchant and the payer; should have charged both like BookMyShow does

3. What are the regulatory hazards in fintech startups?

- Regulatory change, e.g., all firms with INR50M revenue should invoice on government platform only
- Government offering the services free on its own platforms
- UPI

4. What are the challenges in scaling a fintech venture?

- Merchants signed up because the founder was a very persuasive marketer or were offered merchant branded apps and websites for free, but the merchants did not use much
- Refreshing the fee catalogue after the fees expire
- Disruptive events like COVID when over 80% of small business on Fee Plaza shut down

5. Should Indian entity set up a US subsidiary?

- It is very expensive to comply with regulations and implement the solution both in India and in the US, particularly as a bootstrapped venture

CHAPTER 18

NSRCEL at a Crossroads: Scaling Impact in India's Startup Ecosystem

Charu Rastogi and Srivardhini K. Jha

Abstract This case explores the strategic challenges faced by the N. S. Raghavan Centre for Entrepreneurial Learning (NSRCEL), the startup incubator at the Indian Institute of Management Bangalore (IIMB), as it seeks to expand its impact within India's entrepreneurial ecosystem. Originally established to support entrepreneurial learning, NSRCEL has evolved into a multi-sector incubator, working with ventures across domains such as social impact, women-led enterprises, and emerging technology startups. However, as NSRCEL grows, it faces key strategic questions: Should it continue to serve a broad spectrum of entrepreneurs, or should it focus on a few high-potential areas? What should NSRCEL's strategic priority be: scaling incubation, strengthening the ecosystem, or moving into acceleration? How should it position itself relative to other incubators in India's rapidly evolving startup landscape?

The case enables students to analyse the evolution of incubation in India, assess the role of academic incubators, and evaluate strategic options for NSRCEL's growth. It highlights the tensions between breadth and

C. Rastogi (✉) • S. K. Jha
IIM Bangalore, Bangalore, India
e-mail: charu.rastogi21@alumni.iimb.ac.in; srivardhini.jha@iimb.ac.in

A. S. Galande et al. (eds.), *Context-inspired Entrepreneurship*, Sustainable Development Goals Series,
https://doi.org/10.1007/978-981-95-9831-1_18

depth, mission and market alignment, and short-term impact versus long-term sustainability, offering rich ground for discussion on entrepreneurial ecosystems and institutional strategy in emerging markets.

Keywords NSRCEL • Academic incubator • Startup incubation • Entrepreneurial support • Entrepreneurial ecosystem • Scaling incubators

SDG Links This chapter is aligned with SDG 8: Decent Work and Economic Growth, examining how NSRCEL fosters new business creation and job generation through structured entrepreneurship support (SDG 8.3). The chapter also aligns with SDG 9, through its role in strengthening innovation ecosystems, and relates to SDG 4 by supporting entrepreneurship education and capability building.

Established in the year 2000 as a Section-8 not-for-profit entity, the N. S. Raghavan Centre for Entrepreneurial Learning (NSRCEL) at the Indian Institute of Management Bangalore (IIMB) had emerged as one of India's most influential startup incubators.[1] As of March 2025, NSRCEL had impacted more than 5370 ventures and incubated 2910 ventures with a combined value of US$ 7.37 billion. In 2024–2025 alone, it had incubated 1106 ventures across 11 program tracks, covering 82 towns across India, making it one of the most far-reaching incubators in the country (NSRCEL, 2025).

NSRCEL's stratospheric growth had unfolded against the backdrop of a rapidly evolving startup ecosystem in India. Over the past decade, the Indian government had actively pushed for entrepreneurship through initiatives like *Startup India* and *Atal Innovation Mission*. These, along with various individual state-led startup policies, provided funding, mentorship, and regulatory support to early-stage ventures. This period also witnessed an unprecedented surge in entrepreneurial energy, with almost 160,000 startups registered across the country since 2016[2] (Kumar et al.,

[1] An incubator is a form of entrepreneurial support organization that supports early-stage startups by providing them with resources, mentorship, and infrastructure to help them grow. Incubators typically offer office space, networking opportunities, access to investors, business development support, and sometimes initial funding in exchange for equity or a small fee.

[2] Startups registered with Department for Promotion of Industry and Internal Trade (DPIIT) grew from 500 in 2016 to 159,157 in January 2025.

2025). Notably, a growing number of these ventures emerged from tier-2 and tier-3 towns, signalling a shift beyond traditional metropolitan hubs and broadening of the country's innovation ecosystem (Jha & Rajan, 2024a). This decentralization of innovation raised critical questions about how incubators like NSRCEL should evolve to expand their impact—not just on startups, but also on the broader entrepreneurial ecosystem.

Amidst this shifting landscape, in January 2025, the boardroom of NSRCEL buzzed with conversation as the leadership team gathered to discuss the way forward. NSRCEL had evolved into a dynamic entrepreneurial hub, extending its reach beyond traditional business incubation and embracing social enterprises, women-led businesses, and industry partnerships. But now, as the landscape of Indian entrepreneurship continued to evolve rapidly, a critical question loomed: What was next for NSRCEL?

Seated at the head of the table, Anand Sri Ganesh, NSRCEL's Chief Executive Officer, tapped his pen on the wooden surface. 'We've done well,' he began, looking around at his team. 'Our model has worked, our startups are making an impact, and our brand is recognized. But the world is changing. Even though the startup ecosystem is growing faster than ever, demand outstrips supply. We need to decide where we fit in the next phase. Do we scale our incubation model, shift to ecosystem-building to support more incubators, or venture into acceleration and help startups grow beyond the early stages?'

The Indian Startup Incubation Landscape

India's startup incubation network had expanded significantly in the past two decades, playing a vital role in fostering entrepreneurship, supporting startups, and driving innovation. While India had historically been recognized for its strong entrepreneurial spirit, the formal incubation ecosystem only began taking shape in the early 2000s. The first major push came in the year 2000 when the Department of Science and Technology (DST) launched the National Science and Technology Entrepreneurship Development Board (NSTEDB), creating one of the first structured incubation programs in the country. Over the next decade, incubators remained limited in number and scope, primarily housed within academic institutions. However, the period between 2010 and 2020 saw a dramatic surge in incubator activity, with the total number increasing from 170 to 731. This expansion coincided with India's startup boom, driven by policy incentives, increased venture capital activity, and government-backed programs such as Startup India. As of June 2024, there were more than 1100 incubators in India (Jha & Rajan, 2024a). This marked a 200-fold increase in the number of incubators since 2000, reflecting stronger institutional involvement, with universities, corporations, and governments investing more in entrepreneurship.

Despite the stellar growth in the number of incubators, the rate of incubation remained in single digits at 8 percent (Jha & Rajan, 2024a), indicating that a vast majority of startups still operated outside formal incubation structures. Furthermore, a stark disparity existed in the effectiveness of incubators —only 10 percent of incubators supported 98 percent of incubated startups (Jha & Rajan, 2024a), leaving many underutilized. This raises a fundamental question: Are these incubators failing to offer meaningful support, or are startups choosing to grow without them? The answer likely lies in a combination of factors, including the quality of incubation services, the relevance of mentorship, and startups' preference for direct engagement with investors and industry stakeholders instead of structured incubation programs.

Additionally, Tier I cities like Bengaluru, Chennai, and Hyderabad emerged as major startup hubs, benefiting from strong institutional support, corporate presence, and high-quality entrepreneurial talent. Tier I cities housed 48 percent of incubators, while the remaining were spread across Tier II and Tier III cities (Jha & Rajan, 2024a). This signalled progress in extending incubation beyond metropolitan centres and democratizing access to entrepreneurial resources. However, despite encouraging numbers, smaller cities remained underserved, constrained by a lack of experienced mentors, weaker industry connections, and limited access to advanced technology and capital. This was apparent by the fact that even though almost two-thirds (64 percent) of new startups were from Tier 2 and Tier 3 regions (where a large number of incubators were also present), many of them moved to Tier 1 regions to seek incubation support and market access (Jha & Rajan, 2024a).

Types of Incubators: Academic, Industry, and Public Sector Models

India's incubation landscape was primarily led by academic incubators, while industry-backed and public sector incubators had emerged more recently. Academic incubators, primarily housed within universities and research institutions, made up 65 percent of India's incubators. They fostered student entrepreneurship, innovation, and commercialization but struggled with scalability. Notable examples included NSRCEL (IIM Bangalore), SINE (IIT Bombay), and RTBI (IIT Madras). Majority of the incubators in Tier II (74 percent) and Tier III cities (83 percent) were housed in academic institutions (Jha & Rajan, 2024a).

Industry-backed incubators—such as T-Hub and NASSCOM 10,000 Startups—accounted for 29 percent of all incubators (Jha & Rajan, 2024a). They offered stronger market access, investor networks, and go-to-market strategies, helping startups secure funding and scale faster. Public sector incubators (6 percent) were backed by government initiatives like Atal Innovation Mission, Startup India, and Biotechnology Industry Research Assistance Council (BIRAC), focusing on social impact and deep-tech innovation. Industry-backed and public sector incubators were primarily concentrated in Tier I cities.

While academic incubators play a crucial role in fostering innovation, their commercialization challenges could hinder the scaling potential of startups outside major urban hubs. This raises the need for stronger industry partnerships and alternative incubation models to bridge the gap between research-driven innovation and market readiness.

Impact of Incubation

Incubators serve as key connectors in the startup ecosystem, linking startups, investors, universities, and government agencies. Investors view incubators as a gateway to promising startups, while government agencies rely on them to channel investments and track startup progress. As such, it is no surprise that startups that underwent incubation consistently outperformed their peers. They were 2.5 times more likely to attract external funding, secure it earlier, and generate more patents. Incubation also correlated with higher survival rates and stronger revenue growth (Jha & Rajan, 2024a).

Yet, these benefits remain concentrated within a small subset of incubators, raising pressing questions about effectiveness. What distinguishes high-impact incubators from those that remain underutilized? If only a handful are delivering results, how should the rest evolve—or should they exist at all?

NSRCEL

NSRCEL began with a generous endowment of about US$ 3 million[3] from Nadathur S. Raghavan, cofounder of Infosys Technologies,[4] in 1999. Raghavan was the first employee of Infosys and retired as Joint Managing Director in 2000 (Gautam, 2023). He wanted to create a structured support system for entrepreneurs in India. As such, NSRCEL positioned itself as a learning-focused incubator within the academic setting of IIMB. Unlike traditional incubators, it emphasized structured training and entrepreneurial education.

Evolution and Growth

NSRCEL was founded with a mission to foster entrepreneurship at a time when the concept of formal incubation was still nascent in India. Initially it was focused on providing mentorship and guidance to early-stage startups. It also ran two programs for entrepreneurs—an eight-month management program for entrepreneurs and family businesses and a capacity-building management program for early-stage women entrepreneurs (Business Standard, 2016).

In later years the centre steadily expanded its mandate. What began as a generalist incubator evolved into a multi-faceted platform, catering to a diverse range of entrepreneurs. Unlike many incubators that concentrated primarily on high-growth, investor-backed startups, NSRCEL took a broader approach, incorporating social ventures, early-stage entrepreneurs, and underrepresented groups. This diversification reflected a shift

[3] NSRCEL received a grant of INR 130 million, 1$ = INR 43.5407; exchange rate as on 15th December, 1999; Reserve Bank of India - Reference Rate Archive

[4] Infosys Technologies is a global consulting and IT services company based in India. It was founded in 1981 in Pune, India, by 7 engineers.

in India's incubation landscape—from an urban, tech-focused ecosystem to a more inclusive and sector-agnostic model. In an article in The Economic Times (2025), Chaitali Pandey, Marketing Manager, NSRCEL noted:

> When it was founded, India's startup ecosystem was still in its infancy, with limited resources, funding options, and mentorship opportunities. NSRCEL's early role was primarily focused on supporting nascent entrepreneurs with the essential tools to help them turn ideas into businesses, offering incubation, mentorship, and access to networks. As the Indian startup ecosystem matured throughout the 2000s and 2010s, particularly with the rise of technology and digital startups, NSRCEL adapted its offerings, expanding its programs to include sector-specific initiatives and access to investors and industry experts.

Recognizing the untapped entrepreneurial potential beyond India's major startup hubs, NSRCEL had increasingly focused on Tier II and Tier III cities. Programs like the Women Startup Program (WSP) had been instrumental in extending the centre's reach to the North-eastern states and Jammu & Kashmir (IIM Bangalore, 2020). NSRCEL had helped democratize entrepreneurship, ensuring that access to structured support, funding, and mentorship was not limited to metropolitan areas. The push beyond Bengaluru stemmed from the recognition that high-potential ventures in smaller cities often faced greater barriers to scaling due to limited ecosystem support.

NSRCEL's affiliation with IIM Bangalore granted it a distinctive competitive advantage. Unlike standalone incubators, it was embedded within a top-tier academic institution where the academic ecosystem provided mentorship that extended beyond business fundamentals, offering insights into strategy, innovation management, and leadership. Additionally, NSRCEL's positioning within IIMB's broader entrepreneurial ecosystem gave startups access to one of the strongest alumni networks in India. This facilitated fundraising opportunities as well as industry connections, mentorship, and peer learning. The ability to integrate academic knowledge with practical, industry-driven insights differentiated NSRCEL from many other incubators, particularly those that lacked institutional depth.

Core Philosophy of Incubation

Founder-Centric

NSRCEL's incubation philosophy was founder centric. Its programs were designed to understand the world from the founders' perspective and foster a space conducive to sustained entrepreneurial growth. In a podcast with Benu and Sanghvi (2023), Ganesh stressed:

> An incubator has two jobs. First is to provide a safe space for the founder to find their path, while also reducing the risk inherent in an entrepreneurial journey. Second is to accelerate the founder's learning through exposure, peer interaction and incubator support, so they can test and iterate their models quickly.

NSRCEL followed a cohort-based learning model, enabling entrepreneurs to benefit from area-specific mentorship as well as peer interactions. These programs equipped founders with the knowledge and skills needed to transition from ideation to implementation, helping them develop, test, and refine their business models. NSRCEL placed strong emphasis on capability-building, developing an entrepreneurial mindset, and enhancing resilience in its founders. Founders gained insights through workshops, mentorship sessions, and industry interactions, leveraging NSRCEL's network of experienced entrepreneurs, industry practitioners, and alumni.

Broad-Based Incubation with Sectoral Depth

As of March 2025, NSRCEL had 11 programs catering to startups across ideation, prototyping, validating minimum viable product (MVP) and scaling stages. See Table 18.1 for details. NSRCEL's early initiatives were sector-agnostic, laying the foundation for its credibility in the startup ecosystem. It's programs catering to women entrepreneurs and social entrepreneurs fell in this bucket, as did Launchpad, Velocity and Campus founders. As the ecosystem matured, corporations from specific industries increasingly sought to engage with the broader entrepreneurial landscape through NSRCEL, leading to the development of targeted, sector-specific programs. See Table 18.2 for details on NSRCEL programs.

NSRCEL expanded its incubation model by launching sector-specific programs to address the unique challenges and opportunities in specific industries. In mobility, NSRCEL partnered with Maruti Suzuki India Ltd.

Table 18.1 NSRCEL Programs by Stage of Entrepreneurial Journey

Programs / Stages	Establishing my business idea	Refining my prototype	Validating my MVP/POC	Scaling my venture
Launchpad	↔			
Campus Founders (with GPS Renewables)		↔		
Impact Orbit			↔	
Velocity – Kotak Bizlabs				↔
Sustainability Mobility Incubation Program (with ALSTOM)				↔
Goldman Sachs 10000 Women Program				↔
FinTech Centre of Excellence (with Karnataka Government)				↔
Incubation Program for Mobility Startups (with Maruti Suzuki)			↔	↔
Climate Incubation Hub (with HUL)			↔	↔
Healthcare Incubation Program (with DailyRounds)	↔	↔	↔	
Women Startup Program (with Kotak Mahindra Bank)	↔	↔	↔	↔

Source: nsrcel.org

in 2020 to launch the 'Incubation Program for Mobility Startups'. Building on this expertise, NSRCEL introduced the 'Sustainable Mobility Incubation Program' in partnership with Alstom in 2022 to support startups focused on sustainable transportation solutions. In healthcare, NSRCEL launched the 'Healthcare Incubation Program' with DailyRounds in 2024, offering a four-month program for startups working on improving access and affordability in healthcare. In fintech, NSRCEL established a 'FinTech Centre of Excellence (CoE)' in October 2024, backed by the Government of Karnataka. Addressing climate change, NSRCEL introduced the 'Climate Incubation Hub' in 2025, in partnership with Hindustan Unilever Limited (HUL) to foster

Table 18.2 Portfolio of NSRCEL Programs

Sector agnostic programs
Several NSRCEL programs catered to a broad range of startups, while some specifically targeted women entrepreneurs and social entrepreneurs as distinct groups. **Launchpad**, a 100-day pre-incubation program, helped early-stage startups transition from ideation to prototyping. **Velocity**, supported by Kotak Bizlabs, targeted post-MVP, revenue-generating startups. By March 2025, it had engaged 750+ learners and incubated 160 startups[a]. **Campus Founders**, a four-month initiative funded by GPS Renewables, was designed for recent graduates and student entrepreneurs with a working prototype.
NSRCEL's most lauded program in this space was the ***Women Startup Program (WSP).*** Launched in 2016 with support from Goldman Sachs and DST, WSP was designed to enhance entrepreneurial and managerial skills of women leading early and ideation stage ventures. In December 2024, this program was supported by Kotak Mahindra Bank and had inducted its fifth cohort[b] and by March 2025, it had engaged 23,053 learners, incubated 589 ventures across 19 sectors and 24 states of India[c]. NSRCEL has also been a key player in expanding the **Goldman Sachs 10,000 Women program** in India since 2018[d]. Additionally, in 2023 this partnership deepened with the launch of **10,000 Women 'Finance for Growth'** initiative, helping women entrepreneurs raise funds to scale their ventures.
The **Impact Orbit program** (formerly NSRCEL Social) was launched in 2017 to support social enterprises working on high impact solution. The program was supported by prominent foundations and corporates over the years, including Michael and Susan Dell Foundation, Mphasis, Ford Foundation, Capgemini, Acumen Green Growth Accelerator and Pernod Ricard India Foundation[e]. By 2025, the program had incubated 113 ventures, disbursed ₹11.4 crores in grants, and facilitated ₹30 crores in follow-on funding for startups across 10 cohorts[f].
Sector specific programs
Mobility: In 2020, NSRCEL partnered with Maruti Suzuki India Ltd. to launch the **Incubation Program for Mobility Startups.** This 6-month incubation program was designed for automobile and mobility startups in MVP validation and scale up stage[g]. By March 2025, 3 cohorts had graduated and applications were open for the fourth cohort. Deepening its sectoral expertise in mobility, NSRCEL launched the **Sustainable Mobility Incubation Program** in partnership with Alstom in 2022.
Health: Recognizing the growing need for innovation in healthcare, NSRCEL launched **healthcare incubation program** in collaboration with DailyRounds in 2024. The 4-month program designed to provide support to healthcare startups in the ideation to proof-of-concept stage, and working to improve access and affordability of healthcare in India.
Climate: In 2025, NSRCEL launched the **Climate Incubation Hub**, in partnership with Hindustan Unilever Limited (HUL). It is dedicated to fostering ventures that develop tech-enabled solutions to combat climate change.
Fintech: In October 2024, NSRCEL established a **FinTech Centre of Excellence (CoE)** with support from the Government of Karnataka. The centre aimed to run incubation and acceleration programs to drive fintech innovation in the region.

Source: nsrcel.org
[a]Velocity - Kotak BizLabs : Incubation Program for Revenue Stage Startups I NSRCEL
[b]Cohort 5 of Women Start-up Programme gets inspiring welcome – The IIMB Digest
[c]Women Entrepreneurship Program at IIM Bangalore I NSRCEL
[d]IIM Bangalore re-Launches Goldman Sachs 10,000 Women I IIM Bangalore
[e]Impact Assessment Report: An Executive Summary - NSRCEL
[f]Incubation Center for Social Startups I NSRCEL
[g]NSRCEL partners with Maruti Suzuki to launch incubation for mobility startups I IIM Bangalore

tech-enabled solutions for sustainability. These sector-focused initiatives strengthened NSRCEL's role as a catalyst for specialized entrepreneurship across India's startup ecosystem.

Incubation Methodology

From its 23 years of experience, NSRCEL had developed a trademarked incubation methodology which they called 'ECKNA'. The acronym stood for *'Entrepreneurial Capability through Knowledge, Networks, and Assessments'*. ECKNA stressed development of entrepreneurial capability, encircled and supported by three foundational pillars of Knowledge, Networks and Assessments. These pillars formed the inner ring and represented what entrepreneurs received from NSRCEL. An outer ring–comprising supportive components such as Technology, Program Design, Operations and Partnerships–encircled the inner ring and indicated how these critical inputs were delivered to the founders. See Fig. 18.1 for a diagrammatic representation of ECKNA.

The NSRCEL Model: Funding and Institutional Support

As a key player in India's incubation ecosystem, NSRCEL benefited from substantial government and corporate backing. It was supported by the Niti Aayog, Department of Science and Technology (DST) and the Ministry of Electronics and Information Technology (MeitY), reinforcing its status as a government-recognized incubator. Beyond public sector support, NSRCEL's corporate and philanthropic partnerships played a crucial role in shaping its programs. In a round table discussion on the future of incubation (Jha & Rajan, 2024b), Ganesh observed:

> There are several options for creating financially sustainable operations in an incubator. One can have an equity-based model, a pay-for-use model or a philanthropy-based model. NSRCEL relies heavily on CSR, government grants, and philanthropy.

Private sector collaborations had been instrumental in expanding NSRCEL's incubation capabilities, providing startups with funding, industry expertise, and market access. Beyond financial backing, partnerships with corporates served as a bridge between academia and industry, helping startups navigate market validation, regulatory compliance, and scaling challenges. As such, several of NSRCEL's programs were funded

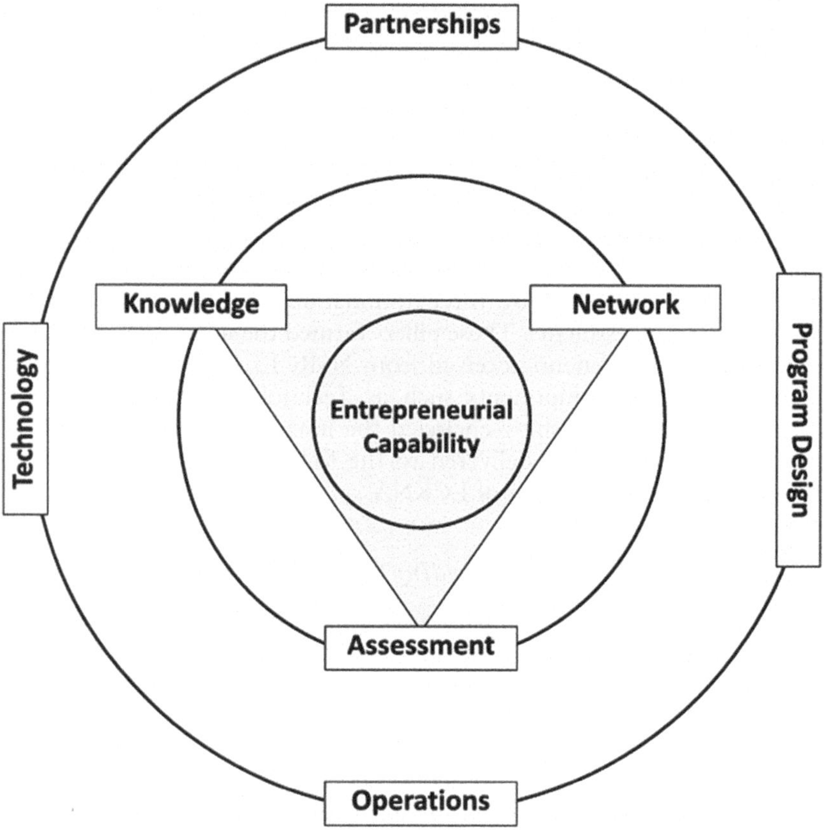

Fig. 18.1 The ECKNA Framework. (Source: NSRCEL)

through partnerships with corporates, driving both business innovation and social impact.

In 2024, NSRCEL forayed into direct investments in startups through a pre-seed fund in collaboration with Small Industries Development Bank of India (SIDBI) (The Hindu Bureau, 2024). The fund aimed to focus on accelerating start-ups in the deep tech and emerging business areas such as healthcare, sustainability and defense innovations.

NSRCEL had stayed relevant by continuously refining its incubation programs to cater to evolving demands such as supporting social enterprises, women entrepreneurs, and startups in deep-tech and fintech. It had also maintained its focus on research, policy advocacy, and creating strong industry connections, ensuring that its impact went beyond just nurturing individual businesses to shaping the overall entrepreneurial ecosystem.

Strategic Dilemma: The Path Forward

As one of India's premier startup incubators, NSRCEL had played a critical role in shaping the country's entrepreneurial landscape. But with the rapid evolution of the startup ecosystem, the leadership team needed to determine how best to position NSRCEL for the future. As NSRCEL stood at the crossroads, three strategic paths emerged, each offering distinct directions.

Option 1: Scale Up Incubation

One possible direction was to solve for capacity constraint at the institution level and expand the annual intake of startups over the next five years. In 2024–2025 alone, NSRCEL engaged with more than 1100 startups through its programs. Given the large number of registered startups in the country (160,000) and the low incubation rate (8 percent), increasing this number to 1500 and eventually to 2500 could be a structured growth objective. Ganesh noted:

> At this point, demand for incubation outstrips supply. There are a larger number of talented founders across the country looking for a competent, safe space to iterate and come up with meaningful business models. However, because of supply constraints, not all founders are able to access high-quality incubators. For example, at NSRCEL we cannot exceed our current selection rate of five to seven percent because of capacity constraints. The upside potential to creating economic or societal impact from incubators is so large that, in my mind, we should not just be optimising but maximising the number of incubators being created.

NSRCEL had established processes, a mentor network, and connections with investors, policymakers, and corporate sponsors. Scaling up would build on these existing strengths, increasing engagement with startups and fostering a larger entrepreneurial community. However, expanding operations would require additional funding, infrastructure, and a larger team of advisors and mentors. It would also necessitate adaptations in mentorship structures and resource distribution to accommodate the increased intake.

Option 2: Strengthen the Ecosystem

Another approach was to focus on enhancing incubation quality in India rather than increasing NSRCEL's own capacity. Ganesh observed:

> We have 1100 plus incubators in the country, but how many of them have brilliant incubation capability? We have had 23 years of learning from our mistakes. We know what not to do. A lot of younger incubators do not have that luxury of learning. I wonder if we should be sharing our learning with the ecosystem, use the opportunity to ramp up their capabilities.

By positioning itself as a "mentor incubator," NSRCEL could work with other incubators nationwide, providing structured training programs, standardized incubation frameworks, and access to its network of investors, corporate partners, and entrepreneurs. In a recent newspaper article (Vaitheeswaran, 2025), Ganesh mentioned:

> We are codifying our incubation methodology, frameworks and templates. We want to increase the knowledge capture for the Indian entrepreneurial ecosystem. We could package these as a consulting capability for young incubators.

This approach aligned with NSRCEL's existing role in the incubation ecosystem. It would address the issue of uneven quality of incubators across the country. By strengthening other incubators, NSRCEL could support a broader range of startups indirectly. However, this transition would involve a shift from direct incubation toward a broader advisory function, requiring engagement with government agencies and institutional stakeholders. It would also require adjustments in NSRCEL's positioning within the startup ecosystem.

Option 3: Move into Acceleration

A third option involved shifting beyond incubation into acceleration. Rather than focusing only on early-stage startups, NSRCEL could develop programs to support ventures at the scaling stage, helping them attract investment, expand into new markets, and navigate growth challenges. Acceleration would allow NSRCEL to engage with startups that had already gained traction, providing targeted support at a critical stage of their growth. Programs could focus on investor relations, market expansion strategies, and sector-specific mentorship.

NSRCEL had already begun expanding into acceleration through targeted programs in collaboration with industry and government partners. Examples included Goldman Sachs 10,000 Women Program, Velocity - Kotak Bizlabs Program and the pre-seed Deep Tech accelerator fund with Small Industries Development Bank of India (SIDBI). NSRCEL could further strengthen its presence in acceleration by expanding existing initiatives and developing new programs tailored to the needs of startups in specific sectors.

However, this shift would require new expertise and engagement with stakeholders in the investment and high-growth startup ecosystems. Acceleration programs often operated with different funding models, and NSRCEL would need to determine how best to structure its involvement in this space while aligning with its institutional mission.

The Decision Ahead

Each strategic path represented a distinct future for NSRCEL. Scaling up incubation would increase reach and engagement with early-stage entrepreneurs. Strengthening the ecosystem would expand NSRCEL's influence by enhancing incubation quality nationwide. Moving into acceleration would provide targeted support for scaling ventures and engage with a different segment of the startup ecosystem.

As the leadership team deliberated, they considered the potential impact of each direction on NSRCEL's role and mission. The decision would shape the organization's future contributions to the entrepreneurial landscape in India.

Conclusion

NSRCEL had established itself as a leading incubator in the country. Its evolution from a generalist startup incubator to a multi-sector, impact-driven platform underscored the changing dynamics of India's incubation ecosystem. However, as it continues to grow, NSRCEL must navigate key strategic choices: how to scale without diluting quality, how to balance competing priorities across sectors, and how to position itself in an increasingly demanding incubation landscape. Its choice will define not only its own trajectory but how incubation in India evolves in the years to come.

Discussion Questions

1. Ho would you assess the strengths and weaknesses of the incubation ecosystem in India?
2. What should NSRCEL's strategic priority be—scaling incubation, strengthening the ecosystem, or moving into acceleration?
3. If NSRCEL decides to take up option 2—strengthening the ecosystem, which strategic approaches should it adopt for effective execution?
4. What are the key success factors for a 'train and support' model?

Supplementary Readings

1. Jha, S. K., & Rajan T. (2024). The future of incubation. *IIMB Management Review*, *36*(1), 48–55. Link: https://www.sciencedirect.com/science/article/pii/S0970389624000090
2. India Incubator Kaleidoscope (2025)—Democratising Entrepreneurial Dreams, https://nsrcel.org/project/india-incubator-kaleidoscope-2024-democratising-entrepreneurial-dreams/

Learning Objectives and Outcomes

This case is designed to help students understand the evolution of India's incubation ecosystem and the unique role of academic incubators like NSRCEL in shaping entrepreneurial outcomes. It encourages students to evaluate strategic options available to incubators such as scaling, ecosystem-building, and acceleration, while weighing the trade-offs involved in each. Through the case discussion, students will critically assess how incubators can align their mission with evolving market needs and develop well-reasoned strategic recommendations for NSRCEL's future positioning within India's startup ecosystem.

This case enables students to:

1. Understand the evolution of the incubation landscape in India, including its drivers, challenges, and key inflection points.
2. Evaluate strategic growth options available to incubators, such as scaling, ecosystem-building, and acceleration, and the trade-offs involved in each.

3. Analyse the role of academic incubators in shaping entrepreneurial ecosystems and explore how they can differentiate themselves strategically.
4. Critically assess how incubators can align their mission with evolving market needs to maximize their long-term impact and sustainability.

Competing Interests The authors have no conflicts of interest to declare that are relevant to the content of this chapter.

Supplementary Material—Teaching Note

Positioning of the Case

This case is well-suited for courses on entrepreneurial ecosystems, incubation, and venture support, offering students a deep dive into the strategic dilemmas faced by incubators in a rapidly evolving startup landscape. It challenges students to evaluate trade-offs between scaling, ecosystem-building, and acceleration, pushing them to consider reach, depth, and long-term sustainability. The case also highlights the unique role of academic incubators, prompting discussions on strategic differentiation and the competitive positioning of incubators within the broader entrepreneurial ecosystem. Through this case, students will critically assess how incubators can maximize impact while aligning with their mission and evolving market needs.

Discussion Questions

- **How would you assess the strengths and weaknesses of the incubation ecosystem in India?**

Open this pasture by asking students to rate incubation ecosystem in India on a scale of 1 to 5, where 5 is excellent. You will get responses between 3 to 4 based on region and sector. Ask students to think of the advantages and challenges from support ecosystem perspective. Responses will centre around the following:

Strengths	*Weaknesses*
Diverse and growing incubation infrastructure in terms of number of incubators	Low incubation rate—probe students for reasons. You may get responses like mentorship quality, lack of strong networks and investor interest
Targeted support for key segments like students, deep tech entrepreneurs, women, social impact startups	Over-reliance on a few incubators as only 10% incubators do the heavy lifting of supporting 98% of the incubated startups
Growing government and corporate backing	Limited reach in Tier II and III cities

End this section by noting that India's incubation ecosystem can be strengthened through a decentralized approach—one that extends quality support beyond metro cities, fosters stronger mentor and investor linkages, and enhances long-term support for startups beyond early-stage incubation.

- **What should NSRCEL's strategic priority be—scaling incubation, strengthening the ecosystem, or moving into acceleration?**

This pasture forces students to weigh the trade-offs between reach, depth, and long-term sustainability while considering NSRCEL's mission and capabilities. Encourage students to think of each option in terms of the impact NSRCEL can create, the challenges it would face, its key operational needs and strategic fit with its context.

Instructors can use this **decision matrix** as part of their board plan for driving case discussion:

Criteria	*Scale up incubation*	*Strengthen the ecosystem*	*Move into acceleration*
Impact	Expands reach, impact and brand presence	Broad systemic impact on incubation quality	Supports high-growth startups and funding access
Challenges	Risk of diluted mentorship and resource strain	Moves away from hands-on incubation	Competes with private accelerators
Operational Needs	Requires additional funding and human capital	Requires new policy engagement, training and outreach programs	Requires investor relations and sector expertise
Strategic Fit	Aligns with NSRCEL's core incubation mission	Positions NSRCEL as an ecosystem leader	Aligns with market demand but shifts focus from incubation

- **If NSRCEL decides to take up option 2—strengthening the ecosystem, which strategic approaches should it adopt for effective execution?**

This question will elicit a range of responses. You can try to coalesce them into the following categories:

- **Build and Operate:** NSRCEL can directly establish and manage new incubators, specific programs, and partnerships in underserved regions. This would ensure structured support and give NSRCEL direct control over quality and outcomes. However, this model is resource-intensive and requires a long-term commitment along with a significant investment in infrastructure and staffing.
- **Build-Operate-Transfer:** This approach allows NSRCEL to set up incubation support structures, operate them to establish best practices, and eventually transfer them to universities, private players, or government bodies, ensuring long-term sustainability. This approach ensures initial quality control while enabling long-term sustainability by embedding capabilities within local ecosystems. The challenge lies in finding reliable partners to take over operations and ensuring consistency in quality post-transfer.
- **Train and Support:** NSRCEL can train incubator managers, mentors, and policymakers, through structured capacity-building programs, equipping them with best practices and resources to enhance startup support across India. NSRCEL can uplift the overall quality of incubation across the ecosystem by standardizing incubation practices, sharing frameworks for venture support, and facilitating knowledge exchange. This model leverages NSRCEL's expertise without requiring heavy infrastructure investment. The drawback is that NSRCEL will have limited control over implementation and outcomes post training.
- **Network and Facilitate:** NSRCEL can act as a connector, encouraging collaborations between incubators, startups, investors, and policymakers, enabling knowledge-sharing and ecosystem-wide improvements. This model is cost-effective and scalable, but its impact is harder to measure since NSRCEL does not directly control outcomes at individual incubators.
- **What are the key success factors for a 'train and support' model?**

NSRCEL can equip young incubators in underserved regions with structured processes, technology-driven solutions, shared services, and ecosystem linkages to enhance their effectiveness and sustainability.

- **Standardized Processes and Frameworks:** Standardized processes can help streamline operations, maintain quality, and make knowledge transfer more effective. Structured frameworks can ensure consistency in program delivery, making it easier for new incubators to adopt best practices.
- **Leveraging technology for scale:** Using digital platforms, online learning modules, and virtual mentorship can expand the reach of the 'train and support' program, particularly in Tier 2 and 3 cities. Technology can enable remote access to resources, reduce operational costs, and ensure continuous learning for incubatees.
- **Centralized services and shared infrastructure**: NSRCEL can offer common services such as legal, financial, and regulatory support through a centralized hub. This would reduce redundancies and improve efficiency. A shared pool of resources, including expert mentors and investor networks can enhance the overall impact of the 'train and support' program.
- **Strategic partnerships and ecosystem integration:** Collaborations with government agencies, universities, corporates, and investors can strengthen the 'train and support' model's impact. Incubators can extend their reach and create sustainable growth pathways for startups by providing funding, mentorship, research access, and market linkages through partnerships.

References

Benu, P., & Sanghvi, D. (2023). How NSRCEL incubated more than 1400 startups in 23 years [Audio podcast episode]. In *The Hindu Business Line Podcasts*. https://open.spotify.com/episode/6L1k3EGD5PTwgooPSEmFKI

Business Standard. (2016). *IIM-B to increase seats in incubator programme*. Business Standard. https://www.business-standard.com/article/management/iim-b-to-increase-seats-in-incubator-programme-116013000305_1.html

Gautam, V. (2023). *Not Narayana Murthy, this man was Infosys' first ever employee who joined in 1981*. Indiatimes. https://www.indiatimes.com/worth/news/infosys-first-employee-n-s-raghavan-620107.html

IIM Bangalore. (2020). *NSRCEL begins the Women Startup Program with an overwhelming response*. https://www.iimb.ac.in/nsrcel-women-startup-program

Jha, S. K., Rajan, T. A. (2024a). *India Incubator Kaleidoscope 2024—Democratising Entrepreneurial Dreams*. https://nsrcel.org/project/india-incubator-kaleidoscope-2024-democratising-entrepreneurial-dreams/

Jha, S. K., & Rajan T. A. (2024b). The future of incubation. *IIMB Management Review*, *36*(1), 48–55. https://nsrcel.org/project/the-future-of-incubation/

Kumar, S., Meena, S., & Kalia, S. (2025). *Nine years of Startup India* [Press release]. Press Information Bureau. https://pib.gov.in/PressReleasePage.aspx?PRID=2093125

NSRCEL. (2025). *Home Page*. https://nsrcel.org/

The Economic Times. (2025, January 8). *90% of deep tech startups don't survive beyond 5-years. NSRCEL's Velocity cohort wants to change that*. https://economictimes.indiatimes.com/small-biz/entrepreneurship/90-of-startups-dont-survive-beyond-5-years-nsrcels-velocity-cohort-wants-to-change-that/articleshow/116703210.cms

The Hindu Bureau. (2024). *NSRCEL IIM Bangalore and SIDBI launch pre-seed deep tech accelerator fund for start-ups in deep tech and emerging businesses area*. The Hindu. https://www.thehindu.com/news/national/karnataka/nsrcel-iim-bangalore-and-sidbi-launch-pre-seed-deep-tech-accelerator-fund-for-start-ups-in-deep-tech-and-emerging-businesses-area/article67794054.ece

Vaitheeswaran, B. (2025). *We want to tie up with incubators, build capacity beyond Chennai*. The Times of India. https://timesofindia.indiatimes.com/city/chennai/we-want-to-tie-up-with-incubators-build-capacity-beyond-chennai/articleshow/118094126.cms

CHAPTER 19

Headstart Network Foundation: Navigating Growth and Impact in India's Entrepreneurial Ecosystem

Ebin Ephrem Elavathingal and Mittu Andrews Tigi

Abstract This teaching case examines Headstart Network Foundation, a volunteer-led nonprofit that has supported entrepreneurship across 23 Indian cities. Set in 2025, the case follows three protagonists navigating an inflexion point: how to remain authentic and volunteer-driven while pursuing professionalization, ecosystem integration, and potential global expansion. Students analyze trade-offs among culture vs. process, financial

E. Ephrem Elavathingal (✉)
Merstra Foundation, Kochi, India

Mälardalen University, Eskilstuna, Sweden

Headstart Network Foundation, Bangalore, India
e-mail: ebin.ephrem@mdu.se

M. A. Tigi
Merstra Foundation, Kochi, India

Headstart Network Foundation, Bangalore, India

Indian Institute of Management Kozhikode, Kozhikode, India

A. S. Galande et al. (eds.), *Context-inspired Entrepreneurship*, Sustainable Development Goals Series,
https://doi.org/10.1007/978-981-95-9831-1_19

sustainability, and mission drift, and evaluate four strategic paths. The case equips learners to apply governance and leadership frameworks to decentralized, community organizations and to assess ecosystem roles beyond incubator/accelerator models. Learning objectives include diagnosing transformation dilemmas, designing context-fit operating models, and articulating metrics that preserve mission while enabling scale.

Keywords Grassroots entrepreneurship • Volunteer-led • Startup ecosystem • Organizational professionalization • Ecosystem governance

SDG Links This chapter is aligned with SDG 8: Decent Work and Economic Growth by examining how the Headstart Network Foundation contributes to startup formation, enterprise growth, and job creation by building and strengthening entrepreneurial ecosystems. The chapter also aligns with SDG 17, through its emphasis on multi-stakeholder collaboration, and relates to SDG 9 by supporting innovation-driven enterprise development.

Introduction

It was a Wednesday evening in March 2025 when Gautham Sivaramakrishnan, Director of Headstart Network Foundation, watched the familiar faces of the other Directors materialize on screen for what should have been a routine strategy call. But nothing about this conversation would be routine. Headstart had evolved over seventeen years from a passionate weekend project into India's largest grassroots startup support network, a not-for-profit entity powered by more than 100 dedicated volunteers alongside just a handful of paid full-time volunteers. The organization had always prided itself on being people-first, where relationships trumped processes and bureaucracy was treated like a communicable disease.

"We've always chosen heart over handbook," Gautham said, running his hand through his hair as he searched for the right words. "Our volunteers don't show up because of KPIs - they show up because they believe in the mission." Netra Parikh, the financial pragmatist and one of the co-founders, leaned closer to her camera. "That's precisely the problem," she countered. "That's precisely the problem, Gautham. Belief alone can't scale us anymore. We're running on sheer goodwill. People are burning out. We can't keep growing on vibes and unpaid labor." Amit Singh, the MD and CEO, the visionary voice, nodded slowly. "We're during that uncomfortable moment of adolescence," he said, his words coming slower, heavier with experience. "Too big to stay scrappy. Too purpose-driven to become another soulless machinery."

As the leadership team grappled with existential questions about Headstart's future, they needed to determine how a volunteer-driven, community-centric organization could evolve without losing its soul. Could they balance grassroots authenticity with institutional rigor in India's increasingly competitive entrepreneurship ecosystem? The organization that had created over 400,000 jobs and nurtured startups across India's underserved Tier 2 and 3 cities now faced its most critical decision: professionalize or preserve, scale up or stay true, evolve or remain authentic.

Background: From BarCamp Roots to National Movement (2007–2025)

From BarCamp Roots to Startup Saturdays (2007–2013)

In the mid-2000s, India's startup ecosystem was still embryonic. Venture capital was scarce, media narratives around entrepreneurship were minimal, and the word 'startup' was spoken in remote corners of India's metros. Within this void, a bunch of passionate technologists and community builders, including Amit Singh, began organizing BarCamps in Bangalore. These unconference-style gatherings offered a platform for peer-to-peer learning and spontaneous startup demos. However, many promising ventures presented at these events disappeared within a year. Amit Singh reflected on this era: "We used to see startups pitch with so much energy, and then they'd vanish. It wasn't about capability - it was about ecosystem support. We needed something more regular, more structured." In 2007, this informal sense of community crystallized into the first "HeadStart" conference, gathering 2500 investors, founders, and enthusiasts over two days, marking the beginning of a quiet revolution.

The transition from informal meetups to formal organization wasn't without tension. When corporate sponsors of the 'HeadStart' conference, who were seeking more structure and formality, demanded legal structure and formality, things the movement had deliberately avoided, the founders found themselves at a philosophical crossroads. The freedom from bureaucracy that allowed their community to thrive is now threatening their growth. After intense debates, they chose compromise over purity. On February 18, 2009, surrounded by legal documents in a registration office, the Headstart Network Foundation was born as a not-for-profit entity.

What made Headstart unique wasn't just what it did, but how it operated. The team rejected corporate formalities in favor of radical openness, creating a culture where anyone could walk in and contribute. "We didn't care about designations; we cared about intent," said Amit. The organization's flagship event, "Startup Saturday," emerged from the realization that early-stage founders needed consistent, accessible, and localized spaces to connect and learn. These monthly meetups became rituals in cities like Bangalore, Mumbai, Hyderabad, and Delhi. Media exposure from platforms like Economic Times helped amplify Headstart's credibility, validating their grassroots approach. This growth model stood apart from institutional accelerators, which are formal programs that provide startups with mentorship, resources, and funding, embodying a bottom-up, community-led startup community driven not by funding cycles but by committed individuals with a shared vision. Amit Singh often emphasized that "this was never meant to be an organization. It was a movement."

Headstart's earliest model was distinctly volunteer-led and city-centric. The founding team operated with zero institutional funding, often covering event costs from their own pockets. By 2013, Startup Saturdays had become one of India's most recognized grassroots entrepreneurship events, catalyzing over 1000 early-stage ventures. Even startups like Flipkart (in very early stages), Ola Cabs, and FreeCharge pitched to validate their early ideas at these gatherings.

Expanding the Volunteer-First Model (2014–2019)

By 2014, Headstart's reputation for fostering local innovation led to rapid geographic expansion. Volunteers opened chapters in underserved Tier 2 and Tier 3 cities, driven solely by local community demand rather than centralized mandates. New leadership figures like Gautham Sivaramakrishnan joined during this phase, bringing fresh strategic vision to the organization.

Gautham, who joined Headstart as a Volunteer after attending a packed Startup Saturday event in Bangalore, vividly recalled the community's transformative impact. "It was the first time I saw so many young founders and people with ideas coming together not in a fancy hotel but in a buzzing college auditorium." As Headstart expanded into new cities, it encountered significant regional disparities in entrepreneurial maturity and institutional support. While cities like Bangalore and Delhi attracted organized venture capital and startup media attention, Tier 2 and 3 cities like Kochi and Pune struggled with fragmented support systems.

Headstart volunteers in cities like Raipur, Coimbatore, or Nagpur often acted as ecosystem generalists, mentors, event managers, connectors, and evangelists, all at once. This deepened dependency on city teams and informal know-how made scaling difficult without draining individual capacity.

Recognizing acute employment and fundraising challenges faced by startups, Headstart introduced initiatives such as "Headstart Higher" for talent recruitment and "Kickstart" for fundraising visibility. These programs weren't just community events but direct responses to gaps that incubators and accelerators were not fully addressing in underserved regions.

However, scaling introduced new dilemmas. Each chapter was deeply decentralized, functioning more like a federation than a single organization. "Some cities were highly productive; others functioned with much less consistency. But the name was the same everywhere," Netra noted, expressing concern over operational inconsistency and brand dilution. Financial sustainability emerged as another growing concern. Headstart's events in Bangalore and Delhi generated 80% of the organization's revenue, while other cities often relied on the central team to take care of unmet expenses. Despite the increasing number of cities (over 15 by 2016), there was no unified revenue strategy.

Volunteer fatigue began to show. "Directors would rotate every three or so years. Institutional memory was lost. Burnout was real," Gautham later reflected. Yet, amidst these challenges, the organization's DNA stayed true: it enabled grassroots entrepreneurship, kept processes light, and nurtured trust over transactions.

At Headstart, leadership was distributed among trusted volunteers without formal positions. Through consistent mentoring and problem-solving, their credibility became their influence currency. However, this model risked leadership vacuums when these individuals exited without succession plans.

Crisis and Digital Pivot (2020–2021)

The COVID-19 pandemic dramatically tested Headstart's resilience. In early 2020, physical events were canceled indefinitely, and the organization's revenue plummeted to near zero, threatening its survival. "It was the first time we were staring into the abyss," Netra recalled. No events meant no money, no community touchpoints, and possibly the end of the road for Headstart."

In response, Headstart pivoted aggressively to digital platforms. Every evening at 6 PM, the core team and city leads would gather virtually, not just to brainstorm but to emotionally support one another and rekindle a sense of shared purpose. These daily calls became a crucible for innovation. The 21-Day Volunteer Development Program (VDP) emerged as a structured sprint to upskill volunteers in community building, digital facilitation, and leadership. Gautham described it as "a gym for ecosystem builders."

Headstart also launched Startup September, a month-long virtual celebration of entrepreneurship, featuring curated panels, pitch events, and expert workshops. This digital event series proved successful, expanding Headstart's reach beyond geographic constraints. It proved that Headstart could thrive digitally, reaching geographies they had never accessed (See Exhibit B: Headstart Culture and Values).

In early 2021, as India started to recover from the pandemic's impact, Headstart Network Foundation encountered a vital turning point. The leadership team recognized a fundamental shift occurring in India's entrepreneurial landscape - the ecosystem was maturing, specialized players were emerging, and Headstart needed to evolve its role to remain relevant and maximize impact.

Headstart strategically shifted from merely supporting founders to becoming "enablers of enablers." This pivot aimed to strengthen the entire ecosystem by empowering key stakeholders essential for entrepreneurial success. In mid-2021, Headstart introduced the "Hubs" initiative, sharing years of expertise in mentorship, networking, and evangelizing entrepreneurship through structured playbooks for new incubators and support organizations.

A major success came in October 2021 when Headstart Bangalore collaborated with five local incubators to standardize mentor evaluation processes and create a shared resource pool, significantly improving mentorship quality across the ecosystem. By December 2022, this model expanded to

32 incubators from India's Tier 2 and Tier 3 cities. During this period, Atal Innovation Mission also roped in Headstart to support the struggling incubators in performing better.

Recognizing the critical role of investments in the startup ecosystem, Headstart launched the "Headstart Investor Circle" in 2022, establishing pathways for successful entrepreneurs, professionals and HNIs to become angel investors. By September 2022, it had enabled over 100+ new angel investors across India, distributing capital beyond traditional startup hubs. Additionally, Headstart developed capacity-building programs for investors from Tier-2 and Tier-3 cities. By the end of 2023, over 100+ new angels were trained, enhancing investment capital availability for early-stage startups. The Headstart Investor Circle has also worked as a syndicate to pool funds into a couple of early-stage startups.

One standout initiative was the "Bharat Pitchathon" launched in June 2022, which improved connections between promising startups in smaller cities and institutional capital. This yearly program included regional pitches leading to national showcases, emphasizing founder-investor fit. By 2024, over 3000 startups had pitched across 40+ towns, raising over ₹200 crore (about $24 million) in early-stage investments, particularly from Tier-2 and Tier-3 cities.

In October 2023, Headstart launched "Headstart Beyond," aiding growth-stage Indian startups in accessing international markets. The initiative started with pathways to the Middle East and Finland, establishing soft-landing programs and market entry resources. Programs like "India-Finland Startup Accelerator", jointly organized by Headstart and Business Finland, enabled 10 startups from India to scale to European markets with Finland as a landing bay. By early 2025, it provided knowledge and mentorship on international expansion for more than 75 Indian startups.

Simultaneously, the leadership began exploring revenue restructuring. Consulting-based engagements with government and private sector entities emerged as an alternate income model. Projects like PM-WANI (in partnership with Meta/Facebook) opened doors to ecosystem-building contracts in Tier 2 cities. These engagements didn't just offer money - they validated Headstart's unique grassroots lens as a professional service, proving that their community-driven approach could deliver measurable policy outcomes that traditional consulting firms often missed.

The Evolving Indian Entrepreneurship Ecosystem

India's entrepreneurship landscape underwent a dramatic transformation during Headstart's journey. In the mid-2000s, the ecosystem was characterized by limited venture capital, minimal media coverage, and social stigma around startup careers. Government attention to startups was minimal, but ecosystems in Bangalore, Hyderabad, and NCR began to bloom organically, powered by talent returning from abroad, increasing digital penetration, and infrastructure developments like Jio and UPI (Tanna & Mandavia, 2024).

The Startup India initiative in 2016 brought increased government attention and incentives. However, these benefits largely favored incubators, accelerators, and government-supported organizations, not lean, community-led, volunteer-driven networks like Headstart. India's innovation ecosystem transitioned from IT services dominance to multi-sectoral vibrancy, with global integration in technology, financing, and human capital (Bhagavatula et al., 2019).

By 2022, India ranked fourth globally for the quality of entrepreneurship, with state-sponsored incubators, corporate accelerators, and professional investor networks dominating the space (Jha & Rajan, 2024). This maturation created opportunities and challenges for organizations like Headstart, which had built their identity on filling ecosystem gaps that are now increasingly addressed by well-funded, professional entities.

The ecosystem's evolution revealed persistent challenges: fragmented support systems, poor access to early-stage funding in smaller cities, and inconsistent mentoring practices. Access to early-stage funding became even more selective post-pandemic, creating bottlenecks for first-time founders and grassroots initiatives. These regional disparities meant that while metro areas attracted sophisticated support infrastructure, Tier 2 and 3 cities continued to rely heavily on community-driven organizations like Headstart.

Current Challenges and Strategic Options

By late 2024, the organization's impact metrics were impressive: 23 cities, 18,000+ startups supported, 400,000+ jobs created. But beneath these numbers lay fundamental tensions. The year-end financial review revealed concerning dependencies, volunteer surveys showed rising burnout, and international inquiries increased. As 2025 began, the leadership knew they could no longer postpone the difficult strategic decisions.

As the leadership team convened for their pivotal March 2025 strategy call, they confronted several interconnected dilemmas that would shape Headstart's future trajectory. The discussion had crystallized around four potential paths forward, each embodying fundamentally different philosophies regarding how Headstart should evolve.

The Four Strategic Paths

The Professionalization Path: Netra's proposal centered on organizational restructuring to introduce professional management while preserving volunteer engagement. Key elements included mandatory revenue targets of ₹5 lakhs minimum per significant event, hiring full-time professionals for operations, programming, and marketing, and implementing robust documentation systems with standardized processes. This would require substantial investment in volunteer management and impact measurement technology platforms.

"Passion is powerful but unsustainable without proper process, structure and accountability," Netra argued, believing the organization could no longer operate on goodwill alone. However, Gautham worried that rigid metrics would transform volunteers' intrinsic motivation into transactional participation. "The moment we start measuring everything, we risk losing the magic that makes people want to be part of this movement."

The Authenticity-First Approach: Amit championed preserving Headstart's volunteer-driven model while making targeted improvements. This approach would strengthen volunteer development through expanded programs like the 21-Day VDP, improve inter-chapter communication through organic means, and maintain flexible, community-appropriate revenue generation without compromising volunteer ethos.

"We're at risk of becoming soulless machinery if we're not careful," Amit warned. "We were raw, community-led, and messy - that made us magnetic to startup founders." This path acknowledged that Headstart's competitive advantage lay in authentic community connection rather than professional polish, though it risked perpetuating operational inefficiencies and volunteer burnout.

However, Amit strongly upholds the belief that metrics define outcomes, as he has echoed numerous times: 'You become what you measure.'

The Global Expansion Vision: The most ambitious option involved expanding beyond India to become a global platform for grassroots entrepreneurship support. Interest had emerged from the US, Japan, Central Europe, UAE and Africa, requiring evolution from an India-centric organization to a globally applicable model while developing frameworks for different cultural contexts.

Philosophical tensions emerged around identity. Amit argued for "strategic dissociation from purely Indian identity" to avoid being "constrained by being seen as an India-only initiative." Netra countered: "Going global doesn't mean we should dilute our Indian DNA. It's our strength, and regional authenticity attracts global partners." This path offered tremendous growth potential but risked resource dilution and loss of domestic focus.

The Ecosystem Integration Strategy: The fourth option involved deeper integration with India's formal entrepreneurship ecosystem through strategic partnerships while maintaining independence. This included expanded partnerships with government agencies (building on existing relationships with seven state governments and two central departments), strategic corporate alliances for CSR impact, and formal relationships with established incubators and accelerators.

This approach could provide financial sustainability through consulting revenue and institutional partnerships while maintaining a mission-driven identity. However, it carried significant risks of co-optation, mission drift, and loss of the independence that allowed Headstart to advocate fearlessly for grassroots entrepreneurs.

Challenges

As the strategy call continued, the three leaders grappled with fundamental questions about organizational identity, social impact, and the future of grassroots entrepreneurship support in an increasingly professionalized world.

Unlike incubators or accelerators funded by state or private entities, Headstart had organically grown within the "culture" and "human capital" domains - building entrepreneurial mindsets, fostering community connections, and developing leadership capabilities through volunteer networks powered by trust and shared passion. This approach had allowed Headstart to create authentic relationships and maintain credibility with founders who often felt alienated by formal institutional processes.

However, this grassroots evolution had left significant gaps in the "finance" and "policy" domains that increasingly defined ecosystem success. While other organizations had direct pipelines to funding networks, government influence, and institutional resources, Headstart remained largely outside these power structures. The irony was stark: Headstart's greatest strength—its community-driven model—was its primary vulnerability in an ecosystem that increasingly rewarded formal partnerships and measurable outcomes.

At the heart of this phase was a dilemma that echoed across many purpose-driven organizations: Could Headstart evolve into a globally respected, financially sustainable platform while still preserving its grassroots, volunteer-first DNA? Or would it need to sacrifice some of its ethos to pursue structure, scale, and stability?

As the strategy call concluded that evening in March 2025, the leadership team dug deep to find the answers.

1. Could a Volunteer-First Model Effectively Compete with Professionally Structured Incubators and Accelerators?
2. Should Headstart Introduce Professional Full-Time Leadership to Enhance Stability and Scalability, Potentially Altering its Volunteer-Driven Culture?
3. Could Institutional Memory and Operational Continuity Be Built without Overly Bureaucratizing Volunteer Engagement?
4. Should Global Expansion Be Prioritized, Possibly at the Expense of Regional Authenticity and Support for Grassroots Entrepreneurs from Bharat, or Should it Remain a Secondary, more Gradual Goal?

The Headstart leadership team faced a pivotal moment in the virtual room. Amit, the visionary, pondered their future, while Gautham, the mission's guardian, felt the weight of purpose. Netra, pragmatic as ever, prepared for critical questions. Their decision would shape Headstart's future and determine its survival in India's evolving entrepreneurial landscape. Could they blend grassroots authenticity with institutional rigor while maintaining their volunteer-driven spirit?

Gautham's eyes scanned the financial calendar, the year 2025–2026 looming. Seventeen years of impact, thousands of entrepreneurs supported, yet the future remained uncertain. Could a volunteer-run organization thrive amid formalized structures? The ticking clock marked the silence. Amit asked, "Are we ready to protect our legacy while embracing

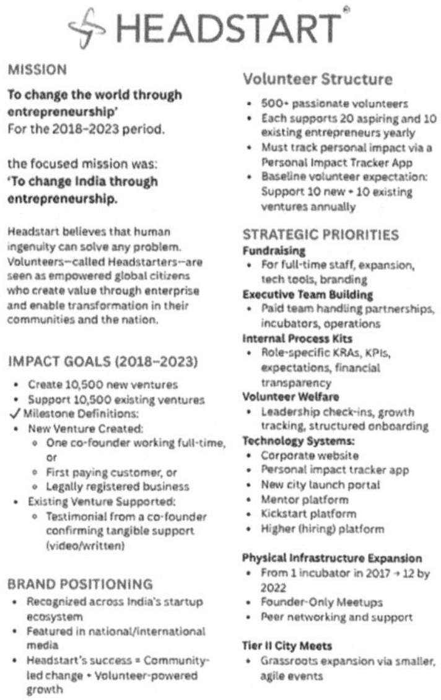

HEADSTART®

MISSION

To change the world through entrepreneurship'
For the 2018–2023 period.

the focused mission was:
'To change India through entrepreneurship.

Headstart believes that human ingenuity can solve any problem. Volunteers—called Headstarters—are seen as empowered global citizens who create value through enterprise and enable transformation in their communities and the nation.

IMPACT GOALS (2018–2023)

- Create 10,500 new ventures
- Support 10,500 existing ventures

✓ Milestone Definitions:

- New Venture Created:
  - One co-founder working full-time, or
  - First paying customer, or
  - Legally registered business
- Existing Venture Supported:
  - Testimonial from a co-founder confirming tangible support (video/written)

BRAND POSITIONING

- Recognized across India's startup ecosystem
- Featured in national/international media
- Headstart's success = Community-led change + Volunteer-powered growth

Volunteer Structure

- 500+ passionate volunteers
- Each supports 20 aspiring and 10 existing entrepreneurs yearly
- Must track personal impact via a Personal Impact Tracker App
- Baseline volunteer expectation: Support 10 new + 10 existing ventures annually

STRATEGIC PRIORITIES

Fundraising
- For full-time staff, expansion, tech tools, branding

Executive Team Building
- Paid team handling partnerships, incubators, operations

Internal Process Kits
- Role-specific KRAs, KPIs, expectations, financial transparency

Volunteer Welfare
- Leadership check-ins, growth tracking, structured onboarding

Technology Systems:
- Corporate website
- Personal impact tracker app
- New city launch portal
- Mentor platform
- Kickstart platform
- Higher (hiring) platform

Physical Infrastructure Expansion
- From 1 incubator in 2017 → 12 by 2022
- Founder-Only Meetups
- Peer networking and support

Tier II City Meets
- Grassroots expansion via smaller, agile events

Fig. 19.1 Snapshot Headstart Vision Document 2023 (from original document)

change?" The room felt intimate as they faced their responsibility. Their choices would define Headstart's role for the next generation of Indian entrepreneurs. With a deep breath, they prepared for the conversation that would shape their future. The stakes were high, and they were the architects of Headstart's destiny (Figs. 19.1 and 19.2).

Discussion Questions

These questions are crafted to spark lively classroom discussions, thoughtful analysis, and deep reflection. They beautifully align with the core themes of the case, the protagonist's dilemma, and Headstart's inspiring vision (See Exhibit A: Headstart Vision Document).

1. How can Headstart institutionalize systems for continuity and accountability without killing the volunteer spirit that makes it special? What processes could retain flexibility while ensuring organizational memory survives leadership changes?
2. What trade-offs should Headstart make to achieve financial sustainability? Can the organization set revenue targets and launch consulting services while maintaining its pro bono ethos, or does this inevitably lead to mission drift?

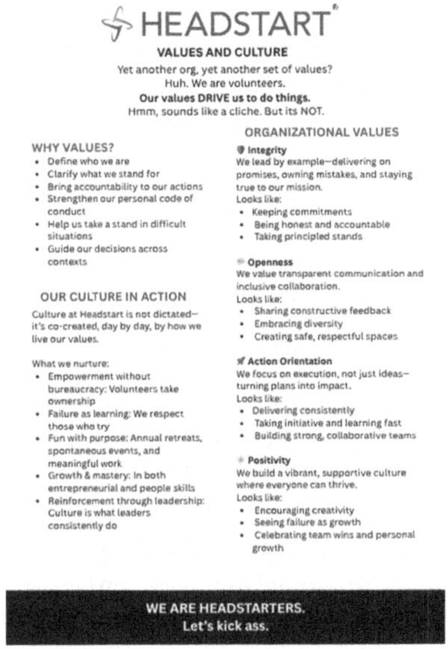
HEADSTART

VALUES AND CULTURE

Yet another org, yet another set of values?
Huh. We are volunteers.
Our values DRIVE us to do things.
Hmm, sounds like a cliche. But its NOT.

WHY VALUES?

- Define who we are
- Clarify what we stand for
- Bring accountability to our actions
- Strengthen our personal code of conduct
- Help us take a stand in difficult situations
- Guide our decisions across contexts

OUR CULTURE IN ACTION

Culture at Headstart is not dictated—it's co-created, day by day, by how we live our values.

What we nurture:

- Empowerment without bureaucracy: Volunteers take ownership
- Failure as learning: We respect those who try
- Fun with purpose: Annual retreats, spontaneous events, and meaningful work
- Growth & mastery: In both entrepreneurial and people skills
- Reinforcement through leadership: Culture is what leaders consistently do

ORGANIZATIONAL VALUES

Integrity
We lead by example—delivering on promises, owning mistakes, and staying true to our mission.
Looks like:

- Keeping commitments
- Being honest and accountable
- Taking principled stands

Openness
We value transparent communication and inclusive collaboration.
Looks like:

- Sharing constructive feedback
- Embracing diversity
- Creating safe, respectful spaces

Action Orientation
We focus on execution, not just ideas—turning plans into impact.
Looks like:

- Delivering consistently
- Taking initiative and learning fast
- Building strong, collaborative teams

Positivity
We build a vibrant, supportive culture where everyone can thrive.
Looks like:

- Encouraging creativity
- Seeing failure as growth
- Celebrating team wins and personal growth

WE ARE HEADSTARTERS.
Let's kick ass.

Fig. 19.2 Summary of Values and Culture of Headstart (from original document)

3. What unique value does a volunteer-led platform offer in an ecosystem dominated by well-funded incubators and accelerators? How should Headstart position itself to remain relevant and competitive?
4. Should Headstart combine rotating volunteers with full-time professionals, or would this destroy its decentralized, people-first culture? What leadership structure best sustains community-driven movements over decades?
5. If you were Gautham, would you prioritize global expansion or double down on serving India's underserved regions? How can organizations balance international growth ambitions with authentic local impact?

Learning Objectives
Students engaging with this case should be able to:

1. Analyze organizational transformation dilemmas in mission-driven organizations, particularly the tensions between preserving authentic community culture and implementing professional systems for scalability and sustainability.

2. Evaluate strategic options for volunteer-driven organizations, including trade-offs between grassroots authenticity, financial sustainability, and competitive positioning in mature ecosystems.
3. Apply leadership and governance frameworks to decentralized, community-based organizations, examining how distributed leadership models can maintain organizational continuity while preserving volunteer engagement and cultural identity.
4. Deeply evaluate the startup ecosystem from a holistic approach and be able to suggest strategies and policies that would shape the economic development of a region.

Supplementary Reading

- Feld, B., & Hathaway, I.(2020). The startup community way: Wiley.
- Foster, W. L., Kim, P., & Christiansen, B. (2009). Ten funding models for nonprofits. Stanford Social Innovation Review.
- Roundy, P. T. (2016). Start-up community narratives: The discursive construction of entrepreneurial ecosystems. The Journal of Entrepreneurship, 25(2), 232–248.
- Senge, P., Hamilton, H., & Kania, J. (2015). The dawn of system leadership. Stanford Social Innovation Review. https://ssir.org/articles/entry/the_dawn_of_system_leadership.
- BarCamp. (n.d.). *FrontPage*. BarCamp Wiki. Retrieved from http://barcamp.org/w/page/402984/FrontPage

Acknowledgements The authors thank the Headstart Network Foundation leaders and volunteers of the Head Start Network Foundation for sharing insights and materials that informed this case.

Supplementary Material

Guidance for Educators on Using this Case for a 90 Minutes Class Discussion

I. **Case Synopsis**

This teaching case examines the strategic evolution of Headstart Network Foundation, India's largest grassroots volunteer-led startup ecosystem support organization. Set in 2025, it features three protagonists—Amit Singh (Co-founder & CEO), Gautham Sivaramakrishnan (Director), and Netra Parikh (Co-founder & CFO) - on a pivotal board call, grappling with an existential dilemma: How can Headstart remain relevant and financially sustainable without losing its volunteer-driven, community-first ethos?

Since 2007, Headstart has supported over 18,000 startups across 23 Indian cities, with flagship programs like Startup Saturday, Headstart Higher, and Kickstart. Amid increased competition from state-sponsored incubators and corporate accelerators, and after a turbulent pandemic pivot, the organization must decide whether to professionalize operations, decentralize power, expand globally, or double down on its grassroots Indian identity.

This case blends storytelling with strategic complexity, which is ideal for exploring themes in entrepreneurship, social impact, volunteerism, innovation ecosystems, nonprofit strategy, and leadership succession.

II. Target Audience

(a) Graduate-level MBA and Master's programs in: Entrepreneurship, Nonprofit Management, Strategic Management & Leadership
(b) Executive education for social impact leaders, incubator managers, or public sector innovation officers.
(c) Advanced undergraduates in entrepreneurship or public policy.

III. Teaching Plan (90-minute class)

Time	*Activity*
0–10 mins	**Opening discussion:** Pose the dilemma: "Can a volunteer-first organization scale without becoming a corporate machine?"
10–25 mins	**Case Facts Recap + Timeline Mapping** (2007–2025)—Break students into pairs and map key milestones.
25–50 mins	**Small group work (breakout groups):** Assign each group one core tension (e.g., people vs process, global vs local) to explore.
50–80 mins	**Class discussion:** Debrief group findings. Ask, "which trade-offs are irreversible? Which ones can be managed through design?"
80–90 mins	**Wrap-up:** Highlight the learning objectives and connect to theory.

References

Bhagavatula, S., Mudambi, R., & Murmann, J. P. (2019). Innovation and entrepreneurship in India: An overview. *Management and Organization Review, 15*(3), 467–493. https://doi.org/10.1017/mor.2019.52

Jha, S. K., & Rajan, T. (2024). The future of incubation. *IIMB Management Review, 36*(1), 48–55. https://doi.org/10.1016/j.iimb.2023.11.005

Tanna, S. S., & Mandavia, N. (2024). Mapping the evolution of campus startup ecosystem: A 25-year bibliometric review (1998–2023). *Journal of Global Entrepreneurship Research, 14*(45), 1–30. https://doi.org/10.1007/s40497-024-00418-z

CHAPTER 20

Unlocking the Marketing Puzzle of a Micro-Entrepreneurship Development Program at Deshpande Foundation

Rakshita Honnatagi, Prakash Satyavageeswaran, and Ashish S. Galande

Abstract The Micro-Entrepreneurship Development Program (MEDP) at the Deshpande Foundation was established to support micro-entrepreneurs through training, credit access, and market linkages. Over time, the program has grown from providing grants to adopting a dual-track approach: I-MEDP for individual entrepreneurs and C-MEDP for collectives. By early 2022, MEDP was working with over 3600

R. Honnatagi (✉)
Warwick Business School, Coventry, UK
e-mail: Rakshita.Honnatagi@warwick.ac.uk

P. Satyavageeswaran
Indian Institute of Management Udaipur, Udaipur, India
e-mail: prakash.satyavageeswaran@iimu.ac.in

A. S. Galande
State University of New York Plattsburgh, Plattsburgh, NY, USA
e-mail: agala009@plattsburgh.edu

A. S. Galande et al. (eds.), *Context-inspired Entrepreneurship*, Sustainable Development Goals Series,
https://doi.org/10.1007/978-981-95-9831-1_20

entrepreneurs across sectors such as textiles, food, and handicrafts. While systems for training and credit had matured, marketing remained a major challenge. Local trade fairs, retail outlets, and small-scale e-commerce experiments highlighted issues of limited manpower, inconsistent product quality, and gaps in digital readiness. As the newly appointed CEO, Aravind Chinchure faced a critical question: how should MEDP design its go-to-market strategy to support both individuals and collectives effectively? Strategic options ranged from building an in-house marketing team to partnering with external platforms or creating a separate marketing entity. The case highlights the trade-offs in designing inclusive yet scalable marketing support for grassroots entrepreneurs and invites discussion on aligning program design with broader development goals.

Keywords Micro-entrepreneurship • Producer collectives • GTM • Grassroots marketing • Institutional partnerships

SDG Links This chapter is centrally aligned with SDG 8: Decent Work and Economic Growth, examining how the Deshpande Foundation builds local innovation and entrepreneurship ecosystems to create employment and strengthen livelihoods at the grassroots. The chapter also aligns with SDG 1, through its focus on poverty alleviation via grassroots innovation, and relates to SDG 4 through skill development initiatives.

Introduction

In March 2022, Aravind Chinchure, the physicist-turned-entrepreneur and the newly appointed CEO of the Micro-Entrepreneurship Development Program (MEDP) (Exhibit I for organization structure), at the Deshpande Foundation (DF),[1] had decided to take the MEDP team for an offsite retreat to understand the team, the program, and issues better. Even though it had been two months since he had joined, he felt the need for deeper clarity on the core purpose and long-term direction of MEDP. MEDP, a flagship vertical of DF, aimed to empower micro-entrepreneurs across rural India supporting over 3600 individuals through a dual model: **I-MEDP (Individual support)** and **C-MEDP (Collective support)**.

[1] Chinchure was simultaneously appointed as the CEO of the Deshpande Startups, but we focus on MEDP in this caselet.

While the retreat gave Chinchure a sense of the impact of MEDP, a recurring concern had surfaced during his interactions with the team: the growing pressure on the program's marketing efforts. With hundreds of entrepreneurs engaged across sectors such as textiles, food, and handicrafts, the team had been struggling to provide targeted marketing support. Constraints related to limited manpower, inconsistent product quality, and gaps in digital readiness had made the task even more complex.

Reflecting on these conversations, Chinchure began to wonder whether MEDP needed a more structured go-to-market (GTM) strategy, one that could have combined existing local trade fairs with emerging digital platforms such as the Open Network for Digital Commerce (ONDC) or Flipkart Samarth.[2] At the same time, he questioned whether the dual-track structure of I-MEDP and C-MEDP was sustainable, or whether a sector-based approach to marketing might have served the entrepreneurs more effectively.

As the retreat unfolded and the scale of the challenges became clearer, Chinchure continued the conversation with Iranna Rotte, Deputy Director of MEDP, and Sandeep Sabharwal, Senior Director of MEDP, to better understand the program's origins and evolution.

Chinchure looked at Rotte and asked,

> Iranna, as someone involved with MEDP from the beginning, could you shed some light on why it was initiated?

Having spent the past 11–12 years with MEDP, Rotte was well aware of the details of the program. Rotte responded,

> The word 'entrepreneur' often makes us think of someone famous for their unicorn or hectocorn startups; but there exists a vast world beyond this. In emerging markets, emphasis should be placed on Micro, Small, and Medium Entrepreneurs (MSMEs), who are often neglected. Over the past 30 years, four out of every five new jobs in the formal sector in emerging markets—80

[2] **Flipkart Samarth** is an initiative by Flipkart (one of India's largest e-commerce platform) to support India's artisans, weavers, and micro-enterprises by helping them access pan-India e-commerce markets. The program offers onboarding assistance, cataloguing, training, and reduced commissions to underserved sellers including women-led and rural enterprises.

percent of all employment—were created by MSMEs. They also contributed to 33% of GDP in emerging economies.[3]

Rotte looked at Sabharwal. Seeing him nod in agreement, Rotte continued,

MSMEs have faced various challenges, from securing finances for their business to conducting research and development (R&D). They have struggled to access credit from banks because of a lack of collateral and a positive income statement. This shortage of finances has led to a multitude of issues. It has constrained the entrepreneurs in spending scarce capital on marketing, advanced infrastructure, and skilled labor as the available money is spent on basic requirements such as raw materials and production equipment, forcing them to focus on short-term needs instead of long-term goals. This constraint on finances also results in MSME owners multi-tasking rather than hiring the required complement of professionals. In the past, MSMEs have also faced a dearth of adequate information on policies and schemes, making it difficult to access the available benefits from government institutions.[4] In 2011, even though institutions were training entrepreneurs and helping MSMEs tackle their challenges, this support was inadequate. Looking at this challenge, the Deshpande Foundation started the MEDP.

Chinchure responded, "Thanks, Iranna, but how are we supporting Micro-entrepreneurs (MEs)? What is our approach?" Sabharwal chimed in, "One is through I-MEDP (Individual-MEDP), where we train, mentor, and support micro-entrepreneurs individually, and the other approach is by forming collectives, C-MEDP (Collective-MEDP)."

Nodding in agreement, Rotte elaborated,

Under I-MEDP, we have an Entrepreneurship Awareness Program (EAP), where we create awareness among MEs about our program. Interested individuals then submit applications, go through interviews, and upon selection, become part of the Entrepreneurship Development Program (EDP). The EDP provides training in various entrepreneurial and practical skills. We also

[3] *UNDESA—Report on MSMEs and the Sustainable Development Goals.* (n.d.). United Nations Department of Economic and Social Affairs https://sustainabledevelopment.un.org/content/documents/25851MSMEs_and_SDGs_Final3120.pdf

[4] Princy Saini, (2014), Study of Micro, Small and Medium Enterprises, Center for civil society. http://easeofdoingbusiness.org/sites/default/files/resources/study-of-micro-small-and-medium-enterprises.pdf

> offer skill development courses to entrepreneurs, such as tailoring, painting, and embroidery, to equip them to earn independently (Exhibit II). After completing the EDP, we connect MEs with banks for credit support and organize *santhes*[5] that serve as marketing support platforms.

Sabharwal added, "C-MEDP adopts a cluster-based approach, where we collectivize MEs and form Off-Farm Producer Companies (OFPO). We nurture these producer companies through skill training, funding, production support, and marketing inputs till they become self-reliant."

After pondering, Chinchure raised a concern, "Do we have a team dedicated to training, mentoring, credit, and marketing linkage? Do we have resources for all these activities?" Rotte replied, "We do have resources for training, credit, and mentoring, but we seem to be lacking in our marketing efforts."

As Chinchure's phone notified him that it was nearing 11 p.m., he realized it was time to conclude the conversation and the retreat. Armed with these insights, Chinchure ruminated on the best course of action to address the concerns on marketing.

The Micro-Entrepreneurship Ecosystem in India

India's micro-enterprise sector was vast but highly underserved. Micro-enterprises, typically businesses with fewer than 10 employees constituted over 95 percent of all enterprises in the country and played a key role in local livelihoods and rural economies (Ministry of MSME, 2022). Yet, most of them operated informally and remained disconnected from formal entrepreneurship and financial ecosystems.

These entrepreneurs, especially those in rural and peri-urban areas, often lacked access to finance due to the absence of collateral or formal income documentation (IFC, 2018). Although the government had launched several schemes like Micro Units Development and Refinance Agency Bank (MUDRA) and Prime Minister's Employment Generation Program (PMEGP) to support them, many micro-entrepreneurs were unaware of such schemes or were unable to navigate the application processes (Government of India, 2023a, 2023b). Even when loans were available, using them productively required business knowledge and support, which many lacked.

[5] *Santhe* is the local word for trade show/exhibition/trade fair.

Another persistent challenge had been market access. Most micro-entrepreneurs depended on local markets or weekly *santhes* to sell their products. However, these were often seasonal or limited in reach or both. With the rise of e-commerce, platforms such as Flipkart Samarth or Open Network for Digital Commerce (ONDC) had created opportunities for broader access, but they also demanded digital literacy, product standardization, and inventory control — areas where micro-entrepreneurs continued to face difficulties (Dalberg, 2019).

Against this backdrop, the MEDP at DF stood out for offering an integrated and field-based approach. MEDP combined awareness generation, entrepreneurship training, credit facilitation, and marketing support under a single umbrella. Its structure enabled it to work with both individual entrepreneurs (through I-MEDP) and groups of entrepreneurs organized into Off-Farm Producer Companies (C-MEDP). This dual-track design allowed the program to tailor its support based on the needs, context, and scale of different entrepreneurs (Deshpande Foundation, 2022; NABARD, 2020).

While many interventions in the ecosystem tended to focus on a single aspect — training, finance, or market access — MEDP attempted to address these holistically. Its focus on tier-2 and rural areas, and its experience in setting up collectives and facilitating sales through *santhes* and small retail outlets, gave it a distinctive position in the landscape of grassroots entrepreneurship.

Evolution of the MEDP

The First Phase

Neelam Maheshwari launched MEDP in 2011 with a two-member team, rolling it out across five districts of north Karnataka. The program initially provided financial assistance to MEs through monetary grants known as Award 1.0. However, at that time, there were no defined expectations of how MEs were to use the grant amount. These grants were intended to give promising entrepreneurs a boost in establishing or expanding their ventures. Additionally, the MEDP team lacked a structured assessment system, leading to the misuse of funds in some cases.

Recognizing these shortcomings, Maheshwari acknowledged the need for certain essential components, including metrics to track fund utilization, and by 2013, the program had established certain procedures to stem these losses. To ensure a more effective selection process, the MEDP team invited applications and shortlisted MEs based on various criteria (mentioned in Exhibit III), including verifying their credibility through bankers and mentors. The shortlisted MEs were then invited for basic entrepreneurship skill training. While 500–800 MEs were trained every year, only 10–20 MEs were awarded the grants. As the MEDP program gained momentum and aimed to reach a larger number of MEs, Award 2.0 was introduced. In this phase, the team expanded its beneficiary base and disbursed funds in stages to improve accountability. This was the first phase of the program, i.e., MEDP 1.0 - characterized by early experimentation, learning, and foundational systems-building.

The Second Phase

MEDP 2.0 was about making the program more sustainable. During the first phase, even after refining the ME selection process, some beneficiaries misused the grant, whereas others lacked clarity on how to use it. This is when the team realized that MEs needed help not only through funding but also through skills training and other knowledge-building activities. In addition, the outreach numbers in the first phase were low. In the second phase, the team wanted to reach more MEs. With these learnings in mind, *Prabhavi Navodyami Pratiyogita*[6] was launched to make the project sustainable; the earlier grant-giving program model was upgraded. Instead of giving grants, they started to connect MEs directly to banks for loans. The Deshpande Foundation supported MEs by paying the interest on the loans directly to the banks. The team supported MEs by training them with the necessary entrepreneurial skills. For example, *Karyagara,* a dedicated training on accounting, bookkeeping, and other business management tools, resulted in MEs improving their financial management, bookkeeping practices, and expense tracking.

As more MEs approached MEDP, the team recognized the need to develop a structured marketing support system. That is when the team opened a retail outlet to help MEs sell their products. However, the outlet saw limited success due to its poor location, which afforded low visibility and resulted in poor footfall. With the retail store not serving its intended purpose, the MEDP team came up with the idea of organizing *santhes.*

[6] A competition which was launched to select needy and enthusiastic Micro entrepreneurs for the program.

Santhes were seen as a scalable way to support hundreds of MEs, offering higher visibility and significant customer footfall. Impact assessment of *santhes* found that 42% of MEs were able to get new customers because of *santhes*, 14.5% were able to get connected with bigger clients, and 36.6% saw an increase in sales and profits (Exhibit 2). However, the MEDP team discovered that not all MEs could attend *santhes*, as some MEs were too busy managing their own retail business, and some others had responsibilities that restricted their travel. However, a key question remained: how could MEDP support MEs who were unable to attend *santhes* due to business or household constraints?

In 2017–2018, MEDP collaborated with the United Nations Development Program (UNDP) to expand the program. Phase one of the UNDP project reached around 10,000 women through awareness programs, with 3000 women attending the EDP. Of these, 1000 women were trained in some livelihood skills and basic accounting. This phase marked the programme's widest outreach to date. In 2018–19, under UNDP phase two, they concentrated on building a sustainable training model, and The *Bizz-Sakhi*[7] was launched. One hundred women were trained and supported. Every woman who participated in the program supported ten more women by teaching them the exact skills they received during the training. However, this collaboration resulted in onboarding more MEs without the resources for marketing support.

The Third Phase

The third stage of the program, i.e., MEDP 3.0, started in 2020, when Vivek Pawar, the CEO of Deshpande Foundation, presented new goals for the organization. The main objective of the organization was to "scale up" that year. During the same year, Sabharwal joined the program, bringing his expertise in the cluster-based approach from his previous experience at AMUL (Anand Milk Union Limited). Given the emphasis on scaling, the team decided to form collectives of entrepreneurs to support a larger number of entrepreneurs under a single company. This idea led to the formation of collectives, thereby creating two verticals in MEDP - the I-MEDP (Individual entrepreneurship) and the C-MEDP (Collective entrepreneurship).

[7] Bizz-sakhi which means Business friend in this context was the name used for a program.

Thought behind Collectives

Collective 1

The I-MEDP team initiated *aari*[8] training in 2018 with 14 *aari*-trained artisans. As *aari* embroidery is quite popular in the region, the team started receiving more demand from the women in the region to conduct such activities. This marked the beginning of a series of training on *aari* embroidery in and around Hubli - Dharwad. After the training, the women artisans started working individually, taking orders from their connections or the already existing customers in their business. However, the income earned by individual women was entirely based on their abilities and their entrepreneurship.

When COVID-19 hit in 2020, there was no income for women trained by the MEDP team. Under these circumstances, the team employed them to manufacture masks. This was the first time MEDP conducted operations at the production level; until now, MEDP had supported entrepreneurs through mentoring, marketing, and credit enablement. This experience boosted the team's confidence in conducting activities at the production level. At this stage, the team saw an opportunity to launch an all-women collective aligned with the scaling objective. Hence evolved, the concept of forming a collective for these women. The collective, Swavalambi Sakhi Producers Company Limited (SSPCL), was registered in October 2020 with 200+ artisans. It had a presence in two cities of northern Karnataka, viz., Dharwad and Hubli. Members who were part of I-MEDP were now enrolled under C-MEDP as a result of the collectivization.

After the demand for masks declined, the MEDP team gradually shifted these women towards *aari* work. They trained these women on advanced *aari* skills and divided them into six neighborhood-based groups. They then provided them with the infrastructure so the women could use the common facility to work. These six groups were assigned six different *aari* products - bags, kids' wear, ethnic wear, home decor, fashion accessories, and office accessories. Even though there was no steady flow of orders, the MEDP team continued expanding the production operation. They identified a company in need of tailors experienced in stitching bags and connected them with a group of women tailors in Dharwad who were trained for the same. They enrolled these women under SSPCL and supported

[8] A type of embroidery training on stretched fabric.

them by giving them the machinery and arranging space to work so that these women could have a steady income. Similarly, a food unit was also registered under the SSPCL Company. By the end of April 2021, the collective was facing a multitude of issues such as inadequate inventory management, free-rider problems, lack of sales, marketing, and quality management. The presence of a free-rider within the units had a demotivating effect on the dedicated members. Some individuals did not actively pull their weight, which led to an uneven distribution of workload and lowered the overall productivity within the units. To address the marketing and sales issue, the MEDP team opened an outlet with the brand name Authentic Karnataka for the products, which was inaugurated in October 2021. While the outlet provided a platform for selling the products, the organization still encountered marketing challenges. The inconsistent quality and lack of standardization across the products created a barrier to attracting customers, building brand loyalty and hampering the marketing efforts. The issues with product quality and inventory management also hampered the marketing efforts. Furthermore, unmanaged inventory resulted in stock shortages or excesses, making it challenging to meet customer demands and maintain a reliable supply. Hence, all the eight units were unable to market their products. Despite the initial plan to focus solely on *aari* products, the organization gradually expanded to include various other product lines. However, this expansion resulted in inefficient marketing communication, as the marketing requirements for each product differed, and the organization had limited resources to fulfill these diverse needs. The E-commerce approach was hard to envision as the company struggled with inventory management and product standardization.

Collective 2

To further expand and scale up their efforts, another collective was initiated by the MEDP team with the aim of creating a larger impact: Santha Haralayya Leather Producers Company Limited (SHLPCL). In 2020, the team sought potential locations to establish an off-farm Producer Company (OFPO), and Madbhavi in Athani taluk, Belagavi district of Karnataka, was chosen for three reasons. First, the village had over 3000 leather artisans. Second, the artisans specialized in the craft of making Kolhapuri Chappals were facing challenges exacerbated by the COVID-19 pandemic, which affected their incomes. Additionally, these artisans were consistently engaged in intra-community competition by selling cheaper Kolhapuris to local distributors, making it difficult for them to increase their profit margins. Last, MEDP had already provided individual training to these artisans.

MEDP felt that forming a collective was an excellent approach to supporting these artisans based on the project feasibility survey they had conducted. MEDP, in partnership with the National Bank for Agriculture and Rural Development (NABARD), initiated this development. The team contacted mentors and designers and helped the artisan company create samples and catalogs. The team also helped set up a common facility center to support the artisans. As the artisans spent a majority of their time in production, it was difficult for them to also take up the additional responsibility of marketing the products. They were wary of causing a lag in production. To solve the marketing issue, an E-commerce approach was taken. The MEDP team launched a website with the brand name The Kolhapur Co., but the team was inept in handling the website, which resulted in marketing issues remaining unresolved.

Reflecting on the challenges faced by both I-MEDP and C-MEDP teams, Chinchure questioned,

> The I-MEDP team is facing difficulties; it is challenging to cater to the marketing needs of such a large number of MEs with a group of 40 members who have to look into every aspect of the program, right from searching, onboarding, and training MEs to handling legal compliances. The C-MEDP team is facing difficulties in marketing and standardizing the products as the team lacks resources and expertise. What kind of marketing research has gone into creating C-MEDP? Does it look like C-MEDP and I-MEDP have a GTM Strategy? Should C-MEDP and I-MEDP remain separate? Is C-MEDP cannibalizing the I-MEDP? What should be the approach for marketing support?

Current Challenges and Strategic Options

By early 2022, MEDP had evolved into a dual-model program operating across individual (I-MEDP) and collective (C-MEDP) tracks. While the Foundation had developed robust systems for entrepreneur selection, training, and credit facilitation, one area remained underdeveloped: marketing. The team increasingly encountered questions around how to support hundreds of entrepreneurs with diverse products, inconsistent digital readiness, and limited market reach.

Key Challenges

Marketing Capacity Gaps

MEDP's existing marketing initiatives such as local *santhes*, the Authentic Karnataka retail outlet, and a newly launched website faced several limitations. The team lacked expertise in branding, digital cataloguing, and sales operations. Quality inconsistencies, inventory tracking, and logistical bottlenecks further hindered scale.

Diverse Product Portfolio

Entrepreneurs across clusters were producing a wide range of items from textiles and *aari* bags to processed foods and handicrafts. Supporting each product line with tailored market strategies was proving to be increasingly complex with the available resources.

Tension between I-MEDP and C-MEDP

While I-MEDP emphasized autonomy and individual growth, C-MEDP pushed for scale through collective production and branding. As both verticals matured, internal discussions surfaced over whether resources were being stretched too thin, or whether a unified marketing strategy was feasible.

Limited Manpower

A core team of around 40 people was managing over 1000 active entrepreneurs across districts, handling everything from mobilization to compliance. Marketing often ended up deprioritized, as field teams focused on immediate training or credit-related responsibilities.

Strategic Options under Consideration

To address the operational and structural challenges that had emerged, particularly around marketing, Chinchure and his team began outlining a set of strategic options. The first was to establish an in-house marketing cell comprising experts in branding, packaging, e-commerce, and sales. This would build long-term institutional capacity and directly support both I-MEDP and C-MEDP entrepreneurs, although it would require upfront investment and stretch the already lean team. A second option involved partnering with external digital commerce platforms such as ONDC, Amazon Saheli, or Flipkart Samarth. These platforms offered broad reach and ready-made infrastructure, shifting MEDP's role to that of an enabler focused on onboarding and basic digital skilling. While cost-effective, this route reduced control over branding and assumed a level of digital literacy that many entrepreneurs had yet to develop.

A third option was to formally differentiate GTM strategies by vertical. I-MEDP entrepreneurs could focus on local *santhes*, WhatsApp sales, and physical outlets, while C-MEDP collectives could be supported through standardized inventory systems, unified branding, and category-specific online listings. This approach aligned with each model's strengths but risked creating internal silos. The most ambitious option was to spin off a dedicated marketing entity, either as a social enterprise or trust, to handle branding, retail partnerships, and digital logistics independently. While this could unlock scale and professionalization, it posed existential questions about DF's role: Would becoming a market intermediary dilute its developmental mission? And could such a unit secure the funding, talent, and governance needed to succeed?

These strategic options highlighted a deeper tension within MEDP: marketing was not just a missing function; it was a structural dilemma. Individual entrepreneurs relied on local *santhes* and informal sales networks, while collectives needed more formal branding and digital distribution. Previous experiments, such as The Kolhapur Co. and Authentic Karnataka, had revealed gaps in internal capabilities and bandwidth. Meanwhile, national platforms like ONDC and Flipkart Samarth offered scale but demanded digital literacy and onboarding support that MEDP had yet to build. As Chinchure reflected on these trade-offs, a core question remained: **How could MEDP design a GTM model that was both inclusive and scalable without stretching its developmental mission or its operational limits?**

Discussion Questions

1. How should MEDP design its marketing support model to serve both individual entrepreneurs and collectives effectively?
2. What are the trade-offs between building an internal marketing team versus partnering with external platforms like ONDC or Flipkart Samarth?
3. Should MEDP segment its marketing strategy by product type (e.g., food vs textiles) or by vertical (I-MEDP vs C-MEDP)? What are the operational implications of each?

4. Is creating a separate rural marketing entity a viable solution, or does it risk diverting from MEDP's development mission?
5. How can digital literacy and local capacity be built sustainably among MEs to support scalable GTM strategies?

Supplementary Reading Resources

1. Kistruck, G. M., Sutter, C. J., Lount, R. B., Jr., & Smith, B. R. (2013). Mitigating principal–agent problems in base-of-the-pyramid markets: An identity spillover perspective. Academy of Management Journal, 56(3), 659–682. https://doi.org/10.5465/amj.2011.0349

   - Essential for understanding challenges in collective entrepreneurship, trust, and behavioural alignment in rural settings.

2. Sutter, C. J., Bruton, G. D., & Chen, J. (2019). Entrepreneurship as a solution to extreme poverty: A review and future research directions. Journal of Business Venturing, 34(1), 197–214. https://doi.org/10.1016/j.jbusvent.2018.06.003

   - Provides a theoretical grounding for entrepreneurship as a tool for systemic development core to the MEDP mission.

3. London, T., & Hart, S. L. (2004). Reinventing strategies for emerging markets: Beyond the transnational model. Journal of International Business Studies, 35(5), 350–370. https://doi.org/10.1057/palgrave.jibs.8400099

   - Frames embedded co-creation strategies useful for building inclusive GTM approaches

Learning Outcomes

4. Apply GTM strategy frameworks in a development-sector context, especially where resource constraints and grassroots entrepreneurs are involved.
5. Critically evaluate trade-offs in designing marketing systems for diverse stakeholder groups (individuals vs collectives, food vs handicraft vs textile).
6. Design organizational structures that balance capacity building, mission alignment, and operational scale, including the possibility of spinning off functions.

Competing Interests The authors have no conflicts of interest to declare that are relevant to the contents of this chapter.

Exhibits

Exhibit I: Basic Definitions and the Organization Chart

Definition in practice: The Government of India's Ministry of Micro, Small and Medium Enterprises passed the Micro, Small and Medium Enterprises Development (MSMED) Act, 2006, which distinguishes Micro-enterprise from Manufacturing-based and Service-based Micro-enterprise. According to this act, a micro-enterprise is one that manufactures or produces goods, processes or preserves them, and whose investment in plant and machinery does not exceed INR 25 lakhs. A micro-enterprise is one that provides or renders services and whose investment in equipment (original cost excluding land and building and furniture, fittings, and other items not directly related to the service rendered) does not exceed INR 25 lakhs (Ministry of Micro, Small & Medium Enterprises, 2022).

Definition in literature: Mehrotra and Giri (2019) have categorized firms based on the number of employees using the Central Statistical Organization's Annual Survey of Industries and have arrived at the employee size distribution in all sizes of enterprises. They defined that a micro-enterprise has less than 10 employees (Figs. 20.1, 20.2, and 20.3).

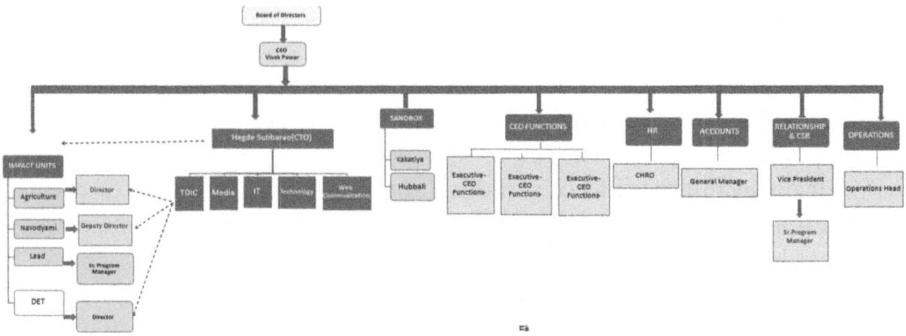

Fig. 20.1 Deshpande Foundation organization management structure. Source: Deshpande Foundation Archives

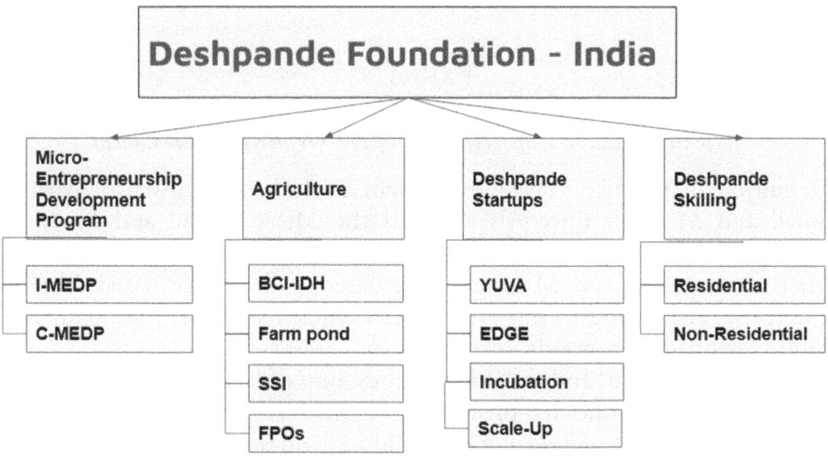

Fig. 20.2 Deshpande Foundation organization structure. Source: Prepared by the Research Assistant based on the interviews with Deshpande Foundation members

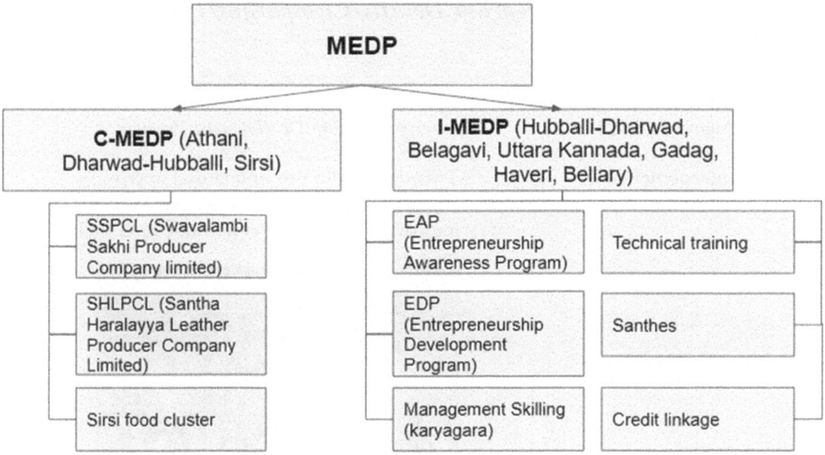

Fig. 20.3 MEDP structure. Source: Prepared by case authors based on the interviews with Deshpande Foundation members

References

1. Q.1. What is the definition of MSME (2022, 25). Ministry of Micro, Small & Medium Enterprises. https://msme.gov.in/faqs/q1-what-definition-msme
2. UNDESA—Report on MSMEs and the Sustainable Development Goals. (n.d.). https://sustainabledevelopment.un.org/content/documents/25851MSMEs_and_SDGs_Final3120.pdf

Exhibit II: Program Details/Campaigns/Photos

I-MEDP

1	*Entrepreneurship Awareness Program (EAP)*	*Orientation to potential members of the Micro-entrepreneurship Development Program.*
2	Entrepreneurship development program (EDP)	Two-day training to onboarded micro-entrepreneurs. This training is targeted to improve financial and communication skills of micro-entrepreneurs 
3	Karyagara	Dedicated training on accounting, book-keeping, digital payments, business registration process, and GST. 
4	Pragati	Sector-specific training targeted to improve the skills of women entrepreneurs. 
5	Credit linkage	The MEDP teams connect qualified micro-entrepreneurs with financial institutions. MEDP team members, along with bank representatives, visit micro-entrepreneurs' premises to assess their creditworthiness.

1	*Entrepreneurship Awareness Program (EAP)*	*Orientation to potential members of the Micro-entrepreneurship Development Program.*
6	Market linkage	The MEDP team connects micro-entrepreneurs with established entrepreneurs in the industry. Additionally, the team organizes trade fairs, locally known as *santhes*, to support the marketing and sales needs of micro-entrepreneurs. 

Source: MEDP archives

C-MEDP

SSPCL: Swavalambi Sakhi Producers Company Limited (Collective)

SHLPCL: Santha Haralayya Leather Producers Company Limited

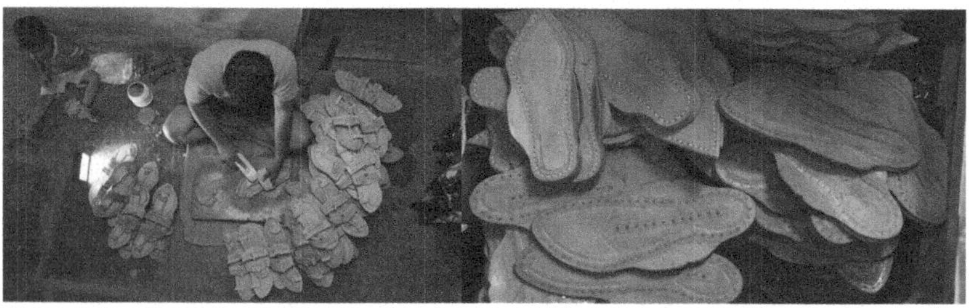

Source: MEDP archives

Exhibit III: Timeline of the Organization and the Data of Santhe *Impact Assessment (Tables 20.1 and 20.2)*

Applicants' Business Evaluation Sheet

Annexure 3:

Checklist for ME executive to screen the application

- Proof of identity
- Proof of residence
- Proof of business for 2 years
- PAN

Annexure 4

Applicants' business evaluation sheet

(Self answering questionnaire to be filled in advance by the applicant and to be brought to EAP venue and share with the Jury)

Applicants Name: **Date: -**

Location: **Business name:-**

Address: **Cell No:**

Here are some of the criteria for you to judge the candidate:-

Score ranges between 1 and 5

1=Poor, 2=Adequate, 3=Good, 4= Very Good and 5=Excellent
Objective of this assessment sheet: To be able to assess the ME potential (existing and growth) and select or reject for onboarding into MEDP

Sl.	Criteria	Score (By Jury)	Comment (by Jury)
1	**Business Idea outline** What is the Uniqueness or innovation quotient of your product/service		
2	**Competitive edge of product/service** What is the "Attractiveness" to the potential customer base		
3	Do you see any Gap due to unmet demand being filled		
4	How do you plan to ensure Sustainability of product/service		
5	**Marketability**		

	Are there any competitors for you in the market		
6	How do you propose to position in relation to competitors		
7	Do you know your strengths and weaknesses as a ME		
8	Can you tell about your ability to reach customer base and retain it		
9	**Management capability (Mentor ratification)** ME possesses the necessary leadership		
10	ME possesses the necessary technical skills		
11	He or she has clarity of the activities, milestones and risks of the business		
12	**Operational Viability** What are the ways to overcome possible operational obstacles?		
13	How will the product/service be distributed?		
14	**Financial Feasibility** How is the present funding of your enterprise (Bank or GoI Loan, MFI etc.)		
15	How do you propose to bring more investment for growth in future (Bank or GoI Loan, MFI etc.)		
16	What is the Long-run profitability quotient in your enterprise		
17	Sensible financial vision in place (financial statements, sourcing of funds and exit strategy explained)		
	Total Overall attractiveness and viability quotient of the business		

Source: MEDP archives

Table 20.1 Timeline of the MEDP program

DF 1.0 (Initiation)	*DF 2.0 (Development)*	*DF 3.0 (Scaling up)*
2011–2013 • Commencement of Navodyami program. • Initiation of financial support. 2013–2014 • Award 2.0 • Grant money released in phases.	2014–2016 • Intermediate financial institutions came into the picture. 2016–2017 • Expansion of Navodyami. • Launch of 'Santhes.' • Initiation of 'Karyagara' 2017–2018 • UNDP project phase 1 2018–2019 • UNDP project phase 2 2019–2020 • Program was renamed from Navodyami to micro-entrepreneurship development program.	2020–2021 • Segregation of I-MEDP and C-MEDP. • Dawn of SSPCL • Dawn of SHLPCL

Source: MEDP annual report 2020

Table 20.2 Impact of local fairs organized by MEDP

Santhe's Support for ME's Business Development

How did Santhe help MEs business	Percent
Helped get new customers	41.98
Connected with bigger customers/ clients	14.50
Reach new locations/regions	2.29
Increase sales	15.27
Increase profit	19.08
Did not help	6.87
Total	100.00

Source: MEDP Impact assessment by KREA university report

Exhibit IV: Short Bios of Key Actors

Dr. Aravind Chinchure

Aravind Chinchure, the CEO of Deshpande Startups at Deshpande Foundation, is a highly experienced physicist with 25 years of expertise in a diverse range of areas such as research and development, innovation, intellectual property, venture investing, business strategy, policy, and education. With a track record of successful inventions and innovations, he has worked with numerous Indian and global MNC corporations, founded his own startup, and provided guidance to business owners both in India and internationally. His technological knowledge spans several fields, including information technology, electronics, renewable energy, chemistry, and physics.

Iranna Shivnand Rotte

After obtaining his master's degree from Walchand College in Solapur, Iranna Rotte joined the Deshpande Foundation as the deputy director of MEDP. He participated in the foundation's Fellowship Program, which had a profound impact on his outlook on life, leading to a positive transformation. Iranna's passion for working with micro, small, and medium-sized business owners was sparked by his experience in the program. He ventured into micro business in 2011 and now manages the Micro-Entrepreneurship program, overseeing business operations in three states with the help of a dedicated team. Iranna has conducted numerous training sessions and workshops and has a thorough understanding of how to scale microentrepreneurs.

Sandeep Sabharwal

Sandeep Sabharwal, an executive at the CEO office of the Deshpande Foundation, is a seasoned professional with 28 years of experience working in both rural and urban settings, demonstrating a flexible and adaptable approach to community engagement. He is well-versed in grassroots program development, execution, and management, as well as the establishment of cooperative institutions. Sandeep has also been involved in managing disaster relief operations in Gujarat in 2001, Uttarakhand in 2013, and J&K in 2014. He has been responsible for recruiting, training, and motivating a team of over 200 experts in areas such as rural development, agriculture, and corporate social responsibility. His knowledge extends to non-timber forest products, traditional Indian farming techniques, dairy farming, and ways to enhance livelihoods through thrift. Sandeep has strong connections to rural communities.

Vivek Pawar

Vivek Pawar, the current CEO of the Deshpande Foundation, had previously served as its Managing Trustee for eight years. Before that, he founded and now holds the position of Chairman Emeritus at Sankalp Semiconductor. As an alumnus of IIT Kharagpur, Vivek worked for Texas Instruments both in India and the USA for over 15 years in various management roles. During this time, he is recognized for developing revolutionary chip devices, for which he received numerous awards and recognition. Over a decade, he established multiple development centers globally, in addition to the four sites in India. In 2005, he established Sankalp Semiconductors, a technology services provider specializing in semiconductor solutions from conception to prototype. Vivek joined the Deshpande Foundation in April 2018 and is responsible for devising a scalable model for the foundation, improving the cost-effectiveness, quality, and execution of its plans.

Source: LinkedIn profiles of key actors and Deshpande Foundation website

References

Dalberg. (2019). India's emerging gig economy: A study of the online platforms and economic empowerment. Dalberg Advisors. https://dalberg.com/our-ideas/indias-emerging-gig-economy/

Deshpande Foundation. (2022). Annual report. https://www.deshpandefoundationindia.org

Government of India. (2023a). Micro Units Development and Refinance Agency (MUDRA). https://www.mudra.org.in/

Government of India. (2023b). Prime Minister's Employment Generation Program (PMEGP). Ministry of MSME. https://www.kviconline.gov.in/pmegp/

International Finance Corporation. (2018). Financing India's MSMEs: Estimation of debt requirement of MSMEs in India. IFC, World Bank Group. https://www.ifc.org

Mehrotra, S., & Giri, T. (2019). The size structure of India's enterprises: Not just the middle is missing (CSE Working Paper #25). Centre for Sustainable Employment, Azim Premji University. https://cse.azimpremjiuniversity.edu.in

Ministry of Micro, Small and Medium Enterprises. (2022). Annual report 2021–22. Government of India. https://msme.gov.in/relatedlinks/annual-report

National Bank for Agriculture and Rural Development. (2020). Producer organizations: Policy and practice. https://www.nabard.org

CHAPTER 21

Entrepreneurship Ecosystem on the Move: Jagriti Yatra Wants to Go Global

Priya Tewary and Sreevas Sahasranamam

Abstract Jagriti Yatra is a unique annual train journey spanning 15 days and over 8000 kilometres across India, designed to bring together participants (Yatris) to engage with social innovators and changemakers across diverse sectors. The initiative is grounded in the concept of 'Middle of the Diamond India' - a demographic conceptualization of India - through which it seeks to inspire youth from Tier 2 and Tier 3 districts to become job creators and build India through enterprise. Set in 2023, this case reflects on Jagriti Yatra's 15-year journey and explores the strategic dilemma of whether the initiative should pursue internationalization. Students will learn about how entrepreneurial ecosystems are created on the move and the role of storytelling and role-modeling in it. The case is well-suited for teaching sessions on entrepreneurial ecosystems, rural entrepreneurship, and narrative-driven entrepreneurship.

P. Tewary (✉)
Jindal Global Business School, O. P. Jindal Global University, Sonipat, India
e-mail: priya1@jgu.edu.in

S. Sahasranamam
University of Glasgow Adam Smith Business School, Glasgow, UK
e-mail: sreevas.sahasranamam@glasgow.ac.uk

A. S. Galande et al. (eds.), *Context-inspired Entrepreneurship*, Sustainable Development Goals Series,
https://doi.org/10.1007/978-981-95-9831-1_21

Keywords Entrepreneurial ecosystem • Entrepreneurship education • Rural entrepreneurship • Role modelling • Internationalization • Storytelling

SDG Links This chapter is aligned with SDG 8: Decent Work and Economic Growth by examining how the Jagriti Yatra inspires and enables young people to pursue entrepreneurship as a pathway to job creation and local economic development. The chapter also aligns with SDG 4, through its focus on experiential entrepreneurship education, and SDG 10, by prioritising participation from non-metro and underserved regions.

Jagriti Yatra, meaning the 'journey of awakening' (in Hindi), is often described as the world's longest entrepreneurship train journey. Spanning 15 days and covering 8000 km across India, it brings together over 500 selected participants, known as Yatris. These yatris travel to 12 destinations, meeting successful entrepreneurs, social innovators, and grassroots changemakers in various sectors. This non-profit initiative that started in 2008 holds a powerful mission of "Building India through Enterprise", with a deep focus on the opportunities and challenges of 'Middle India' as described by Shashank Mani, founder of Jagriti Yatra (Mani, 2023).

However, in 2023, as India held the G20 presidency, with global initiatives like the Startup20, for the Jagriti Yatri leadership team that was attending them, the global spotlight felt both like an opportunity and a prompt. For over 15 years now, Jagriti Yatra's train journey has been serving as a powerful engine for awakening the spirit of entrepreneurship and deepening the understanding among the youth. As they prepared for the next Yatra, the Startup20 initiative pushed them to think bigger. Could the uniquely Indian experience translate globally? Should they actively seek participants from potentially the G20 nations in the next Yatra? What was the value proposition for an aspiring entrepreneur from Brazil or South Africa from a train journey through rural India? If so, how to reach them? How could they manage the more intricate logistics associated with managing a global cohort on a demanding 8000 km journey over 15 days? And more fundamentally, is this the right strategic direction for Jagriti Yatra or a potential dilution of their core mission?

Background on Jagriti Yatra

This initiative was born out of a powerful idea by Mr. Shashank Mani, who first organized the Azad Bharat Rail Yatra in 1997 to celebrate 50 years of India's independence. This journey inspired his book *"India: A Journey Through a Healing Civilization"*. The success of the book led to the birth of the Yatra, now known as Jagriti Yatra, with support from board members Raj Krishnamurthy and Rewati Prabhu, and executed by Gitanjali Bhattacharya and Swapnil Dixit.

Jagriti Yatra was run by Jagriti Sewa Sansthan, a non-profit organization based in Deoria, Uttar Pradesh, with its headquarters in Mumbai. This organization focused on skill development and enterprise-led growth, promoting development across seven key sectors: Agriculture, Education, Energy, Healthcare, Manufacturing, Water & Sanitation, and Arts, Culture & Sports. The vision of this organization was to build India through enterprise by encouraging the youth from smaller towns and villages to lead development through entrepreneurship. It aimed to nurture 1,00,000 entrepreneurs by 2030 and help generate 10 lakh jobs in the process (Jagriti Yatra, 2014).

Middle of the Diamond India Theory

This vision was backed by their theory called 'Middle of the Diamond India', a demographic conceptualization of India. This theory visualized India's demographic landscape as a diamond (see Fig. 21.1), which involved the rich and poor at the two ends of the spectrum, with a middle group, roughly 800 million people from Tier 2 and Tier 3 districts, as Middle India. Jagriti Yatra aimed to ignite the potential among the youth of Middle India, to change their mindset from job seekers into job creators, sparking a movement centered on enterprise-driven growth. Beyond the economic benefits, it also enabled them to discover a sense of purpose aligned with their unique skills.

Three Pillars of Jagriti Yatra

The essence of this entire 15-day journey has been distilled into three anchoring pillars - Innovation, Collaboration, and Transformation. The first pillar, Innovation, involved identifying unique opportunities and taking action towards them. Historically, innovation has mostly come from

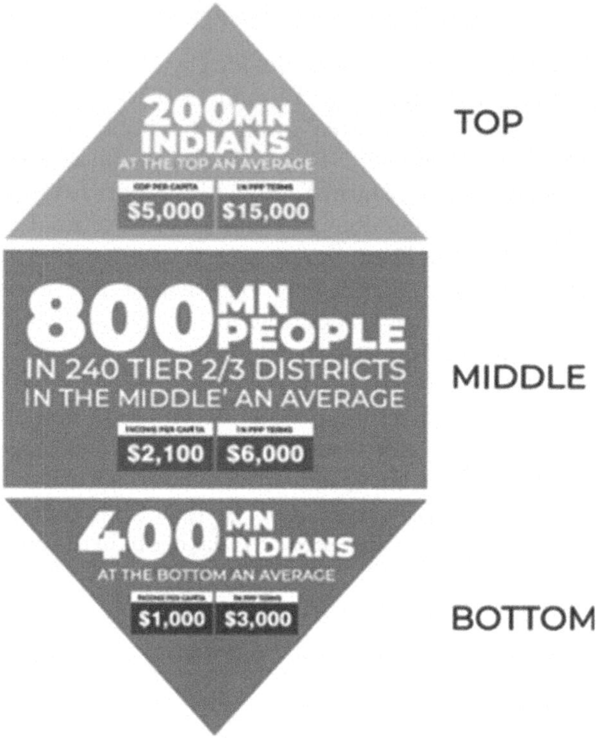

Fig. 21.1 Middle of the Diamond India (Source: Jagriti Yatra team)

the top down, but Jagriti Yatra's vision was that it should become a two-way exchange that included contributions from Middle India. Therefore, the journey prioritized exploring local innovations emerging from Middle India that were making a real difference in their communities. The second pillar, Collaboration, involved working as a team and leveraging each other's strengths to achieve a common goal. The Jagriti institution believed that it was imperative to harness the power of human potential through teamwork in a country like India, where financial resources are often limited. The third pillar, Transformation, involved stepping out of one's context, gaining new experiences, and returning with the drive to create meaningful change. The Jagriti institution compares this transformative journey to that of Mahatma Gandhi, Rosa Parks, and other global leaders who left their surroundings, came back, and challenged the prejudiced status quo during their times. Jagriti Yatra was not just a physical journey across India but was conceived to be a deeply personal one. The Yatris were expected to experience a dual journey, consisting of external learning (through real-world exposure) and internal cognitive shift (through personal self-discovery) that shapes an entrepreneur's mindset.

Entrepreneurial Ecosystem Creation on the Move

To undertake this ambitious project of traveling 8000 km in a train with over 500 participants, Mr. Shashank Mani and his team had to design something top-notch for this to succeed. This train journey planning in itself can be a logistical nightmare, but they also needed to curate the journey to inspire the travelers to undertake development-focused entrepreneurship and help build networks and skills for them. An illustration of what transpired over a typical 15-day yatra is summarised in Table 21.1 with a route map in Fig. 21.2. The journey involved varied engagements, including meeting role models and local communities, panel discussions, and a business plan competition.

Jagriti Yatra fostered collaborative learning by bringing together a diverse group of participants who share knowledge, experiences, and ideas, wherein they not only learn from mentors and role model entrepreneurs but also from each other. The process that brought together the yatris and facilitators is summarised in Table 21.2. This shared journey fostered deep engagement, collaboration, and knowledge exchange that goes beyond traditional classroom learning. Cohorts were the smallest units of interaction during the yatra, and they were formed based on diversity in terms of background, hometown, education, religion, nationality, class, and work experience. Each cohort consisted of 6 participants and one facilitator who was a senior Yatri acting as a mentor and guide for the cohort. 3 cohorts formed groups (of 21 participants) based on the interest areas they expressed while applying for the yatra.

With 500 people from diverse backgrounds coming together from across the country, the biggest challenge was breaking the ice and connecting with strangers. Even though they were put into cohorts based on shared interests, forming bonds in such a short period is not easy. To address this, a unique and engaging activity called the Lifeline activity was used. The lifeline exercise breaks the ice within the cohort and acts as the first step towards peer-to-peer learning. It provided a creative way for

Table 21.1 Illustrative itinerary of Jagriti Yatra

Day	*Location*	*Organization*	*Role model(s)*	*Agenda for the day*
Day 1	Mumbai	Tata Institute of Social Sciences	–	Induction & Introduction
Day 2	Hubli	Kalkeri Sangeet Vidyalaya	Adam Woodward	Understand holistic education, integrating cultural arts with education for rural children.
Day 3	Bengaluru	Mindtree	Parthasarathy N. S.	Panel discussion with IT multinationals, visiting Jagriti Enterprise Mela
Day 4	Madurai	Aravind Eyecare	Dr S Aravind (nephew of late Dr. Govindappa Venkataswamy)	Understanding affordable healthcare for all
Day 5	Sri City	Satyavedu Reserve Infracity Pvt. ltd.	Ravindra Sanareddy	Engaging with a rural region hosting over 200 companies from over 30 countries
Day 6	Visakhapatnam	Akshay Patra foundation	Satya Gaura Dasa	Understanding how 1.5 million midday meals are delivered for children across the country.
Day 7	Behrampur	Gram Vikas	Mr. Joe Madiath	Understanding inclusive access to water and sanitation facilities in villages
Day 8	On train	–	–	–
Day 9	Rajgir	Nalanda University	Gopa Sabharwal	Engaging with the rich cultural heritage of the ancient Indian education system and a panel discussion on entrepreneurial opportunities

(*continued*)

Table 21.1 (continued)

Day	*Location*	*Organization*	*Role model(s)*	*Agenda for the day*
Day 10	Deoria	Jagriti Enterprise Center	–	Testing enterprise ideas, talking to the local community, and having door-to-door interactions with the villagers
Day 11	Deoria	Jagriti Enterprise Center	–	Biz Gyan tree business plan competition
Day 12	Delhi	Goonj; Indian institute of technology (IIT), Delhi	Anshu Gupta	Understanding Goonj's approach to disaster relief and management, and a panel discussion on celebrating entrepreneurship at IIT Delhi.
Day 13	Tilonia	Barefoot college	Sanjit "Bunker" Roy	Engaging with Barefoot's approach of training rural women in solar power, electrical engineering, and handicraft
Day 14	Ahmedabad	Sabarmati ashram; Entrepreneurship Development Institute of India (EDII)	–	Visiting Mahatma Gandhi ashram, followed by an introspective walk beside Sabarmati river; graduation ceremony at EDII
Day 15	Mumbai	–	–	Goodbyes & Deboarding

participants to introduce themselves and connect at a deeper level. Each Yatri was asked to share the story of their life in 5–7 minutes using a line graph, where the *y*-axis showed their emotional highs and lows, and the *x*-axis represented time. Opening up about one's life in front of strangers is not easy. As participants met for the first time, many were hesitant to speak about their personal journeys. However, listening to others, gradually, Yatris, who were initially shy or unsure, shared powerful, moving stories. This activity not only fostered connection but also offered valuable

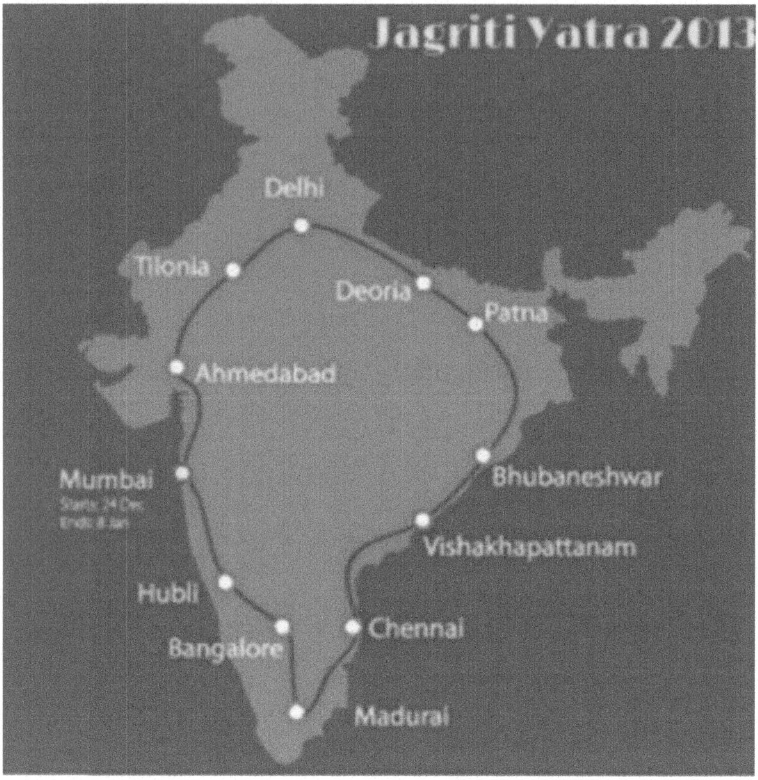

Fig. 21.2 Route Map (Jagriti Yatra 2013)

insights and new perspectives from diverse backgrounds (Jagriti Yatra, 2020).

Peer learning was also fostered through two major group activities during the yatra. These were the AC chair car presentations and the Biz Gyan Tree competition. The AC chair car presentations happened across two AC chair car coaches of the train, having a big LCD panel with live feeds delivered to both coaches while someone speaks. These presentations happened after each role model visit. The first part of these presentations focused on role model organizations and their activities. The real challenge for the groups, however, was to create a viable replication model for those organizations. The Biz Gyan Tree competition involved Yatris

Table 21.2 Selection Procedure

Selection Criteria	*Focus on creativity, passion, and problem-solving rather than exam scores.*
Diversity in selection	Candidates from across India, ensuring geographic & gender diversity.
Yatri composition	Total Yatris on average – 500 – 75 facilitators – 425 participants
Participants	Selected for their entrepreneurial potential and commitment to enterprise-led development.
Facilitators	Experienced professionals (28+ years old) who act as mentors & coordinators for groups of 6 participants. They help with learning, coordination, and bridging communication between participants and organizers.
Facilitator responsibilities	– Support participants in individual and collaborative learning – Ensure cohort follows the Yatra mantra (code of conduct) – Act as a bridge between participants and organizers – Must be fluent in English or Hindi
Selection process	Candidates apply online by filling out an application form with essay-type questions to assess entrepreneurial potential.
Evaluation process	– Applications reviewed by 30+ global experts – Random interviews & reference checks to verify authenticity – Facilitators evaluated separately on experience & leadership skills through an informal telephonic interview
Scholarship consideration	If applying for a scholarship, financial details are required post-selection to identify deserving candidates.

coming up with startup ideas for grassroots-level problems in a sector of their choice, such as agriculture, arts, culture, sports, education, energy and climate, finance, health, manufacturing, or technology. The groups presented their enterprise ideas before a jury in a 5-minute pitch. The jury consisted of sector-specific experts who evaluated the ideas and selected a winner from each sector. The key activities in the train are summarised in Table 21.3.

Storytelling was a key element of the Yatra. In addition to stories shared during the lifeline exercise on Day 2 by participants of the Yatra, there were the stories told by role model changemakers throughout the journey. For each role model, a day of the Yatra was dedicated, which involved the Yatris meeting with the stakeholders impacted by the role model and interacting with the role model directly. Another instance of storytelling happened during the night stay at Deoria, when the story of an old banyan

Table 21.3 Key Activities on the train

AC Chair Car presentations	*After each role model visit, a couple of groups make a presentation discussing the reflections and a replication model for the role model organizations in a 30–45 minute session.*
Compartment sessions	Discussions led by facilitators on specific topics, in formats suggested by the Jagriti team.
Mentor sessions	Mentors and entrepreneurs joining for certain legs of the train journey, and conduct interactive sessions with Yatris.
Arts & Creativity on train	Artists from the Southbank Centre, London & Indian folk artists created visual minutes of discussions. Often this includes documentary makers, photographers, videographers, musicians, and poets.
Yatra Saar	Each group submitted a summary of role model discussions in a format shared by the Jagriti team.

tree in that village was narrated with powerful symbolism. As India's national tree, the Banyan reflected deep-rooted traditions and the strength to grow new roots and expand. Through the story of the banyan tree, Yatris were encouraged to create new ideas and institutions that reflected Indian values and democratic spirit. Yatris were told that just like the banyan tree took root in local soil, strong institutions grew through local leaders who understood traditions and were ready to tackle real-world problems. The stories shared during the yatra provide insights into real-world challenges and triumphs, offering relatable and tangible examples of entrepreneurial journeys.

The visit and night stay at Deoria, the birthplace of the Jagriti Yatra, was the only time when Yatris slept outside the train during the 15-day journey. On that day, Yatris walked around the village to meet with the local community and gathered insights into the problems faced and the current situation of the village. This exploration provided firsthand insights into real-world challenges and opportunities in Tier 2 and Tier 3 districts. That night, Yatris slept on the floor with a mattress kept on straw to deal with the cold, with temperatures close to zero degrees. The smell of earth, the next morning's walk to the banyan tree during the fog, and meditation there gave the participants the taste of middle India.

Another mechanism that brought all yatris together was through the 'Yatra Geet', an anthem that was echoed throughout the Yatra, reflecting its mission. The full English translation of this song is provided in Note 21.1. This choreographed song, taught to the Yatris, is sung with gestures and acts as a constant source of motivation for the Yatris. In the personal experience of the first author:

> The geet worked like an instant energy booster and a wake-up call after a long day's visit for me. Its message was about hope for a better tomorrow and the presence of solutions to the problems faced today. The song also emphasized that everyone present there can count on each other.

Through its unique design, the Yatra became a melting pot of ideas, experiences, and mentorship by bringing together changemakers, leaders, innovators, and policymakers under a single moving roof. In essence, Jagriti Yatra created an entrepreneurship ecosystem on the move where aspiring entrepreneurs, mentors, and investors interacted in a dynamic, high-energy setting while being on a 15-day train journey. The journey itself acted as an incubator, providing networking opportunities, mentorship, and exposure to real-life business challenges. Unlike traditional incubators, which are location-bound, this initiative fostered connections across geographies and industries.

In summary, the Yatra design was anchored in four axes of learning. First, learning through role models. By meeting the role models such as Anshu Gupta of Goonj or Bunker Roy of Barefoot College and listening to their stories, Yatris understood how they built these enterprises. Second, learning from experts through panel discussions. As part of this, participants engaged in panel discussions with the IT industry and on core topics of entrepreneurship, such as marketing, fundraising, and business model canvas. Third, learning through a business plan challenge, which involved participants working as groups to identify a real-world challenge and develop an enterprising solution with support from mentors. Finally, learning from peers on the Yatra, who come from diverse backgrounds.

Reflecting on the four axes of learning, Chinmay Vadnere, the Chief Operating Officer of Jagriti Yatra, said:

> The process of travelling together across the Indian hinterland in the same coach for 15 days while being surrounded by energy, ideas, debates, and collaborations, creates a certain degree of emotional bond between the Yatris, at an occult level or spiritual level! Yatris at the end of the journey are trying to find meaning and purpose, to solve, build, and create selflessly for India. This differentiates Jagriti Yatra alumni from alumni of universities.

Continuation of the Journey

Even after the conclusion of the 15-day yatra, various types of support systems were available for the Yatris to pursue their entrepreneurial journey. For instance, some teams from the Biz Gyan Tree exercise, whose ideas were promising, were invited to Deoria for a 2-week residential program to build a detailed business plan (Jagriti Yatra, 2022). In addition, all the Yatris formed a part of the strong alumni network, the Jagriti Enterprise Network (JEN), that offered mentorship, market access, and investment opportunities to foster entrepreneurship in India's Tier 2 and Tier 3 districts. Besides this, institutional support was available in the form of the Jagriti Enterprise Centre (JEC). JEC created an innovation and incubation ecosystem at the regional level to support small and medium entrepreneurs through market, mentorship, and funding. The first centre, Purvanchal centre (JEC-P), was started in 2017 in Deoria and focused predominantly on North India. Similarly, Jagriti planned to create 3 more such institutions in the southern, eastern, and western parts of India in the future. The Yatris who have an interest in starting an enterprise to solve the problems of tier 2–3 cities can use the resources and guidance from the JEC. The alumni of Jagriti Yatra could also become district ambassadors under the Jagriti Ambassador for District Entrepreneurship (JADE) initiative, an outreach program focused on the youth of tier 2 and 3 districts of India. This initiative, spread across India at the district level, was aimed at building entrepreneurship ecosystems by organizing various events and activities. Prospective entrepreneurial youth identified through JADE are supported by the JEC.

The past Yatris may also volunteer to form the Engine Room Club (ERC), a group of 30 members who were responsible for the smooth management of different departments, including operations, punctuality, programming, water filling, crowd management, media, and branding during the future yatras. This ensured continuous support during the yatra, given that selected ERC members have been part of the yatra and know the 15-day program well. Besides this, the alumni regularly met in various locations across India to discuss the innovations and enterprises created by past yatris, popularly called the 'yatripreneurs'.

Yatripreneurs' Examples

TiTLi (Together in Transforming Learning in India) was founded by a 2012 yatri, Pranjal Modi, in 2015. Being a Chartered Accountant and Chartered Financial Analyst, Pranjal started coaching classes for Chartered Accountants in Ranchi, Jharkhand, in 2011. Through this, he was able to identify foundational issues within the Indian education system, particularly the absence of structured training for Early Childhood Educators and Caregivers. Recognizing this gap, he established TiTLi to offer scalable, affordable, and accessible programs aimed at empowering women to become skilled professionals in early childhood education across both rural and urban settings.

Similarly, OpenGrad Foundation, founded by Sahil Sameer, a 2023 Yatri, got refined and crystallized as a non-profit startup during the Yatra. It was aimed at democratizing access to elite higher education. With a mission to bridge the educational divide for underprivileged youth, this startup provided free, community-driven coaching for various undergraduate and postgraduate entrance exams to engineering, management, and law degrees. Their platform provided video lectures, mock tests, and personalized mentorship from students and alumni of top-tier institutions. Notably, OpenGrad had partnered with the government in Tamil Nadu and Bihar, providing coaching to thousands of students in underserved communities. They have been supported by entities such as The/Nudge Institute and NSRCEL at IIM Bangalore.

Jagriti Yatra, as the world's largest train journey, inspired and supported Indian youth who wanted to build India through enterprise. It has been able to create, on average, 65 enterprises per year across different sectors (Jagriti Yatra, 2018), showcasing strong impact through the creation of a dynamic entrepreneurship ecosystem on the move. In the G20 India year, the team now pondered over whether their journey had a destination beyond Indian shores. They had to weigh multiple operational realities—challenges of international outreach, value proposition for global cohort, complex logistics of global participation, and the fundamental question of whether it's truly aligned with their core mission or risked diluting their hard-won identity. The decision demanded careful consideration, balancing ambition and pragmatism.

Discussion Questions

1. How could entrepreneurship ecosystems be built on the move? What is unique about building entrepreneurship ecosystems in Tier 2/3 or smaller towns of India?
2. What is the role of space and place in entrepreneurship?
3. What is the role of storytelling in driving entrepreneurial action?
4. What are the different entrepreneurship education pedagogies used by Jagriti Yatra?
5. How should Jagriti Yatra conceive its internationalization plan?

Supplementary Reading

Book:

- Mani, S. (2023). *Middle of Diamond India: National Renaissance Through Participation and Enterprise.* Penguin Random House India Private Limited.

Research Papers:

1. Audretsch, D. B., Fiedler, A., Fath, B., & Verreynne, M. L. (2024). The dawn of geographically unbounded entrepreneurial ecosystems. *Journal of Business Venturing Insights*, *22*, e00487.
2. Brattström, A., & Wennberg, K. (2022). The entrepreneurial story and its implications for research. *Entrepreneurship theory and practice*, *46*(6), 1443–1468.
3. Drencheva, A., Stephan, U., & Patterson, M. (2024). Beyond the lone hero: How interpersonal feedback seeking helps entrepreneurs to engage with their social environment. *Applied Psychology*, *73*(4), 1444–1486.
4. Alvarez, S. A., & Barney, J. B. (2007). Discovery and creation: Alternative theories of entrepreneurial action. *Strategic entrepreneurship journal*, *1*(1–2), 11–26.
5. Forte, T. (2021, March 8). The future of education is community: The rise of cohort-based courses. *Forte Labs.* https://fortelabs.com/blog/the-rise-of-cohort-based-courses/
6. Korsgaard, S., Müller, S., & Tanvig, H. W. (2015). Rural entrepreneurship or entrepreneurship in the rural–between place and space. *International Journal of Entrepreneurial Behavior & Research*, *21*(1), 5–26.

Learning Objectives
This case study is relevant for entrepreneurship courses at undergraduate and postgraduate levels. It is also relevant for management development programme discussions with incubator leaders and policymakers in the entrepreneurship ecosystem, as it provides a unique model of enterprise-led development in Tier 2/Tier 3 and small towns of India and highlights how entrepreneurship can be nurtured through experiential learning, ecosystem building, and self-discovery.

- Understand how entrepreneurial ecosystems can be catalyzed through mobile, experiential platforms.
- Evaluate the role of space and place in entrepreneurship.
- Understand how narrative-driven approaches can inspire entrepreneurial action, build community, and shape identity among emerging entrepreneurs.
- Explore the considerations, risks, and opportunities involved in scaling a contextually rooted initiative to international settings.

Acknowledgements The authors would like to thank Chinmay Vadnere, the Chief Operating Officer of Jagriti Yatra, for sharing insights and feedback on the case study drafts. The authors would also like to thank Mr. Shashank Mani and the Jagriti Yatra team for hosting us for field visits to understand their work better.

Competing Interests The authors have no conflicts of interest to declare that are relevant to the content of this chapter.

Exhibits

Note 21.1 English Translation of Yatra Geet (yatra song written in Hindi) (Source: Jagriti Yatra, 2018).

Some of the things are changing, and some we will change.
They will change only when we change;
Some of the things are written, some we will write;
Let's go friends, it's the season of change!
Let's go friends, it's the season of betterment!
The wind is asking us not to stop;
The sky is asking us not to melt,
The earth is asking us to touch and feel it;

Look into my eyes, and don't fear the truth.
Let's go friends, it's the season of change!
Let's go friends, it's the season of betterment.

References

Jagriti Yatra. (2014). *Yatra Saar*. Jagriti Yatra. https://www.jagritiyatra.com/

Jagriti Yatra. (2018). *Yatra Saar*. Jagriti Yatra. https://www.jagritiyatra.com/

Jagriti Yatra. (2020). *Digital Yatra Saar 2020*. Jagriti Yatra. https://www.jagritiyatra.com/

Jagriti Yatra. (2022). *Digital Yatra Saar 2021–22*. Jagriti Yatra. https://www.jagritiyatra.com/

Mani, S. (2023). *Middle of diamond India: National Renaissance through Participation and Enterprise*. Penguin Random House India Private Limited.

CHAPTER 22

Values beyond Wealth: The Making of a Marwari Entrepreneur

Apoorv Arora, Ishan Vats, and Dhruv Dashrath Saidava

Abstract Awanish Agrawal established GreenChem Innovations, a company that operates in the specialty chemicals sector of India. The adhesives line of the firm, which was established on the foundation of family values of trust and reputation, rapidly gained traction. However, the company is currently experiencing significant financial strain. The company's expansion into new verticals, including bleaching chemicals and packaging, has reached a halt, and fixed operating costs are on the increase. Additionally, cash reserves are nearly depleted. Awanish needs to quickly make up a ₹20 lakh shortfall because salaries are due, vendor dues are piling up, and cash flow is running out. He can get money from a bank loan with strict terms, a community (Samaj) loan that is more flexible but still legally binding, or a conditional venture capital note that is linked to ambitious revenue goals. The reputation, long-term strategy, and financial well-being of the

A. Arora (✉) • I. Vats
Indian Institute of Management Kozhikode, Kunnamangalam, Kerala, India
e-mail: apoorva16phd@iimk.ac.in; ishanv16phd@iimk.ac.in

D. D. Saidava
EduNeuro Solutions LLP, Ahmedabad, India
e-mail: dhruv@eduneuro.in

A. S. Galande et al. (eds.), *Context-inspired Entrepreneurship*, Sustainable Development Goals Series,
https://doi.org/10.1007/978-981-95-9831-1_22

community are all impacted by every action. Finding the right mix of formal and informal finance, handling the social obligations associated with entrepreneurial decision-making, and balancing profitable cores against hazardous expansions are all challenges brought to light in the case. It encourages evaluation of GreenChem's financial sustainability, consideration of trade-offs among financing options, and reflection on how community norms influence business choices under pressure.

Keywords Marwari • Informal credit • Community finance • Liquidity crunch • Social capital

SDG Links This chapter is aligned with SDG 8: Decent Work and Economic Growth by examining the social, financial, and institutional drivers of entrepreneurship through the narrative of a Marwari entrepreneur. The chapter also relates to SDG 17, through its focus on family-based business networks and inter-generational partnerships.

Introduction

Awanish sat by the window of his newly renovated office, momentarily disconnected from the quiet buzz of celebration outside. An important customer had just cancelled a large order for speciality chemicals. This deal was worth INR 2 million, which Awanish was counting on a lot. While the contemplative mood loomed large on him, his trance-like state was broken by a sharp ring on the phone on his table. Awanish picked up the phone and responded with practised ease: "Namaste, Mr. Sharma" Already aware of the number in the caller ID, "I heard your son got into a US college. Many congratulations to you and your son." "Thanks, Awanish ji, I wished to talk about the order cancellation." No sooner did the client begin to explain the cancellation than Awanish cut in gently, "This is wonderful news. Please wish him well. And don't worry about the order. We've known each other too long to let this come between us." The caller expressed gratitude. Awanish hung up, appearing calm but secretly quite disturbed. This order wasn't the only one. An underlying change was taking place.

He built GreenChem Innovations quickly and with a big goal: to change the specialty chemical landscape. He started in a small space in Okhla with ₹6 lakhs from Chetan Agarwal, a distant uncle who was known in the business world for being calm and decisive. He built his team around shared beliefs more than credentials. This team included Priya, a marketing strategist and, in some sense, GreenChem's second-in-command. They overcame obstacles like shaky supply chains, restricted margins, and delayed startup times by working together.

The business has seen the light of success in the little time it had existed in the market, but to glow and grow, it required expansion. All of this cost money, but now the numbers were getting tighter. Next to the factory was the vocational center, a skill-building project that started out of a desire to help others. It was running its evening session, which was paid for with the same money that bought raw materials and chemicals. The new line of bleaching chemicals was costing more money than it was making in sales. To make things worse, the employees' pay was due in ten days, but they didn't have the money they needed.

He had just received an offer from a bank to cover only part of his funding needs and on terms that would tighten monthly cash flow even further.

He set the phone down and leaned back in his chair. ₹20 lakhs. That was the shortfall. Between the second unit, vendor dues, and the bleaching line stuck halfway, things were tight. No calls came in. But the silence itself felt like pressure.

Background to the Community Context, Individual, and Case Organisation

Community Context—About the Marwari Community

The Marwari community comes from the Marwar region in Rajasthan, India. They are widely known for their strong business sense and have significantly contributed to trade and industry. Originally, "Marwari" meant people living in Marwar, but now it refers more broadly to business people from Rajasthan who have spread across India.

Marwar's dry environment, lacking many resources, forced Marwaris to become careful and skilled at managing money and resources. Because of this, they learned to plan finances carefully and be cautious spenders. When opportunities opened up in other Indian cities like Kolkata, Mumbai, and Chennai, many Marwaris moved there. They adapted quickly, built new businesses, and became an important part of the local economies.

The joint family concept is one factor that sets Marwari businesses apart. This system lets family members from different generations live and work together. By sharing resources and tasks, they make business function more smoothly and minimize the risk. Family members help each other, which makes it easier to build the firm and make swift judgments. A lot of Marwari families have started to gravitate toward smaller, nuclear households in the last few years because of changes in society and the economy.

The "Parta" system is a specific way that Marwari businesses do things. It's a traditional approach of keeping track of money that involves keeping note of daily income and expenses. This helps firms quickly figure out where they are financially, make quick decisions, and keep their money in order. Marwaris are also known for helping each other through strong networks. These networks help them get money, share important business information, and work together on projects. Groups like the Marwadi International Federation help Marwaris all over the world work together in cultural, social, and economic ways. These kinds of networks help businesses work together and keep their traditions alive, which makes them stronger economically.

A lot of successful Marwari families have had a big impact on India's industrial growth. The Birla family, for instance, started out in the cotton trade and later branched out into other industries, such as jute, cement, and aluminum. They had high standards in both business and giving. Their story is a good example of how adaptable and entrepreneurial the Marwari community is.

Individual - About Awanish

Awanish Agrawal didn't remember a time when business wasn't part of daily life. As a child growing up in a small town in Rajasthan, mornings often began with the rustle of ledger books and phone calls in Marwari, not alarm clocks. His father, Karamchand, ran a textile shop in the town's market, turning over around ₹40–50 lakhs annually. Behind the bolts of fabric and handwritten bills, he also dealt in basic textile chemicals such as softeners, dyes, and processing agents, which were sold in 20 and 50-litre drums stacked near the back office. Karamchand insisted that Awanish should accompany him on weekends and learn the ropes of the trade.

These early exposures weren't just framed as lessons but instead became a form of informal apprenticeship, common in tightly knit family-driven businesses in trading communities like the Marwaris. Learning in such scenarios comes more from observation than instruction, a form of vicarious learning deeply embedded in everyday business life. Between checking fabric stock and greeting regular customers, Awanish learned how credit cycles worked, how tone could shift a deal, and how to let silence do half the talking. During the usual family conversation, his father would often say things like, "A man's word travels faster than his invoice," or "Don't squeeze a customer; make him come back." The message was clear: trust was currency, and relationships were capital.

At home, his mother, Manjula, kept things moving, spanning across accounts, household decisions, and small but steady interventions in the business. She didn't talk much about balance sheets, but she spoke often about reputation. For her, reputation was the credit score within the community. Support was easy to be garnered with a high standing reputation. At the same time, ostracism was widely prevalent. She once told him, referring to an uncle who had defaulted on a ₹30-lakh samaj loan and hadn't been invited to a wedding in seven years, "We belong to a community that remembers things." Consequences, like support, were distributed socially and not legally.

On further probing, Awanish's mother narrated to him the incident that occurred with the uncle in question. He was the owner of a medical gauge-making business. Initially, the business was started from a small shop in the locality where he resided and was completely bootstrapped. The growth curve was exponential, and with time, a strong client base was built, which included multispecialty hospitals down to small local clinics. All this was the result of tireless running and multiple visits to clients, and often being a part of informal ceremonies. It was realised that this business, though thriving well, lacked volume and needed expansion. To that end, two more shops were planned to be set up in neighbouring cities where potential was present, but to finance these endeavours from the earnings alone was challenging, at least at one go. Samaj loans were decided to be the way forward, and a sum of ₹ 30 lakh was garnered. The two shops that were set up with these funds, within a year, needed to be closed owing to a lack of business. The loss-making enterprises were seen eating into the revenue earned from the original shop. The setup also took a toll on the time dedicated to the original business, resulting in a decline in business. The major challenge faced by the new ventures was their alien location. The relationship building in one's locality was easier owing to the already existing social capital, whereas in a foreign location with limited reach and contacts, not to mention already existing players, building a client base was near impossible. All this was the business part. The loss in terms of intangibles was exceedingly varied. The loss of reputation as a businessman, who failed at a venture, was accompanied by the shame and ostracism faced on account of not being able to repay the loan to the community.

Awanish realised that the relationship with the community was a two-edged sword at times, and the chances of nick or even flesh wounds were probable. It wasn't just numbers that Awanish absorbed. It was the rhythm with which the foundation of trust was built slowly over time, favours exchanged quietly, and consequences delivered without paperwork. It was a way of doing business rooted in long-term orientation and shared memory, standing clear as the key features of indigenous entrepreneurial cultures.

Case Organisation—Inspiration and Setup

By the time he finished his commerce degree, it was assumed he would inherit the store. But Awanish was aiming differently. He applied for an MBA, justifying it to his father as "learning how to scale." Karamchand grunted. "Learn what you want, but remember, the market doesn't care for theory. What is the return you expect anyways? A job where you toil away for someone else's dream and for what compensation. Our store pays our accountants ₹70,000 a month. What will you earn after an MBA?" In his heart, Awanish was not altogether oblivious to the fact stated by his father. Neither did he have any inclination to walk the road to a corporate corner office.

Business school didn't replace Awanish's instincts, but it added vocabulary to them. His entrepreneurial ideas found articulation. It was there that Awanish started seriously looking for a market gap to capitalise upon, which came most dramatically. While sitting in the college canteen, Awanish and his group of friends stumbled upon a discussion on the chemical industry in India. Awanish realised through the discussion at once that speciality chemicals was the path forward for him.

He communicated the same to Ravi, his classmate and friend. Ravi laughed. "Your father will have a heart attack if you tell him you're starting a chemical business."

"Not if I do it right," Awanish replied. "And not if I take my time."

Awanish shared the idea among his peer group, but not everyone was convinced. When he pitched the same idea during a classroom showcase, the panel consisting of professors wasn't impressed either.

"Too capital-intensive," one said.

"High regulatory burden," another added.

"Try trading first—it's leaner," a classmate suggested, too.

Awanish nodded politely, but walked out shaken. The numbers made sense on paper. But he couldn't ignore how easily others had dismissed the path.

Awanish had already revealed his intentions about moving into chemicals to launch his entrepreneurial career to his father. That night, he went back to his room and called his father. "Still planning to go into chemicals?" Karamchand asked. "Yes," Awanish said, though his voice lacked its usual edge. At dinner later in the week, he said carefully, "Papa, I don't want to run the family textile business. I want to build something that reflects our values but in a new way." Karamchand looked up from his plate. "Your grandfather once told me that if you believe in your path, follow it." Then he added, "But for the next two years, just focus on building relationships. Don't rush after orders. Trust will bring the business. And always remember that our community supports you, but it also watches closely."

For Awanish, this wasn't just business advice. It was a reminder of the deep-rooted norms of reciprocity and moral obligation that underpinned community support and the quiet sanctions that came with breaking them. He didn't yet know what shape his business would take, but he had his compass: relationships over transactions, patience over speed, and a name his community trusted.

Among Marwari entrepreneurs, financial capital often flowed through informal channels. Loans from community associations like the various Samaj carried low interest rates typically in range of 6–8% and flexible terms but came with social accountability. These financial structures were well-understood in his circles, operating on norms of trust and memory more than formal contracts.

Awanish had grown up witnessing this firsthand. He had also seen what happened when trust was broken. "Baranwal's family was slowly cut off. No invitations. No callbacks." The consequences, like the support, were distributed socially, not legally.

For Awanish, the community remained both a source of strength and a system of watchful norms. "Community loans came cheap... but they came with eyes watching you."

Background to the Industry and Ecosystem

The industrial chemicals sector in India is marked by complexity, regulation, and consolidation. While demand continues to rise, especially from packaging, textiles, and coatings, much of the supply remains import-driven. In his research, Awanish had noted that "India imports ₹6000 crore worth of chemicals each year, and most SMEs can't afford the big players."

The sector presents high entry barriers: capital intensity, price competition, and regulatory burdens such as environmental clearance and safety certifications. Owing to these challenges, small and mid-sized manufacturers remain underserved by dominant players. These clients consist of particular packaging firms in regions like Bawana and Ghaziabad who prioritise flexibility in supply, consistent pricing, and low minimum order quantities. Awanish saw an entry point here. As he explained in their first meeting to Chetan Agarwal, a distant uncle known in the business circle for his calm decisiveness and steady judgment and a doyen of chemical business, "Our first clients will be small packaging units who want flexible delivery and stable pricing. We shall operate lean, and I have plans to source input materials at 10–12% below current rates".

Formal finance brought its own constraints. Banks, like the Commercial Bank of India, typically offered only partial coverage at 11–12% interest with fixed repayment obligations. Venture capital was conditional on performance milestones and often implied dilution. These options existed, but none came without cost—financial or relational.

Current Challenges and the Dilemma

GreenChem Innovations had made early progress, but operational pressures were mounting. The adhesive product line was generating consistent orders and a modest gross profit. Despite this, Awanish was hopeful that over the period, the margins could be increased once a sustainable supply was built. In the latest month, adhesives contributed ₹0.5 lakhs in gross profit. However, newer verticals, particularly the bleaching chemicals, had stalled due to pending environmental clearance and rising raw material costs. The packaging segment remained on hold after a key supplier shut down. Meanwhile, Awanish had launched a vocational training centre named 'ummed' next to the plant as a social initiative. It consisted of two instructors, 15 students from nearby villages, apart from rent and infrastructure maintenance costs, all fell on GreenChem's account. The opening ceremony drew local media attention. That evening, an industry peer texted him: "Noble, but are you sure you can afford to be generous right now?"

The financial picture was tightening rapidly. Gross monthly revenue stood at ₹7.9 lakhs, but the company was losing ₹3.3 lakhs per month. Looking at past years, Awanish knew this wasn't the first time GreenChem had been tight on liquidity, but it was the first time the stakes felt existential. Fixed costs, including salaries and rent, amounted to ₹4 lakhs monthly. With only ₹1 lakh cash in hand and ₹3.2 lakhs in receivables expected within 30–45 days, GreenChem's available liquidity could barely stretch for another month. Payables and equipment dues totalled ₹8.5 lakhs, placing the firm's net working capital at –₹4.3 lakhs. (See Table 22.1).

Against this backdrop, Awanish faced an urgent funding gap of ₹20 lakhs. Salaries were due in ten days. Vendor payments were piling up. The second unit's expansion was half-complete, and the bleaching line continued to draw costs without returns. He needed to act and fast, too. This

Table 22.1 Current Month Operating Snapshot (May 2025)

Metric	*Amount*	*What it tells us*
Gross revenue (monthly)	₹7.9 lakhs	Total income from all product lines
Gross profit (from adhesives)	₹0.5 lakhs	Only adhesives are contributing positively—Other lines are losing
Fixed operating costs	₹4.0 lakhs	Salaries, rent, and admin—Recurring monthly burden
Net burn rate	₹3.3 lakhs	Business is losing this amount every month
Cash in hand	₹1.0 lakh	Immediate liquidity available
Receivables (due in 30–45 days)	₹3.2 lakhs	Short-term inflow, but delayed
Available inflow (cash + receivables)	₹4.2 lakhs	Can stretch 1–1.5 months with this
Payables + equipment dues	₹8.5 lakhs	Immediate financial pressure—Overdue liabilities
Net working capital	–₹4.3 lakhs	Already in shortfall before next burn

Table 22.2 Financing Options and Trade-offs

Option	*Amount available*	*Terms*
Bank loan	₹12 lakhs	11.25% interest, 3-year term EMI ≈ ₹40 K/month
Community loan (Samaj)	₹20 lakhs (assumed)	Soft terms, low interest Flexible repayment
VC convertible note	₹8 lakhs	Only available if revenue hits ₹ 15 L/month Equity dilution likely

Table 22.3 Multi-Year Financial Summary (FY 2023–2025 YTD)

Financial metric	*FY 2023*	*FY 2024*	*FY 2025 (YTD)*
Gross revenue (₹ lakhs)	45	62	79
Gross profit (₹ lakhs)	4	6.5	7
Gross margin (%)	8.90%	10.50%	8.90%
Fixed operating costs (₹ lakhs)	24	35	48
Net profit / (loss) (₹ lakhs)	−2.5	−2.8	−41.0
Capex investments (₹ lakhs)	5.5	10	6.5
Receivables (₹ lakhs)	5	4.8	3.2
Payables (₹ lakhs)	2	4	8.5
Cash in hand (₹ lakhs)	2.5	1.8	1

was not the only crisis presenting itself. GreenChem was not a chemical trading company but a manufacturing unit and to keep the upper hand in the market, it was imperative to focus on creating and launching innovative products, all of which needed substantial money flow to happen in R&D. Hence, Awanish though focusing on the short term need, was not oblivious of his long term financing needs.

He had received an offer from a bank to cover ₹12 lakhs at an interest rate of 11.25%, repayable over three years. The EMI burden, however, would stretch monthly cash flows further. The Samaj loan remained an option that was accessible and affordable, but not without its risks. A venture capital firm had previously offered ₹8 lakhs as convertible debt, but only if monthly revenues hit ₹15 lakhs, a condition GreenChem had yet to meet. Other alternatives included a partial bank loan or a conditional VC offer, each outlined in Table 22.2. It was also important to note that certain trends were present over the years leading to the scenario that presented before Awanish (see Table 22.3).

Each option came with trade-offs that were financial, strategic, and social. The question before Awanish now was: how should he bridge the ₹20 lakh shortfall without compromising his business or the trust it was built on?

Numbers tell stories. The challenge was learning to hear them before the damage was done.

Discussion Questions

1. What do the company's financials and ratios reveal about GreenChem's business model risk and operational efficiency? (Where is the business bleeding money, and why?—Is this a problem of margin, scale, or structure?)
2. Should Awanish protect the profitable adhesives line or continue funding riskier verticals like bleaching and packaging? (What would you advise him to drop or double down on—and why?, Is the bigger risk slowing down and becoming irrelevant, or pushing forward and collapsing?)
3. If you were Awanish, what financing path would you choose out of the three options given your need for liquidity and your community's expectations? (What future are you betting on by choosing this option?, What risks (not just financial) do you take on with each?)

Supplementary Readings

- Cardon, M. S., Wincent, J., Singh, J., & Drnovsek, M. (2009). The nature and experience of entrepreneurial passion. *Academy of Management Review*, *34*(3), 511–532.
- De Carolis, D. M., & Saparito, P. (2006). Social capital, cognition, and entrepreneurial opportunities: A theoretical framework. *Entrepreneurship theory and practice*, *30*(1), 41–56.
- Brush, T. H., Bromiley, P., & Hendrickx, M. (2000). The free cash flow hypothesis for sales growth and firm performance. *Strategic management journal*, *21*(4), 455–472.

Learning Objectives

1. Diagnose the sustainability of a business under growth pressure (Interpret multi-year financials to assess whether the company is scaling efficiently or straining its operating model; distinguish between growth, diversification, and dilution of focus based on cash flow, margin trends, and product-line performance)

2. Make strategic product and resource allocation decisions in constrained environments (Prioritise product lines using financial data and strategic reasoning; evaluate trade-offs between protecting a profitable core and pursuing new but riskier growth areas)
3. Compare and critically evaluate financing options (Analyse formal bank loans, informal community credit, and venture capital in terms of cost, flexibility, and long-term impact; assess how financing structure and timing affect liquidity and control)
4. Understand the role of social capital and community expectations in entrepreneurial decisions (Examine how trust-based ecosystems shape access to capital and accountability; reflect on the influence of family legacy, reputation, and communal norms in financial and strategic choices)
5. Reflect on the ethical and emotional dimensions of entrepreneurship (Explore the personal burden of decision-making when financial logic conflicts with social obligations; consider how founders balance control, speed, and reputation under pressure)

Acknowledgement The authors thank the reviewers for their valuable comments and suggestions, which helped strengthen the case. The names of individuals and organisations have been changed for convenience and confidentiality. Also, Quillbot and ChatGPT were used to improve the draft's language flow and cohesion of sentences.

Competing Interests The authors have no conflicts of interest to declare that are relevant to the content of this chapter.

Supplementary Material

Guidance for Educators on Using this Case for a 90 Minutes Class Discussion

Synopsis

This case looks at the story of GreenChem Innovations, which was started by Awanish Agrawal, a Marwari entrepreneur. Awanish tries to grow his chemical manufacturing business beyond its early success in adhesives. He comes from a community that values trust, reputation, and shared responsibility. But branching out into bleaching chemicals and packaging is expensive, which causes more bills to come due, a lack of cash flow, and operational stress. Awanish is short ₹20 lakh and barely has one month left on his runway. He can secure funding through a rigid bank loan, a socially binding Samaj loan that is both flexible and obligatory, or a conditional venture capital note. Each of these options has pros and cons in terms of financial stability, community reputation, and strategic direction. The case highlights the challenges of resource allocation under pressure, the tension between profitable core products and risky expansions, and the invisible role of social capital in entrepreneurial decision-making.

As a result of GreenChem's story, we are considering how to maintain financial security and strategic concentration in the face of budget constraints. Despite an increase in revenue, the company's margins remain slim and its fixed expenditures have skyrocketed, leaving little room for mistakes. While the adhesives division remains steady and lucrative, efforts to expand into bleaching and packaging have stalled, forcing managers to reallocate resources. Given this conflict, one must wonder if Awanish is dealing with an issue with its structure, its strategy (the lack of scale in diversification), or its execution (the management of its working capital). The case asks students to consider the pros and cons of sticking with a tried-and-true company model vs taking a chance on potentially disastrous innovations that could pay off in the end but could spell disaster in the near future.

In addition, the budget shortage pushes non-financial decisions. Bank loans are credible but have severe obligations, community loans are flexible but connect the entrepreneur to reputational and relational risks, and venture capital offers growth potential but no control or dilution. These choices should be looked at not just in terms of numbers, but also in terms of social capital and community standards. Joining the Marwari Samaj gives you access to low-cost loans, but it also puts invisible constraints on you to be responsible and the danger of social punishment. What matters to Awanish is balancing survival with long-term positioning, innovation with caution, and communal trust with entrepreneurial independence.

Teaching Outline

(a) **Introduction and Situation Analysis (10 mins)**

The instructor can start with a brief introduction to the case, set the context, and ask some participants to summarise the key dilemmas.

(b) **Community and Entrepreneurship (15 mins)**

The instructor can now open the discussion on the floor with a focus on the Marwari community and an overview of what are the unique attributes of the community based on their history, their business ethics and social connections. This is required to help students analyse the critical factors that make up for the success of the Marwari community.

(c) **Expressive Writing Activity (30 + 20 mins)**

The Activity Shall Be Divided into 2 Parts

Part 1 (30 Mins): The students shall have to put themselves in the shoes of various actors, namely the protagonist, community actors and family. They are required to write a short write-up of 100 (max) words for each explaining what their thoughts would be if they were in the situation and how they view other parties in this triadic relationship.

Part 2 (20 Mins): Once the first part is completed, the discussion shall present the systemic factors at play. Considering all that, individual students need to effectively make a case for and against the debt sources Awanish is considering.

(d) **Closing Discussion (15 Mins)**

After the activity, the instructor should discuss and collate all views on debt sourcing and explain how and why Awanish should opt for a particular alternative in a certain case.

Discussion Questions

- What do the company's financials and ratios reveal about GreenChem's business model risk and operational efficiency? (Where is the business bleeding money, and why?—Is this a problem of margin, scale, or structure?)
- Should Awanish protect the profitable adhesives line or continue funding riskier verticals like bleaching and packaging? (What would you advise him to drop or double down on—and why?, Is the bigger risk slowing down and becoming irrelevant, or pushing forward and collapsing?)
- If you were Awanish, what financing path would you choose out of the three options given your need for liquidity and your community's expectations? (What future are you betting on by choosing this option?, What risks (not just financial) do you take on with each?)

CHAPTER 23

Climbing out of the Manhole: The Unrealized Promise of Microentrepreneurship in Tiruchirappalli's Urban Sanitation Ecosystem

K. V. Mukundhan and Sirish Kumar Gouda

Abstract India's sanitation ecosystem keeps its towns and cities clean and healthy. However, many workers in this ecosystem face hazardous working conditions, systemic exclusion, and intergenerational caste-based stigma. When given an opportunity to escape this drudgery, they often choose the certainty of their stable jobs over the uncertainty of entrepreneurship, despite promising government schemes. Entrepreneurship development schemes from National Safai Karamcharis Finance and Development Corporation (NSKFDC) and the World Bank-assisted Vazhndhu Kattuvom Project (VKP) offer several training programmes and low-interest, collateral-free funding. Notwithstanding these efforts, uptake on the ground is low as the sanitation workers find rules and paperwork complex, fear risk and failure, and carry internalized stigma. Furthermore, these schemes often reinforce occupational hierarchies by backing

K. V. Mukundhan (✉) • S. K. Gouda
Indian Institute of Management Tiruchirappalli, Sooriyur, India
e-mail: mukundhan@iimtrichy.ac.in; sirish@iimtrichy.ac.in

A. S. Galande et al. (eds.), *Context-inspired Entrepreneurship*, Sustainable Development Goals Series,
https://doi.org/10.1007/978-981-95-9831-1_23

sanitation-adjacent ventures, limiting genuine social mobility. Entrepreneurship may be the only viable escape hatch toward dignity and self-determination for these workers. To enable this, policy redesign must address deep-rooted structural and psychological barriers to effectively bridge the gap between opportunity, access, and effective use.

Keywords Sanitation workers • Entrepreneurship • Caste-based stigma • Risk aversion • Social mobility

SDG Linkage This chapter is aligned with SDG 8: Decent Work and Economic Growth by examining how entrepreneurship initiatives among Safai Karmacharis create pathways to dignified work and sustainable livelihoods beyond historically hazardous and stigmatized occupations. The chapter also aligns with SDG 1, through its focus on poverty alleviation via livelihood creation, and SDG 10, by addressing structural inequalities and social exclusion.

Introduction

> *By the end of the day, the stench of decomposing garbage sticks to my skin, and every cough reminds me how close I am to the hospital—or worse, my children's grief," says Stanley, clenching a frayed pair of gloves in his hands. "I'm always anxious about infection, but I feel stuck - there's nothing else I can do.*

Stanley has worked in garbage collection for over a decade. Despite the health hazards, social stigma, and utter lack of dignity, he continues in the job. Not because he wants to - but because leaving feels riskier than staying. He has heard of government schemes offering subsidized loans, free training, even startup grants for workers like him. Just last week, an Enterprise Community Professional from the World Bank-sponsored *Vazhndhu Kattuvom Project* (VKP), Rajalakshmi, visited his ward, encouraging sanitation workers to enrol in an entrepreneurship programme.

"*She said I can start something of my own. But who would trust me with money? What if I fail?*" Stanley wonders aloud. The registration deadline is in five days. He hasn't made up his mind.

Stanley's uncertainty is far from unique. Many sanitation workers value the stability of their current jobs - even when it comes at great personal cost.

Lata, a colleague who has worked in sanitation for fifteen years, puts it plainly: "*Leaving this job is not an option. My salary - which has grown from ₹190 to ₹505 per day - probably beats what I'd get elsewhere. I've faced a lot here, but at least I know my full payment will come at the end of each month. No other job can promise that.*"

Their words reveal a deeper dilemma shared by thousands across India's sanitation workforce: Is it wiser to endure a life-threatening but stable livelihood, or to risk everything for a future that promises dignity, independence, and upliftment, but offers little certainty?

On the other side of the equation is Rajalakshmi, tasked with bringing these policy dreams to life on the ground. She faces a different kind of resistance. When she suggested a startup loan to a potential candidate, he replied: "*If this business opportunity is really that great, why didn't you pursue it yourself?*" Even among those interested, support is labour-intensive. "If we help them apply for a loan, we have to do everything - start to finish," she says. "They won't take a single step without us. Even proactive ones show up for every tiny formality. It takes a lot of handholding."

Despite well-intentioned policy frameworks and funding support, the ground reality is far more complex. Cultural stigma, fear of failure, and deep economic insecurity keep many sanitation workers from pursuing a different path. As policymakers advocate for "dignified livelihoods," the big questions remain: How do we translate policy into real empowerment? What can field professionals like Rajalakshmi do to build trust and shift mindsets? And how should programmes be designed to bridge the gap between opportunity and action - for those who have always been last in line?

The Sanitation Ecosystem in India

Among India's blue-collared workforce, sanitation workers are among the most essential yet invisible citizens, responsible for maintaining urban hygiene and public health. They are often the first responders to the waste that cities generate, yet remain the least protected by policy, infrastructure, and social support. According to the World Health Organization, sanitation workers are individuals who are directly or indirectly involved in maintaining sanitation across the full sanitation chain - from the point waste is generated to its final disposal or treatment (World Health Organization, n.d.). Their responsibilities span across the following key components of the sanitation chain: containment of waste (e.g., septic tanks, sewers), emptying and removal of waste from those containers, transportation of waste to treatment facilities and treatment and disposal at designated locations like sewage treatment plants or landfills. Within this broad structure, sanitation workers fall into various occupational categories: de-sludging workers, public and community toilet cleaners, toilet cleaners in schools and offices, domestic toilet cleaners, railway toilet and track cleaners, informal waste pickers, solid waste management workers and drainage and treatment plant workers. Despite the diversity of roles, what unites these occupations is the invisibility, informality, and often intergenerational caste-based stigma associated with them. Some of them are even engaged in manual scavenging, which is banned in India as per the Prohibition of Employment as Manual Scavengers and their Rehabilitation Act, 2013. These workers frequently operate without proper protective gear, health insurance, or job security - making their work not only thankless but hazardous.

Socioeconomic Status and Challenges

Sanitation workers in India embody the defining features of marginalized communities -marked by systemic exclusion, generational poverty, and structural invisibility. Despite performing work essential to public health and urban functioning, they remain on the fringes of social and economic life. They face a range of interlocking deprivations. Most sanitation jobs expose workers to toxic waste, harmful gases, and physical strain - with minimal access to safety equipment or health care. They suffer generational poverty and early entry into labour often prevent upward mobility. Their work is historically tied to Dalit communities, particularly those at the bottom of the caste hierarchy. This leads to persistent discrimination and social ostracization.

Despite constitutional protections, gaps in enforcement, weak unionization, and lack of advocacy leave most workers without meaningful political voice or legal safeguards. As a group, sanitation workers have borne the harshest costs of their marginalization. An estimated 1.3 million sanitation workers exist across India, of whom 58,000 are engaged in manual scavenging, the most hazardous and dehumanizing form of sanitation work. Over half of sanitation workers are women, many of whom combine sanitation duties with unpaid domestic labour. They earn between ₹1000 and ₹2500 per month—well below minimum wage levels (Table 23.1). According to the National Commission for Safai Karamcharis

Table 23.1 Economic status of Sanitation workers

Floor Minimum Wage as per the Minimum Wages Act, 1948	*₹178 ($2.09) per day*
Minimum wages for sweeping and cleaning (unskilled workers)	₹522 ($6.12) to ₹778 ($9.12) per day[a]
Wages paid to sanitation workers in Tamil Nadu	₹1500 ($17.58) to ₹15,000 ($175.8) per month
Cost of living for one person in Tiruchirappalli, Tamil Nadu	About ₹26,800 ($315) per month

[a]As on 1/4/2024 based on classification of cities. For instance, Tiruchirappalli district falls under Area B for which the minimum wages are ₹651 per day

(NCSK), approximately 50 sanitation workers die every year due to illnesses or accidents related to unsafe working environments. Despite government schemes and judicial interventions, sanitation workers remain trapped in an intergenerational cycle of dangerous work, low pay, and social exclusion - conditions that starkly contrast with the dignity promised in India's constitutional ideals (HRW, 2014; Raghavendra & Kumar, 2022). Given this systemic context, how do sanitation workers navigate the trade-off between the certainty of hazardous work and the uncertainty of entrepreneurship?

The Policy Landscape Supporting Entrepreneurship among Sanitation Workers

Recognizing entrepreneurship as a vehicle for both economic upliftment and social transformation, the Government of India has taken several steps to institutionalize support. Successive Governments in India have initiated several policies and targeted programmes, improved access to affordable credit availability, and built support systems at the national and the state level (TNUSSP, 2020). In particular, the Ministry of Social Justice and Empowerment, Government of India set up the National Safai Karamcharis Finance and Development Corporation (NSKFDC) in 1997 to extend loan-based schemes up to ₹25 lakhs for the upliftment of sanitation workers. The schemes have cumulatively accounted for loan disbursals worth ₹7119 lakhs to 11,635 beneficiaries between April and October 2024 (NSKFDC, n.d.). In addition, the NSKFDC has also allied with the National Skill Development Corporation (NSDC) to conduct about 1119 skill-building workshops, and 13,407 skill development trainings to build competencies that will help them take up alternative employment. A list of schemes instituted by NSKFDC to foster entrepreneurship among sanitation workers are provided in Tables 23.2 and 23.3.

While NSKFDC operates at the national level, the state of Tamil Nadu runs its own World Bank-assisted initiative—Vazhndhu Kattuvom Project (VKP), as part of the larger Tamil Nadu Rural Transformation Project. VKP aims to empower rural communities, including sanitation workers, by promoting entrepreneurship, enhancing access to skills and finance,

Table 23.2 Loan Schemes for Entrepreneurship proposed by NSKFDC, adapted from https://nskfdc.nic.in/en/content/schemes-programmes/loan-scheme

S#	*Name of the scheme*	*Maximum limit for loan*	*Rate of interest for beneficiaries*	*Repayment period for loans*
1	Mahila Samridhi Yojana (MSY)	Up to ₹1 lakh	6% p.a.	3 years
2	Mahila Adhikarita Yogana (MAY)	Up to ₹2 lakh	7% p.a.	5 years
3	Micro credit finance (MCF)	Up to ₹1 lakh	7% p.a.	3 years
4	General term loan (GTL)	Up to ₹10 lakhs	8% p.a.	10 years
		Above ₹10 lakh & up to ₹15 lakh	9% p.a.	
		Up to ₹20 lakhs (for studying abroad)	7% p.a.(0.5% rebate for women)	
6	Scheme for "pay and use" community toilets	Up to ₹25 lakhs	8%	10 years
7	Sanitary marts scheme	Up to ₹15 lakhs	7% p.a.	10 years
8	Green business scheme	Up to ₹7.5 lakhs	6% p.a	10 years
		Above ₹7.5 lakhs & up to ₹15 lakhs	7% p.a.	
		Above ₹15 lakhs & up to ₹30 lakhs	8% p.a.	
		For procurement of sanitation related equipment/vehicles costing maximum up to ₹50 lakhs per unit.		

Table 23.3 NAMASTE Scheme, accessed from https://nskfdc.nic.in/en/content/home/namaste

Ministry of Social Justice & empowerment (MoSJE) has formulated a scheme "National Action for mechanized sanitation ecosystem" (NAMASTE). The process of extending the scheme to all the urban local bodies (ULBs) of the country has been initiated. Main features of the scheme to be implemented in all ULBs are:

- Identification: NAMASTE envisages identifying the sewer/septic tank workers (SSWs).
- Occupational training and distribution of PPE kits to SSWs.
- Assistance for safety devices to sanitation response units (SRUs).
- Extending health insurance scheme benefits to identified SSWs and their families under the Ayushman Bharat- Pradhan Mantri Jan Arogya Yojana (AB-PMJAY).
- Livelihood assistance: The action plan will promote mechanization and enterprise development by providing funding support and subsidy (capital + interest) to the sanitation workers, to procure sanitation related equipments.
- IEC campaign: Massive campaigns would be undertaken jointly by the ULBs & NSKFDC to spread awareness about the interventions of NAMASTE.

and creating sustainable and prosperous employment opportunities. Through a network of Enterprise Community Professionals (ECP), VKP supports individuals - particularly women - by offering matching grants, facilitating skill development and training, and guiding them through business ideation and registration. In addition to the above-mentioned programs, various NGOs and advocacy groups such as the Bill and Melinda Gates Foundation, the Sustainable Sanitation Alliance, and Tamil Nadu Urban Sanitation Support Programme, are actively involved in advancing the welfare of sanitation workers.

Barriers to Accessing Support

Despite the existence of encouraging programs, numerous sanitation workers encounter significant obstacles when considering entrepreneurial paths. Kamala, who works in sanitation, describes her challenging home situation that severely limits her options: "*My husband prohibits me from starting a business. He demands that I remain at home to care for our child. He expects to find me at home upon returning from work. Having recently completed rehabilitation for alcohol addiction, he might relapse if I'm not present at home after completing my sanitation duties.*"

The experience of some sanitation workers exemplifies why many policy initiatives fail to achieve their intended outcomes. While policymakers often assume that entrepreneurial ambitions are universal, Vijaya presents a contrasting perspective: "*Contentment matters more than greed. Despite our modest economic backgrounds, we enjoy relative stability in our lives. Our economic circumstances led us to this profession, which enables us to cover our basic needs and set aside small savings for unexpected situations. I find satisfaction in my work here. I cherish the time spent with colleagues, enjoy listening to music while working, and rarely feel exhausted.*"

Risk appetite differs dramatically across the sanitation worker community. Take Marimuthu, who questions his entrepreneurial capabilities despite access to favourable financing and skill development programs. His perspective is revealing: "*If I start a grocery business and my business failed, I would be crushed emotionally. I feel genuine concern watching vegetable sellers struggle as their products spoil unsold. Why would I deliberately place myself in such a precarious position? The reliability of my sanitation employment - with its consistent pay and early afternoon finish - offers security I value deeply. The entrepreneurial path is fundamentally misaligned with who I am.*" Marimuthu's cautious approach illustrates how deeply ingrained risk aversion shapes economic decision-making, causing people to prioritize the certainty of immediate, modest compensation over calculated risks that might yield greater financial rewards and long-term stability.

The small group of sanitation workers open to entrepreneurship often demonstrated a narrow vision of possibilities beyond their current work environment. Bharani, a young worker, exemplified this perspective when asked about his entrepreneurial ambitions: "*I could become a facilities contractor overseeing housekeeping and janitorial staff. It's a business I understand well.*"

Bharani's constrained aspirations are indicative of a broader structural dynamic within Indian social policy, wherein state-led support mechanisms for sanitation workers frequently reproduce rather than disrupt entrenched occupational hierarchies. Programmes such as those implemented by the NSKFDC are emblematic of this trend. While ostensibly designed to promote economic upliftment and entrepreneurship among historically marginalized communities, these schemes predominantly channel beneficiaries into sanitation-adjacent ventures. Typical loan offerings support the construction and management of community toilets, the establishment of sanitary supply outlets, or the procurement of sanitation-related equipment, such as vacuum trucks and cleaning tools. Though these initiatives may improve income stability and working conditions, they often do little to facilitate genuine occupational mobility. Instead, they risk entrenching workers further within the sanitation sector, reinforcing caste-based divisions of labour under the guise of economic development. This policy orientation reflects a latent institutional bias: the implicit assumption that sanitation workers are best suited for roles within the sanitation economy, thereby circumscribing their capacity to imagine - and access - alternative career trajectories. Consequently, what is framed as empowerment may, in practice, amount to a formalization of exclusion.

The Silver Lining: The Need for Social Mobility

Despite their differing views on starting a business and the relative income security of their current jobs, the sanitation workers shared a common underlying motivation: a desire for upward social mobility and a life marked by greater dignity. Their desire to break free from sanitation work was not solely economic; it was deeply entwined with questions of identity, societal status, and self-worth. Many workers spoke candidly about the stigma they faced - not just from the broader public, but often from within their own communities. This stigma, rooted in long-standing caste and class hierarchies, reinforced a sense of marginalization that extended beyond their physical labour to how they were seen and treated in everyday life. Many were acutely aware of how society perceived them, and these perceptions appeared to impact their sense of self-worth.

Take Pushpa, for instance, who expressed guilt about continuing in the sanitation profession: "*My relatives ask me why I continue doing this work and why I don't consider other jobs that offer more dignity. Since no one from my generation is in sanitation work, I find it hard to justify my career choice to those who matter to me.*"

Several workers noted that while their current jobs offered predictable wages, they offered little in terms of respect or recognition. This lack of social esteem weighed heavily, especially among younger workers and parents concerned about their children's futures. This discomfort is echoed by Surya, another worker, who shared that his school-going children feel uneasy talking about his profession with their schoolmates. He worries that his occupation may lead to their social ostracization. For these individuals, the possibility of running a business, however uncertain, carried symbolic value: it offers a break from generational patterns of occupational immobility and a step toward self-determination.

The yearning for respect comes through powerfully in Nakul's words—the youngest among the workers interviewed. "*It hurts when people call me a 'garbage collector' instead of using my name,"* he said. "*I argue with them and insist they call me by my first name.*"

In this context, limited expressions of interest in entrepreneurship - even if clouded by doubt, fear, or hesitation - can be read as subtle acts of resistance against the structural forces that have historically circumscribed their opportunities. These sentiments point to a critical gap in policy design: while programs often emphasize financial inputs and technical training, they may overlook the psychological and social dimensions of transformation - namely, the internalized barriers that must be addressed for true mobility to occur.

Entrepreneurship offers what is arguably the only viable escape hatch for sanitation workers seeking social mobility. The act of starting a micro-enterprise can redefine a worker's identity - from being seen as a "waste-picker" to being recognized as a service provider, small business owner, or social enterprise partner. Such a shift has the potential to dismantle caste-assigned roles and restore dignity through economic agency. Moreover, the entrepreneurial pathway embeds important forms of non-financial support: mentorship, peer networks, and access to market linkages that collectively help overcome bureaucratic hurdles and the social isolation many workers experience. When former sanitation workers evolve into local employers, cooperative founders, or franchise partners, they not only change their own material conditions - they also begin to alter the power dynamics within their communities. With economic independence comes legal recognition, political voice, and social respect.

In a context where both dignity and mobility have been systemically denied, entrepreneurship is not merely an aspirational tool; it becomes a structural necessity- perhaps the only intervention capable of transforming India's invisible sanitation workforce into visible creators of their own futures.

The Decision Situation

As a senior policymaker at the Ministry of Social Justice and Empowerment, you are responsible for redesigning the next phase of entrepreneurship support schemes for sanitation workers. Your team's research indicates that the low participation rate is not due to lack of access, but rather stems from deep-rooted social conditioning, intergenerational trauma, risk aversion, and the absence of role models.

You must now decide on the strategic direction for the programme's redesign. The decisions you make will shape not only the future of these workers but also the credibility of inclusive development policies at a national level.

You are presented with four possible paths, each with its own trade-offs:

1. The current schemes primarily offer subsidized loans, basic business training, and one-time grants. However, many sanitation workers remain hesitant to apply due to rigid loan conditions, bureaucratic complexity, and the perception that the schemes only support sanitation-related businesses. **Redesigning the scheme's core components**, may include more flexible financing models (e.g., smaller grants, milestone-based disbursements), simplified application processes and reduced paperwork, broader eligibility criteria that support non-sanitation ventures and tiered training programs based on readiness and experience. An indicative list of non-sanitation microentrepreneurship opportunities supported by the Vazhndhu Kattuvom Project in Tamil Nadu has been provided in Table 23.4.
2. Even when support schemes are accessible, participation remains low due to fear of failure, internalized stigma, and a lack of visible success stories. A behavioural approach would invest in long-term mindset shifts, focusing on awareness, aspiration-building, and social proof. Interventions can **focus on long-term community engagement strategies**, such as peer-led success stories, behavioural nudges that reframe entrepreneurship as achievable and respectable, youth education and aspiration building through schools and community centres, and community dialogues to challenge caste-based occupational norms. Table 23.5 presents testimonials from two successful NSKFDC beneficiaries.
3. Some in the ministry argue that extensive outreach and handholding might undermine agency or waste resources on unwilling participants. The third option is a **hands-off approach that allows individuals to opt in on their own**. This ensures sanitation workers self-select themselves into entrepreneurship when they are ready. This reduces dependency on programme staff, helps avoid over-engineering the system and focuses public spending on those who proactively engage. However, this approach unfairly penalizes those who lack confidence or exposure but have the potential. Further, this approach is consistent with the goal of breaking intergenerational cycles of occupational immobility.

Table 23.4 An indicative list of microentrepreneurship startups supported by the World Bank sponsored-VKP Project in Tamilnadu

S#	*Business idea*	*Minimum investment*	*Basic skill required*	*Expected profit margins*
1	Panchakavya (biofertilizer) production	₹2 lakhs	Follow production steps	Up to ₹100 per litre
2	Mushroom production and value addition	₹50,000	Follow production steps	Up to ₹25 per kg
3	Operating oil mill	₹3 lakhs	Operate oil presser machine	Up to ₹50 per litre
4	Egg distribution	₹1 lakh	Nil	Up to 10% per egg sold
5	Operating a flour mill	₹2 lakhs	Operate milling machine	Up to ₹17 per order
6	Panjamirtham (fruit/honey mix) production	₹1000/- for 5 kg	Operate packaging machinery	₹300 per kg
7	Pickle making	₹1000/- (for 6–8 kg)	Follow production steps	₹35–40 per kg
8	Snacks (Peanut bar, sesame bar)	₹50,000 to ₹3 lakhs	Operate caking machinery	₹40–50 per kg
9	Millets based health mix, flour)	₹50,000 to ₹1.5 lakhs	Operate packaging machinery	₹40–50 per kg
10	Energy drinks production (Badam mix, Ragi malt, beetroot malt)	₹50,000 to ₹1.5 lakhs	Operate packaging machinery	₹50–65 per kg

Note: The business ideas presented here require a workforce of 2–3 persons at best

4. **Establish a community-led co-creation process** through consultations and participatory design processes. This model involves working closely with sanitation worker collectives, NGOs, and local leaders to co-design entrepreneurship support tailored to community needs. It may result in highly localized or non-standardized programs but has potential for deeper ownership and legitimacy. This may also lead to slower implementation and unequal adoption across states. Table 23.6 presents details of two such community-led co-creation initiatives in the cities of Pune and Hyderabad.

Table 23.5 Success stories and Testimonials from Beneficiaries of NSKFDC Schemes, adapted from https://nskfdc.nic.in/en/content/home/success-story

Sl. no.	*Details of beneficiary*	
Ms. Tatiboyina Ankamma		
1	Name of beneficiary	Ms. Tatiboyina Ankamma
2	Husband's name	Sh. T. Mallikarjuna
3	Address	Dhantholi Nellore Andhra Pradesh
4	Occupation	Collecting domestic waste
5	Name of the agency	*Navajeevan organization, hand holding agency, NSKFDC. AP.*
6	Name of the scheme	Swachchhta Udhyami Yojana
7	State	Andhra Pradesh
"I am Tatiboyina Ankamma (32). My husband's name is T. Mallikarjuna (36). I hail from Dhantholi village in Nellore District, Andhra Pradesh State. I belong to Yanadi Community - one of the most backward communities listed within Schedule Tribes. Thanks to the NSKFDC, Canara Bank (Nellore municipality branch) and Navajeevan organization for making me the owner of a vehicle worth ₹8.48 lakhs. This loan was sanctioned to me under SUY scheme for the financial year 2021–2022. The vehicle was registered under my name with a registration number AP39 TZ5976. The Nellore municipal corporation has hired my vehicle for ten years with a 4% increase in hiring fees after every three years. As per our agreement, the municipal corporation bears the driver's salary, maintenance of the vehicle and diesel expenses and pays me ₹18,936/– per month in hiring charges. After settling the bank EMI of ₹8936, I realize a net income of ₹10,000/– per month. The loan was sanctioned for a period of seven years, with a six-month moratorium period."		
Sl. no.	*Details of beneficiary*	
Ms. Rakhi		
1	Name of beneficiary	Ms. Rakhi
2	Father's name	Sh. Balbir
3	Address with contact no.	Sangam Vihar, New Delhi
4	Name of course	Commercial motor driving training

(*continued*)

Table 23.5 (continued)

Sl. no.	*Details of beneficiary*	
5	Training institute	HIMCON
6	Name of the scheme	Skill development training programme
7	Date of completion	30.03.2015
8	State	Delhi

Ms. Rakhi, 22 years old, is a resident of Sangam Vihar, New Delhi. She was economically-dependent on her father who is a sanitation worker. Her father was not able to provide financial assistance for her higher studies. She came to know about the skill development training programme for Safai Karamcharis, scavengers and their dependants through an awareness camp organized by NSKFDC and enrolled for the course of 'commercial motor driving.'

Ms. Rakhi successfully completed the training programme of 7 months duration and also learnt self defense and soft skills as integral part of the training programme. After completion of training, she continuously practiced driving and after completion of one year, she was able to obtain a commercial driving license. Now, she is a successful commercial driver and is employed in cola cabs, drawing salary of Rs 17,000 per month. She feels proud of her achievement and wants to encourage her peers to come forward and avail the benefits of various schemes meant for them.

Discussion Questions

a) What structural barriers continue to marginalize sanitation workers in India, despite targeted policies and welfare programs?
b) How can meaningful livelihood diversification be achieved for sanitation workers and their families?
c) Given the multifaceted challenges of implementing entrepreneurship programs for marginalized communities, which policy strategy—or combination—offers the most promise? Why?

Recommended Supplementary Readings

In addition to assigning the case for the session, students can be requested to go through the following readings prior to the session:

- *Preparation Support*: WaterAid Report (2020) on the "Status of Manual Scavengers in India"—provides the social and economic context of sanitation workers from the lens of US sustainable devel-

Table 23.6 Examples of two community-led interventions

SWaCH cooperative in Pune
The Solid Waste Collection and Handling (SWaCH) cooperative in Pune is a self-managed, all-women initiative that collaborates with the Pune Municipal Corporation. Over 3000 women provide door-to-door waste collection services, segregating waste into recyclables and compostable materials. The cooperative has developed a significant composting operation, turning wet waste into valuable natural fertilizer.
SWaCH exemplifies a community-driven model where sanitation workers are not just service providers but also co-creators of the sanitation ecosystem. Their active participation in decision-making and operations showcases the power of co-creation in transforming sanitation services.
See https://www.unep.org/news-and-stories/story/empowering-waste-workers-cleaner-safer-city for more information on the SWaCH project.
Empowering slum residents as co-designers of WASH infrastructure in Hyderabad
In Hyderabad, the organization Paani has adopted a design thinking approach to involve slum residents as co-designers of water, sanitation, and hygiene (WASH) infrastructure. Through ethnographic research and community engagement, they identify local needs and co-create solutions, such as user-friendly public toilets and rainwater harvesting systems.
This initiative highlights the importance of involving communities in the design and implementation of sanitation solutions. By recognizing local knowledge and needs, the project ensures that the infrastructure is more effective and sustainable.
See https://jointactionforwater.org/empowering-slum-residents-as-co-designers-of-wash-infrastructure-in-hyderabad/ for more information on the WASH project.

opment goals. The report is accessible at https://www.wateraid.org/in/publications/status-of-manual-scavengers-in-india

- *Policy Context*: The guidelines for the "Self-Employment Scheme for Rehabilitation of Sanitation Workers," by the Ministry of Social Justice and Empowerment, Government of India - provides an account of the policy interventions envisaged to promote entrepreneurship among sanitation workers. The revised guidelines can be accessed from https://socialjustice.gov.in/writereaddata/UploadFile/Guidelines_SRMS_2021_22.pdf
- *Conceptual Foundation*:
  - Frediani, A. A. (2010). Sen's Capability Approach as a framework to the practice of development. *Development in practice*, *20*(2): 173–187—Extends Amartya Sen's capability framework for rethinking entrepreneurship development among sanitation workers by shifting focus from income alone to expanding substantive freedoms and opportunities.

- Lewis, A. C., & Crabbe, R. C. (2024). The entrepreneurship of marginalized groups and compatibility between the market and emancipation. *Journal of Business Venturing*, 39(4), 106,408—Offers two dimensions of market-compatible emancipatory entrepreneurship—ends market-emancipation compatibility and means market-emancipation compatibility, reflecting on the misalignments and constraints encountered by marginalized groups.

Positioning of the Case and Learning Outcomes

This case is ideal for Social Entrepreneurship courses, particularly in sessions examining entrepreneurship development among marginalized communities. It also serves courses in public policy that evaluate initiatives designed to foster economic mobility, social advancement, and entrepreneurial growth within economically disadvantaged populations.

This case helps students of entrepreneurship and public policy understand how context shapes entrepreneurial behaviour, explore the limits of policy in addressing social inequities, and analyse both behavioural and structural barriers to upward mobility. Specifically, readers will:

- Understand the needs, aspirations, and motivations of marginalized communities, with a particular focus on fostering social entrepreneurship and financial independence
- Design policy interventions that address the root causes of marginalization and remove impediments to business venturing
- Apply the capability approach to prioritize building capabilities over mere income generation, and evaluate policy initiatives across multiple dimensions of success

Acknowledgments We would like to take this opportunity to thank the Indian Institute of Human Settlements (IIHS) for giving us this opportunity to understand the complex problem of sanitation. While what we know might have been limited, we learned a lot by being part of this project, and it has been truly transformational. We personally would like to thank Ms. Suganthа Priscilla and Mr. Niladri Chakraborti for their constant support in this project. We would also like to acknowledge the efforts of our Research Associate, Ms. Shanmugha Priya who has been instrumental in collecting formal and informal data from all respondents, collating secondary data from various sources.

Competing Interests The authors have no conflicts of interest to declare that are relevant to the content of this chapter.

References

HRW. (2014). *Cleaning Human Waste: Manual Scavenging, Caste and Discrimination in India*. Retrieved April 4, 2025, from https://www.hrw.org/sites/default/files/reports/india0814_ForUpload_0.pdf

NSKFDC. (n.d.). Loan Schemes and Programmes. Retrieved April 4, 2025, from https://nskfdc.nic.in/en/content/schemes-programmes/loan-schemes

Raghavendra, R. H., & Kumar, R. A. (2022). Sanitation workers: A neglected community of Indian civilized society. *Contemporary Voice of Dalit, 18*, 87–98.

TNUSSP. (2020). *Compilation of Welfare Schemes for Sanitation Workers*. Retrieved April 4, 2025, from https://tnussp.co.in/wp-content/uploads/2021/05/Compilation-of-welfare-schemes-for-sanitation-workers_19-april-2021.pdf

World Health Organization. (n.d.). *Water Sanitation and Health: Sanitation workers*. Retrieved May 19, 2025, from https://www.who.int/teams/environment-climate-change-and-health/water-sanitation-and-health/sanitation-safety/sanitation-workers

CHAPTER 24

Breaking the Cycle—When Entrepreneurial Mindset Outpaces the Ecosystem

Apoorv Arora and Brindha Srinivasan

Abstract Mahalakshmi, a 14-year-old student from a working-class family near Mysuru, grew up watching her parents return home each night from the brick kilns, covered in red dust. When the Zero2Maker (Z2M) program introduced "learning by doing" in her school, she moved from silence and hesitation to building prototypes, presenting ideas, and mentoring younger students. Over six months, she and her peers formed IdeaShakti, a student-led group that sparked a small culture of making in their school.

The real challenge began after the structured program ended. With no clear pathways to mentorship, funding, or scale—and under constant pressure from exams and social expectations such as early marriage—Mahalakshmi and her peers had to decide whether, and how, to sustain the spark.

The case surfaces tensions between early entrepreneurial agency and systems designed for conformity. It explores how gender, family, and local context shape ambition, and provokes debate on whether igniting

A. Arora (✉) • B. Srinivasan
Indian Institute of Management Kozhikode, Kunnamangalam, Kerala, India
e-mail: apoorva16phd@iimk.ac.in; brindhas15phd@iimk.ac.in

A. S. Galande et al. (eds.), *Context-inspired Entrepreneurship*, Sustainable Development Goals Series,
https://doi.org/10.1007/978-981-95-9831-1_24

entrepreneurial intention in low-resource environments is always a gift, or whether it risks becoming a burden when structures to support it are absent.

Keywords Gendered constraints • Ecosystem gaps • Rural education • Peer mentoring • Entrepreneurial mindset

SDG Links This case contributes to SDG 8: Decent Work and Economic Growth by demonstrating how maker-led platforms such as Zero2Maker can enable enterprise creation. The chapter is also aligned with SDG 9, through its focus on innovation and hardware infrastructure, and relates to SDG 4 by enabling hands-on, experiential learning.

Introduction

Mahalakshmi was 14 when she walked into the Zero2Maker workshop in Mysuru. At home, her parents worked long hours at the brick kilns, returning each evening covered in red dust. Education felt like her only possible escape, yet even that path was fragile—college was rare in her community, money was tight, and the expectation of early marriage loomed.

Zero2Maker (Z2M) arrived at her school with a different proposition: two days of "learning by doing," followed by six months of small continuation activities. The program did not ask students what they already knew. It simply asked them to show up and try out problem-solving.

For Mahalakshmi and her classmates, the first days were full of silence. The tools and language were foreign, confidence was absent. But gradually, through trial and error, they began to see themselves differently. By the end of the workshop, they were building simple prototypes and testing ideas. More importantly, they had glimpsed a role they had never imagined for themselves: problem-solvers, not just exam-takers.

Over the next six months, Mahalakshmi and her peers continued experimenting in school, running sessions for juniors, and even naming their small group *IdeaShakti*. What began as hesitation turned into moments of leadership.

Yet when the program ended, the structure vanished. The laptops were taken back, mentors moved on, and the school slipped into its old rhythm. What remained was not equipment, but belief—the idea that they could do more than what was expected of them.

And that is where the tension lies. Sparking agency is one thing. Sustaining it inside systems built for conformity is another. The real case is not just what Mahalakshmi did in six months, but what happens when young people start to think entrepreneurially in places that offer them no next step. Does the spark die out? Or does it quietly begin to change the system itself?

Life of Mahalakshmi

The sun was setting over the brick kilns outside Mysuru when Mahalakshmi's parents returned home, their clothes coated in fine red dust. They both worked in a factory—long hours, little rest. Her father, weary from the day's labor, slumped onto the stone bench outside their one-room house. Her mother joined him, untucking her saree to shake off the dust.

Between sips of lukewarm tea, their conversation drifted to her aunt's upcoming wedding. Dowry. Jewelry. Sarees. The familiar weight of responsibilities. Then, inevitably, to their own daughter's future.

"We should start thinking," her father said, his voice heavy. "What will we give Mahalakshmi in the end? Should she work? Or should we get her married?" Her mother hesitated. Then, in a voice barely above a whisper, she said, "I don't want her to get married. Not now."

Mahalakshmi, standing behind the doorway curtain, held her breath.

Her mother continued, firmer this time, "What life will she have if she marries young, without an education? I want her to work or study further. We will see... there is still time to decide."

Mahalakshmi was 14, an eighth-standard student at the local government high school. Her home stood beside the factory line where her parents toiled—long hours, low pay, no safety nets. She had grown up watching them come home exhausted, their bodies coated in fine red dust, their voices heavy with worry. She had always done well in school, topping her class—not because anyone expected her to, but because she believed it was her way out. And yet, the path ahead was unclear. College felt distant, almost impossible. No one she knew had gone to college.

Mahalakshmi's situation echoed a wider pattern seen across underserved rural communities, where girls often internalize limitations shaped by their environment (see Appendix A).

Then came the Zero2Maker program. One morning, her teacher made an announcement: a new program—something about "learning by doing," making things with tools, and working in teams. Mahalakshmi wasn't sure what any of it meant. She hesitated, but her teacher insisted. "You have potential," she said. "You should give it a try."

Background to the Ecosystem

The Zero2Maker (Z2M) program is not just about tools or machines. At its heart, it is about possibility—about showing students from underserved communities that they can imagine, create, and lead.

Created by Rajesh Nair at the Massachusetts Institute of Technology, an engineer and entrepreneur who grew up in a small village himself, the program is built on a simple but powerful idea: anyone can build self-efficacy, and create solutions to problems, regardless of their background, if they are given the right environment to grow.

In many schools—especially in rural or low-income areas—learning often feels distant from real life. Classrooms are about memorizing, not about building or questioning.

Z2M steps into this gap. It is designed as a pre-entrepreneurship program, giving students their first real taste of what it means to solve problems, to work in teams, and to bring an idea to life. The program doesn't ask students about their skills in design or technology—it starts with the assumption that most aren't. Instead, it asks just one thing: show up, and try.

Phase One: The Two-Day Workshop

Over the course of two intense days, students work in teams to tinker, build, and experiment. They are introduced to basic design and prototyping—using tools like 3D printers and simple electronics—not to become engineers overnight, but to see that they can learn by doing and start to break the fear of learning.

The program guides them through brainstorming ideas, making small models of products, testing them, and presenting them. Along the way, they begin to see that their thoughts matter, they can make decisions, their creativity has value, and they have potential that the schools do not highlight.

Phase Two: The Six-Month Immersion

After the two-day workshop, the program doesn't end. Over the next six months, students return to school and continue small activities with the supplied lab kit and computers, guided by Zero2Maker mentors. These follow-ups are not just exercises; they keep the momentum alive. Soon, students themselves step into mentoring roles—first helping peers in their own school, then reaching students in nearby schools. In doing so, they create a ripple effect of confidence, curiosity, and creativity that spreads far beyond the initial group.

The Shift in Mindset.

What makes Z2M different is not just the hands-on work, but the change in mindset.

For students from communities where futures often feel fixed—where starting a business, building a product, or even speaking in a group seems impossible—this experience is a break in the pattern. It shows them they can take initiative, solve problems, and push beyond what they thought was possible.

Z2M doesn't claim to turn every student into an entrepreneur. What it does is open a door many never knew was there. It gives them a first experience of ownership, agency, and vision.

Z2M Execution

Phase 1 - Day 1: Alienation and Pressure

When Mahalakshmi entered the room, it felt nothing like school. Bright lights. Long tables. Students from six government schools—mostly boys. Every one of them came from places like hers, where computers were rare and machines lived only in textbooks. Almost none had worked with a laptop before, but no one wanted to admit it.

Rajesh didn't hand out instructions. He put a problem on the table: *pets are often left alone at home—how do you keep them engaged?* It wasn't about making a specific toy or following steps. It was about thinking: how does an animal behave when left alone? What happens inside a house when no one is around? What could you build using whatever materials were at hand?

Around the room, students bent over their tables, some grabbing wires, others poking at plastic pieces—acting like they knew what they were doing.

Mahalakshmi froze. She didn't touch anything. A laptop sat in front of her team. She had never switched one on.

Her table was crowded with wires and small devices. She folded her hands behind her back. No one stopped her. No one asked her either. "Pass me the screwdriver?" a boy muttered, eyes still on the table. She handed it over. That was all she did in the first hour.

Mentors moved quickly between teams, talking in English: "design thinking," "prototype," "Arduino." Words that bounced past her, unfamiliar, ungrasped. She nodded anyway, afraid someone might notice her silence.

By lunch, her shoulders ached from standing still. At the washbasin, she told her friends, "This is useless. We should've just stayed in school. At least there, we understand." They nodded. Quietly. No one dared to say, *I don't get it either.* Everyone was bluffing. In a room full of first-timers, confusion was shared, but silence was the rule. For Mahalakshmi, silence also meant invisibility.

Back in the afternoon, the gap between teams began to show. Some had circuits connected, motors humming, ideas taking shape. Her team had nothing. Wires still in the box. The teacher who had accompanied them sat with their group. In a low voice he said, "Everyone else has started. We'll be the only ones left behind."

Mahalakshmi didn't answer. She didn't move. But she didn't walk away either.

That night at home, rolling out rotis beside her mother, she finally spoke. "I don't think this is for me, Amma. It's all machines. I don't know anything." Her mother kept kneading the dough, eyes fixed on her work. No agreement. No comfort. Just: "Eat your dinner." The words landed heavy in Mahalakshmi's chest. Not rejection. Not reassurance. Just silence.

Phase 1 - Day 2: The Spark

She almost didn't return.

That morning, tying her hair in front of the cracked mirror, she rehearsed excuses: headache, stomach pain, anything. None of them sounded convincing. So she packed her bag and went.

The second day felt louder. Faster. Some teams had started testing their models. Lights blinked. Motors buzzed under tables. A few already had rough toys in motion. Her team? Still nothing. Still talking. The teacher folded her arms and warned, "We can't be the only ones stuck. Do something." But no one knew what "something" was. They sketched half-hearted ideas just to look busy.

Then Rajesh pulled up a chair. He didn't give instructions. He didn't hand them a design. He just asked, "What do you think the problem is?" Mahalakshmi's words slipped out before she could stop them: "We don't know what problem we're solving. We're just copying everyone else."

He nodded. "Exactly. So what problem do you want to solve?"

For a moment, silence. Then someone laughed about his dog chewing up slippers. Another said pets get bored when left alone. Slowly, the team began talking like the problem was theirs. Ideas started to take shape. Mahalakshmi's voice, softer this time: "What if it moves when the pet touches it? Like… it starts driving around?" The group went quiet. Then nodded. That could work.

They began building — awkwardly, carefully. None of them had handled sensors or motors before, but together they wired a small car body, attached a sensor, and connected a DC motor. When it finally moved on its own, triggered by touch, the table erupted. It was crude, but it worked.

Teachers leaned over, watching. Some of them were new to the tools too, and students found themselves explaining how wires linked to sensors, how a tiny circuit made the motor spin. The shift was clear: from waiting to be taught, to teaching what they had just learned.

Later that day, as they prepared to present, one of the boys turned to her. "You explain it," he said. "Your English is better. And it was your idea."

She froze, then stepped forward. Her voice shook, but the words carried: the problem they had chosen, the toy they had built, how it worked. How a pet, touching it, would set it in motion. When she finished, there was a pause — not the silence of being ignored, but the silence of a room listening. For the first time, she wasn't invisible.

A Quiet Realization

She didn't become the loudest voice in the room. But something had shifted. She was no longer just handing over tools from the sidelines. She was thinking, questioning, shaping ideas. The tools that had once felt intimidating no longer seemed out of reach.

At the end of the workshop, when her team presented, Mahalakshmi spoke. Her voice was unsteady, her hands gripped the table, but she kept going. She explained the problem, the design, and how they had worked through it. For a moment the room was silent, then the applause came.

A mentor pulled her aside before she left. "Being a Maker isn't just about building products," he said. "It's about seeing a problem clearly and to create a solution." The words stayed with her. Back in school, the change showed. She began speaking up in class, sharing her ideas, collaborating with her peers. Classmates started approaching her for help. The shift was quiet, but visible.

Phase 2 - Six Months of Continuation: From Participants to Possibility Catalysts

The two-day workshop ended, but the journey didn't. As part of the Zero2Maker follow-up, selected students were asked to lead small activities in their schools. It wasn't formal training—just a way to keep the spark alive. But for Mahalakshmi and her teammates, it became much more.

Their teacher gave them a corner in the library on Saturdays. They had access to the kit from the program—laptops, sensors, small motors, toy fans, and other attachments—along with everyday items like cardboard, chart paper, and glue. Each week they picked a theme: "How to make water flow without touching the tap?" "How to build a small game using circuits?" Juniors came in—some curious, some shy, some just skipping class. Slowly, interest grew. Students began suggesting their own problems: "Can we stop the fan when the teacher leaves?" "Can we design a reminder for lunchboxes?"

Mahalakshmi, once silent in a room full of strangers, now explained sensors, led team huddles, and assigned roles. Her teammates had shifted too—more confident, more willing to experiment. They made mistakes, laughed, tried again. Teaching reinforced what they had learned and stretched it further. For Mahalakshmi, it was the first time school felt bigger than textbooks.

As months passed, the sessions grew into something like a student-led maker culture. With their teacher's guidance, they kept a logbook, sketched small budgets, fixed problems with tape and wire, and even started a "Problem Wall" where anyone could post issues to solve. The name *IdeaShakti* stuck—creativity with strength.

By the end of six months, Mahalakshmi's voice carried more certainty. Her hands moved freely as she explained ideas. Peers pointed to her as "the one who knows how to make things." The follow-up didn't give her a certificate, but it gave her something deeper: a rehearsal of leadership, ownership, and the possibility of thinking like a problem-solver.

Present Day Dilemma: From Spark to Step?

It had been a year since the Z2M experience, and Mahalakshmi was now in 10th standard. The group still met occasionally—sometimes at lunch, sometimes by the tea stall after school. Ideas still came easily: a sensor to alert farmers when cattle strayed, a better system for the school's drinking water taps. Talking was never the problem. The harder question was always: *what next?*

Could they actually do more with their ideas? Build something to sell? Take it beyond school?

The obstacles were everywhere—no funding, no mentors, no workspace, and no clear program in their town to support school-level entrepreneurs. Their teacher encouraged them but had no connections. Parents approved of the activity but often asked, "How will this help with exams?" One by one, some teammates dropped out—too much pressure, too little time.

Mahalakshmi stayed. Something in her had shifted too deeply. She didn't just want to pass exams. She wanted to build. Create. Maybe even start something of her own.

One afternoon, sitting on the school steps eating vada pav, she and two friends discussed rebuilding their old prototype—the pet-interaction toy. They knew how it worked. They could improve it. One boy's uncle owned a mobile repair shop; maybe he could help with parts. "But then what?" someone asked. "Make one more? Make ten? Sell it where?" No one had an answer.

That's when the dilemma became clear. They had the spark, but no path.

The real question wasn't which prototype to pursue. It was how to keep moving when the scaffolding disappears. They had belief, but the system around them didn't. Without mentors, funds, or a place to build, would this spirit survive?

Discussion Questions

1. When early agency is sparked in young people, what enables it to grow, and what shuts it down?
2. Can entrepreneurial mindsets be nurtured inside systems that are not entrepreneurial? What is the cost of constantly "believing" without external proof or support?

3. What is the risk of awakening entrepreneurial intention in a context with no next steps? Does agency without structure sustain, or does it fade?
4. How would you design an ecosystem that lets *IdeaShakti* grow without turning it into just another school program?
5. In low-resource settings, what actually makes up a support structure—funding, mentorship, validation, policy? How do we build scaffolding for those who aren't yet founders but are beginning to think like one?

Learning Objectives

1. Examine the role of family, gender, and local expectations in shaping and containing youth ambition.
2. Trace how Mahalakshmi's confidence shifted during the two-day Z2M workshop—from silence on Day 1 to speaking during the team presentation on Day 2.
3. Identify the specific barriers she and her peers faced after the spark: exam pressure, lack of mentors, no funds, no workspace, and family expectations.
4. Examine how gender shaped her experience, both in her family's conversations about marriage and in her initial hesitation in a male-dominated workshop setting.
5. Analyze how the six-month continuation activities turned participants into peer mentors, creating a ripple effect inside their school and nearby schools.
6. Discuss the open dilemma at the "present day" stage: how a group with ideas and energy, but no ecosystem, can (or cannot) sustain entrepreneurial spirit.

Readings

- Kuratko, D. F., Fisher, G., & Audretsch, D. B. (2020). Unraveling the entrepreneurial mindset. Small Business Economics, 57(4), 1681–1691. https://doi.org/10.1007/s11187-020-00372-6
- Teaching entrepreneurship in government schools (IIMA CASE). https://idronline.org/article/education/teaching-entrepreneurship-in-government-schools-idr/
- Stam, E., & Van De Ven, A. (2019). Entrepreneurial ecosystem elements. Small Business Economics, 56(2), 809–832. https://doi.org/10.1007/s11187-019-00270-6

- Porfirio, J., Felício, A., Carrilho, T., & Jardim, J. (2023). Promoting entrepreneurial intentions from adolescence: The influence of entrepreneurial culture and education. Journal of Business Research. https://doi.org/10.1016/j.jbusres.2022.113521
- Schoon, I., & Duckworth, K. (2012). Who becomes an entrepreneur? Early life experiences as predictors of entrepreneurship. Developmental Psychology, 48(6), 1719–1726. https://doi.org/10.1037/a0029168

Acknowledgements We are grateful to the reviewers for their constructive feedback. We extend our special thanks to Professor Sreevas Sahasranamam for his guidance in shaping the framing of this case and for encouraging us to refine it further. We also acknowledge Rajesh Nair for his valuable insights into the Zero2Maker program, which enabled us to capture its spirit more accurately. Also, ChatGPT was used to enhance sentence flow and clarity where needed.

Competing Interests The authors have no conflicts of interest to declare that are relevant to the content of this chapter.

Supplementary Material

Guidance for Educators on Using this Case for a 60–90 Minutes Class Discussion

Synopsis

This case follows Mahalakshmi, a 14-year-old from a working-class family near Mysuru, as she encounters the Zero2Maker (Z2M) program—a hands-on pre-entrepreneurship initiative in underserved schools. In her first exposure to tools, laptops, and problem-solving, she moves from hesitation to proposing ideas and presenting her team's prototype: a responsive pet-interaction toy.

Mahalakshmi and her friends started IdeaShakti, a student-led group that brought the maker spirit to their school, over the course of six months. With continued access to the Z2M kit (laptops, sensors, small motors, toy fans) and help from their teachers, they held sessions for younger students, shared what they had learned, and started to see themselves as problem-solvers instead of just test-takers. For Mahalakshmi, this was a change in her identity: she went from being invisible to being a leader.

When the structured phase was over, it was up to the students and teachers to take care of things. The kit stayed at school, and the student-mentors kept the sessions going. What stayed and grew was faith—early business plans. The case does not inquire if Z2M "functioned"; it demonstrates that it did. The more important question is what happens after the spark: how can early agency survive and grow in situations where there aren't many options, time, or outside help?

This case does not assess the success or failure of Zero2Maker. The program brought problem-solving, teamwork, and prototyping to schools where these kinds of activities were not common. Students like Mahalakshmi kept the momentum going by helping their classmates and making a small culture of making at their school.

There is tension outside of the program. Marks are still important to schools. Parents use tests or early marriage to check on their children's safety. Teenagers are not often seen as innovators in local ecosystems. There aren't many ways to get funding, mentorship, and growth. The question isn't if Z2M worked, but what happens after the spark.

This tension meant more to Mahalakshmi than to anyone else. In the workshop, being a girl among boys and using new tools made her feel invisible. At home, it was because she was expected to get married young. Every little thing she did, like asking a question, sharing an idea, or mentoring younger people, gave her more than just confidence. It was a quiet break in a script that had already been written for her.

Teaching Plan

Theme: Entrepreneurial Mindset Under Constraint.

Phase 1: Entering Mahalakshmi's World (10–15 mins)

Prompt: *"You are Mahalakshmi. A year has passed since Z2M. IdeaShakti still meets, but the big question lingers: 'Should we try again?' How do you feel? What do you say?"*

Goal: Anchor discussion in her lived reality—doubt, pressure, pride, possibility.

Phase 2: Naming the Dilemma (20–25 mins)

Task: In small groups, define Mahalakshmi's dilemma.

What is really at stake?

What are the risks of continuing vs. stopping?

Groups share their articulation of the dilemma.

Phase 3: Ecosystem Diagnosis (20 mins)
Discussion:
What support does Mahalakshmi already have (teacher, peers, juniors)?
What is missing (mentorship, funding, recognition)?
What *minimal scaffolding* could keep IdeaShakti alive inside her school context?

Phase 4: From Spark to Continuity (15–20 mins)
Discussion:
What counts as "success" here—products, mentoring, or simply a mindset shift?
What happens when belief grows but systems don't keep pace?
What role should schools and communities play after the spark?

Web Resources

- **encube.co**
- **rajeshnair.me**

CHAPTER 25

Balancing Tradition and Innovation: The Evolution of Krishna Novelty Stores in Liberalizing India

Kiran Kumar

Abstract This case study traces the evolution of a small-scale enterprise in Kerala, situating its journey within the socio-political and economic contexts of the region and post-colonial India. The Chalakkudy Kamath family, part of the Gauda Saraswat Brahmin (GSB) trading community from Mattanchery in Cochin, began as small-scale traders supplying office and stationery items to colonial and Indian firms. Leveraging their prior connections with the Scottish firms, they diversified into new sectors and product lines. By the late 1980s, R. Nithyananda Kamath, third-generation entrepreneur of Krishna Novelty Stores, was at a critical inflection point as India transitioned towards liberalization, privatization, and globalization of the economy. This case explores the strategic dilemmas a small-scale family business faces in adapting to macro-environment policy changes and the role of partnerships in navigating change. This case is well-suited

K. Kumar (✉)
Jindal Global Business School, O P Jindal Global University,
Sonipat, Delhi-NCR, India
e-mail: kiran.kumar@jgu.edu.in

A. S. Galande et al. (eds.), *Context-inspired Entrepreneurship*, Sustainable Development Goals Series,
https://doi.org/10.1007/978-981-95-9831-1_25

for classroom discussion on family business, small business strategy, and entrepreneurial ecosystem.

Keywords SMEs • Family business • Franchise entrepreneurship • Globalization • Liberalization • Gauda Saraswat Brahmins • Kerala

SDG Links This chapter is aligned with SDG 8: Decent Work and Economic Growth by examining the long-term business journey of Krishna Novelty Stores and the Kamath family to understand how enduring family enterprises contribute to employment and economic growth. The chapter also relates to SDG 9, through its focus on how the firm adapts to industry change and innovation over time.

Introduction

In 1989, Nithyanand Kamath, a third-generation entrepreneur from Kerala, stood at a critical juncture in relation to the future of his family business firm, Krishna Novelty Stores (KNS). As India embraced economic liberalization, opening its markets to global capital, Kamath was confronted with a pivotal decision: whether to scale up KNS's traditional business of stationery and office supplies or embrace a new business model in response to the technological disruptions and increasing competition from the multinational corporations (MNCs). With a legacy rooted in trust, quality, and family control, Kamath had to balance the family's traditional business ethos and the pressing need to innovate in a rapidly changing market. As Nityananda Kamath mentions, 'This multigenerational continuity rooted in its ability to balance between tradition and innovation is the success and legacy of our firm'.[1] Should KNS double down on its established operations or venture into franchise entrepreneurship and explore uncharted models like factory outlets? This case study investigates Kamath's strategic navigation of these dilemmas, offering insights into how Small and Medium Enterprises (SMEs) can adapt and thrive in a globalized economy.

[1] The interview with Nityananda Kamath was conducted on May 4th, 2024.

The Inception of a Business Journey-Historical Background

The business family of Kamath, 'Chalakkudy Kamath', belongs to a traditional trading and banking community of Gauda Saraswat Brahmins spread across the south-west and western coasts. The Gauda Saraswat Brahmins, followers of Kashi Matha migrated from the Portuguese Goa in the late sixteenth century due to a combination of factors such as forceful conversion to Christianity and trading opportunities (Xavier, 2024). The ancestral house of the Kamath's family was in Chalakkudy, a town in the central district of Kerala, Thrissur. The family name 'Chalakkudy Kamath' was given by the locals in the historical port town of Mattanchery in Cochin as they migrated from the nearby town of Chalakkudy where they were the landlords. Recognizing the opportunities in trade and distribution, Kamath's ancestors migrated to the town of Cochin in the first half of the twentieth century as the region was flourishing in the overseas trade during the British period. The global changes in the first half of the twentieth century produced business advantages for the family business firm of KNS. The business family began its entrepreneurial journey with the launch of a moving theater in the town of Mattanchery, known as Krishna theater, in the early twentieth century. Though Krishna theater survived only for a few years, it was during the inter-war period, KNS prospered due to the changes in the colonial policies.

During the interwar period, the colonial state shifted its stance toward trade and industrialization, increasingly favoring the latter. This is reflected in the British policy of import-substituting industrialization in the 1920s, which sought to promote domestic industries while retaining access to cheap machinery, capital, and skilled labor (Roy, 2017). In 1920, the British established a Stores Purchase Committee in 1920 recommending that the colonial government procure goods from Indian sources (Roy, 2018). This policy, rooted in India's contributions towards British during the First World War, benefited Indian industrialists and traders.

Realizing this opportunity, first generation of the business family under the leadership of G Krishna Kamath, grandfather of the Nityananda Kamath, launched a small-scale shop of Krishna Novelty Stores (KNS) in 1935 in Mattanchery in Cochin. Due to the community's influential role as 'portfolio capitalists' (Subrahmanyam & Bayly, 1988), British rulers entrusted the family of Kamath for the wholesale supply of office items such as paper, pins, files, and carbon papers. Sensing the opportunities created by South India's industrialization and expanding bureaucracy, Rajagopala Kamath, son of Krishna Kamath, entered the hardware and furniture distribution business, expanding its unit to Coimbatore to supply leading companies and offices in the princely state of Cochin. One such leading company was Fertilizers and Chemicals Travancore Limited (FACT), a private company started in 1943 by Tamil Brahmins, Seshasayee Brothers, from Tiruchirappalli in Tamil Nadu. Nithyananda Kamath was emotionally moved when he spoke to me about the fact that the furnitures they distributed to the FACT still exist there with the family firm's name KNS still written on it. Kamath continued with their business journey in Kerala for some time until the storm of the first communist government in post-independent Kerala hit their entrepreneurial prospects which focused on social development rather than economic development (Roy & Raman, 2024).

Business Fortunes in the Post-Independent Kerala

The KNS, in the context of the post-independent period shifted their base to Coimbatore in the state of Tamil Nadu where they formed a small production unit of furniture with its head office at Cochin. In the 1970s, Rajagopala Kamath, father of Nityananda Kamath, expanded into textiles by partnering with Madura Coats,[2] supplying chemicals and dyes to its Koratty factory in Kerala for thread manufacturing. One of the peculiar features of the family business of KNS is that they pursued a strategic line of business plan by continuously diversifying and never sticking to a single product or service. In addition, they did not take up each business they were offered, as they rejected the opportunity to distribute tea products to the Scotland company Lipton. As the present managing director of KNS, Nityananda Kamath says, 'Our family business ethos, such as quality, service and trust is more important to us than unethical profits and expansion. We rely largely on future driven businesses'.[3] This can be seen from their persistent ability to adapt and take advantage of the emerging socio-economic conditions.

[2] Madhura Coats private limited is part of the coat's companies founded in the late eighteenth century in Scotland and later in 1986 it was merged with British company Vantona Viyella turning Coats into Coats Viyella.

[3] The interview with Nityananda Kamath was conducted on May 3rd, 2024.

The 1980s marked a transformative decade, introducing policy shifts that encouraged private investment, both domestic and foreign, in industry and trade. While the formal liberalization of the economy occurred in the 1990s amid a foreign exchange crisis, the groundwork was laid during the tenures of Indira and Rajiv Gandhi in 1980s who promoted private investment as a path to economic growth (Tripathi & Jumani, 2013). The economic changes initiated by Indian National Congress (INC) under the leadership of Rajiv Gandhi is argued as 'techno-managerial reforms' (Sharma, 2022) which included restriction of industrial controls and gradual import liberalization through de-regulation especially in the textile industry (Mukherji, 2014). This privatization and globalization of the Indian economy required new skill sets, particularly in education and human capital, to manage and modernize enterprises (Masrani et al., 2021). Recognizing the importance of education, third-generation business leader Radhakrishna Kamath, brother and business partner of Nityananda Kamath, completed a one-year program in All-India Business Management in addition to earning a degree in commerce. This enabled him and brother, Nityananda Kamath, to modernize and professionalize their business within Kerala and beyond.

New Economic Policy and Economic Liberalization

With the liberalization of the economy, new industries emerged producing goods and services, of which Information Technology (IT) was the prominent one. The new scenario led to decreasing demand for the stationery and office supplies market, KNS's original domain. At the same time, the economic policy of dismantling of license raj and easing of restrictions in the foreign investment equipped them with the new business models. One of the dominant business models in the aftermath of economic reforms of globalization and de-regulation was the franchise business models (Bal, 2023). The pro-business rather than the pro-market nature of economic reforms in India resulted in a bias towards economic sectors which involves state for licenses, permits and contracts, and software entrepreneurship in India (Kohli, 2006; Naseemullah, 2020). The economic globalization and entry of multinational corporations resulted in immsense opportunities for micro and small scale businesses where social networks can act as a substitute for 'lack of prior knowledge in franchise opportunity identification' (Brookes et al., 2016). Moreover, urbanization and growth of the Indian economy especially from the post-2000's has resulted in immense opportunities for both franchisors and franchisees equipping them with an entrepreneurial opportunity with reduced risk. The most common franchise outlets in the urban cities in India are in the sectors of education and training, food and beverages and apparels. The Kamath's with their prior relationship with the MNC Coats Viyella adopted the business model of franchise entrepreneurship in apparels and later in gold.

The business model of franchise entrepreneurship was the one chosen by the Kamaths as they had prior relationship with the MNCs like Coats Viyella who were in fact looking to penetrate into India's growing consumer market, particularly in Kerala, where rising incomes due to Gulf migration fueled consumerism. KNS operates within India's vibrant small and medium enterprise (SME) sector, which, as of 2025, includes approximately 5.93 crore registered MSMEs employing over 25 crore people, according to the Union Government's 2025–2026 budget data.[4] The stationery and office supplies market, KNS's original domain, faced disruption in the 1990s due to technological advancements, such as software solutions reducing demand for traditional products. Simultaneously, India's economic liberalization attracted MNCs like Coats Viyella, which sought local partners to penetrate India's growing consumer market, particularly in Kerala, where rising disposable incomes and Gulf migration fuelled consumerism.

Meanwhile, Kerala's retail sector was undergoing change, as urban consumers increasingly embraced branded apparel in emerging 'cosmopolitan' spaces such as shopping malls (Mannathukkaren, 2023). Realizing the shift in consumer demands, KNS responded with a strategic shift to franchise entrepreneurship, leveraging global brands while retaining family control over operations. As a result, Kamath brothers decided to incorporate their wives and nephews into various franchise firms.

Contemporary Challenges and Decision-Making Dilemmas

In the late 1980's, Nityananda Kamath faced a critical dilemma: how to ensure KNS's survival in a globalized economy without compromising their business values centered around family. The stationery business risked obsolescence due to technological advancements, and MNCs posed

[4] https://pib.gov.in/PressReleasePage.aspx?PRID=2099687#:~:text=With%205.93%20crore%20registered%20MSMEsas%20a%20global%20manufacturing%20hub

fierce competition. Kamath's conservative approach, emphasizing hands-on control, clashed with the professionalization demanded by a global market. Below are the expanded options he considered, each with distinct opportunities, financial constraints, risks, and implications for KNS's legacy.

Option 1: Scaling up the Stationery Business

Kamath could scale KNS's stationery and office supplies operations, leveraging its established reputation in Kerala. This involved expanding distribution networks, investing in larger inventories, and targeting new markets like educational institutions and government offices. Scaling could solidify KNS's position in a familiar sector, capitalizing on existing client relationships.

However, this option faced significant challenges. The rise of software solutions, such as word processors and digital filing systems, threatened to reduce the demand for traditional stationery items. Competition from larger domestic and international players could erode profit margins, requiring substantial investments in marketing and infrastructure. Scaling could also have strained family resources, potentially forcing KNS to hire external managers, diluting the family's hands-on control. Kamath had to weigh whether investing heavily in a declining market was sustainable or if it risked overextending KNS's capabilities.

Option 2: Embracing Franchise Entrepreneurship

Franchise entrepreneurship offered a lower-risk path with reduced uncertainity, leveraging KNS's relationship with Coats Viyella. By becoming a franchisee for brands like Van Heusen, introduced in India in 1990 for the first time, KNS could tap Kerala's growing consumer market, driven by Gulf migration and rising disposable incomes. Franchising provided brand recognition, operational support, and marketing from the franchisor, allowing KNS to maintain family oversight while entering the lucrative apparel retail sector.

The risks included dependency on the franchisor's strategy and potential conflicts over operational control. Franchising required aligning with external partners, which could challenge KNS's tradition of autonomy. Additionally, the initial investment for showrooms in prime locations like Mahatma Gandhi Road in Ernakulam was significant, and failure to attract consumers could lead to financial losses. Kamath had to assess whether franchising aligned with KNS's ethos of quality and trust ensured long-term profitability.

Option 3: Innovating with a Factory Outlet Model

Inspired by his travels to the USA, Kamath considered launching India's first factory outlet in 1999. This model offered discounted branded products, appealing to cost-conscious consumers while leveraging KNS's franchise relationships with brands like Pepe Jeans and Reebok. A factory outlet could differentiate KNS in a competitive market, attracting a broader customer base and establishing a new retail trend in India. But this option was high-risk due to its novelty as this was untested in India requiring significant investment in real estate, inventory, and marketing. Convincing Coats Viyella to approve the model was another hurdle, as it deviated from standard franchising. Failure could damage KNS's reputation and finances. Kamath had to evaluate whether the potential to pioneer a new retail model outweighed the risks and aligned with KNS's future-oriented vision.

Option 4: Diversifying into Technology-Driven Solutions

Recognizing the technological shifts disrupting the stationery market, Kamath considered diversifying into technology-driven solutions, such as software distribution or office automation tools. KNS could partner with emerging IT firms to distribute software for document management or collaborate with hardware providers to supply office equipment like printers and computers. This move could position KNS as a modern player in the office solutions market, addressing the declining demand for traditional stationery.

However, this option required significant re-skilling and investment in technical expertise, areas where KNS lacked experience. The technology sector was highly competitive, with established players dominating the market. Entering this space could stretch KNS's resources and require hiring external professionals, challenging the family's hands-on approach. Kamath had to determine if KNS could build the necessary capabilities to compete in a tech- driven market without compromising its core values.

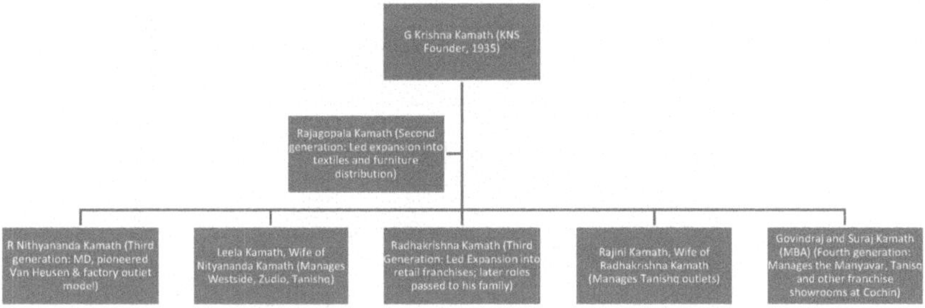

Fig. 25.1 Family Tree

Option 5: Forming Strategic Alliances with Local SMEs

Another option was to form strategic alliances with local SMEs in Kerala to create a collaborative network for distribution and retail. By partnering with other family businesses or small retailers, KNS could pool resources to compete with MNCs, share logistics, and co- develop new markets. For example, KNS could collaborate with local apparel manufacturers to create a regional brand or partner with stationery suppliers to dominate the local market.

This approach could have leveraged KNS's social capital and regional networks, aligning with its tradition of trust-based relationships. However, alliances required complex coordination and it risked conflicts over profit-sharing or decision-making. Kamath had to assess whether partnerships could enhance KNS's market position without diluting its autonomy over decision making or partnering with 'untrustful' partners (Figs. 25.1, 25.2, and 25.3).

Discussion Questions

1. How did Nityananda Kamath's entry into franchise entrepreneurship balance innovation with KNS's traditional family business culture, and what lessons can be drawn from this approach?
2. Was KNS's rejection of the Lipton tea distribution opportunity a strategic decision to maintain focus or is it a missed opportunity for diversification?
3. What were the risks and benefits of launching India's first factory outlet in 1999, and how can SMEs evaluate such novel opportunities?

Fig. 25.2 The picture below shows the inauguration of the first Van Huesen showroom in India. The showroom was opened in the M G road, Ernakulam in Kerala in 1990

Fig. 25.3 The picture below shows K Sukumar of Madura Cots arriving for the inauguration of the first Van Huesen showroom in India in Mahatma Gandhi Road in Cochin in 1990

Supplementary Readings

- Berger, P. L. (2011). *Invitation to Sociology: A Humanistic Perspective*. Open Road Media.
- Grewal, D., Iyer, G. R., Javalgi, R. (Raj) G., & Radulovich, L. (2011). Franchise Partnership and International Expansion: A Conceptual Framework and Research Propositions. *Entrepreneurship Theory and Practice*, *35*(3), 533–557. https://doi.org/10.1111/j.1540-6520.2011.00444.x
- Mani, D. (2019). *Who controls the Indian economy: The role of families and communities in the Indian economy*. Asia Pacific Journal of Management, 38(1), 121–149.

- Ritzer, G. (1983). The "McDonaldization" of Society. *Journal of American Culture*, *6*(1), 100–107. https://doi.org/10.1111/j.1542-734X.1983.0601_100.x
- Roy, T. (2024). *Family businesses in India: History and future*. In *Global Family Capitalism* (pp. 197–2013). Routledge.
- Singh, P. (2022, August). *75 years of Indian business: How we began and how far we have come*. Money Control. https://www.moneycontrol.com/news/business/75-years-of-indian-business-how-we-began-and-how-far-we-have-come-9032091.html
- Stanford Seed. (2022). *Franchising in India: Learning the hard way*. https://www.gsb.stanford.edu/insights/franchising-india-learning-hard-way.

Learning Outcomes

- Balancing Tradition and Innovation: Students will analyze how family businesses can maintain traditional values while adopting innovative models like franchise entrepreneurship.
- Strategic Decision-Making: Students will evaluate trade-offs between diversification opportunities (e.g., Lipton) and high-risk innovations (e.g., factory outlets).
- Adapting to Globalization: Students will explore how SMEs can leverage networks and niche markets to thrive in a competitive, globalized economy.

Acknowledgments I acknowledge the resources and institutional support of IIT Madras, which facilitated this work. The author used an AI language model only for language refinement and checking grammatical errors. All contents, interpretations, and conclusions are the author's own.

Competing Interests The author has no conflicts of interest to declare that are relevant to the content of this chapter.

Supplementary Material—Teaching Note

Epilogue

In 1989, Kamath chose franchise entrepreneurship, opening a Louis Philippe showroom in Ernakulam, followed by showrooms for Peter England and Allen Solly. This decision was based on Kerala's consumer boom, establishing KNS as a pioneer in India's franchise retail sector. In

1999, Kamath further innovated by launching Kerala's first factory outlet in Cochin, introducing brands like Pepe Jeans and Reebok. The outlet's success drew attention from industry leaders like Kishore Biyani, affirming KNS's innovative edge.

Leela and Rajini Kamath, wives of Nityananda and Radhakrishna Kamath respectively managed franchise stores of Coats Viyella like Van Huesen, Peter England Tanishq and Louis Philippe. The nephews of Nityananda Kamath and sons of Radhakrishna and Rajini Kamath, Govindraj and Suraj Kamath are also involved in managing Peter England in the Mahatma Gandhi (M G) road in Ernakulam. While realizing the immense potential of online business for expanding middle class executives, Govindraj Kamath started 'Capsule wardrobe' online venture as an independent firm. As he says 'The Kerala society has progressed a lot materially, but still there is a market for minimalistic clothing in Kerala since there are only very few such initiatives in the state'.[5]

The next generation, led by Govindraj and Suraj Kamath, MBA graduates and sons of Radhakrishna Kamath, too became part of this family business, managing the franchise enterprises of Tanishq, Westside, Peter England, and others. The family business, carrying on for four generations, is rare in the Indian as well as the global context.

Guidance for Educators on Using this Case for a 2-Hour Class Discussion

1. Broad discussion on economic reforms and globalization in the post-1990's India (10 mins)

Educators can begin the class by discussing, with the students, the economic trajectories of the post-independent nation until 1990's and discuss with students about the changes in those periods and its consequences. From here, one can carry forward the interaction with students on 'equal opportunities for all', entrepreneurship, entrepreneurial mindset, innovation, adapting to economic changes and maintaining tradition through going back to communitarian and religious values among others.

[5] The interview with Govindaraj Kamath was conducted on 4th May, 2024.

2. Specific discussion on Krishna Novelty Stores (KNS): Discussion on Globalization and Franchise Entrepreneurship (10 mins)

Build on this discussion to get the class to think about Krishna Novelty Stores and its role in the socio-economic context of economic liberalization in the post-1990's India. Take the forward the discussion by emphasizing both the opportunities and crises faced by the small-scale enterprises in the aftermath of the liberalization and globalization of the economy.

3. Encourage students to think about the various options ahead of them using Peter Berger's concept of 'Sociological Consciousness' (Berger, 2011) by briefing them about its 'debunking-motiff' and 'relativizing-motiff' to do theory by both questioning the taken-for-granted assumptions and contextualizing the realities as multi-layered to reject a fixed understanding (10 mins).
4. Introduce George Ritzer's framework of 'McDonaldization of Society' (1983), and discuss it in the context of economic reforms and globalization of Indian economy and society (50 mins)

Ritzer (1983) through his concept of McDonaldization discusses the rationalities and principles of business organizations in the contemporary globalized world which he calls as '*Grobalization*' to describe the homogenization of the capitalist consumer goods and business models across the globe.

McDonaldization involves four key components;

Efficiency: This is a process of rationalization which stresses the role of finding 'best or optimum means to any given end'.

Calculability: Emphasis on things that can be counted and quanitified.

Predictability: People want to know what to expect while acquiring certain commodity and not have room for any suprises.

Control: Society in general and Economic systems in particular are oriented towards a need to exert greater control over future and uncertainity in the contemporary period.

The concept of McDonaldization (Ritzer, 1983) not only explains the rapid expansion of western firms and models into the global south as a part of cultural homogenization, but also the spread of values and principles underlying the functioning of an organization. This is extremely useful to understand why and how KNS opted for franchise entrepreneurship as a result of economic reforms. Further more, it allows students to learn that small scale business can adapt and infact thrive by entering in partnership with franchisor by acquiring resources in an *efficient* and *quantified* ways and thereby reduce uncertainity and risks through *control* and *predictability*.

Ritzer's concept of McDonaldization produces a profound duality through the mechanism of franchising:

On one hand, franchising is the quintessential instrument of grobalization (growth plus globalization): it carries the complete machinery of rationalized control, predictability, and cultural homogenization across the planet, imposing identical systems and eroding local distinctiveness. On the other hand, entrepreneurs from small scale business families, especially in the Global South, franchising simultaneously functions as a powerful tool of upward mobility and innovation: it dramatically lowers the barriers, risks, and uncertainties of entering the modern capitalist economy, offering small-scale operators a proven, branded, low-failure-rate pathway that would otherwise be inaccessible when competing against chaotic traditional business or starting from scratch. Thus, the very same franchise system that drives global uniformity and corporate dominance is also experienced locally as a liberating, risk-reducing engine of entrepreneurial opportunity.

5. Introduce students to the conceptual framework developed by Dhruv Grewal asking students to engage with their publication (Grewal et al., 2011) to comprehend the franchise strategy and entrepreneurial partnership (40 mins).

Dhruv Grewal et al. (2011) mentions the strategy and operationalizing of the firm by relying on three major factors; Inter-dependence, trust and strong relationship between franchisee and franchisor. This conceptual framework allows students to unpack the decision making and traditional hands-on control approach while at the same innovating in the modern economy. It also gave them the confidence to start factory outlets for the first time in the state of Kerala.

The most important factor in this conceptual framework useful for this particular case study is the inter-dependence and trust developed between KNS and Coats Viyella through a strong historical relationship spanning more than four decades. This was one of the reasons why they could reject the opportunities offered by another company Lipton as they trusted Coats Viyella and didn't entered into business which they had less market knowledge. It also assured a strong relationship wherein trust was not violated by partnering with another Scottish firm, Lipton. This ensured their further entrepreneurial prospects with Coats Viyella in the future. A history of trustful and loyal partnership with a single firm became advantageous for the business family in the long run as the Indian company, Tata and their recent brands like Tanishq and Zudio were entrusted with the Chalakkudy Kamath's in the state of Kerala.

References

Bal, G. (2023). *Sociology of entrepreneurship in India*. Rawat Publications.

Berger, P. L. (2011). Sociology as a form of consciousness. In *Invitation to sociology: A humanistic perspective*. pp. 56–77. Open Integrated Media.

Brookes, M., Altinay, L., Wang, X. L., & Yeung, R. (2016). Opportunity identification and evaluation in franchisee business start-ups. *Journal of Service Theory and Practice, 26*(6), 889–910. https://doi.org/10.1108/JSTP-04-2015-0089

Grewal. D., Iyer, G., & Radulovich, L. (2011). Franchise Partnership and International Expansion: A Conceptual Framework and Research Propositions. *Entrepreneurship: Theory and Practice*. Vol. 35 (3). pp. 533–557

Kohli, A. (2006). Politics of Economic Growth in India, 1980–2005. *Economic and Political Weekly*. Vol. 41(14). pp. 2915–2922

Mannathukkaren, N. (2023). 'Enjoying life': Consumption, changing meanings, and social differentiation in Kerala, India. *Modern Asian Studies, 57*(2), 505–554. https://doi.org/10.1017/S0026749X22000257

Masrani, S. K., Morelli, C. J., & Bagchi, A. K. (2021). The rise of Indian business in the global context in the twentieth century: A review and introduction. *Business History, 63*(1), 1–17. https://doi.org/10.1080/00076791.2020.1803282

Mukherji, R. (2014). *Globalization and deregulation: Ideas, interests, and institutional change in India*. Oxford University Press. https://doi.org/10.1093/acprof:oso/9780198096177.001.0001

Naseemullah, A. (2020). Small Business and India's Elitist Political Economy. *Seminar Magazine*, 734. https://www.india-seminar.com/2020/734/734_adnan_naseemullah.htm

Ritzer, G. (1983). The McDonaldization of Society. *Journal of American Culture*. Vol. 6(1). pp. 100–107.

Roy, T. (2017). The Origins of Import Substituting Industrialization in India. *Economic History of Developing Regions*. Vol. 32(1). pp. 71–95.

Roy, T. (2018). *A business history of India: Enterprise and the emergence of capitalism from 1700*. Cambridge University Press.

Roy, T., & Raman, K.R. (2024). *Kerala, 1956 to the present: India's Miracle State*. Cambridge University Press.

Sharma, A. D. (2022). 'Mr. clean' and his 'computer boys': Technology, technocracy, and de-politicisation in the Indian National Congress (1981–1991). *Commonwealth & Comparative Politics, 60*(1), 50–73. https://doi.org/10.1080/14662043.2021.2001252

Subrahmanyam, S., & Bayly, C. A. (1988). Portfolio capitalists and the political economy of early modern India. *The Indian Economic & Social History Review, 25*(4), 401–424. https://doi.org/10.1177/001946468802500402

Tripathi, D., & Jumani, J. (2013). *The Oxford history of contemporary Indian business* (1st ed.). Oxford University Press.

Xavier, Â. B. (2024). *Religion and empire in Portuguese India: Conversion, resistance, and the making of Goa*. Permanent Black and Ashoka University.

CHAPTER 26

From Stove to Startup: The Making of a Community-Driven Social Enterprise

Sumit Kumar Jaiswal

Abstract This case follows Tanya and Ankit, two fellows in a social enterprise program, as they attempt to co-create a livelihood venture with self-help group (SHG) women in Kotma, a rural subdivision in Madhya Pradesh, India. After months of fieldwork and immersion, they mobilize a team of fifteen women, Annapurna, who express interest in launching a catering business. An immediate opportunity arises when the NGO partner invites bids to provide food services for a year-long training program. While the contract offers short-term revenue and builds confidence, it also poses risks related to financing, operational readiness, and sustainability. At the same time, some women and the fellows envision a more ambitious alternative: developing a small-scale food enterprise producing packaged local delicacies for broader markets. With the bidding deadline approaching, the fellows face a pivotal dilemma: should they pursue the catering contract with immediate but uncertain returns, or invest in building a scalable venture with higher risks and longer horizons? The case highlights

S. K. Jaiswal (✉)
Amrut Mody School of Management, Ahmedabad University, Navrangpura, Ahmedabad, Gujarat, India
e-mail: sumit.jaiswal@ahduni.edu.in; phd19sumitj@iima.ac.in

A. S. Galande et al. (eds.), *Context-inspired Entrepreneurship*, Sustainable Development Goals Series,
https://doi.org/10.1007/978-981-95-9831-1_26

challenges of entrepreneurship in resource-constrained settings, gendered dynamics of SHGs, and the tension between short-term viability and long-term sustainability in social enterprise building.

Keywords Social entrepreneurship • Self-help groups (SHGs) • Women entrepreneurs • Resource-constrained environments • Community mobilization • Sustainable livelihoods • Entrepreneurial decision-making

SDG Links This chapter is centrally aligned with SDG 8: Decent Work and Economic Growth, examining how a community-led small scale food enterprise in Kotma creates sustainable livelihoods and income-generating opportunities (SDG 8.3). The chapter also aligns with SDG 1, through its focus on poverty reduction through collective economic activity.

Introduction

On a starry night, spectacularly beautiful and still, two young fellows sat in quiet contemplation. They had spent months nurturing an idea in collaboration with women from the rural pockets of Kotma, a subdivision in the Anuppur district of Madhya Pradesh, India. They had tirelessly traversed village after village, searching for enterprising women willing to take a bold step toward entrepreneurship. To their surprise, their efforts bore fruit: a team had come together, something they had not anticipated when they first set foot in Kotma.

The team was resolute, eager to seize the opportunity of launching a catering business. Yet, as the moment of execution neared, uncertainties loomed large. Would unseen social dynamics hinder the women from pursuing this venture? Were they truly prepared to run a business for the first time? Crucially, they still needed working capital to start. And with the bidding process for the catering contract fast approaching, time was slipping away. Moreover, there were uncertainties around the sustainability of the idea. As the night deepened, the fellows exchanged a glance. Ankit broke the silence, "Tanya, I am not quite sure which way to go." Tanya smiled and said with a calm resolve, "Let's give tomorrow our best and maybe the path will show itself."

A Fellowship with a Purpose

As part of their fellowship program,[1] Tanya and Ankit had arrived in Kotma with a single mission: to build a social enterprise that could create a meaningful impact in the lives of disadvantaged communities. Their only local contact was Mr. Rajesh, the team leader of the Kotma office of a well-established NGO. With a clean slate and a keen willingness to learn, they approached him. Affectionately called *Rajesh Ji* by the team members, he shared insights about the ongoing development projects and encouraged them to think independently. "Don't worry about success or failure," he reassured them. "Do whatever you believe can add value to people's lives. You have my unconditional support." His words bolstered their confidence, but the road ahead was still uncertain. What idea should they pursue? How would they bring it to life?

The Seeds of an Idea: The Power of Listening

After overcoming the initial uncertainty of their first few days, they devised a plan. During their village immersion program, part of their induction, they had learned a crucial lesson: to build a social enterprise that truly creates value for disadvantaged communities, one must first understand the perspectives of the people it seeks to serve. And so, their journey began. The next challenge was deciding whom to meet. By this time, they had built a good rapport with the NGO team, whose deep knowledge of the field proved invaluable. A team member suggested that they engage with women in self-help groups (SHGs)[2,3] some of whom had been exploring opportunities to start their own businesses. With the team's guidance, the fellows identified specific SHGs, helping them narrow down the villages they should visit. Fortunately, the NGO's goodwill in these villages meant the women were open to meeting the two outsiders. To establish credibility and ease initial interactions, the fellows requested a team member to accompany them to their first meeting, ensuring a smoother introduction to the community.

The first meeting took place at a school complex where an SHG was engaged in the midday meal scheme. After introductions, Tanya and Ankit explained the purpose of their visit and inquired about the group's

[1] https://thebuddhainstitute.org/budha-fellowship-program

[2] https://socialwelfare.vikaspedia.in

[3] https://rural.gov.in

activities, hoping to identify potential business opportunities that could be pursued by partnering with these SHGs. It quickly became evident that most women were hesitant to take risks or step beyond their villages. However, one remark from an SHG member, Tara, stood out. She said, *"If we don't take risks, how will we achieve anything?"* The fellows took note of her statement, gathered her details, and left with a new perspective.

Her words lingered. That night, over dinner, Ankit reflected, "I understand why SHG members are reluctant to risk their savings. But what if there are more women like Tara in other SHGs?" Tanya's eyes lit up. "Then let's find them." With a renewed sense of purpose, they mapped out SHGs across nearby villages, searching for women willing to embrace entrepreneurship. To their delight, they discovered that in nearly every SHG, there was always someone eager for more - someone who wasn't satisfied with merely managing savings and loans.[4] For the first time since arriving in Kotma, the fellows felt they were onto something.

From Idea to Business Model

With a growing interest among SHG members, the discussions became more animated. Some women proposed making pickles, others suggested ketchup or chutneys, and some envisioned food stalls serving local cuisine. While there was no immediate consensus, one thing was evident - food was at the heart of their ideas. Seeking guidance, Tanya and Ankit turned to Rajesh Ji, who mentioned that their NGO had secured a contract to train auxiliary nurse midwives (ANMs). The training program, in its second phase, also required making lodging and food arrangements for the participants, which was scheduled to happen in batches. It sparked an idea. "What if the women set up food stalls for these training sessions?" Tanya proposed. But doubts crept in. Ankit hesitated. "What happens when the training ends? Would the women be willing to step outside their villages? Was it feasible to sustain a business model around an occasional training program?"

By this time, the fellows had also explored nearby markets to assess potential opportunities. The region was known for its rich major (sal, teak, and bamboo) and minor (tendu leaves, gum, harra, lakh, khair, amla, mahua, bhilawa, and various medicinal plants) forest produce.[5]

[4] What do SHGs do?

[5] https://www.alliedacademies.org/articles/climate-change-impact-on-forest-and-agro-biodiversity-a-special-reference-to-anuppur.pdf

Drumsticks, pears, and strawberries grew in abundance,[6] and local delicacies like ***Udad Daal ki Chandiya*** and ***Anaras***[7] were quite famous (see Table 26.1 for more information on Kotma). There was clear potential to develop value-added products, both edible and non-edible, by setting up a small processing unit in the villages. These could then be sold in nearby towns or through broader market channels. Some women had already voiced similar ideas in the past, but several concerns remained. What products should be chosen? Which sales channels would work best? Where would the initial capital come from? And perhaps most crucially, would the women remain motivated, given the long lead time before any profits could be seen? The business model was yet to be figured out. Yet, if the idea could be shaped and sustained, it held the promise of creating jobs and becoming a model that others in the region might one day follow.

Despite several ideas being floated, nothing concrete had taken shape yet. During one of the meetings, the fellows steered the conversation toward the NGO's work - specifically its ANM training program. A woman familiar with the initiative spoke up, sharing how the program had helped the community. In response, Ankit remarked, "And the organization also

Table 26.1 About Kotma

Kotma, a subdivision and municipality in the Anuppur district, is renowned for its rich biodiversity and abundant natural resources. As per the 2001 census, the town had an estimated population of around 90,000. The local economy is primarily dependent on agriculture and forest-based activities. Farmers in the region cultivate key crops such as rice, millets, maize, wheat, chickpeas, and soybeans, with their yield largely influenced by the southwest monsoon.
The area is home to a variety of plant and animal species and provides habitat for several indigenous communities, including the Baiga, Gonds, Panikas, Kol, and Dhanaur tribes. These communities maintain a deep-rooted connection with their environment, relying on both forests and farmlands for their livelihood. Kotma's ecosystem supports an impressive 1527 documented plant species, out of which 518 are recognized for their nutritional and medicinal properties.
Forest produce collection plays a vital role in the local economy, with key resources including char (Buchanania lanzan), tendu (Diospyros melanoxylon), amla (Phyllanthus emblica), bel (Aegle marmelos), karonda (Carissa spinarum), Sal leaves (Shorea robusta), mohlain leaves (Bauhinia purpurea), medicinal herbs, dry wood, and fodder. These natural resources serve as essential means of sustenance and income for the communities living in and around Kotma.

[6] https://anuppur.nic.in/en/produce/

[7] https://anuppur.nic.in/en/culinary-delights/

arranges the food and accommodation." Another woman nodded but quickly interjected, "Yes, they do, but the quality of the food was very bad. We received a meal box, but it tasted terrible." Intrigued, the fellows later asked Rajesh Ji about this. He explained that the organization had previously outsourced the catering to a local food vendor. It triggered a thought. Ankit turned to Tanya and said, "You had mentioned setting up food stalls run by the women for these training programs. What if they took it a step further by taking the entire food contract instead?" The three of them paused, considering the possibility. Finally, Rajesh Ji said, "If they can manage it, why not?" Tanya smiled and asked, "Shall we run it by them?"

Taking the Leap: The Birth of *Annapurna*

The next day, the fellows organized a meeting and proposed an idea to the group: What if they had the opportunity to improve the quality of food provided in the training program this time? Tara asked, "You mean we would be delivering the food?" "No," Tanya clarified. "We mean the group taking on the entire catering contract for the year-long training program." A silence followed. Many of these women had rarely ventured beyond their villages, and now they were being asked to take full responsibility for something entirely on their own. Breaking the silence, the eldest and most seasoned woman, Manju Devi, spoke with quiet conviction: *"If we confine ourselves to the comfort of our villages, we will never accomplish anything truly significant."*

With that, the group had found its leader. Some women immediately agreed, while others asked for time to discuss it with their families. Over the next few days, a few members dropped out, while others joined in, eager to take on the challenge. Eventually, a determined group of fifteen women committed themselves to this bold new venture. They called themselves *Annapurna,* the giver of food and nourishment, a name that reflected their purpose and hope.

The Challenges Ahead

Everyone was excited that a team had come together, but a bigger challenge lay ahead—how to execute the plan. There were three key hurdles: securing the contract, obtaining funds to fulfill it, and ensuring the group was operationally ready. Neither the fellows nor the women had any prior experience in these areas. To find a way forward, the fellows approached

Rajesh Ji for guidance. He explained the application process and the necessary documentation. First, the group needed to open a bank account in a nationalized bank to be eligible for the contract. Then, they had to submit a competitive bid, as other caterers would also be invited to apply. If they won the contract by offering the lowest bid, they would still need to secure funding to manage operations. Additionally, preparing food at scale was an entirely new challenge for them.

The fellows felt a bit anxious and called a meeting with the women to discuss the situation. They expected hesitation or doubt from the group. However, to their surprise, the women were unfazed. One member spoke up, "Until now, we were not even sure if we would go through with this. But now that the opportunity is in front of us, we must try. I am sure something will work out." Another woman added, "We do so much household work, yet we never receive respect or appreciation from our families. If we succeed in this, people will finally see us differently." Many others nodded in agreement. Their words dispelled any lingering doubts and infused the entire group, including the fellows, with a renewed sense of purpose. The fellows realized this was no longer just about starting a business; it had become something much bigger.

That meeting resulted in a clear blueprint for executing the idea, outlining the following key responsibilities:

1. **Bidding Process**: The fellows would handle all the necessary paperwork and, with the group's consent, submit a competitive bid for the contract.
2. **Securing Funds**: The fellows would explore funding opportunities and seek external financing to support the initiative.
3. **Execution by Annapurna**: The women's group, Annapurna, would take charge of the entire operational aspect, including designing the menu, procuring raw materials, preparing the food, and ensuring timely delivery (see Table 26.2 for projected financials).

The Dilemma

While forming the group was an achievement in itself, the real work was only just beginning. Yet something continued to trouble the fellows. The idea of securing the catering contract seemed like their best shot, but was it the right move? After all, this was not just any contract. It was linked to a captive audience assembled by the NGO. What would happen if that support

Table 26.2 Projected Financials for the Catering Business

Training demand, scope, and cost estimates
Over the next 18 months, the NGO planned to organize one training batch per month, each accommodating 100 participants for a four-day program. Each participant would receive two meals per day.
The fellows were considering a bidding price of Rs 200 to Rs 250 per participant per day. The estimated operating cost per batch - including raw materials, cook wages, fuel, transport, and basic consumables - was approximately Rs 60,000. An upfront investment of around Rs 1,50,000 was required to launch the initiative.
Note 1: Annapurna consisted of 15 women members, who would operate on a rotational basis. For each training batch, five women would manage the kitchen operations. The operating cost also included a stipend of Rs 300 per day per woman to compensate them for their time and effort during the four-day training.
Note 2: The NGO was running this training program for the government, and the payment was expected every 2 months.

disappeared? Would the women still stay together and explore other opportunities? Would they learn enough practical skills to carry forward into their next venture? And most importantly, was this model truly sustainable?

Although there was shared clarity on the group's original intent, exploring the possibility of a catering business, the fellows had not entirely dismissed an alternative path: setting up a small-scale food manufacturing unit targeting a broader market. Some women had even floated the idea of producing packaged food items like ***pickles, papad, and other local specialties*** that captured the distinct flavors of Kotma. But this path was far more ambitious. The "what," "how," and "why" of that business were still unclear. It would involve a longer gestation period and significantly more risk. At the same time, if it succeeded, the potential for long-term sustainability and broader impact was much higher.

Time was running out. If they chose to pursue the catering contract, the fellows needed to act quickly, resolving issues related to funding, logistics, and execution. But if they opted to explore the food enterprise route, they would have to return to the women's group, revisit the idea, map the market, and prepare for an entirely new set of challenges Annapurna had not yet confronted. The fellows knew that the catering idea had traction, a clear revenue opportunity for at least a year and a half, and the backing of the women. The food enterprise was more distant, but if nurtured, it could create more profound and longer-lasting change.

Tanya and Ankit had come a long way since their first visit to Kotma. They had built trust, mobilized a team, and uncovered a real opportunity. Yet, with the bidding deadline fast approaching, a quiet uncertainty hung over their next steps. *Should they pursue a funded catering contract with immediate returns but uncertain longevity, or build a more scalable food enterprise with higher risk and slower returns?*

As they stood at this crossroads, one thing was clear: whatever path they chose, this journey had already begun to transform them, and the women of Annapurna, for good.

Discussion Questions

1. **Opportunity Development**

    - What entrepreneurial opportunities emerge in this case? Were they discovered, created, or co-created?
    - In what ways did the fellows and community members contribute to identifying and shaping these opportunities?

2. **Challenges and Entrepreneurial Roles**

    - What are the key challenges in launching a community-driven, for-profit venture in a socio-culturally unfamiliar environment?
    - In such a setting, should the entrepreneur primarily act as a decision-maker, facilitator, or change agent? Why?

3. **Stakeholder Engagement Strategies**

    - Who are the critical stakeholders in this venture, and what roles do they play in its development and sustainability?
    - What strategies can be employed to build trust, secure community buy-in, and ensure long-term engagement?

4. **Opportunity Evaluation**

    - What criteria should be used to evaluate and select among multiple potential opportunities?

Learning Objectives

1. Understand the dynamics of opportunity development and opportunity evaluation in a rural context.
2. Analyze entrepreneurial roles in resource-constrained and culturally complex settings.
3. Evaluate strategies for building inclusive, sustainable ventures through stakeholder engagement.

Supplementary Readings

1. Two keys to sustainable social enterprise (https://hbr.org/2015/05/two-keys-to-sustainable-social-enterprise)
2. How Social Entrepreneurs Make Change Happen (https://hbr.org/2015/10/how-social-entrepreneurs-make-change-happen)
3. Brumme, Cait, and Brian Trelstad. "Should Your Start-up Be For-profit or Nonprofit? A Guide for Social Entrepreneurs." Harvard Business Review 101, no. 3 (May–June 2023): 136–145.
4. Corner, P. D., & Ho, M. (2010). How Opportunities Develop in Social Entrepreneurship. *Entrepreneurship Theory and Practice*, *34*(4), 635–659. https://doi.org/10.1111/j.1540-6520.2010.00382.x (Original work published 2010)
5. Sarasvathy, S. D. (2001). *Causation and Effectuation: Toward a Theoretical Shift from Economic Inevitability to Entrepreneurial Contingency.* Academy of Management Review, 26(2), 243–263. (15 pages)
6. Dees, J. G. (1998). *The Meaning of Social Entrepreneurship.* (8 pages)
7. Venkataraman, S. (1997). *The Distinctive Domain of Entrepreneurship Research: An Editor's Perspective.* Advances in Entrepreneurship, Firm Emergence and Growth, 3, 119–138. (12 pages)

Acknowledgement I am grateful to Prof. Sreevas Sahasranamam for his encouragement and guidance in developing this case. I also thank the anonymous reviewers for their insightful comments, which greatly improved the quality of this case.

Competing Interests The authors have no conflicts of interest to declare that are relevant to the content of this chapter.

Supplementary Material: Teaching Note

Guidance for Educators on Using this Case for a 75 Minutes Class Discussion

I. **Case Summary**

This case follows the journey of a group of rural women and a cohort of fellows as they attempt to establish a community-driven food enterprise in Kotma, a resource-constrained environment. It explores themes of entrepreneurial decision-making, social enterprise development, stakeholder engagement, and business model configuration in a rural socio-cultural context.

II. **Teaching Plan (75-minute Session)**

1. **Introduction & Context Setting (10 mins)**
   - Ask participants to summarize the case
   - Ask what the dilemmas are faced by the fellows
   - Provide background on rural entrepreneurship in India
2. **Case Analysis & Discussion (45 mins)**
   - Ask participants to reflect on the key dilemma.
   - Note down their responses on how the class would address the dilemma.
   - Facilitate discussions using the questions provided in the Discussion Questions section.
   - Break students into small groups to come up with a business model for this case.
3. **Application & Wrap-Up (20 mins)**
   - Relate learnings to broader theories of entrepreneurship and social innovation (effectuation in a resource-constrained environment).
   - Discuss real-world implications and similar case studies.
   - Encourage students to design their own community-driven business models.

III. **Discussion Questions**

1. **Opportunity Development:**
   - How did the opportunity emerge in this case? Was it created or discovered?
     1. Opportunity: An opening into creating a new equilibrium (an entrepreneur identifies a gap in the market, an unmet need, or a problem that can be addressed through a new product, service, or business model)
     2. If opportunity is created, how? It emerged through the interactions of multiple actors. SHGs, NGOs, and even other stakeholders had been there. But what made the difference? The arrival of fellows: They brought a fresh perspective. When they went out to discover an opportunity, they created one in the process. Some other fellows may have started a different business with the same set of people or may have reached a different conclusion about which idea to pursue or the gaps or problems they saw.
   - How did the fellows and community members contribute to opportunity development?
     1. SHG women as co-creators: Willingness to take risk, shaped the direction of the enterprise, skills, experience and community trust played an instrumental role
     2. NGO as a legitimizing partner: Facilitated access to SHGs and ensured credibility, provided logistical and institutional support
     3. Fellows as facilitators of effectuation: Leveraged existing resources rather than imposing a plan, fostered co-creation by involving SHGs and the NGO
     4. External factors: The Government scheme was instrumental
2. **Challenges and Entrepreneurial Role:**
   - What are the key obstacles in launching a community-driven for-profit enterprise in an unfamiliar socio-cultural setting?
     1. Trust Deficit and Legitimacy Issues
        - Entrepreneurs entering a new socio-cultural environment often struggle with credibility
        - Communities may be skeptical of external interventions
        - Gaining acceptance requires deep engagement and alignment with local aspirations

2. Resistance to Risk and Change
    - Many marginalized communities prefer stability over entrepreneurial risk, especially where failure can have dire financial and social consequences.
3. Stakeholder Coordination and Buy-in
    - Community-driven enterprises require collaboration among diverse stakeholders—NGOs, SHGs, local institutions, and government bodies
    - Misaligned incentives and differing expectations can delay progress
4. Resource Constraints and Infrastructure Challenges
    - Limited access to capital, supply chains, and logistical support makes execution difficult
    - Entrepreneurs often have to make do with existing infrastructure and social capital
5. Gender Norms and Cultural Constraints
    - In traditional communities, women may have restrictions on mobility, financial independence, and business decision-making
    - Overcoming these barriers requires tactful engagement and role model identification

- Should the entrepreneur act as a decision-maker, facilitator, or change agent in this scenario?
  1. Decision maker
      - Entrepreneurs make key calls on strategy, funding, and execution.
      - This role is necessary when quick, high-stakes decisions are required.
      - However, in community-driven enterprises, a purely top-down approach may alienate stakeholders.
  2. Facilitator
      - Instead of dictating decisions, the entrepreneur enables stakeholders to co-create solutions.
      - In this case, the fellows leveraged SHG women's insights to shape the business model.
      - Encourages local ownership, making the venture more sustainable.

   3. Change Agent
      - Entrepreneurs challenge existing norms and introduce new possibilities.
      - Example: Tara's statement about risk-taking subtly shifted the group's mindset.
      - However, change must be gradual and embedded in the community's realities.

3. **Stakeholder Engagement Strategies:**
   - Who are the critical stakeholders in this case, and how do they influence the venture's success?
     1. SHG Women—Core partners; their participation and risk appetite shape the business model.
     2. NGO Team—Provides legitimacy, field insights, and logistical support.
     3. Local Community—Acts as the primary customer base; their trust determines market acceptance.
     4. Government & Institutions—Policies, funding schemes, and regulations impact viability.
     5. Entrepreneurs (Fellows)—Act as facilitators, aligning stakeholder interests and driving execution.
   - What strategies can be used to ensure community buy-in and long-term commitment?
     1. Co-Creation—Engage community members in decision-making rather than imposing solutions.
     2. Trust-Building—Leverage existing networks, demonstrate quick wins, and maintain transparency.
     3. Skill Development & Ownership Transfer—Equip SHG women with business skills to enhance autonomy.
     4. Iterative Experimentation—Start small, prove viability, and scale gradually.
     5. Cultural Sensitivity—Align business activities with local norms and values.

4. **Opportunity evaluation:**
   - What criteria should be used to evaluate and select among multiple potential opportunities?

Frameworks that could be used.

Framework 1- Adopted from Timmons (1989).[8]

A balance between opportunity, resource, and team

- **Opportunity**: Is there a real and pressing need (e.g., food for training batches)? Is the market large or growing?
- **Resources**: What is currently available (women's time, NGO support, small capital)? What else is needed?
- **Team**: Do the women and fellows have the capabilities and commitment?
- **Stakeholders**: How much is the dependence on non-core stakeholders to pursue this opportunity?

Application: The catering contract may score well on opportunity and resources (short-term), but the team's long-term vision could align better with a scalable unit.

Framework 2: Effectual logic, Sarasvathy (2001).[9]

Particularly useful in uncertain, resource-poor settings.

- **Bird-in-Hand Principle:** What do we already have (skills, relationships, basic kitchen tools)?
- **Affordable Loss:** What can we risk (Rs 1,50,000, time of 5 women per batch)?
- **Lemonade Principle:** How can we turn surprises into advantages (e.g., if NGO demand declines)?
- **Crazy Quilt:** Who are our partners/stakeholders (NGO, fellows, local market)?

Application: The women might prefer starting with what they have (catering) and co-creating a larger business as they learn.

[8] Timmons, J. A. (1989). *The Entrepreneurial Mind.* Brick House Publishing Co., 3 Main St., PO Box 512, Andover, MA (clothbound: ISBN-0-931790-84-0; paperback: ISBN-0-931790-85-9, $18.95)

[9] Sarasvathy, S. D. (2001). Causation and effectuation: Toward a theoretical shift from economic inevitability to entrepreneurial contingency. *Academy of management Review*, *26*(2), 243–263.

Framework 3: Screening opportunities.
Comparing the two options (Catering business and small-scale manufacturing unit).

Criteria	*Catering contract*	*Manufacturing unit*
Ease of implementation	High	Low–medium
Capital required	Low	Medium–high
Time to cash flow	Immediate	Delayed
Scalability potential	Low–medium	High
Social impact	Moderate	High (long-term)

Application: Helps in facilitating a comparative discussion

IV. **Framework to learn**

Effectuation in Resource-Constrained, Community-Driven Social Enterprises.

Sarasvathy's (2001) *effectuation theory* argues that entrepreneurs create opportunities using available means rather than relying on predictive planning. This approach becomes even more critical in **resource-constrained environments**, where uncertainty is high, and traditional business logic often fails.

Note: The key discussion question below each head is not meant to be asked to the class but only to guide their thinking when they apply effectuation in a resource-constrained context.

In this case, effectuation manifests in the following ways:

1. **Bird-in-Hand Principle (Start with Available Means)**

Instead of waiting for ideal conditions, the fellows leveraged existing resources:

- Human Capital: Women from SHGs with prior experience in small-scale food preparation.
- Social Capital: The NGO's goodwill helped them gain access to communities.
- Physical & Financial Constraints: Lack of capital meant relying on existing infrastructure like school kitchens.

- **Approach in a resource-constrained setting:** In a resource-constrained setting, available means often include informal networks, social capital, and frugal innovation rather than financial resources or technology.
- **Key Discussion Question:** How do social entrepreneurs identify and mobilize unconventional resources to create value?

2. **Affordable Loss (Minimize Risk Instead of Maximizing Returns)**

Rather than making large upfront investments, the entrepreneurs:

- Focused on small, low-risk experiments (e.g., starting with SHG-based food supply).
- Partnered with women who were willing to take risks, mitigating broader community hesitation.
- Used the NGO's support to absorb initial uncertainties rather than securing external funding.
  - **Approach in a resource-constrained setting:** Unlike venture capital-backed startups, social enterprises in rural contexts prioritize sustainability over rapid scaling and rely on small, iterative steps.
  - **Key Discussion Question:** How does the affordable loss principle shape decision-making in social enterprises compared to traditional startups?

3. **Crazy Quilt (Co-Creation with Stakeholders)**

The entrepreneurs did not have a predefined business plan but instead:

- Engaged SHGs early on, allowing them to co-develop the business model.
- Relied on existing trust within the community rather than forcing top-down strategies.
- Used partnerships (NGO, SHGs, local institutions) to mitigate operational challenges.
  - **Approach in a resource-constrained setting:** In resource-constrained environments, *collaborative entrepreneurship* is often more effective than individual-led ventures. The co-creation pro-

cess ensures higher legitimacy, stronger stakeholder commitment, and shared risk.
  - **Key Discussion Question:** How does co-creation with marginalized communities shape the design of social enterprises?

4. **Lemonade Principle (Leverage Contingencies Instead of Avoiding Surprises)**

   Unpredictability was a given in this case:

   - Women's reluctance to leave their villages initially seemed like a barrier but led to the realization that a hyper-local business model was more viable.
   - A chance remark from a woman in the SHG—*"If we don't take risks, how will we achieve anything?"*—helped the fellows identify natural leaders within the group.
   - Using alternative opportunities to generate working capital by partnering with the FPC when other funding opportunities, like taking bank loans, were not working out.
     - **Approach in a resource-constrained setting:** In highly uncertain environments, setbacks often reveal hidden opportunities, making flexibility and rapid adaptation critical.
     - **Key Discussion Question:** How can social entrepreneurs train themselves to recognize and capitalize on unexpected opportunities?

5. **Pilot-in-the-Plane (Control the Future Instead of Predicting It)**

   Instead of waiting for external validation, the entrepreneurs:

   - Took small, iterative steps to refine their business model.
   - Did not rely on long-term predictions but adjusted based on real-time feedback from SHG women and stakeholders.
   - Focused on influencing the local ecosystem (e.g., building a network of reliable suppliers and customers) rather than waiting for ideal market conditions.

- **Approach in a resource-constrained setting:** In rural and underdeveloped regions, external dependencies (government policies, market access) are often unreliable. Social enterprises must shape their environments rather than passively reacting to them.
- **Key Discussion Question:** How can social entrepreneurs develop control-based strategies when operating in unpredictable environments?

How do entrepreneurs shift the equilibrium while developing a social enterprise by using effectual logic?

Need to transform the socioeconomic equilibrium to achieve the social mission. It is usually done by change agents. Social entrepreneurs, as change agents, focus on changing two features of an existing system, the economic actors involved (social entrepreneurs often add new actors to existing systems—customers and government) and the enabling technology applied (replace a key technology with a lower-cost one), to create sustainable financial models that can permanently shift the social and economic equilibrium for their targeted beneficiaries.

Questions to be asked by social entrepreneurs

- Who is the current equilibrium benefiting?
- How can the social entrepreneur shift the current equilibrium?

V. Conclusion

This case serves as a practical tool for students to understand the nuances of community-driven social enterprises. By engaging with the themes of opportunity development, entrepreneurial decision-making, and opportunity evaluation, students will gain valuable insights into the challenges and opportunities of launching sustainable social ventures in underprivileged regions.

Index[1]

[1] Note: Page numbers followed by 'n' refer to notes.

A. S. Galande et al. (eds.), *Context-inspired Entrepreneurship*, Sustainable Development Goals Series,
https://doi.org/10.1007/978-981-95-9831-1

The manufacturer's authorised representative in the EU is Springer Nature Customer Service Centre GmbH, Europaplatz 3, 69115 Heidelberg, Germany. If you have any concerns regarding our products, please contact ProductSafety@springernature.com

Printed and bound by CPI Group (UK) Ltd, Croydon, CR0 4YY

21/09/2026

02219962-0003